2

RED CIRCLE

Calligraphy by Stephen Songsheng Chen

RED CIRCLE

CHINA AND ME
1949-2009

STEPHEN SONGSHENG CHEN

AuthorHouse™
1663 Liberty Drive
Bloomington, IN 47403
www.authorhouse.com
Phone: 1-800-839-8640

Red Circle Publishing &
Cultural Exchange International
美国红圈出版文化交流国际公司
707 Radio Drive
Lewis Center, Ohio 43035
www.redcircle.me

First published by AuthorHouse 10/08/2009

ISBN: 978-1-4490-3365-1

Printed in Canada

This book is printed on acid-free paper.

Cover Design by Andrew Mays
Cover Illustration by Stephen Adam
Interior Design by Adalee Cooney

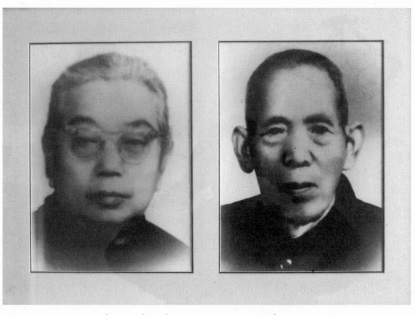

Dedicated in loving memory of my parents
Professor Chen Pinzhi
Madame Fu Junying

I have longed to tell my family's story for many years. My most important goal in publishing Red Circle: China and Me, 1949-2009, *in the year of the People's Republic of China's 60th anniversary, however, is to enhance understanding of China around the world through recounting the true stories of ordinary Chinese people. It is essential to know China's history to appreciate where it is today and to create a better future, not only for China, but also for our world.*

— Stephen Songsheng Chen

Contents

Author's Note

I WAS 10 YEARS OLD when, in 1949, the People's Republic of China was founded. For the next 60 years, my family and I experienced China's great upheaval, witnessed its suffering and awakening, its despair and hope, and participated in its transformation and the remarkable progress that has brought it to where it stands today. I was and am a part of that history. My life story mirrors that of my country.

As China developed from a woefully backward and impoverished nation into a superpower, the world's attention has focused on its economy. Little does the world know, however, that during the 1950s, China had already tried its "Red Capitalist Road." Since 1979, Deng Xiaoping's "socialism with Chinese characteristics" has moved the nation forward along a new capitalist road under the Communist banner. In its long march to achieve a prosperous and harmonious society, China has faced tremendous social disharmonies and unprecedented challenges caused by the unresolved problems of the past and by its startlingly rapid economic growth without fundamental political reform.

I am a survivor who has come through many difficult, even life-threatening, events, campaigns, and persecutions, and I've been lucky enough to emerge as one of the pioneers who helped develop the economic ties between the United States and China. As China struggled, so did my family. As China progressed, so did my family. The progress has been remarkable.

Forty years ago, I would have been sentenced to life in a labor camp if I dared to write *Red Circle*.

Thirty years ago, I would have been placed under house arrest if I dared to write *Red Circle*.

Twenty years ago, I wouldn't have been allowed to reenter China if I dared to write *Red Circle*.

Ten years ago, I would have been spurned in China if I dared to write *Red Circle*.

Today, in the year of China's 60th anniversary, I am fortunate and pleased to be able to put *Red Circle* into your hands, the story of a man, a family, and a nation.

Stephen Songsheng Chen   *August 3, 2009, my 70th birthday*

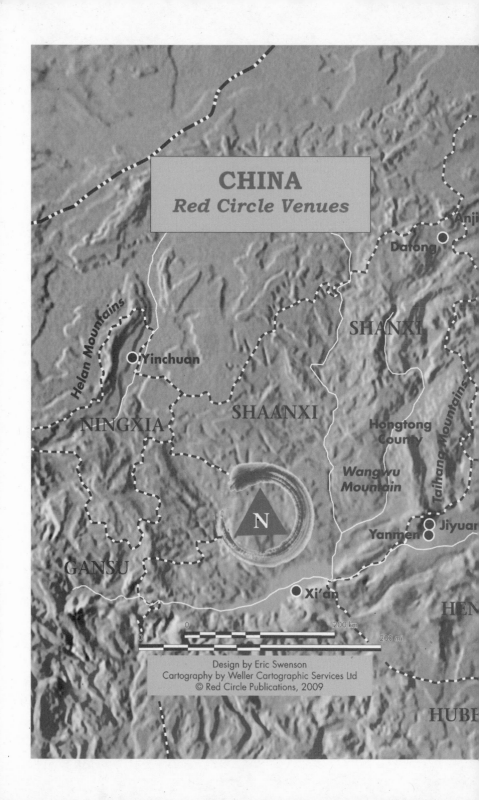

CHINA
Red Circle Venues

Anji

Darong

SHANXI

Helan Mountains

Yinchuan

SHAANXI

Hongtong County

Wangwu Mountain

Taihang Mountains

NINGXIA

Yanmen

Jiyuan

N

GANSU

Xi'an

HEN

200 km

200 mi

HUBE

Design by Eric Swenson
Cartography by Weller Cartographic Services Ltd
© Red Circle Publications, 2009

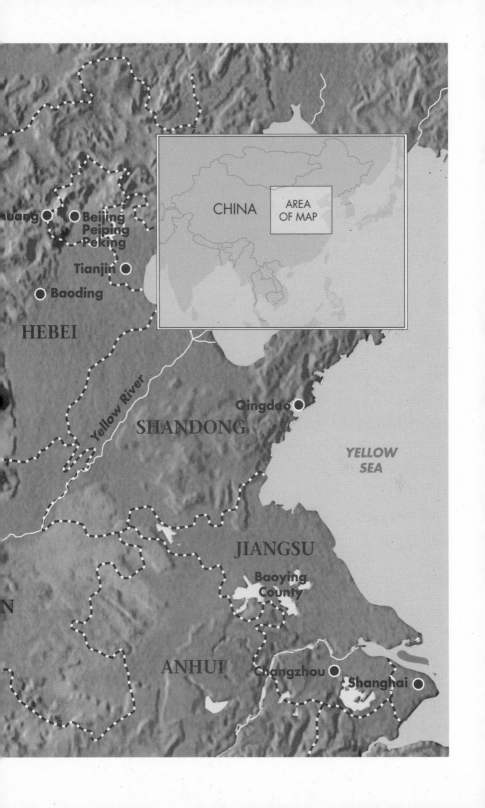

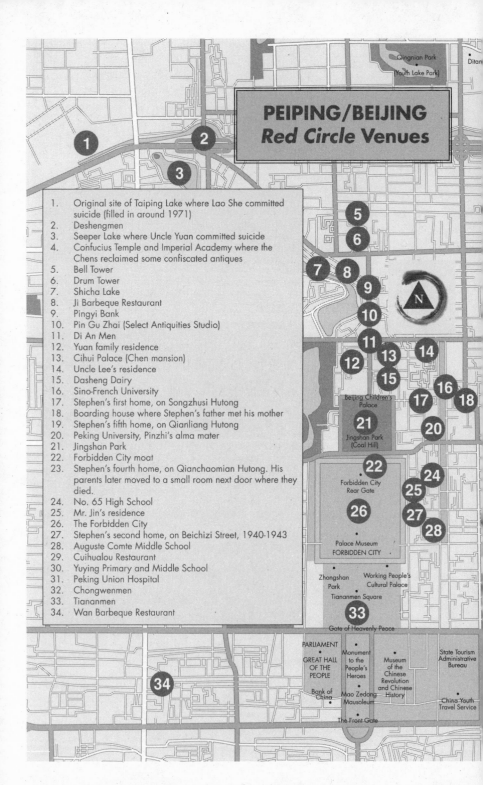

PEIPING/BEIJING *Red Circle* Venues

1. Original site of Taiping Lake where Lao She committed suicide (filled in around 1971)
2. Deshengmen
3. Seeper Lake where Uncle Yuan committed suicide
4. Confucius Temple and Imperial Academy where the Chens reclaimed some confiscated antiques
5. Bell Tower
6. Drum Tower
7. Shicha Lake
8. Ji Barbeque Restaurant
9. Pingyi Bank
10. Pin Gu Zhai (Select Antiquities Studio)
11. Di An Men
12. Yuan family residence
13. Cihui Palace (Chen mansion)
14. Uncle Lee's residence
15. Dasheng Dairy
16. Sino-French University
17. Stephen's first home, on Songzhusi Hutong
18. Boarding house where Stephen's father met his mother
19. Stephen's fifth home, on Qianliang Hutong
20. Peking University, Pinzhi's alma mater
21. Jingshan Park
22. Forbidden City moat
23. Stephen's fourth home, on Qianchaomian Hutong. His parents later moved to a small room next door where they died.
24. No. 65 High School
25. Mr. Jin's residence
26. The Forbidden City
27. Stephen's second home, on Beichizi Street, 1940-1943
28. Auguste Comte Middle School
29. Cuihualou Restaurant
30. Yuying Primary and Middle School
31. Peking Union Hospital
32. Chongwenmen
33. Tiananmen
34. Wan Barbeque Restaurant

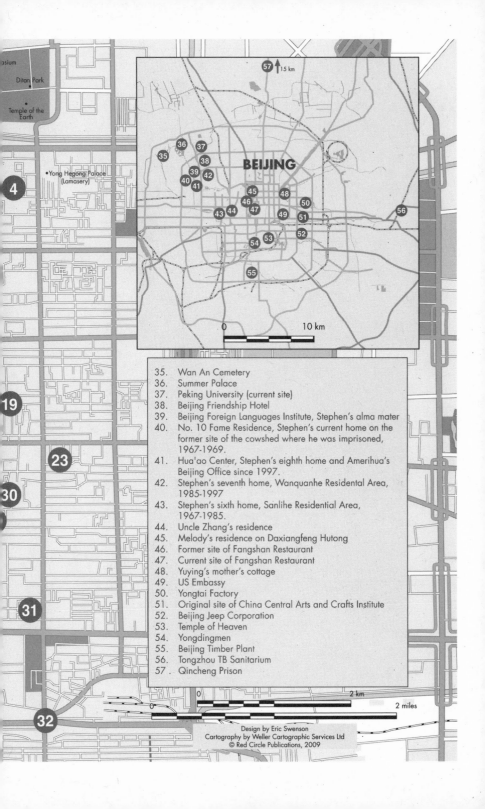

BEIJING

57 ↑ 15 km

0   10 km

0   2 km

0   2 miles

Design by Eric Swenson
Cartography by Weller Cartographic Services Ltd
© Red Circle Publications, 2009

LEAVING GOOSE GATE

1918-1948
Yanmen Village, Jiyuan County,
Henan Province; Peking/Peiping, China

IN THE EARLY YEARS OF the twentieth century, Henan was the poorest province of a thoroughly impoverished country, and Jiyuan was one of its poorest counties, but both were rich in history and legend. The village in which my father lived, Yanmen, lay near Wangwu Mountain, where the legendary first Chinese ancestor, the Yellow Emperor, built the original Temple of Heaven, making it the birthplace of China. Supposedly starting with Laozi himself, who is said to have sojourned there, Wangwu Mountain became the center for Daoism. Emperors of many dynasties made the arduous pilgrimage to this sacred place to offer sacrifices to their ancestors and implore the heavens for a bountiful harvest for the whole land.

Far below the mountain, Yanmen was so desolate that even the songbirds seemed to avoid it. The isolation and stark hardship of life in Yanmen were captured in the village's name, which translates as Goose Gate. Only wild and foolish geese flew through the high, narrow pass into the desperation of Yanmen.

As far as the eye could see and beyond, the earth was made of a fine, yellow, silty loam called loess. Loess sediment, carried by the mighty Yellow River, gave the river its name. The soil is fertile but erodes easily without vegetation. With no irrigation and in the dry, wind-eroded terrain of Henan, there were vast stretches where nothing grew—no trees, no shrubs or native grasses, not even weeds. Parts of the land were like a desert but without sand or oases.

Deposited by the winds over millions of years, the loess would rise quickly when the winds came up. If the gusts were strong, dust filled the air, the sun disappeared, and darkness descended, separating Yanmen even from the heavens above.

The village had two parts. At the time my father, Weizhen, lived there, upper Yanmen consisted of 10 families who lived in the hills and 20 families who lived in the lower, flatter part of the village. All the families in Yanmen were surnamed Chen, Yue, Liu, or Lee.

My father's family rented and then bought what natives considered to be some of the poorest land in Yanmen on the parched, terraced slope of a small hill. Ten years earlier, my grandfather, Chen Fayuan, had brought the whole family there from neighboring Shanxi Province to escape widespread famine. They had fled with virtually nothing and over the years carved three large caves into the face of a loess cliff to house the family and their belongings. No one else in the region had three caves in one location. Most families had to satisfy themselves with one small cave, basically a domed room. The arched ceiling provided structural stability to the dwellings, but cave-ins occurred with some regularity. Most dwellings had a built-in oven that served for cooking and heating.

In front of the caves, the Chens had a spacious courtyard with a hard, compacted dirt surface. It was enclosed by a clay wall and, outside the wall, pine, poplar, and persimmon trees grew, irrigated by water from the nearby well. As there were no windows in the cave—the only opening was the main entry—the dwellings were dark and not roomy enough for family gatherings. The courtyard was where all the family— the parents and the four unmarried brothers and three sisters still at home—and other relatives and neighbors could come together. When friends such as Father Clement, a French missionary with whom the family grew close, were passing through, they would always join the Chens for a simple meal and pleasant conversation. Father Clement learned some Chinese words from my father, who learned quite a few French phrases and correct pronunciation from Father Clement. They became close friends.

The most important resource in the high and dry environment of northwest Henan Province was water, and the Chens had it. Before purchasing the property, my grandfather had offered the landlord a higher price if he would include a small adjacent piece of land. It was there that he began to dig for water. His first two tries yielded only occasional trickles, but then he struck a bonanza. The well the family dug in the spring of 1914 near their courtyard was a steady producer of pure and sweet water. Even in times of drought, the well ran full. To this very day, it holds water. The Chens were generous, sharing their good fortune with relatives and neighbors alike, especially their former landlords, the Lius. All called it the "sweet well."

Early one morning in the first lunar month of 1918, Weizhen opened the door of his cave with barely a sound and, just as quietly, shut it behind him for what would be the last time in almost five years. The Spring Festival had just passed, and he paused to glance at the occasion's remnants.

He had written three sayings on red paper and pasted them above and on either side of the main cave's entry, where my grandparents lived. They were not at all like the scrolls purchased from shops for the occasion and displayed by other villagers. My father took a long, last look at his calligraphy. Even though he was considered a modest lad, he took pride in his free-flowing, strong, and, he thought, bold and elegant characters, which proclaimed:

In the New Year, we enjoy the blessings of our ancestors.
The joyous festival portends eternal spring.
An auspicious star shines on high.

While some might find the sentiments conventional, they stirred Weizhen. During Father Clement's many visits, my father had learned that Peking University was reforming its courses and would soon offer a modern curriculum. From *New Youth* magazine, begun by Chen Duxiu, later one of the founders of the Chinese Communist Party, my father had also learned about the New Cultural Movement to modernize his country. He made up his mind that he would walk to the capital, 800 kilometers away; sit for the entrance exam; and, if he passed it, begin to educate himself and, he hoped, play a role in the new China that would join the world beyond its borders.

The short, slender 20-year-old with closely cropped hair, thick eyebrows, and jug-handle ears turned away from his home and made his way across the courtyard. He wore an old sheepskin jacket, tight-fitting cotton trousers, and a pair of homemade cotton boots. He tightened a gray bag across his shoulders and pushed the courtyard gate ajar. He stuck his head out and looked in all directions. Nothing stirred, not even a chicken or a dog. He carefully closed the gate behind him and strode toward his future down the rugged, narrow path toward where the sun would rise within the hour.

To reach the road that would take him to Jiyuan Town and from there to Peking, he had to cross the deep ravine that separated upper and lower Yanmen. Even walking at a quick pace, it would still take more than an hour. In the face of the chill wind, he put his head down and began his journey with a confident stride.

"Weizhen!" a deep voice suddenly and unexpectedly called out.

Startled, and in the lingering darkness, my father did not immediately recognize the old man squatting in a nook on the leeward side of a ridge. In his old black handmade cotton trousers and jacket, he was barely visible. But when the stooped figure slowly rose and extended two trembling hands, Weizhen cried, "Father!" He dropped his shoulder bag and stepped forward to support his father. "What are you doing here?"

The old man pulled his son closer to the sheltering ridge, out of the path of the February wind. "I've been waiting here for you for nearly two hours."

"On such a cold day, what are you . . . ?"

"I just knew you were going to leave for Peking. I didn't sleep a wink. When you are troubled, I feel even worse."

"I am more excited than troubled. I know my journey won't be easy. But it will certainly be easier than your bringing our whole family from Shanxi to Yanmen."

"You are not going to a poor place like Yanmen. You are going to the capital."

"I know. But 'where there is a will there is a way,' as you always taught us. The only thing that bothers me is I have to leave you and Mother. I can hardly bear the thought."

"We won't get in your way. Mother and I are happy that you have such bold plans for your education. Who in our family is more deserving? Who in our village? Only you in Yanmen made it to middle school in Jiyuan Town. I have faith in my heart that you will succeed."

While he was talking, the old man undid his waistband and pulled out a small, black leather pouch from deep inside his jacket. "Here you are."

"What's this?"

The old man gestured for his son to untie the pouch. When my father opened the still warm pouch, he found it filled with large, shiny silver coins.

"These 20 silver coins were left by your grandfather. It was his life savings. I buried them under the oldest persimmon tree outside our courtyard. During the worst time of floods and famine, of drought and the plague of locusts, no matter how much trouble our household was in, I didn't touch it. This is what our Chen family ancestors bequeath to you. Take it. On the long road to Peking, you must have money for the journey."

"Father, I can't take this! I'll work as I make my way to the capital. I'll do odd jobs for people. Don't worry; I'll be able to earn enough to get there."

"But what will you do when you get to Peking? You don't know the city or what life is like there. You don't know the people, and you won't have any relatives to rely on. With this money from your forefathers, you might be able to stand on your own two feet and start a new life."

My father clasped the pouch tightly to his breast, fell to his knees before the old man, clutched him, and began to weep. Then as the sun broke over the mountains, its beams began to pierce the morning haze, bathing the two in soft sunlight.

"Son, don't cry." The old man pulled his son to his feet and brushed the dust from his pant legs. "Come on, if you cry now, what will you do later? Always remember, if things are going well, keep fighting your way forward. If things don't go well, you can come home. Yanmen is always your home! Our little village, it made you, didn't it? Your roots lie here."

Despite his admonishment to his son, the old man's voice became hoarse and he failed to stop several hot tears from falling down his cheeks. He tightened his grip on his son's hands.

My father thought about his roots and the hard physical work that was such a part of life in Yanmen. He remembered how his family had cleared the land, dug wells, planted crops and trees, carved caves, and sunk their homes into the earth. Life was a struggle, always on the edge. Any harsh act of Nature could push the Chen family to the brink of disaster. Living close to the edge had honed my father's desire to branch and flower beyond his roots.

"I know that, Father, but if I don't make something of myself in Peking, I would have a hard time coming back and facing you." Still holding the old man's hands tightly, my father used his hands to wipe the tears from his cheeks.

"Aim high, think big, and take your first step without hesitation. Always have hope." The old man gave the young man's hands one last squeeze. "Time is wasting; you should get on the road." The old man stooped down to pick up the bag and put it over my father's shoulder. "Keep the money safe."

My father put the little leather pouch into his jacket, close to his chest, and looked at the old man, unable to bring himself to leave. "Father, I didn't dare to talk about leaving with Mother. I was worried it would hurt her too much. Would you comfort her and make sure you two look after yourselves?"

"We will. Don't worry. Go on, you should get going." The old man nodded and waved awkwardly, his hand close to his heart.

My father turned around and took a few hesitant steps before turning again and saying, "Father, I can't take all of this money. How about I just take half?"

"So what would I do with the rest? Put it back under the persimmon tree? Money is something that you do not bring with you when you are born and you won't take with you when you die. It is to be used where and when it is needed most, Son. In the capital city, let these silver coins help you to make something of yourself. In ten years time, you'll be able to bring Mother and me to celebrate the New Year with you in Peking."

My father stepped forward and again took his father's hands into his own. "I sure hope that I'll be able to bring you and Mother much sooner than that."

"I'll look forward to that day! Come now, it's getting late, you should get on your way."

"Yes, Father, I guess I'd better be going," he said, forcing a smile but not wanting to release the old man's hands. Looking

8

deeply into his father's eyes, he finally let go, backed up a few steps, bowed deeply, and then turned and strode away.

The morning sun seemed to have risen quickly. Thousands of rays of light passed through unusually red clouds, casting a glow on the earth and the old man. When my father next turned to look, his father was a distant figure but appeared somehow to be standing straighter, taller.

My father walked on. Ahead, the rising sun shone full on the long, narrow mountain pass he needed to cross. He took one last look at Yanmen, at his father. He could barely make out the old man standing on the ridgeline far below. But by squinting and looking hard he could still see his father slowly waving his right hand in the morning sun, in the rosy light that fell through the morning's remarkable red clouds.

———————

IT TOOK MY FATHER OVER two weeks to travel the 800 kilometers from Yanmen to Peking, hitching an occasional ride on a passing cart and doing odd jobs along the way in return for food and lodging. He could have taken the train, but wanting to save every bit of money he could, he walked. His only expense for the trip was buying two pair of cloth shoes from a street peddler to replace the ones he wore out.

After his journey, my father entered Peking through the Yongdingmen Gate. (This magnificent and imposing structure was built in 1553, torn down in 1958, and its replica constructed on the same site in 2004.) He found a small inn in the Tianqiao area, which had only one wide bed for all its guests. Late on his second day in the city, quite by accident, he found the Preparatory French School. Father Clement had told him he must attend it before he could be admitted to the University.

With his heavy Henan accent and ragged clothes, my father was almost rejected at first sight. However, Father Clement's patient tutoring and my father's diligent study paid off. His accurate French pronunciation astonished the examiners, and he was admitted.

When he filled in the registration form, my father changed his first name from Weizhen to Pinzhi to signify a new beginning to his great expectations. Adding to one's name was not unusual, especially for intellectuals. Traditionally in China, all first names have a meaning. Weizhen meant "containing treasure." Pinzhi, a very literary name, was harder to interpret. I didn't ask my father but rather learned its meaning from Mr. Sun, a close friend of my father who was also my tutor. Pinzhi means "an invitation to accomplish great achievements." Mr. Sun told me that when he and my father attended the same school not far from Yanmen, he could already predict that my father was destined for lofty things.

My father was a natural and devoted student, full of curiosity and high ideals. His first year in Peking passed quickly. Aside from his studies and part-time work as a classical Chinese tutor, he cared deeply about helping to build his nation. He saw the need for educating the masses, emancipating women, securing individual freedoms, and promoting science and democracy. Only then could China break the chains of imperialism, stand strong, and join the modern world on equal footing. To work toward these goals, as soon as he got into Peking University he joined the New Culture Movement that he had first learned about in Yanmen.

Sunday, May 4, 1919 began bright and early for my father and turned out to be the dawning of a new age in China, a red dawn. That morning he arose with the sun and finished work on three large protest signs he had volunteered to prepare. His bold calligraphy read: "Don't sign the Treaty of Versailles," "Struggle for sovereignty externally. Get rid of traitors at home," and "No more imperialism."

Once he had washed his brushes, he hurried to join his fellow students from Peking University and a dozen other universities in a meeting. He was eager to see what steps the protest would take next. The gathering combined youth and nationalism for the first time in China's history. The sparks that kindled such revolutionary and nationalistic fires in China began with the terms of the Treaty of Versailles, which ended World War I.

Despite its stated goals of advancing democracy and self-determination, the Paris Peace Conference awarded China's resource-rich Tsingtao region on the Shandong Peninsula—formerly a German leasehold—to the Japanese. This was bad enough, but then it was learned that the Chinese government had already given the Japanese rights to the area in exchange for a large loan.

When news of this treachery reached China, the students were outraged at their spineless and corrupt government, at the hypocritical and double-dealing Western powers, and at imperialistic Japan. After meeting and drafting resolutions and a manifesto, more than 3,000 students assembled in Tiananmen Square to demonstrate. My father was filled with feelings of strength, pride, and confidence. He had never felt such energy before. It was electric as it surged through the crowd. He felt like a true pioneer helping to take his country where it had never been before.

The students waved their banners, flags, and placards. They shouted slogans and cheered their leaders. In vain, the police chief and education minister pleaded with the students to disperse. Speakers brought the crowd to a frenzy, reserving their harshest words for the Chinese officials who had collaborated with the Japanese. Especially reviled was Communications Minister Cao Rulin, one of the Cabinet's leaders. The crowd called for all of the collaborators to be sacked and the treaty to be rejected.

En masse, the students then moved to the capital's diplomatic quarter, where they submitted petitions to the legations of the great Western powers, but the demonstrators were not through yet. Amidst cries of "On to the traitor's house," they marched to Cao Rulin's compound on nearby Zhaojialou Lane. The militia and police assembled there tried and failed to protect the residence.

My father was short and thin but strong and nimble. He was one of the first half-dozen students who climbed over the residence wall and opened the main gate, allowing the crowd to pour into the compound. They used bamboo poles to knock off roof tiles and break windows, through which they entered the house.

Cao Rulin had escaped, but inside the students found Zhang Zongxiang, Minister Plenipotentiary to Japan, who had been involved in turning over Tsingtao. They took him outside and roundly beat him. Then in their calculated rage, the students methodically sacked and burned the place. During the melee, more than 30 protestors were arrested and imprisoned. As dusk descended and the flames began to die down, the troops and civil authorities finally restored order and the crowd disbanded.

A slow drizzle fell from the darkening sky, and occasional gusts buffeted my father as he returned to the boarding house where he lived. Despite the wind, the smell of smoke was strong all the way home. It permeated his hair and clothes and filled his nostrils.

May 4 was the most exhausting and exhilarating day of his life. Although he had no way of knowing how quickly and how far the unrest would spread throughout the rest of China, he had played a role in setting in motion the greatest social, political, and cultural change his country had yet seen. Without undressing, he lay down on his bed and fell asleep immediately.

IT WAS AT THE BOARDING house that my father met his wife-to-be, Fu Junying, my mother. She had been born into a very poor family near Baoding in Hebei Province. Along with her two younger sisters and a brother, my mother had come to Peking with their father, who was the chef in the boarding house that served as dormitory and dining hall for many college students. The sisters helped in the kitchen and cleaned up after meals. My mother was just 15 years old when my father met her and had blossomed into such a beauty that every boarder gazed on her with admiration, some with lust.

For her part, my mother saved her shy glances for my father, the poorest boarder in the house and 10 years her senior. My father always arrived late for meals, entering only after the other students had left and my mother had already started cleaning up, so that they could be alone together. For a long time, they never spoke to each other, communicating only through their eyes and smiles. They felt an immediate attraction, a powerful connection, a non-verbal meeting of minds that grew into profound love. They had so much in common, including their poverty, their simplicity, and their hunger for a better life.

My mother and father wed in 1923. Within a year, my father graduated from Peking University, began teaching French language and literature, and fathered his first son, Jisheng. As a poorly paid beginning lecturer, he had to take as many jobs as possible to provide for his growing family. He bought a German-made bicycle to travel between his four different university posts, two middle-school positions, and one tutoring job with an autistic adolescent. Each day, he commuted up to four hours between his various places of employment, returning home each evening exhausted. By 1929, my parents had saved enough money to buy and thoroughly renovate a small house for a very low price, a dilapidated wreck in a good neighborhood on the east side of the newly renamed Peiping. Three sons and a daughter were then part of the family, so the move to larger quarters was timely.

After 10 years of teaching and translating writers such as Anatole France and Madame de Lafayette, my father had established himself as a leading intellectual, inspiring teacher, and distinguished professor at the Sino-French University. During his summer vacation of 1935, he produced China's first bilingual French textbooks. With my mother's full support, he sequestered himself in a small room at the Auguste Comte Middle School, a part of his university. For two months, my father never went home, never even left the school grounds. His only outdoor activities were running in the playground and bathing in the outdoor bath. Twice a day, my mother sent a meal over. Otherwise he worked day and night writing and compiling his *magnum opus*. Before the vacation ended, piles of his manuscript filled the desks of his editors at the university press.

The three volumes of *La Langue Française* were published in 1936 and quickly became widely used by universities and middle schools throughout China. His productive tenure in the ivory tower, however, was soon to end. China was on the verge of a long, cruel, and costly war with Japan that would turn out to be the largest Asian war of the 20th century. Suffering through eight years of brutal attack and occupation, 35 million Chinese lost their lives.

———·•·———

ON JULY 7, 1937, OFFICERS of Japan's Guandong Army manufactured an incident outside of Peiping at the Marco Polo Bridge. This ploy was part of their well-designed plan to launch an all-out invasion of China. They took Peiping the next day, and, with the arrival of reinforcements from Manchuria, easily occupied the entire region. Nine days later, Chiang Kai-shek announced that China was at war with Japan to the finish. China's struggle for national survival had begun.

Not long after, my father suffered a deep personal tragedy. His mother, still in Yanmen, broke down from her constant overwork. By August, she was dead. My father brought my grandfather to Peiping before the situation in our occupied hometown deteriorated.

Unwilling to teach in universities and schools controlled by the Japanese, my father resigned all his academic positions and looked for other employment. After extended conversations with my mother, my father joined professors from Peking University, Tsinghua University, and Nankai University intending to travel to Kunming, Yunnan Province, to join the Southwest United University, which was formed in April 1938. My father made the long, tough journey all the way to Hong

Kong and then by boat to Vietnam, but never got as far as Kunming. When he learned of my mother's illness, he returned home, jobless.

In an instant, our family was in uncomfortable financial straits. To raise money, my father even sold the copyright to his textbooks. My parents decided to move out of our newly renovated house and rent it to a German family. With the half-year rental deposit, the copyright sale, and years of savings, my parents entered the real estate business.

During the war with Japan, refugees flooded Peiping and were eager to buy inexpensive homes. My father's creative approach was to buy old, even collapsed and deserted houses at low prices, restore them to decent condition, and sell them at reasonable prices. In order to start his venture, he needed a trustworthy construction team. At this critical moment, my father met Uncle Lee. From the beginning, they talked with each other like old friends. Uncle Lee, 12 years younger than my father, was from a poor village in Miyun, a county to the north of Peiping. Their village and Shilipu Township nearby didn't produce many agricultural products, but they did produce many skilfull handymen, carpenters, and masons. My father explained his idea and the tenuous financial condition he was in to Uncle Lee. Uncle Lee told my father that his men would be pleased with only room and board to start the venture. All wages could be paid after my father sold the first renovated house. This generous offer significantly reduced my father's initial cash investment and started the ball rolling.

Uncle Lee's team made the first old house that my parents bought into a residence for the workers. My parents' first foray into real estate, a business with which they were almost totally unfamiliar, became a very prosperous model. Uncle Lee also helped to obtain raw materials from his hometown where they were cheaper than what was generally available. It turned out that my father's first renovation job was completed much better, faster, and cheaper than he expected, and the house quickly sold for much more than he expected. When Uncle Lee and his workers received their first lump-sum cash payment in big red envelopes at the end of the year, it took them a long time to count out all the bank notes.

A sound concept, savvy strategy, and good friends enabled my father to soon become the most competitive builder in Peiping's housing market. At first, their main customers were relatives, friends, and university colleagues, but soon new customers were attracted by affordable prices for good quality residences in safe areas. Business boomed. At its peak in the mid to late 1940s, the family business sold dozens of houses monthly and had many others under reconstruction in inventory. It was one of the largest realties in town.

When I, the youngest son, was born on August 3, 1939, however, my parents were still a poor couple. Overjoyed to have such a fine boy—and so big—they were also disappointed that they couldn't afford the traditional first-month birthday party for me. However, my father was pleased that he found a very good name for me, Songsheng. "Song" means "high" and "mountain" and "sheng" means "born." "Song" is the first word of Songzhusi Hutong, where we lived at the time. More importantly, it is also the name of Mount Song in Henan Province, one of China's five sacred peaks. There the Shaolin Temple and almost 250 pagodas are located amidst such a remarkable landscape that Mt. Song has been designated as a UNESCO International Geological Park.

My parents believed very strongly that my birth was an auspicious sign for the family's prosperity. The casting of my *bazi*, or birth chart, was most propitious. In the Chinese lunar calendar, 1939 was the year of the rabbit. I was born exactly at 2:00 PM and weighed nine pounds even. These factors, my astrological determinants, and the eight characters that marked my birth all indicated that I would have a most fortunate lot in life and that my birth foretold a turning point in the family fortunes.

Those beliefs quickly began to be realized as, even under Japanese occupation, my parents' business flourished. A Japanese general took a fancy to our much-beloved home along the moat on the east side of the Forbidden City. He forced my parents to sell it to him and gave them an extravagant sum as a display of his wealth. My parents used the proceeds and their savings to purchase the former residence of a Manchu aristocrat, a relative of China's last emperor, Puyi. Although completely dilapidated, it was the largest palace in Peiping in private hands: 120 rooms, seven courtyards, and extensive gardens. Late in the fall of 1941, my father toured the palace for the first time with the broker and Uncle Lee. It was literally breathtaking. The place had been abandoned after the downfall of the Qing dynasty and had become a flophouse for transients and worse. The stench from human excrement and urine so befouled the air that breathing was difficult at times. The prince's palace had turned into the proverbial den of iniquity. Prostitutes and drug dealers openly plied their trades. In the huge parlor, about 20 people sprawled on the floor, smoking opium and taking other drugs. Off to the far side, several young men attacked an older man, who from the sounds of things owed them money for drugs. They kicked at him as he writhed on the floor. Before my father could try to intervene, the broker steered him and Uncle Lee out of the parlor and further into the decayed remains of the once magnificent palace.

The gardens had also been ruined by neglect. They were thick with weeds, and the stark limbs of dead trees stood out across the landscape. The only building in the garden, a large complex with several adjoining rooms, was almost completely collapsed. Even the addicts and derelicts kept their distance from this dangerous structure.

Despite his own doubts and against the advice of his friends and family, my father finally told the prince's broker that he would pay the asking price but only if all the people staying in the palace were relocated within one month. Once the sale was final, my father invited architects from the Imperial Museum to advise his design team. One major challenge was maintaining the integrity of the prince's palace while outfitting it with modern facilities and equipment. The heating system and bathrooms, for instance, were imported from Europe. It took two full years for him and his workers to rebuild the palace.

My grandfather, even shorter and thinner in his old age than in his Yanmen days, spent all his time at the various construction projects with me and the other children of the household. We collected nails and wood shavings and scraps into baskets and performed other tasks. Used nails were hammered straight and the wood was carried to the kitchen to cook the workers' meals. We ate while chatting happily with the workers. Many of them didn't even know that this old man was the father of their boss.

What I liked best of all about living in the palace was playing in the gardens. My father lovingly restored and expanded them, turning the huge garden space into two parts. The front was landscaped elaborately and imaginatively. The back became a large vegetable garden called the kale yard. At one edge was a manual windlass to draw water from a newly excavated well for irrigation. My father dug it shortly after we moved in. It reminded him of the well at home, of the sweet water that had been the source of our family's good fortune in Yanmen.

A good-sized building was located between the two gardens, which my father named Xanadu from Samuel Taylor Coleridge's poem. The poem was inspired by Marco Polo's description of Shangdu and Kublai Khan's summer palace. My father's Xanadu consisted of two halls, a study, a suite of eight adjoining rooms, and a basement. Here my cousins and I had our very own "preschool" and could play in bad weather.

A small stream and pond spanned by a stone bridge were my favorite part of the front garden. Ornamental flower parterres guarded the entrance to Xanadu. Throughout the compound stood seven stately jujube trees, the date-like native of China. Along the high walls of one side of the garden was a stand of bamboo and an amphitheater for performances.

My family cultivated a wide variety of vegetables in the back garden. I learned how to prepare the soil, plant seeds, draw water from the well, weed, and harvest. After calluses appeared on my little hands, I had a greater appreciation of the children's poem, "Farmers weeding at noon, Sweat down the field soon. Who knows food on a tray, thanks to their toiling day?" Lots of food, much of it home grown, graced our dining table. There were never any leftovers. We shared the vast amounts of food produced in our garden with family and friends, even strangers.

After one year in the kindergarten, I went to primary school in 1944 when I was five years old. Two years later, I was transferred from Auguste Comte Primary School to a missionary school, Yuying Primary School. It was a very nice and also a very expensive school. I still remember how Old Zhu, our pedicab driver, had to put two big bags of the fast-depreciating banknotes in the pedicab to take my mother and me to the school to pay my fees. I started learning English and got my English first name, Stephen, from a kind woman teacher. She gave all her students English first names that started with the same letter as their Chinese first names. She told me she chose Stephen for me from the Bible. I'm glad I didn't learn until later that Stephen was stoned to death.

I spent most of my time after school in the gardens. I often played in or near the stream and pond and learned how to swim there without my mother ever learning of my derring-do. I loved the seven jujube trees. I often got stomach pains and the "runs" from eating too many dates. They were so good, I just couldn't stop myself. I was an excellent climber and the only one in the family who could reach the sweetest dates remaining on the highest branches after harvest. If the jujubes fell by themselves or were shaken from tree branches, most would break. I always saved those especially sweet whole dates for my parents; for Nanna Ma, my former wet nurse; and, most importantly, for my favorite playmate, Lifen.

With my schoolmates, I enjoyed playing field hockey on the palace's broad grass field. Just before the end of summer vacation, all the parents and close family friends would be invited to the championship games and an outdoor barbecue afterward. The happiest years of my life were the carefree times in the palace. Neither the occupation by Japan nor the fierce civil war that tore the country apart afterward spoiled the joy of childhood for me.

My grandfather died in the summer of 1943. I was heartbroken at his death, but it ended months of bedridden misery and several unsuccessful surgeries. Whenever the old man had felt well enough, he loved to have me sit close to him on his bed. He would tell me story after story about Yanmen village and Wangwu Mountain. My favorite was about the Mountain of the Temple of Heaven. Emperors of the Ming and Qing dynasties so disliked making the arduous pilgrimage to Wangwu Mountain that they built their own Temple of Heaven in Beijing.

Another of Grandfather's stories that I loved was "The Foolish Old Man Who Removed Mountains." The Foolish Old Man didn't like that the Wangwu and Taihang mountains obstructed his way and decided that he and his sons would begin removing them. The Wise Old Man told him that he could never complete the job. To this day, I remember every word of the Foolish Old Man's retort: "You are so conceited that you are blind to reason. Even a widow and a child know better than you. When I die, there will be my sons, who will have their sons and grandsons. Those grandsons will have their sons and grandsons, and so on to infinity. But the mountains will not grow. Why is it impossible to level them?"—to which the Wise Old Man had no reply. It was clear from the way that Grandfather told the story that he admired perseverance.

The day of the funeral was a sad but exciting one for me. The ceremony had created quite a stir in Peiping. In deference to our family, from morning to afternoon an endless stream of people came to the memorial service in Jiaxing Temple. I was fascinated by the chanting of the Buddhist monks and Daoist priests. When the burial procession set off in the afternoon, its head arrived at Di An Men Gate while its tail was still inside the temple, two kilometers away. An abundance of tables provided a continuous feast for all in attendance.

My parents had prepared themselves well for the turning point following the surrender of Japan. They had established an excellent reputation and had more houses in inventory than any other realty in town. Thousands of families flooded Peiping, and the real estate market quickly boomed. My parent's diligence and foresight were amply rewarded, and our family fortune was made. My birth chart had correctly foretold this turn of events.

I loved watching my mother and father work together, especially when they sat at their special desk, built for the two of them. I learned the lessons of a lifetime watching my parents at work and remembering my father's and grandfather's stories. I marveled that the wonderful life we led had all started with 20 silver coins. It made me think of one of my father's favorite sayings: "Everyone has opportunities. Only those who are prepared to seize them benefit." I vowed to be prepared in my life.

Chapter 1

TREASURES IN TROUBLED TIMES

1948
Peiping, China

DUSK FELL UPON DI AN Men Street. All about, strewn flyers urged residents to "Destroy the Communist bandits and suppress the rebellion." Because of the blackout, the street lamps stood dark like sullen sentinels. Shop lights were covered with thick black paper or cloth. Pasted to every window in sight were crossed strips of paper to limit damage in case the city was bombed. The imposing Drum Tower, unmanned ever since the deposed Emperor Puyi had left the Forbidden City, loomed silent at the far end of the street.

Distant gunfire punctuated the steady whistle of the frigid northwest wind. The Communists were advancing and the Nationalists retreating everywhere. The rickety trolley cars with their grating bells made the only other sounds.

Many stores on Di An Men Street had already closed. A desperate few, still hoping to lure one or two more customers, stayed open. Signboards promised "Sacrifice Prices," "Closing Sale," or other fortunate opportunities for buyers, but the streets were empty. Even the vagrants and beggars who frequented the arcade of the Di An Men Gate had disappeared. The city was under attack, in the midst of a severe winter, and would soon be pitch dark. New Year's Eve 1948 in Peiping had no air of festivity to it at all.

An antiquities dealer on the west side of the street still had his lights on. It was a small storefront, with a magnificent sign above the door for which my father had provided the calligraphy. Against a black background, three raised characters painted gold—Pin Gu Zhai—stood out and proclaimed Select Antiquities Studio. My father and I entered the dimly lit establishment and joined a scholarly looking group of my father's friends already assembled around an elm wood table. I often accompanied my father to this shop, but tonight was special. After greetings were exchanged, the shop owner got right down to business.

"You would be acquiring quite a treasure, a national treasure really, Professor Chen. But I fear at quite a price. The owner's chamberlain said if they took it abroad, they would make an absolute fortune from it. They know full well its value," the bony, middle-aged man said.

"Have you had the experts verify it, Mr. Qi?" My father was considering a staggering investment and needed everything to be in order.

"Absolutely. Quite a few authorities, in fact, including your friends from the Imperial Museum."

"It is unquestionably authentic," said Chang Weijun, the Imperial Museum's senior researcher and my father's friend since college. "Its owner is named Jin, a descendant of a close relative of the Aisin Gioro imperial clan of the Qing Dynasty. Only such a family would be able to acquire such a treasure. Mr. Qi told him that you have rebuilt the Prince's residence. That's why he agreed to consider you as a buyer."

"You know the adage as well as I do. 'Invest in times of peace and hoard in times of trouble.' Thirty gold bars is a lot of money, especially given the situation we're in now," my father replied. He liked being able to propose the apt aphorism for any situation.

Mr. Chang's head bobbed in agreement. "How true. Thirty gold bars. Fifteen kilograms of gold." After a pause, he added, "For which you could buy two-and-a-half million kilograms of rice. Does it make any sense to spend so much money in such turbulent times? Lots of people with rare items in their pockets are begging for food today."

Mr. Qi sighed and said, "But then there's the question of having a national treasure go abroad, where we may lose touch with it."

"Mr. Liu." Mr. Qi turned and spoke to the short, stout man beside him. "What do you think?"

Liu Bowen, one of China's most renowned antiques brokers, adjusted his glasses, wheezed, and cleared his throat. "I think Professor Chen should meet Mr. Jin and see this treasure with his own eyes before we reach a decision."

"Exactly, Mr. Liu," my father nodded.

"The sooner the better," Mr. Qi said at once. "Mr. Jin needs a prompt reply. The family plans to flee south within the next few days."

"Mr. Qi, please pay another visit to Mr. Jin. See whether we can call upon him this evening. Mr. Liu and Mr. Chang, if you don't have other plans, please join me at my home for a simple meal. We can wait there for Mr. Qi's message."

"Let's go, Mr. Liu," Mr. Chang said as he helped his portly companion up and took his arm. Liu was not yet 50, but he had the look and bearing of someone far older. He was not in good health and rarely left home. When he did, he was impeccably and elegantly dressed. Tonight he looked especially well-attired.

Chang helped his friend out of the shop and into my father's black Dodge sedan. After a short drive, the car pulled up to the wall outside No. 3, Cihui Hutong. We walked through the gate, along the gray brick corridor, and up the steps through the deeply carved inner gate. We then crossed the porch, went through a third gate, and finally arrived at the big parlor of the main courtyard.

My mother was waiting at the doorway. "How are you, dear friends? You certainly are a fine sight for these sore eyes. We should see each other more often."

"You might see us more frequently if it weren't such a hard journey to get here."

"What do you mean?"

"I feel I've walked a full kilometer from the first gate to this doorway," Mr. Liu said with a smile but breathing heavily.

"Now don't tease me after all this time. Let me help you," said my mother as she guided the men into the large parlor.

My parents had kept the room to the same dimensions it had been when the palace served as the Prince's residence. It was much broader, higher, and five times longer than parlors of normal mansions. Inside were elegant eight-leaf screens, a hallmark of the Chen family, including four landscape paintings and four traditional calligraphy scrolls. All were done by noted Chinese artists and calligraphers of the time, each an intimate friend of my father.

The centerpiece of the eight screens was a picture of splendid plum blossoms in winter, so full and evocative that visitors often found themselves trying to catch a whiff of their fragrance. The panel above showed four pied magpies singing happily in the plum tree's upper branches. It was a tour de force by Master Qi Baishi and displayed his special, luminous red ink. The four birds represented the four Chen sons, while the blossoms were a reminder that the warm lushness of the autumn fruits started with the hard winter's flowers. My father liked to get to the heart of the matter and to be succinct. Sometimes when we asked about the picture, he would simply say, "No sweat, no sweet."

In the middle of the parlor was a huge bed of elaborately carved rosewood that was used for seating when it wasn't used for sleeping. It was my grandfather's place of repose. Behind it now was a long, narrow rosewood table on which my father had placed a large photograph of my grandfather after he died in 1943.

Sometimes just passing by my grandfather's picture put a lump in my throat and made me feel like crying. I also took joy, however, from looking into my grandfather's kindly eyes, so accurately portrayed in the picture. It brought back fond memories for me of wonderful stories about Yanmen, my grandfather's home, so far away from the noisy and busy city. I never tired of hearing these tales, and my grandfather had never tired of telling them.

The eastern hall contained my favorite piece in the mansion—a tall clock with a long pendulum, the gift of a French businessman. A little toy man mounted on a horse rode around the top of the clock when it rang the hour. And in this hall, sitting behind the small desk my mother had arranged for me so she could watch me doing my homework, I liked to watch my parents work at the large rosewood desk they used every day. It had drawers on both sides and a marble top with patterns resembling swirling clouds and tranquil water. My parents appeared very much in love as they shared the desk and their thoughts and took care of their business. My father said he liked to read and write while listening to the clicks of my mother's abacus. The western hall was decorated in the modern style. Large garden pots of tall pomegranates, osmanthus, and balata brought vitality and a delightful scent to the surroundings.

The group walked into the parlor where an older and a younger man were conversing. My mother made introductions. "Mr. Liu, Mr. Chang, this is Mr. Yu, my husband's closest colleague and the wonder worker who oversees our finances. And this handsome young man is Zhijie, Pinzhi's nephew from his hometown in Henan."

"When did you get here, Zhijie? I haven't seen you for ages." My father smiled affectionately.

"Hello, Uncle. I just arrived. It's been a rough trip. The Reds are everywhere. They control the Northeastern provinces and almost all the north. Jisheng says Peiping will be completely overrun within the month. I couldn't have made it here without his help."

"Where is Jisheng?" My father asked after my eldest brother.

"He's with General Yuan in the salon. They have something to discuss with you."

My father turned to Mr. Yu and said, "Please show our guests to the dining room. People must be hungry after this long day. Junying, Songsheng, and I will join you shortly."

The salon was in the western end of the main parlor. My mother knocked lightly on the door and Jisheng let us in. I smiled and nodded at my brother and quietly made my way to a corner as my parents had directed.

"Sorry to have kept you waiting, General Yuan," my father greeted the middle-aged man. Yuan had an obvious military bearing but was traveling in civilian clothes. He had known our family for years and was aide-de-camp to General Sun Lianzhong, Chief of Staff in President Chiang Kai-shek's Office. General Sun and his wife, Yufeng, were among my parents' closest friends.

"I pay this unannounced visit with orders to tell you specifically what is happening in Nanking. While we were waiting for you, I briefed General Chen in some detail."

My father had a hard time accepting my brother's rank. "Jisheng's too young to be a general. He got promoted only because General Fu needed to expand the army."

"You are too modest. Your son has what it takes to lead—he showed that in his service against the Japanese—and he has graduated from military school."

Jisheng was in the 14th graduating class of the Whampoa Military Academy that Chiang Kai-shek once headed and where Zhou Enlai had been director of the Political Department. It provided many leaders to both sides of the civil war. After graduating, Jisheng was appointed a platoon leader in the Nationalist Army to fight against the Japanese. Within three years, he was promoted to a battalion commander and critically wounded at a battle in southern Henan Province. A Japanese bullet went through his chest, but he survived.

My father sat down on the sofa next to the general and listened intently as he said, "The current situation is deteriorating daily. Chiang Kai-shek plans to submit his resignation soon. General Sun and his wife sent me a confidential telegram from Nanking, asking me to get word to you and Mrs. Chen that they are determined to leave the mainland for Taiwan."

"Oh, my!" exclaimed my mother, still with some surprise despite the inevitability of the news.

"They urge you to decide without delay whether to stay or leave. Tickets for Taiwan are getting harder and harder to obtain. But the Presidential Chief's Office can help," Yuan said gravely.

Jisheng said, "The end can't be far. We heard that General Fu has been in contact with officers of the Communist Party through his daughter, who is an underground member of the Communist Party here."

General Yuan confirmed the rumor. "Yes, it is true. General Fu even asked the Communist Army to bomb the airport in the Temple of Heaven to prevent Chiang Kai-shek's son from flying in. General Fu had built this temporary landing strip to accommodate his own evacuation should he need it."

"Really?" My father was pleasantly surprised by this piece of news.

"Absolutely true. General Fu doesn't want to be bothered by Generalissimo Chiang and his Nanking government."

"Then a peaceful turnover of Peiping is truly possible." My father had never given up this hope.

"Be that as it may," Jisheng said, "we still should be wary of the Communists. They don't keep promises and always turn against friends! I've given it long and serious consideration, and my family and I have decided to leave Peiping for the south."

"How?" my mother asked.

"First to Tsingtao and then Shanghai. We'll pick our steps."

Jisheng's revelation proved to be a conversation stopper. Finally, General Yuan broke the uneasy silence that had fallen upon the group. "The question is not just what is going to happen next week or next month, but what will happen down the road. Dear friends, you must think about whether you can trust the Communists with your future!"

The room fell quiet until General Yuan broke the silence again.

"If you intend to leave, General Sun is the one person who can help. Please ask Jisheng to stay in contact with me before I leave Peiping. I would spare no effort if I could be of service to you." General Yuan rose to leave.

"How can we ever repay you for your kindness?" My mother took his hand.

"Don't mention it, Mrs. Chen. Mrs. Luo also asked me to tell you that she's eager to play mah-jongg with you as there aren't many good players in Nanking."

"She's always such a joy to be around. Please do remember us to General Sun and Yufeng."

"Jisheng, ask Wu to get the car ready for General Yuan," my mother said.

"It would be more discreet to have Zhu take General Yuan back by pedicab," my father said. "Let us see you off, General Yuan."

"Professor Chen, Mrs. Chen, don't bother. Let Jisheng do it for you."

"Just to the doorway," my father insisted.

My father and mother accompanied General Yuan to the entrance foyer. I kept back, but as my brother opened the door, I could see Old Zhu waiting by a covered pedicab, holding a flap open.

"I wish you a safe trip, General Yuan." My father grasped Yuan's hand.

"Take care of yourselves. I hope we may meet again soon and under happier circumstances." Yuan inclined his head in their direction, waved his hand in a salute, turned sharply, and walked out.

My parents, Jisheng, and I made our way to the dining room in the main courtyard. People around the table were enjoying aromatic pork hotpot and drinking Huadiao yellow liquor while listening to Zhijie talk about his journey to Peiping.

"We could smell this wonderful dinner from afar." Jisheng took his seat and right away raised a glass. "Before I dig in, though, I'd like to toast to Uncle Zhang, Uncle Liu, and Cousin Zhijie."

"I want to toast too," I said.

"Children should not drink alcohol," my mother said, removing my cup.

"It's not liquor, mum. It's just tea." I took my cup back.

"You are so quick, Songsheng." My mother smiled with pride.

"Where are the other children?" my father asked.

"They're skating on the rink in the back garden," I replied.

"This is how children should be, without a care in the world," Mr. Chang said. "They bring a touch of joy to our New Year, which otherwise is pretty bleak."

Mr. Liu said, "Carpe diem! Even in troubled times, we must take the time to enjoy life."

"That's for sure." Zhijie stood up and topped everyone's drink. "For now, let us toast to the moment, friends and family together."

"Speaking of family, Zhijie, how are things at home?" my father asked.

"Very bad, Uncle. Most young men have left Yanmen and Jiyuan and headed south, leaving the elderly, women, and children to fend for themselves. Between wars and lousy harvests, people are living on dried sweet potatoes and wild potherbs."

My father looked sad. "I want you to take some gold back to Yanmen and buy food for the families who need it."

"Auntie has already told Mr. Yu to take care of it, to have the gold hammered into flakes and sewn inside wadded jackets so I can take it back safely."

Jisheng said, "Zhijie will go by way of Baoding. My friends at the Military School can get him a rail ticket to Jiyuan Town. Someone from Yanmen can meet him there."

"Mr. Yu, tell our counting room to prepare more gold flakes for Zhijie. This is literally a matter of life or death."

"Please put your mind at rest, sir; it will be done. Excuse me, everyone," Mr. Yu said as he walked out.

The hot pot was steaming and wonderful aromas filled the dining room, but nobody had an appetite except me. Again, conversation lapsed. The company was preoccupied and, for the moment at least, content to drown their sorrows. Zhijie took a new bottle from the sideboard and filled everyone's glasses. The telephone broke the silence.

My mother answered, said a few words, and replaced the phone in the cradle. "That was Mr. Qi. He asked you to come promptly to Mr. Jin's place. He'll await you on the corner of Beichizi Avenue."

"Zhijie, I have some important business to attend to with Mr. Liu and Mr. Chang. Your auntie and Jisheng will help you get things ready. Let's talk more when I get back," my father said.

"Let me go too!" I pleaded.

"You'd just be getting underfoot when there are serious matters to discuss," said my mother.

"Oh, it's alright. Let him see something new." My father was strict with his children, but he always wanted us to learn more about the world, so he often took me along when he went to Select Antiquities Studio or met with his old friends. I loved listening to adult conversation. So, at my father's words, I ran out of the room to get his coat. My father, Mr. Chang, and Mr. Liu followed.

"Pinzhi," my mother caught up and whispered to him, "Don't forget that you have an appointment to meet Hanchen in the garden study tonight."

"I won't. If I am a little late, please talk with him first."

The Dodge left Cihui Hutong and crossed East Jingshan Street. It didn't pass another car on the dark streets all the way to the west side of the Forbidden City where Mr. Qi awaited them at the appointed corner. As the car was too wide to get into the lane, Wu parked it and turned off the lights. Mr. Qi led the car's occupants down the alley until they saw Mr. Jin standing in front of a red double door.

My mouth dropped open and my eyes grew wide. An old man in a fur cap and fur coat greeted us. He smiled warmly at me. Never in my life had I ever seen such a display of finery. By contrast, my father had the money to wear fancy clothes but was a simple man who dressed in the simplest ways. He never wore leather shoes—preferring his cotton-padded footwear— or a suit, as did most of his colleagues.

Mr. Jin admitted them into the main parlor. I thought it looked very old-fashioned and almost empty. A long straight table with a damask runner and several chairs stood in the center of the room. The old man asked everyone to take a seat. A servant poured each of us a cup of fragrant jasmine tea.

"You are Mr. Chen, I presume?" Mr. Jin nodded to Mr. Liu.

"No, no. I'm Liu. My friend here is the buyer." Mr. Liu gestured to his right.

Mr. Jin turned and apologized to my father. "Please excuse my presumption."

Mr. Qi broke in at once. "You know the old proverb, 'The wise buyer never shows his silver.'" The gentlemen all smiled, and I thought about what I had just heard. The saying was new to me.

"Mr. Jin, this is Professor Chen Pinzhi, about whom I have spoken at such length. Professor Chen spent two years restoring your uncle's palace."

Mr. Jin made a reverent bow to my father. "My family owes you a debt of gratitude, Mr. Chen. Most of my relatives are in quite desperate shape, not even able to support their own families. Without you, my uncle's residence would have fallen into utter ruin."

My father returned the bow with folded hands and said, "Mr. Jin, please allow me to thank your family for the opportunity to fulfil my dream, to bring such a magnificent structure back to its glory. I believe that the Chen family has been allowed to borrow the palace for a time and enjoy its beauty."

Mr. Jin looked at me. "And who might this young master be?"

Mr. Qi said, "This is the youngest son of Professor Chen, Songsheng."

Mr. Jin beamed benignly. He seemed to take an immediate liking to me.

Mr. Qi said, "Mr. Jin, in view of the hour, could you please bring out the treasure? I must confess I can hardly contain my excitement."

"Certainly. Let me show you my family's most valued possession."

Several servants in gowns and jackets put on pairs of white gloves and lit sandalwood. One placed an embroidered cushion on the table. Another lay a cushion on the floor directly in front of the table. The head man walked slowly to the table, holding in both hands a rosewood box set on all four sides with deep emerald jade. He gently put the case on the cushion and then stood aside.

Mr. Jin rose and said to us, "This rosewood case bears the imperial seal of Emperor Qianlong, my great ancestor. According to my family code, I must perform a short ritual before opening this case. Please allow me."

Mr. Jin walked slowly to the table and slowly knelt down on the cushion. He folded and lifted his hands above his forehead and kowtowed three times. Then he stood up and put on white gloves. After taking off the box cover, he withdrew a wood dowel and laid down the four sideboards of the box. This revealed an inkstone case made of dark yellow wood. Mr.

Jin gently took the cover off, and everyone saw the ancient inkstone, quite worn.

"This is the inkstone of Chu Suiliang, the famed chancellor, calligrapher, and poet of the Tang Dynasty, whose writings have been admired for 1,300 years." Mr. Jin lifted it carefully. "This treasure is precious not only for itself but also for these rosewood side boards. Each board displays the imperial seals of emperors from the Tang, Song, Ming, and Qing Dynasties." All eyes were upon the opened box and the four seals impressed upon its yellow satin liner.

Mr. Jin continued, "As far as I know, there's nothing like it in the world, one piece with four imperial seals." He called for a servant to bring a magnifier for his distinguished guests and a footrest to help me see it more clearly.

I was allowed to examine the treasure first, and as I carefully scrutinized each of the seals through the glass, Mr. Jin explained, "The earliest seal is from Emperor Gaozong of Tang. Chu Suiliang began his service with Gaozong's father, Taizong. When you open the four side boards of the box, you'll see the Tang seal on top, then seals of Emperor Shenzong of the Song Dynasty, Emperor Chengzu of the Ming Dynasty, and Emperor Qianlong, my revered ancestor."

At that moment the room was so quiet that everybody's breathing could easily be heard. Taking turns, everyone held the magnifier and enjoyed the four imperial seals, practically ignoring the inkstone.

My father raised his head and asked sadly, "How can you part with such a family treasure?"

"To be honest, parting with this makes my heart ache. I would give up everything else we are fleeing with in exchange for this treasure. But our trip is perilous, fraught with all sorts of dangers. I could not face my ancestors if anything happened to this precious family possession. I've turned it over in my thoughts again and again and made up my mind. The safest thing to do is to leave it here, entrusted to a man of perception and honor. I think you are that man."

"Mr. Jin, I believe that Professor Chen cherishes this treasure with a depth exceeded only by your own. We know it is impossible to overvalue a priceless object. But, amidst the chaos of war, in these times of trouble, do you think it is possible that we discuss the price?" Mr. Qi asked politely.

My father shook his head vigorously in disapproval. "I accept Mr. Jin's price. Not even one ounce of gold is to be deducted. Mr. Jin, I appreciate more than you might know that you trust me with this treasure."

Mr. Jin was instantly moved to tears by my father's words. "No, Professor Chen. It is my honor to have met so generous and true a person as you. Please take it at half the price that my man quoted to Mr. Qi."

"No, quite impossible," my father said immediately.

"I will rest in peace, my heart satisfied, if this treasure goes with you to the prince's residence. Please don't refuse me."

Mr. Chang thought about it a bit and then said, "Why don't you two just split the difference?"

My father shook both his head and his hands this time. "No, I insist. It must be the original price. Thirty gold bars, plain and simple, or else I would have qualms of conscience."

Mr. Jin looked up through tears at my father. Then he slowly stood up, wiped his face, and turned to face his head man. "Bring me the Cabbage and Cricket."

The servant walked to an adjoining room, returned with a rosewood box, and handed it to his master.

Mr. Jin walked over to my father. "I'm so fortunate to meet you today. I have never met a buyer like you. So I will accept the terms you demand, the original price, but you must accept one request of mine."

"Ask and you shall have it," my father said as he stood up quickly.

"You must take this present." With those words, Mr. Jin opened the beautifully carved rosewood box with the soft patina that comes only with age. Inside was an ivory cabbage with a green cricket carved from bright emerald jade. I could hardly believe my eyes. The cricket looked so real with its two long, slender antennae feeling the tip of the white-green leaf of the cabbage. I wasn't the only one in the room spellbound. This was another treasure of incalculable value and incomparable beauty!

My father was taken aback. "How could I allow this? We historians and collectors knew that such a piece existed, but then it just disappeared. And now we are face to face with it. How can I accept such a valuable present?"

"Treasures are expensive; principles are beyond measure," Mr. Jin said. "You would shame me if you decline my gift."

Mr. Qi said firmly, "You must take it, Professor Chen. Mr. Jin is expressing his deepest feelings."

My father agreed. "I accept your most remarkable gift, Mr. Jin, even though I have no way to express my deep gratitude. I'll have Mr. Yu, of my counting room, come here with Mr. Qi to bring the 30 gold bars to you by 9:00 tomorrow morning."

"It is settled then," Mr. Jin said.

My father stood up to leave. "Put your heart to rest, Mr. Jin. I pledge to safeguard your treasures. Would you please honor me by visiting my house before you depart?"

"I would surely like to pay you a visit. I've wished for some time to see the rebuilt palace. But in these uncertain times, I cannot promise. Safeguarding the inkstone was the last task keeping us in Peiping. It is best for us to say goodbye here." Mr. Jin accompanied us to the doorway.

On the way home, I asked, "Daddy, how much do you think the cabbage and cricket is worth?"

"It's hard to say," Mr. Qi jumped in. "It's a treasure of the realm."

"I really like Mr. Jin and feel sorry for him," I said softly. "It must be very hard for him to part with his beloved treasures. He was crying."

"You're right, but his tears were not for the treasures alone," Mr. Qi said.

The Dodge drove by the red wall of the Imperial Palace. As my father gazed up at the corner tower of the palace, he said, "Mr. Qi. I must pay Mr. Jin ten more gold bars. What do you think?"

Mr. Qi shook his head and answered, "I'm afraid that simply won't work. It will offend and hurt Mr. Jin, and he would never accept it anyway."

The car drove into East Jingshan Street, leaving behind the Forbidden City and its surrounding moat. Its occupants should have felt joy at acquiring these two priceless treasures, but the ride home was quiet, even solemn. I couldn't stop thinking about the tears in Mr. Jin's eyes.

Chapter 2

PEIPING LIBERATED

1949
Peiping, China

IT WAS PAST 11:00 PM when we returned from Mr. Jin's house. I
scurried immediately off to bed while my father walked through
the arched door of the main courtyard and into the garden,
making his way to the garden complex. For most of the past
three years, it had been the secret home of Zhang Hanchen,
my father's close friend from Jiyuan County. It also served as
a frequent meeting place for the underground branch of the
Communist Party in Peiping, of which Hanchen was an official.

My father told Uncle Zhang that many relatives and friends
had witnessed horrible scenes with their own eyes in the
Northeast and outside of Peiping. The Communists had already
killed many landlords. What made Uncle Zhang think that our
family would be spared?

Uncle Zhang said we were different. We did have a large parcel of cropland outside of Peiping and many other properties, but we'd delivered our title deeds to the Land Reform Committee and my father had been designated an "Enlightened Gentryman." As a professor and national bourgeoisie, my father was a natural ally of the Communists, he said. My father then recapped the critical part of their conversation to my mother.

"Do you really mean what you say?"

Uncle Zhang answered earnestly, "You gave me this safe house from the moment I started my underground work in Peiping. Think of all the money and other support that I've received from you and Junying. And you provided my comrades with secret dwellings, donations, places to meet. The Peiping underground party and the higher leadership realize and appreciate what you have done for us. I'm talking to you not only as a compatriot from Jiyuan County, but also as a senior officer of the Communist Party."

My father listened in silence.

Uncle Zhang continued, "Besides, our Northeast Field Army is poised to enter Peiping and Tianjin. Fu's troops are trapped. Leaving Peiping is by no means easy. Indeed, it's downright dangerous. And how will you deal with all your family properties?"

"Is it really possible for Peiping to change hands peacefully?"

"Let me tell you that as directed by the Peiping underground party, Fu Dongju, General Fu's daughter, is now living with her father in Zhongnanhai, persuading him in our direction while reporting his actions to Communist headquarters. Just to let you know, the Peiping People's Government will be founded later today. Ye Jianying, Chief of the General Staff, will be the mayor and Xu Bing the deputy mayor."

"Xu Bing? Mr. Xing, one of my neighbors who have advised me many times not to leave, has also mentioned this person."

"Yes, Xu Bing is very close to Xing's family."

"All right, Hanchen. Your words give me comfort. It truly seems that staying is a wiser choice than fleeing. Thank you for your counsel. Now it's time for your rest. Sleep well."

My mother was much encouraged by Uncle Zhang's information and advice. In the dim light of a kerosene lamp in their bedroom, my parents spent the rest of the night discussing their immediate actions. As I lay in my bed across the room, I overheard them quickly agree that they would stay in Peiping, but they differed on whether Jisheng and his pregnant wife should leave for Shanghai. My mother was totally against it. Although undecided, my father saw the need for our family to establish a branch beyond the control of the Communist army.

Once my father and mother finally decided to stay in Peiping, our whole family plunged into preparing for the upcoming Spring Festival. The very first thing that we thought about was whether our close relatives and friends would be able to have Laba congee on their table this year.

The first holiday season event was the eighth day of the twelfth lunar month, supposedly the day Buddha received enlightenment. Called Laba, it was traditional that day, among even the poorest families, to eat congee, a kind of rice porridge with eight ingredients. However, this year, almost half of the two million people in Peiping could not afford this simple meal. Rice was too expensive. A professor's monthly salary didn't even buy 10 kilos of rice. Where would you find extra money even if you could procure the other ingredients—cowpeas, rice, millet, peanuts, mung beans, adzuki beans, jujube, and walnuts—to say nothing of all the other foods that made the day so special—almonds, melon seeds, pine nuts, lotus seeds, water chestnuts, and red cowpeas?

Peiping's residents were beset by soaring prices and the rapidly declining value of banknotes, which were not as valuable even as toilet paper. A full bag of large denomination banknotes might buy a few kilos of corn flour if you could find it. Factories and stores were closed. Thousands of professors and teachers in colleges, high schools, and primary schools went on strike because they could not afford the next meal for their families.

While the sporadic gunfire in Peiping's outskirts was unsettling, people got used to it. Little did they know what a desperate battle was going on in besieged Tianjin, only 120 kilometers away. Their biggest concern was eking out their daily existence. Even with money—and very few had any—it was hard to find food, cooking oil, and all the other staples of life.

Thanks to Mr. Zhao, who was in charge of our 15 acres of cropland in the western suburbs of Peiping, and with Jisheng's help, rice, flour, corn meal, pork, and vegetables were regularly delivered to us, although in much less quantity than in previous years. These foodstuffs were more precious than anything else at this moment. For years, my parents had shared their bounty with at least 30 families. Their tradition of sending holiday food to the families of their relatives and friends before the Laba feast became much more important in 1949 than ever before. Our whole family worked day and night preparing for more than 50 deliveries.

One of our first deliveries was to our close neighbors, the Yuans, and I went there with my mother. The owner of a Peking Opera troupe, Uncle Yuan had a big house with front and back yards located in the street opposite Cihui Hutong. Mrs. Yuan was a famous Peking Opera actress. Yuan Lifen, the family's only child, was two years older than I and my best friend. We were such a lively and good looking couple that we were often sought as bridal attendants for weddings. We had fun at these events, but our favorite activity was watching, learning, and singing Peking Opera. Usually, as soon as I entered the Yuan house, I'd choose an opera prop—a sword, spear, or wand—and begin to move it through the air and act out roles. However, this time the gate was closed, and no one answered our repeated knocking. My mother and our servants were ready to leave when Mrs. Yuan finally opened the door and walked out, Mr. Yuan a few steps behind, followed by Lifen.

"So sorry, Mrs. Chen. Hello, Songsheng. We were all in the back yard and didn't hear your knocking at first. Please come in." Mr. Yuan apologized over and over.

My mother told the attendants to unload the vehicle. "Please accept this token of our regard and in celebration of Laba."

Mrs. Yuan put her hand to her heart and said, "My goodness! So many wonderful things! We are really overwhelmed."

"Lifen," my mother called, "Songsheng has a little something for you." I gave Lifen a packet of folded red silk.

"What is it?" Lifen was wide-eyed with curiosity.

"Let's open it up and have a look," I said eagerly.

"Wait! Let Lifen open it herself." My mother stopped me. Everyone walked into the living room.

Lifen quickly opened the packet to reveal a feather scarf with a red flower design. She grinned happily from ear to ear as she unfolded the scarf and draped it over her dress.

Mr. and Mrs. Yuan were so moved by our gifts that they didn't know how to respond until Mrs. Yuan said, "You'll never know just how timely your assistance is!" She was almost moved to tears. "To tell the truth, Mrs. Chen, we have not been able to pay our troupe for several months now. Who is in the mood to listen to opera in these troubled times? We often have more actors on the stage than people in the audience. And half of them are maimed soldiers or local ruffians who don't pay for their tickets."

Mr. Yuan continued. "Just now we were searching in our backyard for anything to hock. We must care for the elders in our troupe and not allow them to suffer hunger."

"Don't worry. I'll have someone bring more food here tomorrow," my mother said.

"There is already quite a lot," Mr. Yuan said. "Many people in the troupe have left. If I were still just an actor and not the manager of the troupe, we would have returned home to Tsingtao months ago."

"From what I understand, conditions are almost as desperate there as here. Few places are spared the turmoil of war. We just hope that Peiping can escape the disaster of open warfare." My mother rose and said, "I regret that we must leave now. We've another delivery to make, and it's quite far."

Night had already fallen when we arrived at Uncle Lee's house. I ran through the yard of the house shouting, "Uncle, I'm bringing you your favorite Northeast tobacco leaf." I rushed in and unexpectedly came upon my father in deep conversation with Uncle Lee at the table.

"It's Songsheng who cares about me most, isn't it? You bring me my tobacco every year! I've been missing you, too. Look, I've made you a broadsword." Uncle Lee gave it to me. It was a wooden sword tied with a red cloth. After a sincere but quick thank you, I brandished my newest gift and ran off to a corner to practice my dueling moves.

Aunt Lee poured tea for everyone. "We will never be able to pay back your favor to our family. You gave us this house, and you've taken care of us all along."

My mother broke in, "We are so close, dear friends. We do for you only what you would do for us were our roles reversed."

"We see you as our older brother and sister. As family, will you join us for dinner? Some fresh homemade corn cakes," offered Uncle Lee, pointing to the dishes on the table, "plus wonderful pickles we preserve ourselves."

"Time for dinner for everyone. Come on!" My father called Lee's three sons, two daughters, and me.

"Uncle Lee's corn cakes are my favorite." I dropped my sword, dashed to the table, and reached for a steaming hot corn cake.

The two affectionate families ate as if one household and relished the baked cakes and corn meal porridge with pickled radish, preserved potherb mustard, and boiled salted cabbage. The adults spoke of war's woes and their worries and hopes, while the children simply enjoyed their meal. I managed to finish three bowls of porridge. As simple as the fare was, my father and mother said they had not enjoyed such a delicious meal for a long time.

By the end of January, the war outside of Peiping was largely over. Most civilians didn't know the exact details of how peace came so suddenly. From Jisheng, my father learned of the negotiations whereby 520,000 soldiers of the Kuomintang North Army had peacefully surrendered to the Red Army and were being reorganized. Without a battle for the city, Peiping's civilians were saved. The universities and historic sites were spared, especially the Imperial Palace, although a lot of precious antiques had been carted away to Taiwan by the Kuomintang.

While war did not, fortunately, break out in Peiping, our family and other citizens of the city were still in a state of suspense about their future. No one had yet seen the Red Army, also called the Eighth Route Army. Kuomintang propaganda depicted the Communists as barbaric and inhuman. However, my father and mother had seen with their own eyes Uncle Zhang and his colleagues of the underground Communist Party. They were reasonable, plain people. My parents didn't quite know what to believe.

On the last day of January, my parents and I started out for the Ji Barbecue Restaurant and a gathering of relatives and friends. The Dodge was still on Cihui Hutong when it came to a sudden stop.

"Look!" Old Wu was astonished. "The street is full of soldiers with dogskin caps."

My father leaned out to check. It was true. "Turn back. Hurry up!"

Cihui Hutong was narrow. We backed the car up carefully and then returned to the residence.

"Wu, go and look around nearby," my mother urged.

"I'm going, too!" I said.

"No, you are not! You are staying at home!" my mother declared resolutely.

Wu was barely out of the house when Zhu returned on his pedicab.

"Sir, Madam! Eighth Route Army soldiers are everywhere in town," Zhu announced breathlessly. "Di An Men Street was full of soldiers with leather hats, cotton uniforms, and rifles. Master

Jisheng's orderly in plain clothes was coming in our direction, recognized me, and asked me to bring you this letter."

"How is it outside?"

"It's actually quiet and in good order."

My parents went to the parlor and opened the envelope. The scrawled letter showed the marks of being hastily written.

> *Dear Father and Mother:*
>
> *Our division headquarters and troop are going to march out of town and accept reassignment by our agreement with the People's Liberation Army. The specific conditions and completion date are not yet known. We have been very well treated, so don't worry about me.*
>
> *It is really fortunate for Peiping and its residents that a peaceful settlement could end the conflict. Still I advise that you stay home in the coming days. Try to get in touch with Uncle Zhang as soon as possible. If any members of the Liberation Army pay you a visit, be sure to treat them with courtesy.*
>
> *Best wishes and take care!*
>
> *Your son,*
>
> *Jisheng*   *Jan. 30, 1949*

No sooner had my father folded the letter and put it back on the desk than Wu came in quickly and said some officers of the Liberation Army were at the gate, requesting an interview. "Talk of the devil, and he is sure to appear. Hurry up and let them into the reception room," my father instructed Wu. "Junying, I am going to meet with them. Please have someone invite Mr. Yu and others there."

My father made his way to the reception room next to our front gate, where he saw several soldiers wearing gray cotton army uniforms. One of them stood up and came over, dragging his left leg.

"Hanchen, is that you?" My father was surprised; he'd never seen Uncle Zhang in uniform before.

"I'm visiting you openly and in my official capacity this time." Uncle Zhang chuckled and held tightly onto my father's hands. "Let me introduce you. This is Professor Chen Pinzhi, about whom I have told you so much. And this is Division Commander Liu and his assistants from the Northeast Field Army."

"Hello, Commander Liu and everyone. Welcome!" My father invited them to be seated. Wu served tea. My father was surprised to see a division commander who looked just like an ordinary soldier, while Commander Liu was surprised to see a rich professor acting like an ordinary civilian and dressed in such simple garb.

"Pinzhi, Commander Liu's birthplace is Nanyang of our Henan Province."

My father looked amiably at Liu. "Nice to meet you. I know Nanyang well. When I was a boy, I liked to visit there."

"You wouldn't recognize it today. People have plunged into an abyss of misery. Suffering greets the eye everywhere," Liu said with emotion.

Uncle Zhang said, "Pinzhi, as you are well aware, until recently my work was all underground. Now I'm an official in the Peiping Military Control Committee, so I won't have to hide anymore, going from place to place. Since we are old friends, I'll come straight to the point. I have a favor to ask of you."

"Please do."

Uncle Zhang pointed to Commander Liu and said, "The Liberation Army is advancing on the city, and Commander Liu's division needs to find a provisional residence for his headquarters. Would you mind . . . ?"

"How many people? How large should the location be?"

"About 60, including those of division headquarters and the garrison platoon. It's better if the unit can stay together."

My father quickly ran over his inventory, but nothing large enough was available. Only the large garden and garden complex of our mansion would work.

"Pinzhi, we would like to hire the garden of your house for a few months. It shouldn't be long before Commander Liu and his troops are assigned a formal residence, but in the meantime . . . ."

"We're of similar minds," my father said quickly. "There's lots of space here, and the building where you used to hide has not been in use since you left. As you know, it has many rooms and the garden has its own gate."

Liu was a little hesitant, "Are you sure we're not making too much trouble for your family, Professor Chen?"

"No trouble at all," my father answered. "The garrison platoon may live in the line of houses at the end of the kale yard. Commander Liu and other officers of division headquarters will live in the guest room and side rooms. The study may serve as Commander Liu's office. Preparation will take only two or three days."

"Wonderful! That is a great favor to us! Many of our soldiers are now living in the open." A broad smile broke out over Liu's face. "Tell me what you will charge us for the rent, and we'll pay what you ask."

My father shook his head. "Rent? What rent? That's not possible. Hanchen knows me well. You may ask him whether I charged him any rent."

"Times have changed. Things are different," Liu insisted. "Business is business, while you two are old friends. The rent is a must."

Uncle Zhang said, "Let's iron out the details later. For now, let's go to the garden and have a look around."

Led by my father, the group walked out the main gate and entered the garden.

"Good lord! I had no idea that there was such a huge garden in a mansion in downtown Peiping. It could hold a full reinforced company besides division headquarters and a platoon." Commander Liu paced the space, full of praise and amazement.

"So it is settled. Today is January 31. Everything will be ready by February 2, or at the latest the 3rd, Thursday. You may move in then."

"You are really most generous, Professor Chen." Liu was moved. He sighed and nodded, "You have solved a big problem for us. Thank you. Thanks a lot!"

"You are welcome, Commander Liu. Indeed, it is I who should be thanking you. We Chens will fear nothing as long as your division and garrison live in our garden," my father joked.

In a few days, Commander Liu and his unit moved in. I helped show them around the garden and find a place in the northeast corner to build a huge open-air toilet for about 60 people. Luckily, there were no ladies. I quickly fell in with

Commander Liu and many of the soldiers. When I had finished my winter vacation homework, brush and pen calligraphy, I would slip into the garden and tag along with the soldiers, asking them to show me their weapons. My favorites were the shining Japanese .38 caliber rifles and the German Mauser pistols.

Soon after came the Lantern Festival, the 15th day of the lunar year's first month. My parents decided to celebrate a happy Rice Glue Ball Feast all together with family members, servants, and Commander Liu's division and garrison. They chose a menu featuring dumplings and sweet, glutinous rice balls, which could be ordered from a snack store. The big job was to make enough dumplings for nearly a hundred people.

Everyone got involved. The soldiers scrubbed their bed boards on which we would prepare and serve more than two thousand dumplings. In the back kale yard, two firewood cooking ranges were set up temporarily. The dumplings were put into huge pots and stirred with shovels. Outside, the parlor walls were hung with festive red lanterns. Inside were three tables of food and drink.

After the guests and hosts were seated, my father toasted first: "To Commander Liu, my dear friend Hanchen, and every honored guest, the Lantern Festival this year is so much different from those past. Our family members, both old and young, are enjoying this happy time together here with Commander Liu and his men. We celebrate not just the festival but also the peaceful settlement of recent hostilities. It is on festive occasions when we miss our dear ones the most. Every one of you is far away from your hometown and missing your family. Now I'd like to toast you on behalf of my whole family, wishing you and your family good health and happy lives." To loud applause, my father lifted up his cup and drank its contents.

Commander Liu stood up eagerly. "Professor Chen, Mrs. Chen, dear little Songsheng, and each friendly host. We have been at war for so long, from the Northeast to Peiping. This is the first time in years that I have been able to taste such good liquor and delicious food, especially these dumplings, and enjoy such amiable entertainment. We can hardly express our appreciation for this festival and your warm-hearted hospitality. Professor Chen, Hanchen, and I are Henan countrymen. So I want to say it in Henan dialect: 'Come across a compatriot, and tears will flow.' We'll never forget this moment. We will forever be the army of the people of China. I wish to show my gratitude with this cup of liquor. Division personnel, garrison platoon leaders, stand up! I offer a toast to Professor Chen, Mrs. Chen, and every one of the Chen family!" Commander Liu and the officers drank to warm applause.

"Sergeant Dong," Liu ordered, "sound the order." Dong filled his cup and ran out of the garden complex, transmitting the order to officers and soldiers in the bungalows of the back kale yard. The officers and soldiers walked out of their rooms with cups, shouting loudly and tidily in line, "To Professor Chen, Mrs. Chen, and the entire Chen family!"

My parents, other members of the family, and servants, accompanied by Liu and Uncle Zhang, walked out with their cups and expressed thanks loudly to the officers and soldiers outside the bungalows, "Thank you all! Thank you very much!" Firecrackers exploded and rockets soared. Commander Liu and my father held each other's hands tightly. Heartfelt laughter and happy tears melded with the sounds of the fireworks and cheerful voices.

I didn't understand what liberation was all about, although I heard my parents discuss it many times. They didn't seem to understand it either. I did know, however, that whatever liberation meant, I was having one of the best times of my life.

Chapter 3

BIRTH OF A NATION

1949
Peiping/Beijing, China

DESPITE THE PEACEFUL TRANSFER OF power in Peiping from the Nationalists to the Communists, my parents remained anxious and uncertain about just what "liberation" entailed. Who or what was being liberated and to what extent? I would sometimes hear them talking when they didn't know I was listening.

Of course they understood that Communism meant taking from the rich to give to the poor. They were resigned to the fact that the new government would eventually target us, one of the richest families in Peiping. They hoped that Uncle Zhang's promises would be honored, that their past service to the Communists and their well-known generosity and support of the poor would give them some protection. But they knew in their hearts that their time was coming. For my sake and for my sisters', they tried, not always successfully, to keep up a good front.

Immediately after Peiping's liberation, we didn't dare go outside the mansion's grounds. At night, even a dog's barking could put my parents on edge. My family felt a great sense of impending doom interspersed with brief moments of hope. Looking back on those days, I think we sometimes were in a state of suspended animation—"waiting for the other shoe to drop," as they say in America. When my sisters and I returned to school after winter vacation, however, it was to the same classes and teachers as before. The routine of school helped to restore a sense of normalcy, however temporary, in our family.

My two older sisters attended middle school. Old Zhu took me to Yuying Primary School and my younger sister to Boshi Kindergarten in his pedicab. Around noon, my little sister and I would have lunch at Cuihualou, a nearby restaurant. The owner of Cuihualou was a good friend of my parents. After school Old Zhu fetched us home. Everything seemed to be just the same as before. The only thing out of the ordinary that I remember was one time when some policemen visited us to reregister the household and check on each occupant, including all the servants. Each one of us filled out two registration cards. One was kept by the local police station. The other served as our identification card in the new China. We didn't know until much later that this was a critical tool for managing internal travel. Everyone had to stay where they were registered and could not move to any other place without permission from their local police and their work unit. The hard-and-fast household registration system, which restricted personal freedom of travel and transfer, was in place until 1988, when China began issuing ID cards. Currently, Chinese citizens are allowed to travel and find jobs at any location in China with their ID cards, but only as visitors. It is still hard to secure permanent residency in all big cities.

My parents' greatest worry was how my oldest brother, Jisheng, would fare under the new government. They thought that as the youngest general in the Nationalist Army, Jisheng stood out as an easy target. In fact, all of Fu Zuoyi's troops were going through a smooth reorganization outside Peiping. In late February, Fu Zuoyi and his close staff flew to Shi Jiazhuang, 200 miles south of Peiping, and offered a humble apology to Mao Zedong and Zhou Enlai. Mao commended General Fu for "doing a good job that the people will never forget" and promised him that all prisoners of war would be set free so Fu could meet with them if he wished. His troops could either stay in the Communist Army or leave. Those staying would be treated equally with those already in service, and those leaving would receive travel expenses to return home or to other destinations. My brother and most of his senior staff mustered out of the army and went their own ways.

That spring, Mao moved his headquarters from Hebei Province to Fragrant Hill, in the Western Hills suburb of Peiping. The Liberation Army marched south and on April 23 occupied Nanking, the capital of the Kuomintang government. Before the end of May, they liberated Shanghai. My third elder brother was set to graduate from the Aviation Department of Shanghai Jiaotong University, but we totally lost contact with him for several months.

After seven months' residence, Commander Liu prepared to move his division headquarters out of our garden. Before they departed, the officers and soldiers cleaned up everything inside and out, including the garden and kale yard. My parents were touched when the soldiers pulled down the toilet they had built in the back kale yard. They dug a large pit, carried away their waste by truck, and brought back truckloads of clean soil in which they planted quite a variety of vegetables.

The last night before the detachment departed was one of the saddest and also happiest of my life. I was very unhappy to see my soldier friends leave but also felt I was the luckiest boy in the world. It was the night I fell in love.

Commander Liu invited all of us and our servants to the garden parlor and hosted a dinner party. He prepared several dishes, doing much of the kitchen work himself. To express my family's deep appreciation to the detachment, Lifen and I performed the last scene of the popular Peking Opera "Farewell My Concubine." Although Lifen was two years older than I, she was shorter than most girls her age and looked just like my younger sister, small, exquisite, and charming. She and I often sang Peking Opera together, but this would be the first time for us to perform with full accompaniment, costumes, and makeup. During the final rehearsal, Lifen did fine, but I had a big problem performing as a tender lover with Lifen with other people watching. I didn't hold hands with her, much less take her in my arms and caress her. Lifen knew exactly what was wrong. She asked the accompanists and others to leave, including her parents who were directing the scene. She showed me how those touching scenes must be played, how I must hold her as we prepared to say good-bye forever. I don't think either of us realized until that moment how much we both had grown up. We were no longer innocent playmates, mere neighbors.

We sang on the garden's outdoor stage for about 100 soldiers and guests that warm autumn evening. Costumed and painted, the 10-year-old ruler and his 12-year-old concubine performed so well that the cheering and applause sometimes drowned out our singing. I had never before so appreciated Lifen's beauty as I did that night. Neither had I fully appreciated her extraordinary dramatic abilities. Lifen performed her swordplay dance, her last entertainment for me, and sang her way into my heart. When Lifen committed suicide in my arms, she was crying copious tears. As I gazed at them and at Lifen's artfully accentuated eyes, I realized what love for someone other than my family or Nanna Ma, my former wet nurse, was. I held Lifen tightly, relishing the touch, reluctant to let her go. I had never felt such feelings before. Finally we left the stage, only to return for several curtain calls. Many in the audience had never seen such a performance before and their cheers thrilled me. My dream of becoming a Peking Opera star blazed.

My warm feelings toward Lifen were further kindled later in the evening. Performers used to skip their dinners for the sake of their evening show. Following tradition, Lifen's parents invited me and my parents to their house for an after-show meal since Lifen and I had not eaten since lunch. We walked ahead of our parents. It was pitch dark and a little chilly. Lifen kept edging closer and closer to me. I felt so warm in my heart. I held her hand and wished the short distance between our houses was far longer.

Before he departed, Commander Liu gave me a wooden pistol tied with a red tassel as a souvenir of his stay. I hated to say goodbye to the troops and Commander Liu. I had learned many things from them at a very impressionable age. Their hope and commitment were contagious. Despite my parents' apparent doubts about the future, I had high hopes.

Once the troops decamped, the garden parlor stood eerily empty and quiet. But soon it became the chosen place for my family to secretly discuss what we should do about "Liberation." Our most pressing concern was whether Jisheng and his wife, who was five months pregnant, should leave Peiping and flee the mainland. My brother decided to take his wife to Tsingtao via Tianjin and then to Shanghai on their way to Hong Kong or Taiwan. I watched as Mr. Yu hammered gold bars into leaf and had it sewn into my brother's underwear to take on the trip. It was hard for my father and mother to see part of their family leave for such an uncertain and possibly risky future. But, as my father concluded, it was worth the risk. My father instructed Jisheng that when he found my third elder brother in Shanghai, they should try every way to leave Shanghai for Hong Kong or Taiwan, striving to give our family some options if the situation at home deteriorated.

After my brother left, change greatly accelerated around us. Peiping and all of China were suffering severe shortages of capital, foodstuffs, and other commodities. Everything became incredibly expensive, if you could even find anything for sale. The rocketing prices in Peiping caused its residents much anxiety. The new government replaced the Nationalist banknotes with their own, Renminbi or RMB, the People's Currency. Ten of the old notes, Jinyuanjuan, equaled one of the new, although the amount that could be exchanged was small. Virtually no one except small businesses used cash. Gold and silver coins were banned. The basic units of exchange in Peiping became calico and millet.

My father's old friends at Peking and Tsinghua Universities, along with everyone else there, drew their salaries in millet based on the academic pecking order. Then they exchanged the millet for cash. Communist government officials and People's Liberation Army soldiers were paid the same way. In general, life was hard; however, before long, people finally realized that they did not have to worry as much about whether they would find their daily food. Employed workers, clerks, and teachers were entitled to 1,000 to 2,000 RMB and 15 kilograms of foodstuff, which was deducted from their monthly wages on payday. At that time, 2,000 RMB could buy about 65 kilograms of flour. People in Peiping came to understand that one meaning of "liberation" was freedom from worry about the source of their next meal. Friends at Peking University kindly informed my father that there was no need to send them foodstuffs anymore. Regulated by the Peiping Social Affairs Bureau, a professor's monthly salary was 436 to 493 kilos of millet, enough to support his whole family, although the equivalent RMB could buy only two thermos flasks of grain.

As for business deals, especially those involving large sums, calico was the accepted method of payment. All negotiations were carried out in *pi*, a traditional Chinese measure for cloth, about 33 meters. Then the calico was converted into the current rate of currency, which fluctuated widely from day to day or even within a day. Whenever I was along, my father would ask me to do the calculations for the transaction, so I learned to do sums in my head quickly. I was so proud to come up with the right number as accurately as my mother, who used her abacus.

My formal schooling continued during these desperate times. But it was through accompanying my father to the market, restaurants, and antiquities dealers that I learned practical arithmetic, street economics, national and local history, and other valuable lessons. I learned new words and new ideas and met new people. The lasting impressions, however, were about the realities of life in hard times. I had enjoyed a very privileged childhood, but by the age of 10, my eyes were beginning to open to new facts of life, including my feelings for Lifen.

After many thorough discussions, my parents decided to sell, very quietly, most of their real estate holdings. They knew that in these hard economic times, it was far better to have cash in hand than houses in the inventory. I remember my father saying, "Oaks may fall when reeds withstand the storm." A lower profile might help us survive dangerous times. I liked my father's frequent use of such sayings. Usually I understood them at once, but sometimes I had to puzzle out their meaning and see how it applied.

Once the terms of a house sale were agreed on, the parties would meet at the Pingyi Banking House on Di An Men Sfreet to conclude the deal. Afterward, Mr. Xu, the bank manager, almost invariably hosted a luncheon at the Ji Barbecue Restaurant or Heyizhai Restaurant. Whenever I wasn't at school, I attended these banquets with great gusto. I was big for my age and growing fast. I loved to eat and to try new things. I believe that the broad tastes and hearty appetite I have today were shaped by my culinary adventures as a child.

During this time, my father became the deputy chairman of Peiping Preferential Treatment Committee. The group's goal was to help the poor. They set up Relief and Investigation Committees to create a list of donors' names and to provide millet to old and poor residents. My father's main job was collecting donations and raising funds to support the city government and civil administration departments, which suffered from massive capital and cash flow problems. With no staff support for the committee, my father called upon his employees to collect contributions and otherwise support relief efforts. Our family quickly became one of the largest donors in all Peiping. Occasionally, I accompanied my parents when they took huge piles of currency to the committee officials. I was proud to see how impressed the officials were by my parents' good work and those stacks of cash.

I remember these times fondly. They were, however, the calm before the first real storm clouds appeared on our family's horizon.

One day in September, we had visitors from the China National Federation of Supply and Marketing Cooperatives. Uncle Zhang had called in advance to set up the appointment. At the appointed hour, three jeep loads of Red Army officers in gray uniforms, but without badges on their collars or caps, assembled in our reception room. Uncle Zhang introduced everyone, briefly explained the work of the federation, and then came right to the point. The federation consisted of grass-roots—city, county, and provincial level—supply and marketing cooperatives. It had 10 million individual members and was growing. It helped the people buy and sell agricultural and other items and promoted exchange between urban and rural areas. The federation was relocating to downtown Peiping and urgently needed a sizable office location. Our home would be the ideal location. Would we sell it?

Perhaps fearing that my father's generosity to the new government would cause him to agree to sell our home immediately, my mother quickly thanked the officers for their visit and interest, but replied that we needed time to consider the proposal and talk with our friends and tenants who currently lived with us. She promised to get in touch with the federation through Uncle Zhang.

The prospect of losing our beloved mansion unsettled my parents so much that they could muster little enthusiasm for the upcoming celebration of the founding of the People's Republic of China. But their doubts had little effect on my hopes and excitement. I got up before sunrise on October 1 and hurriedly washed. After donning my carefully laid out blue trousers and white shirt, I gulped my breakfast, scurried to Old Zhu's pedicab, and headed to Yuying Primary School. The crowds in the street soon grew so thick that I had to exit the pedicab and make my way on foot. Finally, I reached the school playground and joined about 50 other selected students wearing the same blue pants and white shirts. We stood in lines and listened to the teachers' instructions. I was only in the fourth grade, but because of my height, I was placed in the last row. Originally, no primary or middle school students were scheduled to join the crowd on Tiananmen Square. Fortunately for me, an influential friend of Yuying School pleaded our case and a small delegation of students was chosen to attend.

Just as we linked up with other student teams in Dongdan Square, about two miles from Tiananmen, rain began to fall. We ate steamed bread and boiled water in the rain for lunch. The lead teacher warned us many times that there were no toilets anywhere in the square, so each of us went to the toilet before we moved on. Then every student got five candies for dessert.

It was already past 1:00 PM when the student teams arrived at the specified site south of East Three Gates in front of Tiananmen. Immediately all the students and their teachers surged into the crowd. Everyone was sitting on the ground. The student teams were placed at the front, but from the back row I could see only the dazzling banners, the colorful flags, and the faint figures in the distance on the gate tower. A giant portrait of Mao Zedong was suspended above the central gate of the tower, hung with banners on both sides announcing "Long live the Central People's Government" and "Long live the People's Republic of China."

The official ceremony started at 3:00 PM. Mao solemnly declared in his broad Hunan accent: "My fellow countrymen! The People's Republic of China and Central People's Government are founded today!" His words were followed by the national anthem and a 28-gun salute, symbolizing the 28 years of struggle since the Communist Party was founded. The cannonade was deafening, far more powerful than the distant gunfire I had heard while the civil war still raged. Mao pressed the button and the bright five-star flag of new China rose slowly up the tall pole in front of the gate tower.

Then an impassioned Mao read the *Notice of People's Republic of China Central Government*, renaming Peiping as Beijing and selecting it as the capital of the new China. Afterward, a grand parade began. Zhu De, commander in chief, paraded army, navy, and air forces and proclaimed the command from the People's Liberation Army headquarters. He swore to mop up quickly the rebellious troops of the Kuomintang, liberate all the remaining non-emancipated territory, and annihilate the bandits and other counter-revolutionaries as well as suppress any rebellion or other disturbance. More than 16,000 soldiers then marched by the reviewing stand as 26 fighter and training planes flew overhead from the East. This parade took three hours in all.

Next was the people's parade. First were the workers, followed by peasants from Beijing's suburbs. Then came teams of government officials and young college students. Soon it was dark. Lamps on the gate tower were suddenly turned on, and multi-colored lights brightened the square. Giant searchlights roamed the sky. Paper and cloth lanterns were also lit. The square was a sea of light. The ceremony didn't end until 9:30 pm. The majority of the city's residents didn't know very much about the Red Army, the Communist Party, or the central and municipal governments. Their passionate desire to attend the grand ceremony was based on their hope, and their joy and relief at having escaped from the worst disasters of war. Without knowing what would happen tomorrow, they celebrated today.

After standing there for nearly 10 hours with no water or food except the steamed bread and five candies, I was hungry and tired. When I returned home, all my family, including several relatives and friends, were discussing the grand ceremony. Without even washing my hands, I sat right down and began to stuff myself.

The talk focused on renaming Peiping as Beijing and selecting it as the capital. Mr. Chang Weijun, known as an "Old Beijing Hand" and quite the local historian, had warmed to the topic of Beijing's many names. Frequent swigs of his favorite sorghum liquor probably helped to loosen his tongue and led to some repetition, but I loved learning about history and followed every twist and turn in the naming of the city in which I had been born.

Beijing was one of China's six ancient capitals and had gone by many different names over the centuries. It was first called "Ji" in the Zhou Dynasty 3,000 years ago. The second name was "Yanjing" (Capital of Yan) after the Yan state moved to Ji and built up the new capital. The third one was "Youzhou" (Ji City) during the Sui and Tang Dynasties. In the last years of the Tang Dynasty, the Liao Kingdom briefly occupied Youzhou, naming it "Nanjing" (Southern Capital) or again "Yanjing." By the early 12th century, it was called "Zhongdu" (Central Capital). The sixth name was "Dadu" (Great Capital) chosen when Kublai Khan founded the Yuan Empire. After troops of the Ming Kingdom captured Dadu, they changed its name to "Peiping House" (Northern Peace). The great achievement of the Ming Dynasty was to build the Forbidden City and the Imperial Palace. The city was actually called "Beijing" starting in 1421, later written in English as Peking. In 1928, the Kuomintang government renamed it Peiping. The Japanese occupiers changed Peiping back to Beijing, and after their surrender, the Nationalists restored Peiping. Beijing was the city's most long-standing name, the most commonly used in literary works, and the most popular with the local people.

I was too sleepy to hear all of Mr. Chang's seemingly endless discourse. Nanna had to ask Old Zhu to carry me to bed. By then it was late and the party ended soon after. Several hours later, I awoke to go to the bathroom. I was surprised to hear my parents still up discussing the offer to buy our mansion. As tired as I was, I was determined to stay awake and learn our fate if I could.

My father said, "The government officials came on the recommendation of Hanchen. It won't be easy to turn down their request."

My mother asked father whether it would be a sale or a donation.

"Hanchen promised it would be a sale, but not like selling in the open market. If I understand correctly, one half is to be bought by the Federation, and the other is to be our donation."

"What kind of deal is that and how much will they pay?"

"I cannot tell. Their first offer will probably be their final offer. We don't get the chance to bargain."

"That's not right!"

"It's better than nothing. What can we do even if they take away our house without a penny of payment?"

"Nothing. They have the authority." My mother heaved a heavy sigh.

"By the same token, they have used their authority with discretion so far. Market prices are stable. Even with land reform, we, as Enlightened Gentrymen, have not been bothered. We have no choice but to accept our lot."

"You're right," my mother said with resignation.

Money was not the only issue. Although we would be allowed to keep the gardens and some buildings on that side, losing our much-loved mansion was a bitter pill to swallow. As tired as I was I couldn't fall asleep. I wondered how soon we would have to leave our home and where we would go. What would happen to all the people who lived with us? Dawn was breaking before I finally dozed off.

Chapter 4

Expelled from the Palace

1950
Beijing, China

THERE WASN'T MUCH TIME FOR further discussions between my father and mother about selling the house. An Army messenger delivered an official letter from the President of the All China Federation of Supply and Marketing Cooperatives (AFC) to our residence five days after the meeting. Uncle Zhang also passed on whatever he learned from the leaders of the Central Government Administration Council. To my father's surprise, neither the letter nor what Uncle Zhang was told mentioned any amount, although the extreme urgency of the matter was stressed.

Not long after the letter arrived, my father let me tag along to a meeting he had with his financial advisers in the accounting room.

"It's a strategic move on the Federation's part," Mr. Yu said. "They know this house is not for sale. They want to take it but just don't want to make an offer."

"Obviously," Mr. Chang agreed. "They also realize that the Chens are in no position to ask a price based on fair market value."

"They know very well how much the main residence of this mansion is worth. I have handled hundreds of real estate transactions, and this is the first time that the buyer didn't make an offer," Mr. Yu added.

My father viewed it from a more practical angle. "We are in no position to ask for any price. As the saying goes, 'Under the eaves of another's house, you have to lower your head.' We certainly don't want to offend any high-ranking government officials."

Mr. Liu said, "The government has already seized many houses whose owners were closely related to the Kuomintang regime. They have also purchased many houses below value and are using them for offices and official government residences."

"How much did they pay?" my father asked.

"Between a third to half the market value."

No one said anything. The only sound in the room came from Mr. Yu's abacus. I learned from him later that Chen Lifu, a member of one of the Big Four Families under the Kuomintang regime, had once tried to buy our mansion and that a very rich American entrepreneur had made an even higher offer, but Father had rejected both. Using those offers as a reference, Mr. Yu calculated the fair market value and showed his abacus to my father. "This is roughly how much you will get for the mansion alone, not including the garden."

My father stood up. "Well, our hands are tied. We simply need to accept and await our fate. Mr. Yu, please ask Wu to drive Mr. Chang and Mr. Liu home."

We walked from the parlor and met my mother on the porch. "You look exhausted. How did your discussions go?" she asked.

"It's hopeless. There's nothing we can do but let all this take its own course."

"You mean selling our house without an offer or a price?"

"Yes."

"How soon must we move?"

"Very, very soon."

"My goodness! Seven families of friends and tenants have to be relocated. So much furniture and so many items need to be moved. I need time to do all this."

"Regrettably, this is not our decision. We must vacate our house within a month after the sale."

"One month?" My mother was incredulous. "Impossible! I need at least three months."

"I'll try my very best to extend it to 45 days. No more."

Mother nearly collapsed. My father supported her as they walked slowly through the veranda to the big parlor of the main courtyard. After two years of rebuilding and refurbishing and five years of enjoyable residence, my parents could not believe that all this would be gone forever.

"Mother, don't worry. I like the garden much better than our main court. We don't need all these rooms. I have so much fun in the garden." I couldn't help interrupting.

"I know it will suit you. It's exactly what you wished, isn't it?"

"He has a point though," my father laughed. "We'd have to get rid of the big house sooner or later. 'A tall tree catches the wind.' Under the new system, the richest people will be the first to bear the brunt of the storm."

I felt that as long as I had the jujube trees, the stream, the playfield, the well, and the kale yard, I had nothing to worry about.

Exactly as my father expected, the Chen family "sold" the main compound of their mansion to AFC for about a third of its market value. But AFC's lump sum payment was all in cash. My parents never let their other children know how much money they got from this transaction. I knew, however. Mr. Yu and three clerks from the bank spent the whole afternoon behind the locked door of the accounting room counting the banknotes. Then he let me in to see all the stacks of bills before they were put into stitched, white moneybags. Old Wu drove Mr. Yu with all the money to the bank.

A 50-member relocation team was established under the overall planning and leadership of my mother. The toughest job was helping the seven families find new residences. Mr. Yu and his assistants prepared two houses from the Chen's real estate inventory as temporary living quarters for the families who needed them. Uncle Lee's construction team undertook the biggest job. They cleaned, washed, and repainted the rooms of the main garden compound and renovated the other rooms into two new bedrooms for my elder sisters. They built a big new dining room, a large kitchen with stoves, a water supply, and a sanitation system, three living areas for home workers (the new term for servants), three new bathrooms, and a separate three-room courtyard for my older brother, Yansheng, and his wife, the newlyweds coming to Beijing from Shanghai. They traveled with my other brother, Jisheng, his wife, and their one-year-old son.

In early 1949, Jisheng and his then-pregnant wife had left Beijing. They traveled first to Tsingtao, a coastal city of Shandong Province, and then took a boat to Shanghai. It was hard to get the boat tickets, and even at the outrageous prices they paid for them, their two seats came without a berth. The couple had to sit up on the small boat for 16 hours as it steamed to Shanghai under cover of darkness to avoid being attacked by Kuomintang bombers.

Their ordeal was far from over when they arrived in Shanghai. Jisheng found Yansheng, my third elder brother, who was suffering from tuberculosis. There was no way for Yansheng to take the risk of going to Taiwan or Hong Kong. Besides, all ship ticket offices were closed. Jisheng contacted all his friends and acquaintances without success. Worried about his wife, due to give birth to their child at any time, Jisheng called on his last resource, his friends in the Thirty-Eighth Corps.

Before Jisheng was transferred to General Fu's troops, he had served as an officer in the 208th Division of Kuomintang's Youth Army, which was later expanded to become the Thirty-Eighth Corps. After they captured Nanjing, the Communist Army annihilated the Corps outside of Shanghai. The remnants of the Thirty-Eighth Corps retreated to Shanghai and prepared to escape to Taiwan. With the help of his friends, Jisheng finally obtained two tickets to Taiwan. Just when they were about to depart, their son was born, and they had no other choice but to cancel their travel plans.

Jisheng gave his priceless tickets to the two brothers of Yansheng's fiancée and stayed in Shanghai until it was captured by the Communists on May 27, 1949. Instead of heading toward Taiwan, Jisheng, his wife, their son, Yansheng, and his fiancée came back home to Beijing just as the storm clouds were beginning to appear on our horizon. Nevertheless, we had a wonderful family reunion. My parents were so glad to welcome their sons back home and to meet their first grandchild and beautiful daughter-in-law to be.

Without waiting for the newly repainted rooms to dry thoroughly, my mother promptly started moving us from the main house to the garden. Yansheng and his fiancée stayed with us while Jisheng's family found a house only a short distance away.

Unlike his usual practice, my father spent very little time reviewing the renovation blueprints with Uncle Lee and his people. He concentrated on finishing his two most important jobs. Accompanied by Uncle Zhang and Chang Weijun, my father and I went to the Forbidden City to pay a courtesy call on Mr. Ma Heng, the Dean of the Palace Museum. My father deeply respected and admired Mr. Ma both for his 25 years of devoted service to the Palace Museum and for his courageous efforts to protect and prevent so many treasures of the Palace from being shipped off to Taiwan by the Kuomintang. According to Uncle Zhang, Mr. Ma had taken great risks by rejecting Chiang Kai-shek's personal invitation to leave Peiping for Taiwan. Mr. Ma continued to serve as the President of the Imperial Palace Museum after the liberation of Peiping. In Mr. Ma's old-fashioned office, my father informed him of his intention to contribute a major portion of his antique collection to the Palace. Mr. Ma was overjoyed when he read the items my father had listed on a piece of rice paper in his meticulous script.

"All rare treasures. A heaven-sent fortune. This is unbelievable. Truly unbelievable."

"Take my word for it. You can believe it, sir." Mr. Chang said. "These are some of the finest pieces from Professor Chen's collection, which he began acquiring in 1928."

"Undoubtedly," Mr. Ma replied respectfully. "And it's presented in such elegant calligraphy."

"I take that as a high compliment, coming as it does from such a master. My long dream has been to return these possessions to where they belong. This is just my first step," my father said cordially.

Uncle Zhang added, "Professor Chen's family will soon move out of his mansion, and he is concerned about some of his bigger paintings that need large walls to be displayed. They would fit only in the palaces of the Forbidden City."

"You would set my heart to rest if I could donate these items to the Palace Museum," my father continued.

Mr. Ma was deeply touched. He stood up and shook hands with my father without saying a word, nodding his head.

Shortly after, my father and our workers carefully wrapped dozens of paintings, calligraphy scrolls, and pieces from my father's ceramic and bronze collections and put them on a long, flat cart. Zhu, the pedicab wheeler, pulled the cart from the front while Wu and I pushed it from behind. My father walked at the side with two Palace Museum officials. It took us 30 minutes to get to the Forbidden City. Mr. Ma and his assistants examined each donation, took notes, made marks in different colors, and moved the items to the storehouse. Mr. Ma had already written his letter of thanks. Together with a neatly written donation item list, he handed the letter to my father in a big envelope. Mr. Ma and his people saw us off at the back door of the Forbidden City, which was very unusual, according to Mr. Chang. As we made our way home, my father seemed quietly happy, as if a burden had been lifted from him.

Weeks later, Mr. Ma invited my father back to his office. He issued my father a certificate of honor with the official seal of the

Palace Museum and signed by Mr. Ma. He also gave our family a lifetime free admission pass in recognition of my father's contributions to the museum, and, to express his personal appreciation, gave my father one of his renowned horse paintings. I didn't know too much about the certificate, but I liked Mr. Ma's horse painting a lot. Two big horses stood under a large tree on a hill while three colts cavorted in the meadow below. And I really enjoyed the lifetime free pass. My father used it often, taking me and various cousins, nephews, and nieces to the Forbidden City, Jingshan Park, and Beihai Park.

I felt real special when I used the pass by myself. I held it high and led our whole group through the gates of these parks. At first, the gatekeepers checked the pass carefully. Soon they knew me well and just smiled and let us enter. Without my father's knowledge, I used the pass to bring my classmates to the parks, a privilege that made my friends envious.

Jingshan Park had been the Imperial Garden, facing the back door of the Forbidden City, and was the highest point in Beijing. While my father practiced his Tai Chi, also called shadowboxing, we children would climb up to the highest pavilion on the hill and enjoy a bird's eye view of the whole city. After finishing his exercises, my father would take us to Beihai Park, one of the oldest and most authentically preserved imperial gardens in the world. I liked the white pagoda and boating on the lake. But I liked most eating at the Fangshan Restaurant, which we often did during these excursions.

The restaurant was established originally for the royal family and had been open to the public only since 1925. I was fascinated to learn that, according to surviving records, it used to serve the Dowager Ci Xi 108 different dishes for one meal. My father never ordered those expensive dishes. He told us that the simple foods based upon the royal recipes were much more nutritious and just as tasty.

Once my father had found a safe home for our artwork and antiques, he turned his attention to other responsibilities brought on by having to dismantle our household. He made an appointment with the President of the AFC, but when he and Wu drove to the meeting place, they could not find the AFC's temporary office. Wu asked many people for directions, but no one had the slightest idea. A young clerk finally saw our car and led my father to the President's office in the basement of a bank building.

The results of their meeting were that the China All Federation of Supply and Marketing Cooperatives took over a third of our furniture and the Dodge sedan, and Wu became the chauffeur for AFC's President. Moved by my father's generosity, the AFC's President extended our moving deadline by another month. He said he had too much work to attend to before the National Day anyway.

Later, Mr. Yu would joke, "They gave us one-third of the fair price for our house, and we gave them one-third of our furniture in return." Needless to say, Mr. Yu did not repeat his witticism in front of my father.

Although the tasks my father had to perform before moving were important, they were not nearly as complicated as my mother's. She had to make the really tough decisions about which of our home workers to let go. These people were more like Chen family members than servants. None of them wanted to leave, and my mother honestly wanted to keep everyone, but we all knew that some workers would have to go. I think my mother was most concerned about Nanna Ma, my former wet nurse, and Old Zhu, the pedicab driver.

My mother had suffered from mastitis after giving birth to my second elder sister, so she could not suckle me. Nanna Ma came to us by way of a good family friend. She had recently lost both her husband and baby girl when their farmhouse caught fire in the far west suburb of Beijing. Nanna Ma had gone to the farmers' market that day and, upon her return, found only the remains of the farmhouse. Compassionate neighbors had already removed and buried the charred corpses of her daughter and her husband, the village shoemaker, so she would not have to witness such a grisly sight.

Nanna Ma couldn't bear to stay in her former village, so she went to stay with a friend who happened to know our family well. Nanna Ma's grievous loss was certainly our most fortunate gain. The deep love that would have naturally flowed to her husband and daughter now came to the Chen family, especially me. And I returned her love and devotion as fully as I knew how. I spent more time with Nanna Ma than I did with my mother. I think our wonderful relationship consoled her. She was always proud of me as I grew up and became a big boy, but I know she wished deep in her heart that I will still an infant in her arms.

When my mother and I first talked about Nanna Ma's leaving, I cried. I told my mother that I would use my pocket money to support her. My mother said she thought this was a good plan, but when she told me her long cherished dream for Nanna Ma, it made me smile through my tears. I persuaded her to give me the pleasure of telling Nanna Ma and went immediately to her room.

"Nanna, what are you doing?"

"Making you another pair of shoes. Come here. I have some of your favorite snacks." Nanna Ma always used to buy me peanut brittle.

"May I tell you something secret?"

"Of course. What?"

I closed the door and began to whisper in her ear.

"Speak up. There's nobody here."

"OK! Will you marry Zhu?"

"Nonsense! What are you talking about?"

"I'm serious. Will you marry Zhu?"

Nanna Ma waited for a moment and then asked, "Where did you get that crazy idea?"

I searched her basket on the bed and found a pair of large shoes. "Whose shoes are these?" I asked, holding them up in front of me.

Nanna cheeks reddened instantly.

"I know," I said. "These are for Zhu."

Nanna laughed. "Nothing escapes your sharp eyes."

"Nanna, Zhu is strong, honest, and gets along well with people. And he is single, never even married before. I know he likes and cares about you a lot."

"Why are you suddenly telling me this?"

"Nanna, it's high time for you to have your own family."

"Is this your mother's idea?"

"It's hers, but I happen to think it's a great idea."

Nanna's cheeks went from rose to a deeper red. She brought me close to her and held me tightly in her arms.

Nanna Ma and Zhu were soon married with all Chen family members and house workers in attendance. The newlyweds moved to their own house and shoe shop in the West District of Beijing. The front part of their new home was their shop and the back their bedroom, workshop, and small kitchen. At their wedding, Nanna Ma proposed a toast to my father, mother, and all the guests. Then, crying happy tears, she said, "We certainly could never have married or be moving into our own shoe shop and home without the Chen family and without you, our friends. And I want to show you something that symbolizes this generosity, something that I will treasure for the rest of my life."

She held a small red purse high for everyone to see and, through her tears, managed to say softly, "This is a gift from Songsheng. He bought me the purse and put all his saved pocket money into it. I know this because I've been keeping Songsheng's savings for him and now he has given them all to me."

I felt it was the least I could do to show my love to my dear Nanna and help her with her transition. My parents gave three years of wages as severance pay to all the servants who were leaving and a lump sum payment of 18 months of wages beyond their regular salary to those who stayed. Nanna Ma and Old Zhu managed their tiny shoe shop well, but they never had a child. Almost all the hand-made shoes in the Chen family were from their shop. I visited them often until Nanna Ma died of a sudden heart attack in early 1958. Old Zhu closed his shoe shop in 1959 and went back to his home village in Hebei Province.

My mother and father also made a major decision about where to put much of the remaining family fortune, especially the money from the sale of the mansion. Despite being sold for a fraction of its value, we received AFC's payment in currency. How to handle that enormous amount of cash in hand became a demanding question. We bought a huge amount of the PRC's first government-issued bonds, setting a record for a one-time subscription in Beijing. These bonds offered 5% annual interest and full repayment of the principal in five years. Every "share of point" of the bond was weighted to the prices of 3,000 grams of rice, 750 grams of flour, 1.33 meters of woolen fabric, and 8,000 grams of coal in six cities across China. The government published these numbers every 10 days.

Although my mother might not have understood the economic policies of the new government, she felt certain it would keep its promise on the first bonds it sold. No one could predict what might happen to money in the banks, while the 5% annual interest on the bonds was something you could count on. This proved to be a wise investment, indeed a life-saver. Years later, these bonds rescued the Chen family in ways we could never have begun to imagine in 1950.

My mother's plan dovetailed neatly with my father's appointment by the municipal government as the Vice Director of Beijing's Bond Sale Promotion Committee. My mother's proposed subscription exceeded my father's quota as assigned by the Committee, but to set a good example, he encouraged her to subscribe even more. I think this was also what my mother had in mind.

One event relating to our subscriptions became a story often retold in our family. My father had received a call from the Bond Committee asking if they could meet with him briefly to discuss a financial error they had detected. Error? How could that be? Father set up the meeting for the following hour and went immediately to the accounting room. Mr. Yu broke out in a cold sweat and quickly began to check his figures. My father certainly didn't want to lose face in front of the government, the Committee, and all his colleagues. I'm sure that Mr. Yu and his assistants were holding their breath, hoping there might be some mistake about the mistake. They knew that Father didn't tolerate careless errors, especially on such an important and public issue.

When the Committee officials arrived, they quickly disclosed that the mistake was not that we had paid too little, but that we had paid too much. Mr. Yu had not included the interest on savings deposits that had been transferred. Our mistake was in their favor. The officials had brought along a large sack of money to reimburse us for the difference. My father was relieved, but refused to accept it, saying it could go for additional bonds in the names of our workers. My mother said that in all the years he had been with us, Mr. Yu had never made a single mistake, but that he ought to get a bonus for making this one with such good results all the way around. Everybody ended up having a hearty laugh at Mr. Yu's expense, even Mr. Yu.

Mr. Yu was good-natured and very smart. I liked being around him and learned a lot from him, not just about numbers. He liked to give me assignments. Concerning the worker subscriptions, he suggested to my parents that I calculate the portions to be given to each worker. He said that he should not be involved since he was one of the beneficiaries. I suspect this was just another way for him to test my mathematical skills. I presented my parents with a neat and accurate accounting of the apportionments, then distributed the bond coupons to each worker, making sure they knew how to check their principal and cash their interest payments on due dates.

I accompanied my parents to see Mr. Yu in his small office in the garden. When I handed him his share of the bond, he declined it and seemed a little embarrassed.

"I am sorry," he said, "but I can't take it."

"How come?" I was surprised.

"I made the mistake of not counting the interest due. Mistakes shouldn't be rewarded."

My mother said, "You must take it."

My father quickly added, "Mr. Yu, you deserve much more than this."

After a short silence, Mr. Yu acquiesced, "I accept it, but please allow me to host a farewell dinner for my co-workers who are going to leave us."

Mr. Yu hosted a big dinner at the Ji Barbeque Restaurant. It was not only a farewell party for his co-workers, but also for himself. He soon retired and left us despite my parents' urging him to stay. Mr. Yu knew his workload had been decreasing since my father had gradually withdrawn from the real estate business. He didn't want to be a burden on our family.

The more I got to know Mr. Yu, the more I liked and respected him. Now I understood why my father always called him Mr. Yu. For all my life, I would remember him as a gracious gentleman and a true mentor, a model for me to learn from forever.

Under the cloud of the war to resist US aggression and aid North Korea, a huge military parade became the main event of new China's first National Day celebration. Four hundred thousand people gathered together in Tiananmen Square. The two slogans on each side of Mao's portrait had been changed to "Long Live the People's Republic of China" and "Long Live the Great Unity of the World's People." But nobody in the Chen family was in the mood for the holiday festivity. Although we and our remaining home workers had settled into the garden, everyone still felt dispossessed. After school, I sometimes forgot and by habit ran toward the gate of the main compound, only to find it tightly locked.

Before turning all our keys over to the AFC, my father took me and my little sister for our last tour of the mansion, the ultimate farewell to the palace. It was late afternoon on a cool, late autumn day. My mother and other sisters were out shopping. Only a few trees still held on to a scattering of leaves. The typical hustle and bustle of the old days had been replaced by a definite air of sadness. My father took us slowly to the main compound through the front moon gate from the garden. The other two moon gates between the main compound and the garden had already been blocked off by Uncle Lee and his people.

"Let us tour the whole compound inside and out," Father told us. "You tell me what you remember best about our home, alright?"

"Alright!" I got excited because I had many stories to tell.

I think it was the first time in years for my father to go around to every nook and corner of the huge place. He seemed much less familiar with it than I was. When I showed him and Jiahui my secret paths from one courtyard to another, they were quite amazed.

"Father, to answer your question, I love the jujube trees and the stream and pond the best, but as far as architecture goes, I like the second inner festoon gate the best," I said, sitting on the threshold. The gate displayed marvelous, carved lotus leaves and flowers and was brightly painted.

"Why?"

"It was so beautifully done. Besides, when we opened all the gates during festivals, we could see from this gate to the corridor, the main courtyard, the parlor, and all the way to the rear line of rooms." I prided myself on my powers of observation.

"Splendid. But do you know how much time it took Uncle Lee and me to build it?"

"No."

"The better part of two years." Father sighed with emotion. "How about you, Jiahui?"

"I know what she likes the most." I jumped in before Jiahui had a chance to answer.

"No. I want to tell Dad myself," Jiahui shouted in a hurry. "I like the tree house in the cherry-apple tree."

"I knew it. I knew it," I laughed. "She always begged me to help her get up to the tree house."

Father spent a fair amount time in the accounting room and the parlor. Quite a bit of our furniture remained there. We sat on the leather sofas in the empty parlor while Father was lost in deep thought.

"Let's go. It is getting cold here." He finally stood up and led us silently back to the front moon gate.

"Is this moon gate also going to be blocked off?" I asked when we got to our garden.

"Yes. The main compound belongs to the government now," Father said softly.

"Don't worry, Father. When I grow up, I'll build a bigger house for you and Mother," I said earnestly.

"And I'll help Songsheng do it," Jiahui added.

"Wonderful!" Father smiled wholeheartedly. "But we don't need a big house anymore." He locked the moon gate. Looking at Jiahui and me with deep love, he added, "Heroic children make glad parents. Keep up your spirits and you will have many other ways to make your parents happy."

In my own private bedroom, on the huge, elaborately carved, rosewood bed that had been my grandfather's, I couldn't fall asleep. I was already missing our old home, but I was thinking more about my father's words. I wanted to be heroic with high spirits. But what were the many other ways to make my father and mother happy? I was only 11 years old, but I felt I was nearly grown up.

Chapter 5

ANSWERING THE CALL FOR
RED CAPITALISTS

1951-1953
Beijing, China

IN ADDITION TO PROMOTING GOVERNMENT bonds, my father passionately backed the new government in many other ways, notably during the Korean War, which the government portrayed as an invasion of North Korea by the US Army and its allies. In China, the conflict was known as "Resist America, Aid Korea; Protect Nation and Home." What started as a civil war between North and South Korea in June of 1950 escalated into a major flare up between the East and the West, the hottest spot in the Cold War, right on our border.

The Chinese People's Volunteers advanced across the Yalu River and deep into the Korean Peninsula to fight against the Americans. Even children showed their support for the Korean cause. My schoolmates and I wrote and played in many street shows to participate in the campaign. I was usually chosen for a leading role, but I refused to play the American general in our little dramas. It was not so much because I hated Americans. I just hated playing a loser. And we were going to beat those Yankee imperialists, of that I was sure. I loved my country. I thought what we were doing would help us to win the war. It was an exciting time to be alive.

My father was appointed Vice Director of the Beijing Resist America, Aid Korea Contributions Committee. Without talking with my mother, he donated a large amount of cash, almost enough to pay for a fighter plane for our forces. That made him, at the time, the biggest lump-sum donor in China. My mother was choked with silent annoyance. She was not against my father donating to the cause, but thought it was too much, and it used up all our family's gold and US dollars. My father viewed it differently. He often reminded my mother that he had had only 20 silver coins when he left Yanmen. As my grandfather had said, money should be used where and when it was needed most.

The Beijing government issued my father many certificates of commendation. His story was reported in many newspapers. He kept none of the articles and only a few of the receipts for his donations. He pasted these receipts with some other items in an old copy of *La Revue de Pekin*. Nobody knew anything about this little treasure until Jiahui, my younger sister, found it in March 2009 and gave it to me. I thought I had struck gold. The receipts were often annotated in my father's distinctive hand. He could have followed the advice of my mother and his friends by using the money to buy some land or houses in Hong Kong. His friends who had made such investments there soon became multimillionaires, but my father invested in his country.

Ironically, my parents' support for the government made them feel less secure, not more. They came to fear that their generosity would eventually mark them as targets because they were so clearly wealthy. My father said later that when Mr. Yu told him that his total donations could buy meals for 200,000 people for a whole week, he felt guilty to be rich for the first time. While my parents tried to shield me from their worries, it was obvious they had a lot on their minds.

Their biggest concern was my brother Jisheng. He had staged a popular "uprising," meaning he had surrendered to the Red Army, but he was actually suspected of retaining his earlier allegiance and being a Kuomintang spy. Jisheng had been detained and interrogated during the campaign against counter-revolutionaries, which started in 1950 after the war in Korea began. By the end of that year, US forces controlled all of the Korean Peninsula and stood poised at the Yalu River, the Chinese border. The Americans had actually bombed China's Northeast. In the spring of 1951, 2,000 KMT troops calling themselves the Anti-Communist National Salvation Army and backed by the CIA attempted the first of several invasions of Yunnan Province. Coastal raids were common, and former KMT soldiers, bandits, and saboteurs still roamed parts of the countryside.

China felt it had to respond to these threats ruthlessly, and it did. Former KMT officials and military officers and even mere "sympathizers" were rounded up and executed. All Nationalist army officers, battalion commanders and above, had been and were being routinely executed. My parents never knew whether the next campaign would put Jisheng squarely in its sights, or when someone might decide to accuse him falsely of acting against the state or even harboring such thoughts. My eldest brother's fate would inevitably have a direct effect on our family.

My parents became even more anxious after Yehu, our guard dog and companion to Mr. Wu, our gardener and gatekeeper, disappeared one winter night. Everybody loved Yehu; he was such a gentle, playful, and pleasing animal, except with strangers. Then he could be fierce; then he was so protective of us and our property. While other residences in the neighborhood had been burglarized, we felt secure knowing that no intruder would ever get past Yehu, our Night Tiger.

We were devastated by his loss, but Mr. Wu was disconsolate. He methodically searched the whole surrounding area and then far beyond, inquiring of everyone he met if they had seen his dog. He searched every day for three months and then just seemed to give up. During a warm spring evening, my father took me for a walk along the banks of Shicha Lake. Suddenly I saw Yehu on a leash behind a middle-aged, bald man crossing our path not far ahead. I ran toward them yelling, "Yehu! Yehu!" at the top of my lungs.

Yehu spotted me and immediately began tugging at his leash. By the time my father caught up with me, the bald man was having a hard time controlling Yehu.

"Excuse me, sir," my father exclaimed. "Excuse me, sir!"

The bald man looked up blankly and asked, "Are you talking to me?"

"Yes, I beg your pardon. Is this dog yours?"

"Of course. What kind of silly question is that?"

"I don't believe this is your dog, sir." My father was still trying to be polite.

"Nonsense! I have owned this dog since he was a puppy."

Yehu kept trying to free himself from the bald man's grasp. More and more people, including two policemen, gathered, curious about what was causing the commotion.

"Very well," my father said. "There are police officers and quite a few people here. Let us ask someone to take the dog to a mid-point between the two of us. You and I then call the dog and see to whom the dog responds. How does that sound?"

"Ridiculous! Why should I do that?"

My father turned to the two policemen. "Officers, we lost this dog four months ago. We believe that he was stolen from us. Do you think my request is reasonable?"

"Yes, I think so. It doesn't hurt anyone at least," the elder policeman replied.

The other policeman said, "Mister, do you agree? There shouldn't be any problem if you truly are the owner."

The man neither consented nor refused. After a moment the elder policeman stepped forward and said, "Okay, I'll be the judge," as he directed my father and the bald man where to stand and led Yehu between them. "As soon as I say go, start calling the dog."

"Ready? Go!"

"Yehu!" my father thundered. I could hardly believe such a deafening shout came from my calm and soft-spoken father.

Yehu was upon us in a second, pouncing on Father and me, wagging his tail, licking our faces, and letting out little joyful yelps. The crowd cheered. Yehu barked. It seemed everybody wanted to pet him. When we looked around, the bald man had disappeared.

"Don't worry about it, officers. We have Yehu back. That's the important thing." My father shook hands with the two policemen. "Thank you on behalf of the whole Chen family."

Mr. Wu bought 10 big bottles of white liquor for the party to celebrate Yehu's return and drank more than half of them himself. The chefs prepared quite a feast. More than 30 Chen family members, home workers, and close friends gathered in the garden for the occasion. We washed the embroidered collar and cord Nanna Ma had long ago made for Yehu. Mr. Wu and I bathed him from top to bottom. We hadn't had a party for a long time, and this was a good reason to be happy. The household stayed joyful for several weeks, indeed right up until the day the Beijing government announced its "Killing Dogs" campaign.

Dogs had never fared well under the Communists. They were banned in the PRC's first year, although the ban was rarely enforced. Dogs were seen as a sign of wealth, linked to bourgeois sentiments, and branded a "symbol of decadence and a criminal extravagance at a time of food shortages." Newspapers portrayed keeping dogs as "uncivilized and unhealthy" because they spread disease, polluted the environment, and frightened and bit people.

We didn't know what to do. We had just gotten Yehu back and now we might lose him to the government's latest campaign for the public good? Mr. Wu was terribly upset. For the first time, he actually entered my father's study to propose that he leave and hide Yehu in his home village. Since that village was still under Beijing's jurisdiction, my father suggested that the safest thing to do was to send Yehu to Yanmen.

This plan was kept so secret that I knew nothing about it. Mr. Wu departed. Yehu disappeared. Three weeks later, Mr. Wu reappeared with a longer beard, thinner face, and sad eyes; he looked like an entirely different person. Mr. Wu finally answered my ceaseless questions and told me he had left Yehu in Yanmen.

Mr. Wu's health deteriorated rapidly. He drank more and ate less, and then one day he just resigned his position with us and went back to his home village. It apparently didn't take Mr. Wu long to spend every bit of his severance pay on his favorite white liquor. Sometime later, we learned that Mr. Wu had died and been buried in a straw mat by a poor and distant relative. Without telling my parents, Mr. Yu, Uncle Lee, and all our home workers bought him a coffin and reburied him behind his hut.

That summer, my parents grew more and more concerned over whether they had put our whole family in harm's way by failing to leave Beijing when they had the chance. They decided to consult with Uncle Zhang and invited him to dinner. I remember how joyful Uncle Zhang was when he revisited the garden where he had stayed for so long. He and my parents had a long talk at the dinner table. Many of the dishes were prepared in their Jiyuan hometown style. My job was to refill their cups with white liquor and I stayed busy. I kept my ears open and learned a lot that night.

When they took the reins of government, the Communists took over all the enterprises formerly owned by the Nationalists, but all private business remained in the hands of their owners. Indeed the new government took immediate action to calm the fears of business owners and investors that they were in any jeopardy. On May 2, 1949 Vice Chairman Liu Shaoqi, Chairman Mao's second-in-command, invited 128 capitalists to a meeting in Tianjin to explain the role of the private sector in the new China. He told them that the nation needed them, and that progressive Red Capitalists could do their patriotic duty and earn a profit at the same time. Liu emphasized that private business was needed to supplement the socialist economy. Liu's view was later formalized in a resolution of the CCP's Seventh Central Committee.

Uncle Zhang stressed the word "resolution" several times to make sure my parents understood what the CCP's resolution, now in black and white, meant. He said the resolution was the most authoritative law not only for the Party, but also for the country. The positive results Uncle Zhang cited put my parents' minds at ease all the more. Beijing's privately owned companies had jumped from around 5,000 in 1949 to almost 6,400 in 1951. And these companies hired about 80,000 employees, 260% more than 1949.

Being a progressive Red Capitalist carried prestige. It meant you were patriotic and responsive in answering the call of your nation. You were looked up to. My father first became involved in 1950 with the founding of the Beijing Xingye Investment Company Limited, the first private investment company in new China. He was a shareholder, and for a short time, directed the Real Estate Department.

My parents joined Red Capitalist clubs, where the gentlemen studied government policies and discussed how to expand their businesses and the ladies prepared and launched employee welfare programs. I really liked going to my mother's meetings. Everybody seemed to have fun and, best of all, at the end they always served a potluck of great food. I can still remember how much I enjoyed Mrs. Tao's hot and sour soup and Mrs. Ding's Sichuan-style shrimp.

Late in the summer of 1951, at the invitation of his close business friends, my father took the train to Tianjin to attend an internal meeting of top-ranking capitalists in North China.

This meeting followed by two days of open discussions played an important role in reaffirming my father's determination to answer the call of the new government to get more involved as a Red Capitalist. When he returned, my father briefed us on what he had learned at the gathering.

Mr. Wang, a well-known entrepreneur close to the central government, had chaired the meeting. He and a few other capitalists who had been present at the earlier meeting with Vice Chairman Liu in Tianjin passed on surprising news to the attendees: "Exploitation is meritorious."

"You mean exploitation contributes to society?" My father didn't trust his ears.

"It's not what *I* mean. Those aren't my words," Mr. Wang said.

"Whose are they then?" my father asked.

"Liu Shaoqi's," Mr. Wang replied.

"Does that mean capitalists and their enterprises are allowed to exist in new China?" someone asked.

"As long as they are progressive," Mr. Wang replied.

"What does 'progressive' mean?" quite a few people asked in chorus.

It seemed nobody at the meeting was able to answer the question. At home, my father did, however, have his explanation. He told us that to be progressive meant to follow the directions of the Party. Father's idea was to sell our garden, move the family to a smaller house, and invest in a manufacturing business. My mother fully supported this plan and added a new wrinkle. She wanted to buy a dairy business to diversify our investments.

Soon they held a meeting in the huge garden hall. All our family members and home workers gathered to hear my parents announce their decisions. First my father spoke about their hopes for becoming Red Capitalists and helping China grow. Clearly my father loved China very much and wanted the new government to succeed. He said that the war against the imperialists in Korea was draining our national treasury and that we needed to support China in every way we could.

Then my mother spoke about our need to move. "Now even the garden is too big for us," she said. "All of Songsheng's older brothers and sisters have moved to their work units or their colleges. We don't need such a large place anymore. We hope we will be able to sell it soon."

"Don't worry about your future, however," my father added quickly. "Junying and I are already making arrangements to take good care of each and every one of you."

With the help of the AFC President—who was very happy with the cooperative's new quarters, our old mansion—we quickly sold our garden compound to the Communist Central Government Administrative Bureau. The Bureau was anxious to find residences for top CCP and government leaders who had been transferred to Beijing, and the garden fit their needs perfectly. After our experience of having to sell the mansion so far below market value, my parents were surprised at the Bureau's offer. It was actually a fair price, my father said, and he accepted it immediately.

In August 1951, we moved out of the garden compound and into our new home, which was a well-kept older house in the East District, quite some distance from the mansion. One of the few home workers we took with us was Nanna Yang, my little sister's former wet nurse who now served as one of our housekeepers. The main structure had a wing on either side and a total of 11 rooms. My parents added a full bathroom next to their bedroom. A paved path led from our front door to the courtyard. My mother soon made it all into a very comfortable and beautiful residence and filled the courtyard with an array of flowers. As nice as the new place was, though, I really missed our garden, with its brook, the playfield, and those seven jujube trees.

At that time, most companies—public and private—had tight cash flow problems. Knowing that my parents intended to invest in private businesses, friends and brokers flocked to our house. There were actually quite a few good investment opportunities, such as printing plants, flour and grain mills, and wine and white liquor plants. My mother and older brothers and sisters didn't understand why my father chose to acquire the Yongtai Machine Tools Factory, but once he set his mind to something, my father would not be deterred. After completing the move from the garden, my father bought the tool plant in an undeveloped area on the eastern fringe of the city surrounded by farms. My mother established Dasheng Dairy in a northern suburb of Beijing.

It took my father an hour and a half to get to the plant from home, changing buses three times and walking on a dirt road for 15 minutes. My father invited Mr. Yu to help manage the plant's finances. They worked closely with the chief engineer and sales manager to develop a plan to expand and modernize the manufacturing lines. After ordering new equipment and machines to replace the ancient ones then in use, the next investment my father made in the plant surprised everyone. He told Uncle Lee to draw up plans for a new dormitory for their single workers. My father couldn't tolerate the desperate conditions in the typical workers' shelter and also felt that a business owner had to win the hearts of his employees before he could succeed.

The factory had one main product: files. My father and his team of engineers expanded the plant, adding a foundry and a heat treatment shop, and began producing other hand tools and metal fixtures as well. When I visited the plant with my father, the two things that impressed me the most were the earsplitting racket coming from the stamping shop and the thick black smoke that bellowed from the foundry smokestack.

The plant turned out to be a sinkhole for our family's remaining funds. I knew that whenever Mr. Yu came to our house, it was for nothing else but more money. I overheard my parents' worried conversations. Neither of them could guess how much more money must be invested before the plant generated a profit.

In contrast with my father's entry into the challenging heavy industry sector, my mother's Dasheng Dairy, like many other dairies in that district, was flourishing. With the quick improvement of living standards, more families could afford milk for their babies. My uncle, Mother's younger brother, managed the business, which also had a small sales office not far from our old mansion.

I remember one other significant event that summer. Lifen told me that her parents had entered her name for the National Academy of Chinese Theater Arts. She asked me to accompany her and her parents to the audition. For all her talent, Lifen was shy, and I think she wanted someone else she knew in the audience. It was hot early that Sunday morning in July. When we got to the Academy, a crowd of parents and kids waited outside the audition hall under the scorching sun. The few trees on the street offered little shade.

After what seemed like hours, one of the examiners finally stepped out to the sidewalk and called Lifen's name.

We followed him into the building, where he pointed her to the stage and asked, "What would you like to sing for us?"

"Phoenix Returning to Her Nest," Lifen replied nervously. She looked unbelievably uncomfortable up there.

After the accompanists had set the pitch and begun to play, Lifen rose to the occasion and sang beautifully. I sat in my seat in the front row and beamed with pride at my girlfriend's performance. Her soulful solo earned her hearty applause.

"We would like to hear another piece from you. What would you like to perform?" the Head Examiner asked.

Lifen seemed flustered by the request and stared hard at the floor and then gulped. After a few moments, I asked, "Lifen, why don't you sing a piece from 'Farewell My Concubine?'"

"Would you sing with me, please?" she begged.

I didn't know what to do and looked to the group of examiners for direction.

"That would be fine," one of the examiners replied.

I climbed to the stage, cleared my throat, and began to sing—the overlord starts the duet. Lifen and I had our roles down pat but performed with a passion that must have been rare in such a setting. As soon as we finished, everyone in the audience, each of the examiners, and even the accompanists applauded enthusiastically.

"That was simply splendid!" said the Head Examiner. "Young woman, I think you can look forward to matriculating at the Academy. Young man, you have a strong and mature voice for someone your age. Would you like to be a student of the Academy?"

"Yes. It's my dream to go into Peking Opera, but I'm afraid my parents wouldn't approve."

"I understand. But just to be sure, why don't you talk to your parents immediately? If your parents consent, you and your friend could be schoolmates."

I walked home with the Yuans on a cloud thinking sweet thoughts about going off to the Academy with Lifen. Our friendship had ripened wonderfully. While we had not yet kissed, we had held each other closely while performing and had recognized without words the romantic feelings we had for each other ever since we first sang "Farewell My Concubine" that night three years ago. To my surprise, Uncle Yuan and Auntie Cheng had no encouraging words for me. Before we said good-bye, Uncle Yuan told me in a serious tone that I must talk with my parents immediately.

When I got home, I went promptly to talk with my father and my mother. I told them I had gone to Lifen's audition and been asked to apply to the Academy myself. Quietly but firmly, my father told me that it was totally out of the question. My mother added that I would continue my education through middle school and then go to the university like all my older brothers and sisters. The discussion lasted only moments.

And so that fall, riding my father's old bicycle, I started the new semester as a junior high school student at Yuying Middle School. Lifen began her studies at the Academy. After that, we didn't see much of each other, and I missed her. I was walking proof of the old adage my father often used to describe his feelings about Yanmen, "Absence makes the heart grow fonder."

Another memorable event took place before the end of the year. On December 21, 1951, Mr. Lao She, the writer I admired the most, was named the "People's Artist" by the Beijing Government and Beijing People's Congress. I must confess that

I have so much respect for this esteemed master that I cannot say or write only his two names. I must always add "Mister." Mr. Lao She had come back to Beijing from England in 1950. Encouraged by the significant changes in his hometown, he chose one of the poorest and dingiest areas in the southern part of Beijing, Longxu (Dragon Beard) Ditch, as the setting for his three-act drama. It depicts the miserable and the hopeful life of four families in old and new China. After its premier in February 1951, I saw the play three times. I was so fascinated by the drama that I could recite many of its lines. I badgered my father to invite Mr. Lao She and their mutual friends, Uncle Chang Weijun and Zhao Shaohou, for a dinner to celebrate his wonderful play, but Father declined, saying Mr. Lao She was too busy for such an evening because he had a heavy schedule as Chairman of the Beijing Literary Federation.

Another piece of year-end good news was that both the Yongtai Plant and the Dasheng Dairy were certified as Basic Law-Observing Enterprises by the workgroups of the Three-Antis Campaign. It and the Five-Antis campaign that followed a year later were supposedly aimed at eliminating corruption, waste, and bureaucracy and then targeting bribery, tax evasion, cheating on government contracts, theft of state property, and stealing the country's economic intelligence. In reality, they served to consolidate Mao's power, punishing political opponents, the bourgeoisie, and capitalists. Few of those charged were actually put to death—most incurred harsh fines, some were tortured and imprisoned—but the campaigns drove many thousands to suicides. So many people plunged to their deaths from Shanghai's skyscrapers that they came to be called "parachutes."

Mr. Yu brought the official assessment certificate for the Yongtai plant to our home together with his resignation letter. He told my parents that he had done his very best for the plant to earn its Basic Law-Observing Enterprises certificate while many other private companies suffered heavy fines that bankrupted their businesses. Mr. Yu said his health didn't allow him to continue with such an exhausting job. My father immediately accepted his resignation with grateful appreciation for his big contribution to the plant. At my mother's request, Mr. Yu had dinner with us. He drank quite a lot of white liquor with my father and me. He laughed, laughed as if relieved of a heavy load. My mother told me later that my father awarded Mr. Yu a generous pension. Before long, Mr. Yu and his whole family returned to his hometown in Hebei Province.

Beginning in 1953, China launched its first Five-year Plan. Based on Russia's economic development model, the Plan concentrated on heavy industry and capital-intensive technology. In the next six years, over 10,000 Soviet engineers and advisors came to China to assist in building and modernizing almost 150 major projects. Russian became the only foreign language taught in middle schools and colleges.

Under the collective leadership, preparations for China's first central and local People's Congress progressed smoothly. Mao chaired the committee to draft China's constitution. Liu Shaoqi led the Central Election Committee. Zhou Enlai headed the committee to draft the Central Election Regulations. On July 27, the Korean Ceasefire Agreement was signed. Except for an internal anti-party movement relating only to senior Party officials, there were no political campaigns in the nation. For the first time in years, there were no anti-this or anti-that movements that sought to expose and destroy "dangerous" elements and cliques.

By 1953, China's population had reached almost 600 million. Two hundred and twenty thousand students attended 182 universities and colleges. Gambling stopped, banditry vanished. There was no more prostitution, no more opium. Red Capitalists, the national bourgeoisie, were represented by one of the four small stars surrounding the big CCP star on the national flag. (The other three stars represented workers, peasants, and the petty bourgeoisie.) Red Capitalists continued doing their patriotic duty while theoretically also continuing to earn their profits. In October, my father was invited to attend the National Industrial and Commercial Federation conference. Mr. Chen Shutong, a friend who lived nearby, was elected its Chairman. There was a lively atmosphere to the event, and the delegates heard of progress across the board.

When the nation is at peace, it is easier for its citizens also to be at peace and happy, and my family was. My father's efforts at the Yongtai Plant looked like they might finally start paying off. My older siblings were teaching or studying at universities in Beijing and Baoding. Jiahui, my little sister, started her first year in Peiyuan Primary School. I was in my second year in Beijing No. 25 Junior High School. My parents often told us they had never lived such a carefree life. It was absolutely true. We could park our bicycles anywhere without locks, and we often forgot to bolt our front door at night.

Looking back on those early years of the new China, I wish that the spirit, momentum, and political climate of 1953 could have prevailed through the following decades instead of the darkness that descended. What a different and better China we would be looking at today.

Chapter 6

The End of the Road

1954-1956
Beijing, China

In 1954, WE CONTINUED TO enjoy our simpler, quieter life, free of trouble. The new China was surmounting its early difficulties. Effective price controls held inflation down. Costs of daily necessities and other commodities had fallen and social order was restored. Gone were the days when it took a wheelbarrow full of currency to feed a family for a day. My older sisters, Siwei and Wuquan, went to the China Agricultural University and the Beijing Medical University without having to pay tuition, room, or board. The very expensive private schools that Jiahui and I attended were converted to public schools in 1952. We paid no more tuition.

A memorable example of how low prices were at this time is that it took only a tenth of my father's monthly salary from the factory to host a New Year's dinner for the whole Chen family at an expensive restaurant. Relatives from Yanmen could afford to visit Beijing more frequently, always bringing my father's favorite foods from home. Whenever they came, it was my job to entertain them and guide them in the big city. I used my father's free admission pass to take them to the Summer Palace, the Forbidden City, and the Temple of Heaven. There I would tell them the story I had heard from my grandfather about how the lazy emperors didn't like the long pilgrimage to the real Temple of Heaven on Wangwu Mountain, so they built a new one in Beijing. My cousins felt so proud. In spite of the magnificence of Beijing's Temple of Heaven, it simply didn't measure up to the original temple in Jiyuan.

As 1954 began, my father was happily engaged in turning his Yongtai Plant into a profitable enterprise. Even though the plant was still operating at a loss, it was on the right track to start returning my father's investment soon. The management team's projections and numbers had proven true in the past, so there was reason for optimism.

Meanwhile, my mother was diversifying the Dasheng Dairy product line. She had been very successful at raising chickens when we still had a large garden, and she decided to introduce a new variety of Leghorn to the booming local market. More and more customers overcame their initial prejudice and invested in the new Leghorns. They were easy to raise, reached maturity quickly, and were prolific layers, far out-producing other hens. Mr. Lee and some of Father's engineers built incubators at the dairy sales office, and soon my mother was doing a brisk business in Leghorn chicks.

After careful consideration, my brother Jisheng declined a job offer from the new government and enrolled at Hebei Agricultural University in Baoding, majoring in agronomy.

Jisheng never forgot the scenes of rural poverty he had witnessed during his army days and believed that modern agriculture offered the best way to better the lives of China's hundreds of millions of peasants. He was eager to earn a degree as was expected in our family. Interestingly, that year, our sister Siwei began teaching there. Instead of earning a decent salary, he had to be industrious and thrifty during his college years. My parents helped him by giving him a lump-sum payment for his expenses as well as for his family. My sister-in-law, a middle school teacher, shouldered the burden of raising their two sons. Siwei and her new husband often asked Jisheng to join them for meals in their small dormitory room. My other brother, Yancheng, was married, had a son, and was a lecturer at the Beijing Aeronautic University.

Although we didn't know much about the Communist Party, "New Democracy," or the "New Democratic Revolution," my family and our friends mostly liked what we saw, heard, and experienced under the new government. All of us loved Chairman Mao. My father admired Mao from the bottom of his heart. He regularly bought Mao's books. When Uncle Zhang gave him all of Chairman Mao's poems that he had collected, many of which were unpublished, he was as excited as if he had found a rare treasure. Father never tired of reading Mao's poems to me and explaining how great they were, abiding by the metrics of traditional poems but having powerful new meaning. Very quickly, I learned most of Mao's poems by heart. I can recite them still today. Believe it or not, after 20 long years of persecution, my father wrote a passage from Chairman Mao's "Chanting the Plum" on a scroll in his gorgeous calligraphy at age 80 and gave it to my second brother-in-law. It is the only piece of his brush calligraphy left in our family.

The peaceful time, however, was short-lived. "A storm may arise from a clear sky," as my father would say, and he felt deep foreboding when he was invited to an advisory meeting about tearing down Di An Men to improve traffic in the area. Tear down Di An Men?! My father could not believe his eyes when he saw the invitation.

Father arrived at the meeting early. Several of his acquaintances from architecture, real estate, and academia were already assembled, including Professor Liang, the leading light of Tsinghua University's Architecture Department and Vice Director of the Beijing Planning Committee.

My father was glad to see his old friend again. Although these two professors didn't see each other often, their high mutual regard kept their friendship intimate and warm. Their companionship had deepened after both decided not to flee to Taiwan before Beijing was liberated. Uncle Zhang told my father that as soon as Tsinghua University was taken by the Liberation Army at the end of 1948, Professor Liang made a detailed map, identifying all the important ancient sites in the city. The CCP Central Committee headquarters distributed copies of the map to the Liberation Army so that these sites were well-protected, and none sustained damage. When my father took visitors to Beijing's historic sites, he would speak with great respect of Professor Liang's efforts to preserve them.

After exchanging greetings and inquiring about friends in common, Professor Liang told my father that he was frankly worried about their prospects of saving Di An Men. He felt that even as a leader on the Beijing Planning Committee, his objections would be for naught.

"Professor Chen," he said, "You can speak to both the ideals of the university and the realities of the marketplace. I hope you will make an eloquent plea on our behalf."

"I will try my best, but if they do not heed so eminent an authority as you, why would they pay any attention to me?"

The meeting was intense. My father did make a powerful speech, which he concluded by saying:

"Di An Men has been a prominent feature of our city since 1420. It is far more than simply a great architectural treasure, however. It is an essential part of our city's structure and integrity, helping to secure the central axis of Beijing. This gate was designed according to a code of rites and hierarchy that acknowledges the power of divine alignment. It balances Tian An Men (Tiananmen). Tian, the heaven, and Di, the earth, are two parts of a whole. What happens to heaven after the earth is gone? If Di An Men falls, the city becomes unbalanced and loses its stability. Let us not take these risks when we have such thoughtful alternatives. Please save Di An Men."

"Professor Chen, don't you think you are being superstitious?" a government official quickly asked.

"I don't think he is at all," an older lady immediately interrupted. "We should respect and preserve the ancient sites of our ancestors. That is our duty."

A young bespectacled man rose and said, "I am an architectural engineer. Please allow me to express my ideas from a technical point of view." He placed a drawing on a large easel and explained, "This magnificent brick and wood palace gate contains seven spaces. The central open space is 7 meters wide and 11.8 meters high. Its two adjacent side spaces are 5.4 meters high. They provide more than enough room for pedestrians and bicycles. We could easily build a road around

Di An Men for cars and trolleys. Why should we have to knock down this magnificent piece of architecture?"

Following the engineer, many citizens spoke, protesting the government plans and pleading that Di An Men be saved.

"May we ask Professor Liang to tell us his view?" my father suggested.

"Ladies and Gentlemen, I have already written a letter to Premier Zhou. This issue not only relates to Di An Men, it relates to all of Beijing. With its large number of high quality historic sites, Beijing is perhaps unrivaled in the world. We must cherish our unique heritage. I am not saying that Beijing should forego reconstruction, which sometimes involves destruction. But we have many options for rebuilding Beijing while preserving our inheritance from the past. We could, for instance, build a new city outside of the old downtown. Instead of pulling down the city wall, we could develop parks and other amenities along it. We have to remember that once these historical sites are gone, they are lost forever. Any later attempts to reconstruct them would be nothing more than historical and architectural fakery."

The officials then declared the meeting over. Despite the unanimous agreement of the citizens who had gathered, a sense of fighting for a losing cause pervaded the room.

This was the last meeting between Professor Liang and my father. Uncle Zhang told my father that Professor Liang was severely criticized because of his staunch insistence on historical preservation. He said that Mao had decided that Beijing's development was a political issue to be determined by the CCP Central Committee alone and said that he would love to see many more smokestacks all over the city.

Di An Men was pulled down by the end of 1954. Visiting the scene was distressing, but I couldn't stay away. I went there often with my father, the Yuans, or my schoolmates, but most often alone. No machinery or explosives were used to destroy the building. This huge structure—38 meters wide and about 12 meters high and deep—was knocked down by hand with all kinds of mallets, sledge hammers, and pry bars.

Our mansion was only a five-minute walk from Di An Men. I had passed through that gate hundreds of times on foot or on my bicycle. I always liked the building, but only when it was about to be destroyed did I really appreciate just how much it meant to me. There was nothing I or anyone else could do about this desecration. The people were helpless to stop it. I visited the site as often as I could before the last remnants of this treasure could be removed and all signs of its existence erased.

The last time I visited Di An Men was a chilly autumn afternoon after school. I walked alone to the site but didn't take Cihui Hutong because I could not bear to see our old home again. Long before I got there, the steady pounding beat of the destruction grew loud. Suddenly I saw Lifen and her parents in the crowd that had gathered to watch and mourn and headed their way.

We gazed sadly and silently at the workers taking out the last standing wall and breaking the rubble into smaller pieces to be carted away. For as many people as were assembled there, it was very quiet, a solemn and somber scene. The sounds of the wrecking crew, of course, continued unabated. Finally Lifen spoke up.

"Mother, I can't stand to watch or listen anymore. Let's go home."

"Yes. Let's go. My ears are pounding. My heart is aching," Auntie Cheng said. As was the new practice under the Communists, wives started using their maiden names, so instead of Auntie Yuan, I now called her Auntie Cheng.

As we walked away, I knew I would not return to watch now that only rubble was left. I turned around to look over my shoulder for one last look at the remains of our beloved Di An Men. I saw a hundred holes and a thousand wounds. It might have been the shriek of timbers being pulled apart, but I seemed to hear Di An Men crying. I didn't want to cry in front of Lifen, but it wasn't easy for me to hold back my tears.

On February 3, 1955, the new crossroad was completed. The traffic sign still said Di An Men, but the real Di An Men had ceased to exist. As a concession to those so strongly opposed to the destruction, the Beijing government promised to preserve all the architectural elements they had removed—doors, windows, beams, columns, poles, bricks, tiles, anything that could be salvaged. They planned to rebuild Di An Men near the Temple of Heaven. Unfortunately, a huge fire consumed everything, so even a fake Di An Men couldn't be "rebuilt."

Next to fall to the municipal modernization plan were the magnificent 12-meter-high city walls, unequaled in the world. The inner wall was 22.5 kilometers long and the outer 14 kilometers. Dating from the Yuan Dynasty, the walls had been planned, built, modified, and reinforced over the following six centuries. Each brick weighed 24 kilograms. Hundreds of millions of bricks were made in Shandong and Henan Provinces and transported by boat along the Grand Canal to Beijing. If Di An Men and the city walls could be eliminated so easily, what sites were safe?

Our family didn't have a very happy New Year celebration in 1955. All the destruction and what it might foretell of the future cast a heavy shadow across our minds. In the course of the last year, the situation at my father's factory had gone from promising to dismal. A touching incident occurred at this time. My father told his management that he would not draw any salary until the company began to make a profit. Only then did he learn that his top staff—nine people, including Uncle Lee—had been drawing only half their salaries for the previous three months as a voluntary contribution to keep the plant running. They believed so strongly in my father and had such high hopes for their company and their nation. My father immediately brought in a briefcase full of currency to make up the difference to all his employees and pledged fresh investment in Yongtai. The management thanked my father on behalf of the staff but said that the situation was dire, that any new investment would simply carry the company over to the next brink. Long-time customers were canceling orders without warning. When pressed, a few companies said that the authorities had told them to deal only with state enterprises or private-public joint operations.

Hoping that his old Henan compatriot, Zhang Hanchen, might be able to give him some good advice, my father decided to meet with him. Uncle Zhang had recently been promoted to a very senior position in the central government. My father had to call his secretary to make an appointment even to meet him at his new residence. Armed soldiers patrolled around his big house day and night. Although it was not what Uncle Zhang wanted at all, it was not easy for his old friends to see him anymore.

When my father arrived he was greeted by Uncle Zhang, his 18-year-old son, Taiming, and seven-year-old daughter, Taiqing.

After warm greetings between such dear friends long absent from each other, everybody made their way into the parlor, which reminded my father of the main parlor of our mansion, only smaller.

Taiming poured a cup of tea and said, "Uncle Chen, please have some of Henan's fine green tea."

My father looked the young man up and down. "Taiming, you've become an adult. I wouldn't recognize you if I met you on the street. And Taiqing, what a lovely girl you are," my father said as he hugged Taiqing. My father always had a sweet spot in his heart for his best friend's daughter.

Both Taiming and Taiqing were born in Zhicheng, about 10 kilometers from Yanmen. Taiming was now a college student in the History Department of Peking University. Taiqing attended a primary school for children of CCP senior officials. Hanchen told my father that he felt so guilty about the little time he had been able to spend with his wife, Yulian. They were married in 1935, and Hanchen calculated that they had spent a total of only 160 days together. Early on, he was fighting the Japanese in the Taihang Mountains. After Japan surrendered, he returned to his hometown, Zhicheng. Before Hanchen was transferred to the Peiping underground committee in 1946, he actually stayed at home for three months. His wife died soon after giving birth to Taiqing in 1947. Because of his duties to the Party, Hanchen was unable to go back home to hold a simple memorial ceremony for Yulian. The next year, Hanchen asked his colleagues to bring both of his children to live with him in Peiping. Hanchen never remarried, although many young women had set their sights on him.

"Taiming and Taiqing, run tell your aunt to cook up some genuine hometown noodles quickly for your Uncle Chen. Then come tell us when dinner is ready."

"Oh, please, don't bother. I can't take up your time like that," my father said.

"Bother? How could you say that?" Hanchen seemed disappointed. "How much bother have I caused you, if we talk about bother? Are you treating me as a stranger now, just because we haven't seen each other for a while?"

"You have so many important matters to attend to."

"Important matters? What matters more than meeting with my best friend, a compatriot from Henan to boot? Weizhen, I truly miss you. Oh, sorry, I didn't mean to call you by your old name."

"That makes me even more comfortable." My father smiled.

"Pinzhi, I truly miss where we grew up and want to return there, away from all these campaigns and movements. I am so tired of politics."

"I miss you too," my father said. "You are the only one with whom I can speak frankly about everything. So I regret that what I'd like to consult you about is politics."

"Please be as straightforward in asking your questions as I will be in giving my answers."

"It's about my plant and the dairy. We keep on putting in more money, but both businesses are on the verge of bankruptcy. What should we do now?"

Hanchen didn't reply immediately. He stood up and closed the door to the dining room.

"Let me share this very confidentially with you." When Hanchen had something important to say, he would write it out in his bold calligraphy. Hanchen spread a large piece of paper on the tea table, took up his brush, and wrote:

> *No more capitalist trial. No more Red Capitalists.*
> *China capitalism turns into China state capitalism.*
> *China state capitalism turns into China socialism.*

"No more Red Capitalists? I can't stay abreast of all these fast changes." My father didn't seem willing to accept this fate.

"We'll see even more changes in the near future, I believe."

"But it was the central government that asked us to become Red Capitalists."

"The government obeys the Party and the Party obeys Chairman Mao. Let me try to explain."

Hanchen sketched Mao's plan to convert the economy to complete state ownership and some of the strategies he was using. In the current movement, the first step, "Eating Apples," had already been taken, turning carefully selected big and influential privately owned "Apples" into public and private joint companies. The second step, "Eating Grapes," was being implemented on the numerous remaining, privately owned "Grapes," the medium and small firms with more than 10 employees.

"Pinzhi, the writing is on the wall. You have no choice but to turn your factory and the dairy into public and private joint operations."

"What will happen to Red Capitalists like me?"

"The bourgeoisie will be eliminated as a class. Red Capitalists will be transformed into ordinary workers."

"What will happen to our employees?"

"They should be safe after becoming employees of the new public and private joint companies."

"As long as they are safe and sound, I am much relieved."

"I am afraid it is still too early to use the word 'relieved.'"

"Why?"

It seemed Hanchen couldn't produce an easy answer.

Just at that moment, Taiqing knocked on the parlor door and announced, "Dinner is served, Uncle Chen."

"Let us go enjoy some hometown food," said Hanchen, pointing my father to the dining room. "Pinzhi, let me introduce you to Liandi, my beloved wife's younger sister. Liandi, this is my best friend, Professor Chen from Yanmen."

"From Yanmen?" Liandi was surprised and delighted.

"Yes, we were neighbors. So glad to meet you. Ah! Handmade noodles with pounded garlic! What fond memories this brings back!" My father was eager to dig in.

"I knew you'd love it." Hanchen turned to Liandi. "See, what did I tell you? This is what my friend likes best."

Liandi still felt a little uncertain. "But it's so simple."

"That's the beauty of it. With fried eggs and sesame oil? How could you beat that? Only on holidays did we have it that way in Yanmen," my father said. Then he continued.

"Let me tell you a wonderful story about my grandma. My father bought her a full bottle of sesame oil every year before the lunar New Year. But he always found the old bottle of sesame oil still full. Do you know why, Taiming and Taiqing?" my father asked.

"She didn't use it," Taiqing quickly replied.

"No." My father shook his head.

"She poured other cooking oil into the bottle." Taiming made a reasonable guess.

"No." My father smiled. "My grandma always used a chopstick to put a bit of sesame oil into her pot of water. But before she put the chopstick into the oil bottle, she put it into her pot. Only then did she dip it into the oil bottle, quickly withdraw it, and plunge it into the pot."

"Oh! The water got some oil and the oil got some water," exclaimed Taiqing, laughing.

"What happened to the old bottle of watery oil?" Taiming inquired.

"My grandma gave it to my old sister-in-law for their small family." This was not a funny story to my father, but a revealing tale of poverty and frugality.

Everyone enjoyed their noodles. Hanchen and my father finished three big bowls. My father didn't want to hold up Hanchen any longer. Hanchen walked him to the front door.

"Hanchen, please don't bother to see me out."

"Pinzhi, I want you to be careful. The wind sweeping through the tower heralds a rising storm in the mountain."

My father apparently didn't comprehend Hanchen's warning. "Be careful about what? Can you be more specific?"

"I just don't know what they," Uncle Zhang said, pointing one thumb upward, "are going to do next. I don't know many of the things that are happening, but from what I have seen and what I can guess, we are facing some rough times ahead. Just be careful."

On that note, the two old friends from Henan parted.

The very next day, my parents delivered their requests on behalf of the Yongtai Plant and the Dasheng Dairy to their respective district governments. On February 28, 1955, each district's Industrial and Commercial Bureau approved their requests, and by March 1, 1955, the Yongtai Plant and Dasheng

Dairy were duly registered as operating under their new structure. One week later, Mr. Diao Gejun, the plant's Party Secretary, and his team were assigned to the plant. My father still held the title of General Manager. Mr. Diao became the Deputy General Manager. Mr. Diao's team members took key jobs in every department, section, and workshop. My mother used her high blood pressure as a pretext to apply for her resignation from Dasheng Dairy.

When I overheard my parents' business friends discuss the Public and Private Joint Operation movement, they often made a joke. Red Capitalists saw the movement as "getting onboard the pirate ship," while government officials saw it as "pirates getting onboard our ship." As a matter of fact, getting onboard was the one and only option. My parents bought and took over the Yongtai Plant and Dasheng Dairy on February 26, 1952. Under the new plan, they would own only a quarter of the stock in their businesses. The other three equal shareholders were the state, the company's reserve fund, and the company employees, although the state actually controlled these funds. At the same time, my parents were supposed to receive annual five percent buy-out payments, which would be calculated on the basis of their total assets in their businesses. The value of their assets, however, was determined solely by the government agencies. The five percent buyout payments were from the government no matter whether the new companies were profitable or not and would continue for seven years beginning in 1956.

With the shrinking of our investment, the Chen family circle shrank again. Only our grandaunt continued staying with us. We let go the last of our home workers, including Nanna Yang, Jiahui's former wet nurse. My mother offered her two rooms next to the diary office to live in with her relatives. My mother, younger sister, and I often visited her there and regularly left her with some cash for treats beyond her basic needs.

Other changes occurred at this time as well. The fears Uncle Zhang expressed to my father quickly came to be. My father was shocked to learn that Hu Feng, China's leading literary theorist, a prominent poet, and a revolutionary since the 1920s, had been arrested. Hu had come under attack as early as 1952 for his "capitalist, bourgeois, individualist literary thoughts." Otherwise an orthodox Marxist, Hu deviated from the Party line that literature must always reflect the class struggle. He defended his views in a 300,000-word report to the Party that only brought him further difficulties.

Hu was assailed at public meetings and in the press. Over 2,000 articles or essays were published criticizing him. A nationwide hunt began for members of "Hu Feng's Anti-Revolutionary Clique." By mid-May, Hu was arrested and more than 2,100 others were implicated as being "anti-party" and "anti-people." Only a fraction of them were investigated, stripped of their positions, or arrested, but uncertainty and terror reigned as the campaign to liquidate Hu and his suspected sympathizers spread. The lines were now even more clearly drawn between Mao's government and China's intellectuals. My father knew several of those implicated. Hu was quickly sentenced to 14 years in prison. My father said he had similar feelings when Hu was arrested as when Di An Man was razed. If such icons could fall, who or what would be next?

Before I started my last two years of middle school, Lifen and I set up a system of communicating without our parents knowing. Instead of using our home addresses, we sent letters to her Academy or my school. Occasionally, we talked from public phone booths at a pre-arranged time. My classmates always made fun of me when they passed Lifen's letters on to me from our school reception room, although I never told anyone that I had a girlfriend.

Occasionally we'd go see a movie or a play. It was easy for me to get the free time but tough for her. She had to make up an excuse to get away for a few hours between dinner and bedtime. The movie theater we went to was pretty far away from her Academy. We definitely didn't want to bump into one of her schoolmates or teachers. There in the dark, watching the movie and enjoying the ice cream I'd buy for us, we'd sit close but dared not even touch each other's hand.

In one of the letters I got from Lifen she sent me a ticket to see a play in which she had a small role. The theater was on the east side of Chang An Boulevard. The play was pretty boring and didn't give Lifen any chance to display her talent. The best part came after the show, when I got to take Lifen back to her Academy. We decided not to take the bus and trolley but walked all the way through Tiananmen Square and Qian Men to Tao Ran Ting.

"Hungry?" I asked.

"I thought you'd never ask."

"What would you like to eat?"

"Anything you like."

"No. I want you to tell me what you like to eat."

"How about fried pancakes?"

"That is exactly what I like the most."

"I know that, and I also know the best fried pancake booth around," Lifen replied with a sly smile.

When we reached the booth, several customers lounged on long wooden benches.

"My classmates and I come here often when we're sick of the bland food at the Academy. This is cheap and tasty."

Some customers, apparently regulars, recognized Lifen, the beautiful Peking Opera student of the Academy, as we entered. They smiled at us and then the dynamics changed.

A tall young fellow asked Lifen, "Is that your boyfriend?"

"Oh, nonsense. He's my brother," Lifen replied.

"Oh! A big brother, eh? Do you think he can protect you?" he asked as he came toward us.

"Hey! Are you forgetting your manners? I wouldn't get any closer if I were you." My deep, loud voice caught everyone's attention. "Lifen, let's go."

I was relieved that no one followed us out. Lifen and I were the only ones on the unlit street. I don't know if she was actually afraid or not, but she said she felt safe with me at her side. For the first time, Lifen gracefully linked her arm with mine and leaned her head against my shoulder as we walked slowly to her Academy. It was my first time to be with a girl this way and at such a late hour. I just wished our walk could last forever, but despite our pace, all too soon we stood before the Academy front door.

"It's so late. The buses have stopped running. How will you get back home?" Lifen was worried.

"Walking. I like walking."

"Let me walk you as far as Qian Men Boulevard."

"Then I'd have to walk you back to your school again."

"Could I just walk you part way?"

"If that is your desire, who am I to say no?" Lifen's words warmed my heart.

I took off my jacket and wrapped it around Lifen's shoulders. We went back the way we had come, arm in arm and without a word almost all the way back to the pancake booth.

Lifen resolutely declined my request to walk her back to her school. We faced each other but avoided direct eye contact, our glances downcast. It seemed especially hard for us to part with each other that night.

"Take good care of yourself."

"You too!" I couldn't find any better words.

Lifen helped me put my jacket back on and then I turned toward her. We stood so close we could feel the ragged rhythms of each other's breathing. I was enveloped in her fragrance. Suddenly Lifen kissed me. I was so surprised I barely had time to respond before, just as quickly, she turned around and ran toward the Academy. It was our first kiss.

Unfortunately, it was also our last.

Chapter 7

LABELED AN ENEMY

1957
Beijing, China

EARLY IN 1957, I ACHIEVED a goal previously denied to me and was flush with revolutionary fervor. In my middle school, I was a triple good student—excelling in study, attitude, and health—a leader in and out of the classroom. Yet I had been denied admission to the Communist Youth League because of my "landlord" family background. I persisted and was finally accepted as a League member. The school's League secretary encouraged me to redouble my efforts to serve and also to help my parents make ever greater contributions to Beijing's socialist agenda.

One test of my family's revolutionary zeal came when my father's tool plant and my mother's dairy became state-private joint ventures overnight. My parents were no longer in control of the companies they had taken over, financed, and poured their energies and talents into. At first, my siblings and I were concerned that it would be hard for my parents to accept the fact that they had completely lost their authority over their own businesses. In truth, after the initial shock, confusion, and disappointment, my parents both felt liberated, freed from the yoke of trying to make something work in a system that was increasingly showing signs of being broken. My father was about to turn 60 and was tired of trying to make the Yongtai Plant work. He was looking forward to retirement.

As soon as Mr. Diao was assigned by the local government to the Yongtai Plant as Party Secretary, my father's General Manager position became a mere title. Diao ran the show. Despite this turn of events, my father told us that the Communists were better than the Nationalists. New China was better than old China. He was a sincere supporter of the government even though he saw its flaws.

Whatever losses were suffered when the Communists took over, by the mid-1950s China had gained stability. Food supply was steady, there was no inflation, and many of China's past travails—civil war, foreign occupation, bandits, and warlords— no longer troubled us. We all supported the government, and life seemed mostly good.

My carefree middle school years were some of the sweetest of my life. I was the son of a patriotic Red Capitalist and happy at home and in school. During my last semester at Beijing No. 65 Senior High School, my only worry—the same as all my classmates—was the upcoming college entrance examination. Everybody said this year's exams were going to be much more difficult than the previous year's. I was confident that my consistently high test scores would gain me admission to the school of my choice, but I didn't have an answer when people asked me what I planned to major in.

Mother was most involved in my studies. Father only asked me what my final exam scores were and my ranking. As long as I was among the top five, he said nothing. My mother would buy me new clothing, a wrist watch, or something to mark my achievement. If I failed to reach the top five, my father would again not say a word, but he gave me a look as hard as flint. God forbid if ever I wasn't in the top 10. For sure, I knew not to expect my usual reward. Nevertheless, my mother would still buy me something small, a new schoolbag or a fountain pen. One semester, however, I didn't get anything but a long, difficult conversation with Mother when I failed a physics exam. Mostly, school was easy for me, but I depended more on my native wit than hard study—my lifetime weakness. As the Chinese saying goes, "It is easier to move a mountain than to change a man's character."

Starting with my last semester in February 1957, my father unexpectedly began talking with me frequently about my education as well as other topics. These several unforgettable months of intimacy with my father are among my most treasured memories. Father had the time for me and was in a good mood. Sometimes we'd talk for hours. Occasionally, we would share two or three small dishes and some of his favorite vermouth or white liquor. A frequent subject was my college major. He never told me what to choose but delicately guided me in reviewing the options that would best match my skills, interests, and expectations.

I certainly agreed with his assessment that a career in science or engineering wouldn't suit me even though my scores in mathematics and chemistry were pretty good. The liberal arts soon became the focus of our conversations. Gradually reading between the lines, I came to understand that he hoped I might follow in his footsteps and major in foreign language and literature. Although he never voiced this wish, I believe his dream was that I might assume his mantle and become a writer, an academic, an intellectual.

I listened attentively to my father as he considered my future, but I still yearned to be a Peking Opera actor. I knew it wasn't realistic. I knew how my parents had reacted when I wanted to enroll at the National Academy of Theater Arts with Lifen. But it was my dream, my passion, and I was confident of my talent. By 16, my powerful bass voice in "painted face" roles had already won me wide notice and lavish compliments in opera circles. I was invited to perform by professional troupes in Beijing, Tianjin, and other cities. My six-foot figure helped to make up for my lack of experience and my adolescent awkwardness. Wearing my costume helmet and platform boots, I was over seven feet tall, dwarfing everybody in sight. I enjoyed showing off the money I earned from my performances. I'd take several of my schoolmates to an expensive Western-style restaurant and would even sometimes sing for them. I was puffed up and sailing along with dreams of my quick success and future glory.

My parents would often attend my performances and on this thin thread I based my faint hope. Now that they had seen how good I was, already at such a high level of professionalism, might they reconsider their opposition to the idea of my becoming an actor? I thought it best to tell Uncle Yuan and Auntie Cheng about my intention first, thinking they might be able to help me plead my case with my parents.

"Do your parents know about your plans?" Uncle Yuan immediately asked.

"Not yet."

"You should tell them right away," Auntie Cheng said.

"I will."

"While you are here, however, let us explain the big differences between being a professional and an amateur," Uncle Yuan said.

I knew Peking Opera was a difficult profession, but I had no idea that Uncle Yuan and Auntie Cheng experienced such hardships to practice their art. They spent most of their mornings doing physical and vocal exercises. Days were given over to rehearsals. Most of their evenings were spent on stage, leaving little Lifen with her nurse at home. In sickness and in health, they had kept to this routine for more than 20 years.

"Then why did you let Lifen follow in your footsteps?" I asked.

"We couldn't stop her. She has such talent, but I still have serious misgivings," Auntie Cheng said.

"Besides, I am not a professor," Uncle Yuan added. "Your father is. You have the world at your feet. Why would you be thinking of taking the most difficult path when a wide highway lies in front of you?"

They didn't let me leave until after dinner. Uncle Yuan knew his pancakes with fried eggs were a favorite of mine. At the table, they again urged me to go to college and pursue Peking Opera only as a hobby. Before I left, Auntie Cheng made me promise that I would talk to my parents that night.

My mother's response was firm and simple: "Don't you even think about it! You know that everyone in this family must graduate from college. Besides, I thought we had discussed this thoroughly already." My father just shook his head in disbelief and then nodded in agreement with my mother.

Despite my father's rejection of my dream, we continued our wonderful intimate conversations. He opened many doors for me that spring and summer. He gave me several books on Western civilization and history to read. I didn't know exactly what his aim was at first but came to know that he simply wanted to help me as best he could as I stood at a crossroads facing one of the most important decisions of my young life. Choosing a college major often dictates the course of one's remaining years. My father told me how important it was for him, a young man from a small, provincial village, to get into Peking University in spite of the many more probable roads he might have taken. He was much obliged to Father Clement, who had inspired his dream and stirred his sense of responsibility. My father was determined that all his children should go to college as an essential step in preparing them to become responsible and contributing members of society.

Once I had finished the books my father had given me, he gave me a long list of Western—mostly English—novels and plays to read in translation. I remember some "must reads" at the top of his list: Dickens' *David Copperfield*, Hardy's *The Return of the Native* and *Tess of the d'Urbervilles*, and Shaw's *Heartbreak House*.

I got copies of the books my father suggested and plunged into the new and fascinating world of English literature. Every moment I could spare, I read voraciously. One day when I was lying on my bed, deep into Thomas Hardy, my father came to my room with a few more books in his hands. They were his translations of well-known French writers—*Sur la Pierre Blanche* by Anatole France, *La Question d'argent* by Alexandre

Dumas fils, and *La Princesse de Clèves* by Marie-Madeleine de La Fayette.

He put the books on the desk, sat on my chair, and motioned me to sit next to him, saying, "You will enjoy literature even more if you can read it in the original language. But the highest pleasure for me was translating these wonderful works so that Chinese readers could enjoy them. Unfortunately, when the Japanese occupied our country, I had to discontinue what I thought would be my life's work."

"Do you want me to choose a foreign language as my college major?"

"Son, it's not what I want. You must make your own decision. But you have a real talent for learning foreign languages, and I hope I can help you see your options."

The more I thought about what my father had said, the more certain I was that I would be an English major. I aimed to attend Peking University, my father's alma mater. Quite a few of his colleagues and former students taught there. About two months before the national examination, the Beijing Foreign Languages Institute (BFLI) offered its admission exam. I took it to double my chances of getting into a top school. Beyond preparing for these exams in a dozen courses, I had one other important goal that semester: I wanted to help my school take the top prize in the annual Beijing Middle Schools Theatrical Contest.

At my middle school, I regularly played the leading role in the extracurricular drama troupe, acclaimed as one of Beijing's best scholastic dramatic programs. Coached by actors from the China Youth Art Theater, we frequently gave public performances. During New Years, our energetic shows at the Yuanensi Theater generated an enthusiastic response and real income to expand our program. That year, I bought tickets for the best seats in the house at a quarter of a yuan apiece and invited my whole extended family, our former home workers, Nanna Yang, Old Zhu and Nanna Ma, and the families of Uncle Lee, Uncle Yuan, and Uncle Zhang.

Uncle Zhang and his son, Taiming, and daughter, Taiqing, couldn't attend, but everyone else was there and thrilled to see each other again on such a wonderful occasion. Lifen looked so petite and pretty in her colorful New Year's dress. People who hadn't seen me for a while expressed surprise at how tall I was. I got many compliments on my performance and my knack for comedy.

After the show, my parents invited everybody to have dinner with us in a nearby restaurant. I didn't know it at the time but that night was the "Last Supper" for this Chen family circle. These old friends would never gather again. Lifen had to skip the dinner to return to her Academy, so I walked her to the bus station and we began to talk about our futures.

"What's your plan after high school?" she asked.

"I'll study English and literature."

"I think you'll be good at that."

"What's your plan?" I asked.

"I want to join a provincial Peking Opera troupe after graduation."

"Wouldn't you rather stay in Beijing?"

"No. I can get more experience faster and earn better pay by leaving the city." Then Lifen asked, "Who was that girl?"

"Who are you talking about?"

"The girl with two long plaits in the blue dress who followed you from backstage."

"Oh, she's a schoolmate and my makeup girl," I answered as the bus pulled up.

"She looks very sweet and beautiful," Lifen said as she got on the bus, then turned and waved at me with a knowing smile.

Lifen was dead on target with her sharp eyes. She had picked up on something that I thought was well hidden. The girl was Meng Yuying, certainly the greatest bonus to come from my dramatic activities, even including the top prize our school won at the municipal theatrical contest that year.

Yuying lost her father when she was 12. Her family relied upon the small income of her elder brothers. She lived with her third elder sister's family—including their four children— who supported her schooling. Her sweetness, beauty, and quiet demeanor made her quite an attraction at school. None of the boys could pass her without stealing another look at her. She often served as the announcer for our school ceremonies and meetings. In those days, youngsters were generally very shy and naïve about the opposite sex. Dating was unusual, and couples would soon become an item of gossip, sometimes scandal.

Yuying had also captured my attention, but we had no opportunity to get to know each other until the drama troupe director invited three girls who were good in arts and crafts to help improve our makeup and costuming. Two of them took care of the extras and minor players. Yuying was assigned to me and the other principal players. She was a godsend to me because I couldn't see well enough to paint my own face without my glasses, but I couldn't very well paint my face while wearing glasses. The first time she made up my face, I was sweating heavily. She had to repaint my eyes three times because the makeup was smeared by my sweat. Sitting there in a T-shirt, I hoped it wasn't unpleasant for Yuying. For me, I certainly liked sitting so close that I could hear her breathing and smell her body. After the show, she always brought me a cup of water and helped me remove my makeup.

Since she lived only a 10-minute walk from my home, the director asked me to escort her home when it was dark. Sitting on the back saddle of my bicycle, she had to hold me from behind. When we made a sharp turn, she grasped me tightly, leaning her head against my back. So natural! So intimate! So innocent! It thrilled me, and I wished the way to her home weren't so short.

One night after a dress rehearsal, Yuying was not feeling well. I let her sit on the bicycle seat and held her with one hand while gripping the handlebar and guiding the bike with the other. It was slow going but I was blissful. When she leaned her head on my shoulder, I could feel she was running a fever. We didn't talk much. When we got to her home, she thanked me in a very weak voice and said, "You must be exhausted." She didn't know how refreshing our long walk was for me. Afterward, Yuying and I became very close to each other.

That spring was a momentous one. Khrushchev made his secret speech condemning Stalin as a "tyrant," "headsman," and "dictator." By the fall of 1956, popular uprisings occurred in Poland and Hungary. Khrushchev invited the senior CCP delegations headed by Liu Shaoqi and Zhou Enlai to Moscow. In early 1957, Zhou Enlai secretly visited Poland and Hungary. Although uprisings were suppressed and Khrushchev was seriously criticized by Mao and the CCP leaders, all these unexpected events had put the CCP on alert to the fact that people living under totalitarian communist governments could take only so much. Pent-up emotions could explode. Internal conflicts within the CCP bubbled up from underground. For these and other reasons, China began a rectification campaign to improve the lot of its citizens and to solicit comment and criticism aimed at bettering governance and making the bureaucracy more responsive to the people.

At the same time, the Hundred Flowers Movement was coming into its fullest, if short, bloom. Taking its name from a line in classical Chinese poetry—"Let a hundred flowers blossom; let a hundred schools of thought contend"—the movement called for free and open discussion about the party and the government. In early April, the *People's Daily* published an editorial calling on intellectuals to voice their suggestions and criticisms to the Party. Many people responded. In May, the CCP's Central Committee invited non-Party members, especially intellectuals, to help on its Rectification Campaign, which was often termed "housecleaning." My father was asked to participate and did so on many occasions.

This unprecedented warm political climate did not last long. Much of the criticism the government received was deemed "unhealthy" or "destructive." By May 15, Mao had heard enough. He issued an internal directive alerting the CCP to an impending crackdown. He estimated that up to 10% of Party members were Rightists, with many more to be found among non-Communist party intellectuals. Some wondered whether the Hundred Flowers Campaign was nothing more than an effort to entrap citizens, a means to "lure the snakes from their holes," as Mao put it. If so, it was extremely effective.

On June 8, the *People's Daily* published an editorial that launched the Anti-Rightist Campaign, which continued until the summer of 1958. The paper labeled all the people who had criticized the government as anti-CCP and anti-socialism, and the purge was on. Based on unofficial statistics, more than three million citizens, 275,000 of whom were Communist Party members, were labeled as Rightists. Almost a million and a half were labeled "Mid-Rightists." During the campaign, more than 4,000 of the accused died of "unnatural causes." Beyond these numbers were tens of millions of relatives and friends who also suffered persecution, simply because of their relationship with the victim.

Many victims were guilty of nothing more than being out of the room when their colleagues were deciding who should be named a Rightist so that their unit could fill its quota. Academia and the legal profession were especially targeted. Often the people named were prominent, and taking down these enemies of the state served as an example to others: "Killing a chicken to scare the monkeys," as the phrase went. The campaign began a reign of terror that would last two decades. It broke up many families. Husbands divorced wives to spare them from being incriminated. Wives renounced their husbands and changed the family names of their children to their mother's name. Lovers split up. Long friendships ended quickly.

Even with all the fast changes and turmoil surrounding me, after I took my exams, I could think of little else besides whether I would be admitted to BFLI. I was pretty sure that I had done well, especially on my oral exam, where I benefited from all my performance experience. My responses were quick and fluent, and my pronunciation was accurate. One warm day in early June, when I came back from the Beijing Library, my mother greeted me in the courtyard with a big smile, holding up an envelope. My letter of admission! I was light-headed with joy. I read the letter three times and didn't really comprehend much beyond that one word—acceptance. We couldn't wait until my father came back from his plant to have our traditional family celebratory meal of dumplings. For the first time, both my father and mother toasted me with glasses of red wine and white liquor.

With my letter of admission in hand, I could now "coast." My classmates were jealous that while they were studying hard day and night for the upcoming national entrance exams, I had already gone to the Imperial Mountain Summer Resort in Chengde for my summer vacation. When I came back, my mother and grandaunt prepared all I needed for boarding at the college dormitory. Strangely, after our many months of cordial conversation, I found my father withdrawn and silent most of the time. I barely ever saw him. Before I left home for school, he quietly gave me two volumes of an old Chinese-English dictionary and told me to take good care of myself.

As soon as I got to BFLI on September 1, I was shocked by the tense atmosphere and the constant, strident criticism of Rightist professors, other Institute employees, and even senior students. I shared a dorm room with five other students. Day and night, loudspeakers blared accusations and screaming diatribes, making it difficult to either concentrate or fall asleep. A roommate told me that the English Department was the most severely affected one in the school. Several professors had already been named as Rightists.

In the middle of October (four fortuitous months after I received my letter of admission!), my father was named a Rightist. He learned later that he had been on a list of "candidates" for the label for months and was "elected" because his district needed a Rightist of some note; he met the qualifications.

When I learned of my father's new status some weeks later, I just couldn't believe it! How could such a patriotic citizen, respected professor, and successful entrepreneur, someone who had contributed so much to his country, come to such an unjust designation? Every weekend when I rode my bicycle back home, I found my whole family was oppressively subdued. Very seldom did my father talk to my mother and then only in a low voice, words that I couldn't understand. My father lost a fair amount of weight during this period, and his hair was quickly turning white. Strangely, he started wearing a worker's uniform to go to the plant. Nobody in our family except my mother knew that my father was now a common laborer in the boiler shop of the plant he used to own. He went to work early in the morning and came back late at night. I was in school Monday through Saturday, when I would return home as soon as school was out. I always tried to be close to Father, but he almost seemed to be hiding from me. About the only thing that appeared to interest him was when I spoke of my courses and teachers. He spoke to me about his troubles only once when we were alone in the courtyard.

"Son, you know pretty much what has happened to me," he said. "Just remember, he who is ready to believe is easy to deceive. Your survival depends on not letting your tongue say what your head shall pay for. Heaven punished me but spared you! You avoided a dangerous situation by a mere four months."

I knew what Father was talking about. If he had been marked as a Rightist before my college admission exam, who knows what my fate might have been.

One Saturday night weeks later as I was going to bed, I saw my father sitting behind his desk writing. When I awoke at midnight, he was still there, working under a dim reading lamp. My mother was worried but dared not interfere with him. She put a cup of tea on his desk and then left without a word. Finally, I broke the heavy silence.

"Father, what are you doing there at this hour?"

My father raised his head and said, "I'm writing something."

"Can't it wait until tomorrow? Mother is very worried about you."

He sighed, "No. it can't wait. I must finish it today and prepare my next one tomorrow."

"What is it about?"

After a long pause, he said, "It is my self-criticism."

Self-criticism! That was exactly the term they used in the Institute when I attended the anti-Rightist rallies. More than 200 students and the department CCP branch officials attended one assembly criticizing a professor, a Harvard graduate who had taught Medieval British Literature at the Institute for more than 20 years. The terraced classroom used to be where the professor gave his lectures. Now he was being lectured to and denounced as a criminal by his colleagues and students. He stood with his head down on the platform. The Party Branch Secretary sat behind a desk, chairing the meeting. Before the long rants against him began, the accused Rightist read his self-criticism, confessing how he had misled his students, taking them down the wrong road to becoming "White Intellectuals."

One result of the Anti-Rightist Campaign was the clear dichotomy between "Red Intellectuals" and "White Intellectuals." Red meant a socialist heart and mind that loved the CCP and Red China, listened to the Party's words, and followed its orders. White meant a bourgeois heart and mind, opposed to communism and progress in the PRC. The professor admitted that he encouraged his students to read literature rather than political books. He was against the policy of sending students to the countryside to do farm work during the school year. He believed students should focus on their studies rather than take two months a year to plant trees. He had told his students that hard and persistent study, not tree planting, had made him proficient in English, Italian, French, German, and Latin. To me, everything he said made good sense.

To the Anti-Rightist campaigners, however, these were crimes that deserved to be punished. The professor was later sent to the countryside to be reformed under supervision. When he had volunteered to present his opinions publicly as part of the CCP's Rectification Campaign, he had become an enemy of the state, a criminal who had broken no laws.

And now my father was in the same boat. I could not believe it, but it was true. My heart ached. I could see him standing in front of a rally, reading his self-criticism, listening to the audience excoriate him. These dreadful images began showing up in nightmares.

I couldn't just step aside and do nothing.

"Father, let me at least write that for you." I sat down on the other side of the table and took the pen and paper from him. "Just tell me what you want to write."

"Secretary Diao told me that my self-criticism must address my greatest mistake, suggesting that unprofessional Communist Party leaders and members should not interfere with plant operations guided by professional managers and engineers."

"What's wrong with that?" I felt indignant and aggrieved. My father's plant—with its foundry, forging, stamping, welding, heat treatment, and machining—needed technicians, engineers, and skilled workers to function, not Party functionaries and doctrinaire ideologues. How could non-professionals lead professionals?

Father interrupted me immediately, "No. That's just a Rightist's point of view."

"But it's the truth."

"Now you understand why this is so difficult for me to write."

"Father, let me do this for you. I don't feel comfortable writing it in front of you. I'll finish it in my room. You just go to bed."

"Are you sure?"

"I'm positive. In our political study course, we read a lot of articles in the *People's Daily*. I know how to handle this. Rest easy."

It was tough for me to write that black was white but not that hard to copy words from the newspaper. I was good at composition and imitating the tone of the anti-Rightist rhetoric. It didn't take me long to finish, but I was scandalized upon reviewing what I had written. What rubbish! I had to go against all my convictions to get it done. To survive, I had to learn how to say and do the "correct" thing, even if it was terribly wrong. Where was the justice?

Early Monday morning, I found Father at the dining table, waiting for me to have breakfast.

"Father, here is your self-criticism. But I may have written something you can't accept."

"Oh, never mind," Father said. "Remember that you are writing something not for your father, but for a Rightist."

Father and Rightist. I just couldn't link these two words together. My heart was aching, but I had to hide my pain in front of my even more pained father. Against my will, I had to portray my dear father as an enemy to complete this difficult task.

My tears dropped on the paper. Father quickly took out his handkerchief to wipe them off carefully.

"Father, please forgive me for what I have written and have a look at it."

"No. It is I who has brought trouble for my family. I don't have the strength or desire to read it," he said sadly. "It bears your tears and my broken heart."

That week at the Institute I couldn't stop thinking about whether my writing had been accepted by Mr. Diao and what was happening to my father. On Saturday afternoon, as soon as I finished school, I rode my bicycle back home as fast as I could. Father was not back yet. Mother, Jiahui, and I waited and waited until we saw Father walk in with his tired face and sunken red eyes. He told me that Secretary Diao had taken his self-criticism and hadn't summoned him back to the office, so it must have passed muster.

Before the lunar New Year's Eve, my mother and Wuquan, my second elder sister who was in her last year in the Beijing Medical University, encouraged me to invite Yuying to our house for the first time for a family dinner. In those days, it was quite a significant event to bring a female friend home. It confirmed a romantic relationship, subject to one's parents' concurrence.

I went to fetch Yuying. Wearing a multicolored padded jacket, she seemed a little nervous as we stood together and I knocked on our door, which was quickly opened by Wuquan.

"Welcome! Welcome! Come right in." From her eyes, I knew she liked Yuying at first sight.

Yuying nodded at her in greeting. I was so nervous, I forgot to introduce them. We walked through the courtyard. Standing outside of the living room, Mother and Jiahui welcomed Yuying.

"You must be Yuying. Welcome! Come in!" Mother said with a sweet smile.

Father stood up from his desk. "Please sit down and make yourself comfortable."

Then I introduced Yuying to everyone. We sat enjoying our jasmine tea while my mother, Wuquan, and Yuying talked. Jiahui sat close to Yuying, and Father just listened and looked at Yuying with a smile; it had been a long time since I had seen him smile. And then, Grandaunt came in and said dinner was served. She took Yuying by the hand and led her to the dining room.

The table was laden with tasty dishes to welcome Yuying. We usually didn't have that many dishes, even on weekends. Father opened a bottle of his homemade plum wine.

"What would you like to drink?" he asked Yuying.

"Anything you serve," she answered timidly.

"Try a little of this then." Father poured Yuying a small glass of his special wine, raised his glass, and toasted, "To your family."

Yuying stood up and toasted my father back. The whole dinner came off wonderfully. Everyone was happy, especially my parents. It was clear that they liked Yuying immediately. She told my parents some stories about her father that she hadn't even told me. A learned scholar, Yuying's father, 16 years older than my father, had died in 1953. He was the senior secretary for several officials of the Nationalist government in Beijing. Knowing of my father's interest, Yuying told him that her father was also good at calligraphy.

After dinner, Yuying said she had to go home before it got too late. My parents and sisters asked her to come back soon. I escorted her home. She told me that she liked my sisters and parents and said being with them made her miss her father all the more. We made plans to see each other over our vacation and said good night.

As uncertain as our situation was, my family was looking forward to spending some time together over the holidays. But on New Year's Eve we received sad news from Yanmen. Our relatives wrote that after more than five years of a happy life in the country, our big yellow dog Yehu began to act strangely. He barked and howled toward the north, straining against his collar and the long leash with the golden silk embroidery. After a few days of this miserable existence, he rejected all food and drink and finally died with his eyes wide open. My family was stricken as if a beloved relative had died. I am quite sure that Yehu knew he was dying and wanted to come home to be with us. The Chens would suffer far more grievously from the fanaticism then beginning to scour our country, but this was an early taste of it and a real, irredeemable loss.

Chapter 8

SON OF THE CRIMINAL

1957-1960
Beijing, China

WHEN I FINISHED SENIOR HIGH school, I was the third tallest
and second heaviest of all the graduates. I was a record-setting
shot-putter on my track team. At six feet and 170 pounds, I
was pretty much fully grown, but in many ways I was still a boy,
naïve and trusting. I thought people generally were decent and
straightforward. I thought everyone was my friend. I couldn't
conceive of people who feigned friendship and then stabbed you
in the back. I didn't understand why Chairman Mao repeatedly
exhorted us to "Never forget the class struggle." In a seemingly
non-violent society where "Serve the people" was a motto and a
goal, who was struggling against whom?

It didn't take long for me to learn about struggling. After I
got to the Institute, I was jolted from my naïve idealism by cruel
reality. Just about everything I saw was different from the life I

had experienced up until then. Mao's Anti-Rightist Campaign was going full force. Once I was identified as the son of a Rightist, my ordeal began. I was 18 years old and only one of the campaign's millions of innocent victims.

As a result of this movement, all Chinese could see for the first time the miscarriage of justice perpetrated against so-called enemies of the state, and it scared them. In colloquial terms, the accused enemies of the people were "capped" as Rightists. The Rightists' caps, just like those placed on tens of millions of landlords, rich farmers, counter-revolutionaries, and bad elements before them, were like steel bands tightening around their heads and those of their families. All these "evil" capped individuals were defined, classified, and punished according to the CCP. Assisted by the central and local governments, Party committees and branches implemented the public labeling process at huge mass rallies.

Like other declared enemies before them, Rightists were widely and publicly reviled and condemned. Even old friends and relatives would shun them for fear of being implicated. The charges against them were kept in their personal files forever and stayed with them wherever they went. Relatives and associates of the Rightists might not be charged, but they still suffered. Even if the caps were later officially removed, these former enemies of the state were assigned new titles: "Cap-taken-off" Landlord, Rich Peasant, or Rightist. They were no longer criminals, but they were second-class citizens, and their damaging files still shadowed them and their offspring. I heard from Uncle Zhang that someone had mistakenly put serious accusations into the file of an innocent Red Army officer who was then arrested for being a Kuomintang spy. He was tortured to death. Many years too late, the mistake was "rectified," and he was cleared.

As the Anti-Rightist Campaign raged on, the people soon learned that they'd better say what Mao said and do what Mao told them to do; otherwise, a cap could easily be put on their heads. "Be the Party's obedient tools" became dogma and the accepted practice throughout China. I didn't dare express my repugnance at the thought, but I just couldn't compare a human being to a tool, let alone an obedient tool. In this way, however, Mao paved the way for his rule of one, his brand of socialism, and the "Great Leap Forward." Perhaps no other economic plan in history was as ill-conceived or would prove to be as catastrophic. It was a major contributing factor to the Great Famine of 1958-61 in which 35 million Chinese reportedly perished.

When I chose to attend BFLI, it was because it was one of the best colleges directly under China's Ministry of Education. The required five years of coursework included intensive and extensive reading, writing, written and oral translation, listening, speaking, world history and geography, Western literature, and a second foreign language. In addition to the rigorous study, BFLI could boast of several noted professors. To my great surprise, when all the new students were introduced to the faculty, several of the better-known professors and lecturers weren't there.

It wasn't long before I saw them, however. Starting the next day, they were regularly hauled up to be harangued and criticized at huge repudiation rallies at which our attendance was required. Classes were canceled to give way to all these events. After several weeks of enduring these rallies, the Institute's accused Rightists were assembled and banished from campus. I saw it happen. It was late at night when I was awakened by noises outside the dorm. Looking down from my third-floor window, I saw a small group of people loading baggage onto an open truck. As my roommates gathered around me, we recognized them as the denounced Rightists from the English and French departments. We learned later that they were sent to labor farms in the far west.

Not long after, academic classes were again canceled (but not our political classes!) so students and faculty could participate in what was called the "Great Debate" about the Red Experts who followed CCP orders and the White Experts who still espoused the old educational system. This was not a debate in the Western sense, with two sides arguing over the strengths and weaknesses of their positions. It was a discussion to which all were expected to contribute. We were encouraged to voice our opinions without reservation. The Party Secretary of our second grade English Department even helped me prepare key points of my speech. My argument was very simple and direct: The traditional foreign language courses of our Institute should not be criticized for following the White Expert Road in view of our fruitful history of accomplishments. How could a wrong-headed, bourgeois educational system produce so many top professors, teachers, ambassadors, and government officials?

What a fool I was! I thought my persuasive, well-documented points would win support. I never imagined that I had been set up, that my speech was planned as a negative example, and I had been designated as the villain of the piece beforehand. The next day, I saw hundreds of new big-character posters all over the Institute. They criticized me for following in my Rightist father's footsteps and called me many bad things—dangerous, bourgeois, anti-Red, degenerate. This was the first time I saw my name in big letters. The posters condemned me for enjoying bourgeois literature and achieving top marks in my English classes but poor grades in my political courses. The English Department Party Secretary berated me publicly, saying, "Chen Songsheng can recite long soliloquies and sonnets of Shakespeare, but he can't provide a simple explanation of socialism. If anyone still doesn't understand what the White Expert Road is all about, just take a look at him."

I felt betrayed. I was constantly watched, in full public view, with no place to hide. I couldn't wait for the weekends to be with my parents, Yuying, and Jiahui, but I was too ashamed to tell them what was happening to me at the Institute. Since there was nothing they could do about it, I didn't want to worry them. I didn't feel pity for myself. When I sat up all night writing Father's self-criticisms, I felt deeply the greater hardships my father had suffered. As I became more circumspect and cautious in my speech, I understood why my father had become withdrawn and silent.

My father had always taken the lead in answering the calls of the Party and the government. How could he become the enemy of his homeland that he loved beyond words? What could he say? Silence was the only way he could show his bitterness and resentment. In this sense, I did follow in the footsteps of my father. I fell silent.

As the higher education system was reformed across China to follow the Red Expert Road, all college students had to go to the countryside to do physical labor for at least two months every year. Our English Department selected Anjia Village, about 100 miles west of Beijing, as our labor base. Our main work there was digging holes and planting chestnut seeds on the barren mountains close to the village. In contrast with some of my schoolmates who didn't like physical labor, I loved it. My frequent work in the vegetable garden of our mansion had prepared me well for this sort of manual labor. I knew how to handle tools, stayed on task, and dug at least twice as many holes in a day as my average classmate. Besides, the two months on the mountainside afforded me an escape from the endless political events at school.

Early in the morning, we'd pick up some steamed buns or corn cakes, salty pickles, and a big canteen of water for our whole day of labor on the mountain. The higher up the mountain I went, the fewer people I encountered, so I always climbed as high up as I could. There I was close to heaven, planting seeds in the designated spots, breathing fresh, cold mountain air, and singing my Peking Opera. Not a soul ever bothered me. It was nothing but blue skies, white clouds, wild flowers, and the birds that joined me in song. My glorious solitude in such a beautiful natural setting lifted my spirits.

At these moments, I felt a wonderful sense of freedom. While my future was clouded, there was nothing I could do about it. Rather than worrying about something totally beyond my control, I often let my mind carry me back to the past, savoring those carefree times and the wonderful stories my grandfather told me. In my rucksack, I always carried a pencil and a notebook. During my breaks, I wrote long love letters to Yuying, most of which were never sent. Yuying was still a senior high school student, and I dared not cause her any trouble. Except for occasionally going to some out-of-the-way place on a weekend evening, we never got together. Another pastime on the mountain for me was writing old-fashioned poems. My first serious try was a verse for my grandfather. Though it was very juvenile, I felt good to have written it and read it aloud with my thoughts flying far to my grandfather's home near Wangwu Mountain.

In 1958, National Day and the Mid-Autumn Festival came almost simultaneously. In the lunar calendar, the Mid-Autumn Festival, also called the Moon Festival, falls on the 15th day of the 8th month. At that time, the moon is supposedly at its brightest and fullest. Families, poor or rich, always gathered together under the full moon to enjoy moon cakes, fruit, and wine after a sumptuous reunion meal. We were told that Anjia Village planned a big celebration on October 1, including a great Moon Festival feast, followed by an evening party featuring entertainment.

After I finished my work for the day and was returning to our quarters, I heard Old Shun, the Institute's venerable gatekeeper, call me over to the kitchen where he was working. He and several others were preparing braised pork in brown sauce, vegetable dishes, steamed buns, and rice for the evening's feast. The delicious smells hung in the air, making my mouth water.

"Xiao Chen, come in. I have something to tell you." Everybody else called me Big Chen, but Lao Shun called me Xiao (little) Chen.

"I'd better stay outside. The smell makes me too hungry."

"Secretary An has said the whole village wants you to sing some Peking Opera at tonight's show.

I was taken totally by surprise. "Did our English Department Party Secretary approve this?"

"He didn't agree at first, but Secretary An told him that in Anjia Village, he, the Party Secretary, has the final say."

Old Shun could tell from my face that I was troubled. He quickly added, "Secretary An also said that while your father may be a Rightist, you are not. So there is nothing wrong with letting you sing Peking Opera to entertain the villagers."

"But who will accompany me?"

"Unaccompanied singing. The Secretary could not find you an accompanist."

I was usually quite relaxed singing in front of large audiences. That night, however, was so unusual for me that I was uneasy. I dared not drink any wine or liquor at the feast, although I couldn't help taking some of that delicious pork, but just a little. "Play wind instruments when full, but sing when hungry." That's the rule in Peking Opera circles. I wanted to sing my best for the farmers and Secretary An, who had entrusted me with the task.

Hundreds of villagers and students were seated in front of a temporary stage in the big area where wheat was threshed. Several gas lights hung above the stage. After the singing of the national anthem, the evening show began with a chorus that sang several rousing patriotic songs. Then came the dancers and finally my Peking Opera. After my last encore, the audience applauded and cheered wildly. The sound reverberated between the surrounding mountains, producing the most electrifying sound I had ever experienced. I felt as if my whole body was on fire. I loved performing Peking Opera!

After the show, Secretary An asked Old Shun to invite me to his cottage. Both Old Shun and I were pleasantly surprised to find a dozen or so people waiting for us around a table full of food and drink. Secretary An pointed us to a kang, a sitting bed made of bricks that could be heated. It was clearly the place of honor.

"Boy, I know you didn't eat much at the feast. Join us now for some homemade drinks and some of our local specialties.

Please make yourself at home with the An family. We are all Ans here—uncles An, aunts An, An brothers and sisters. That is why this village is called An Family Village." Secretary An laughed warmly.

A beautiful young woman poured everyone a full cup of white liquor.

Secretary An raised his cup, "We haven't heard such wonderful Peking Opera singing for a long time, if ever. Let us drink to Xiao Chen."

"I am not worthy of such compliments. Let me toast to Secretary An and all of you for giving me this undeserved honor and uncommon opportunity."

Secretary An shook his head and said, "We cannot allow the offspring of Rightists to be shut out of society, nor the Rightists themselves. The Rightists I met in our labor farm are all good people."

"Uncle, you are drunk." The young woman tried to stop Secretary An from continuing.

"I am not drunk. My head is very clear. Boy, do you know why we applauded your singing so enthusiastically?"

"Why?" I was anxious to learn the reason.

"You have a strong voice and you sang well. But there is another reason." Secretary An slowly emptied his cup. Everyone wanted to know what he would say next.

"Because you sang how Lord Bao achieved justice by executing the emperor's son-in-law who had betrayed and plotted to kill his first wife. There is a lesson there for us today about the misuse of power."

"You sang just what we wanted to hear," Old Shun added.

I knew immediately what Secretary An and Old Shun were referring to. There was a growing disconnect between reality and the policies and practices of the government as the effects of the Great Leap Forward began to be felt across the land. The peasants saw what was happening and there was growing discontent.

The twin pillars of China's development were grain and steel, and Mao's plan was to jumpstart a huge increase in production for both. The plan was for China to double its steel output within a year by relying on a network of "backyard furnaces." The collectivization of agriculture, which would increase production, and government control of grain would provide the capital to speed industrialization, or so the Chairman thought. Never-proven and totally bogus methods to increase agricultural production were immediately implemented. The weather was good and 1958's harvest promised to be bountiful, but Mao's policies ensured that that was not to be. Farm laborers (and workers from many other sectors) were diverted to steel production and large construction projects, including huge buildings to commemorate the PRC's tenth anniversary. Grain rotted in the field. Plagues of locusts, their numbers swelled by the removal of their natural predators during Mao's Great Sparrow Campaign, devastated crops. During this time China continued to be a major exporter of grain because Mao didn't want to lose face or have the rest of the world know his master plan was a failure.

Despite diminished production, local and provincial authorities were encouraged to exaggerate their harvest numbers to "prove" how well the new policies were working. In our political classes we often read those fabulous claims. I remember one ridiculous report that Zuotou Village in Anguo County, Hebei Province, had harvested 15,300 kilograms of wheat per acre. I knew this was nonsense. In my father's home village, it would be a miracle if an acre produced 1,000 kilograms. What I didn't know were the terrible consequences of these boastful lies. Secretary An explained to me that the more output that was reported, the more public grain the peasants had to contribute to the state, leaving the villagers with little or nothing to show for their work.

After our two months of labor in Anjia village, I thought we could return to the Institute and concentrate on our academic studies. I was wrong again. As soon as we got back—even before we had time to unpack—all the students were called to the huge dining hall for a mobilization meeting to kick off the Big Smelting Steel and Iron Campaign. We were answering Mao's call for the nation to produce 10,700,000 tons of steel that year, on our way to surpassing Britain. Quickly, "Everybody, make steel," "1070," and "Surpassing Britain, catching up with USA" became our new slogans, reminders of our responsibility to our homeland.

Our class sessions were shortened so that we had more time to dig pits on our playground and basketball courts for constructing steel and iron smelting furnaces. These pits were much bigger, wider, and deeper than the little holes we dug on the mountain. We called them hollows. One full basketball court was barely large enough for two hollows. Old Shun was invited to be our construction instructor, but he declined. He told the Party Secretary of his branch that he knew very well how to dig a hole in the ground, but he knew nothing about constructing furnaces for making steel.

All of the male students and teachers were assigned to build the furnaces. We worked around the clock in three eight-hour shifts. Female students and teachers collected and transported coke, scrap metal, and other raw materials for the furnaces. Our English Department, the biggest department in the Institute, was in charge of five furnaces. A few actual iron workers were detailed to help us, but by and large, this whole campaign, which kept furnaces across the nation burning 24 hours a day to meet their assigned quotas, was a strictly amateur production. No one, including Chairman Mao, knew anything about metallurgy. But we were excited to see our homemade furnaces being completed and erected, ready to smelt iron and steel. No classes. No homework. No exams. What fun!

I went back home to get some fresh work clothes and was surprised to find a big pile of metal objects in the courtyard and my mother rummaging through cabinets, cases, and boxes.

"Mother, what are you doing?"

"Songsheng, I'm so glad you're back. I've got some jobs for you." My mother had worked up quite a sweat.

"What?"

"Collecting metal for the Big Smelting Steel and Iron Campaign."

"What?"

"We must search everywhere, find all the metal objects we have, and donate them to the street committee."

"What kinds of metal objects?"

"Metal bed stands, bedsprings, lamps, pans, woks, cooking utensils . . . ."

"How will you prepare your meals without cooking stuff?" I was confused.

"We have no need to cook anymore. Our street committee opened a public dining hall for all the residents. There's no more private cooking. We just go there and take what we need." My mother answered firmly, but she too seemed a little confused.

"Where is our grandfather clock?" I exclaimed with alarm when I entered our living room. It was a long-time favorite of mine.

"Don't get upset," my mother stopped me. "The Party Secretary of our street committee told me that it could contain many metal parts, which would be good as raw materials to smelt iron and steel."

I couldn't believe it. Our big grandfather clock was a gift from a French friend to my father. We had had it since before I was born. On its top, a little toy man on a horse would travel around a full circle when the clock rang the hour. How could the Big Smelting Steel and Iron Campaign benefit from sacrificing such a beautiful piece of craftsmanship?

At dinner that night, everyone was subdued. My father looked thin and weak, his eyes sunken. He seemed too tired even to pick up the steamed bun that my mother had brought from the community dining hall. I was worried, but, even in his weakened state, he still retained his spirit of perseverance. After dinner he invited me into our living room.

"Son, there is no need for you to write confessions for me anymore. All this same old stuff really ticks me off, but I can handle it. I don't believe Secretary Diao even bothers to read these things. Let us talk about your studies."

"There's not much to say. We spend more time on our labor course and now smelting iron and steel." I truly had nothing to report about my studies at the Institute.

My father said, "You can't go with the stream. You must have your own ambition and goals in your life under all circumstances."

"What do you mean?"

"Struggle to live in the crevices. Struggle to live in the gaps and margins," Father said in a low but forceful voice. I wasn't sure I understood what he was trying to tell me.

"When you dug holes on the mountain, did you see small trees growing from tiny crevices between barren rocks? While big trees nearby may wither and die, those small trees survived and will grow into big, sturdy trees."

"What should I do?"

"Absorb every drop of water and nutrient whenever and wherever you can."

"Could you please be more specific, Father?" I asked with a little impatience.

"You have to find your own way, because there will be no more easy roads for you to follow. Let me give you some advice about your English studies."

When my father talked to me, he rarely addressed specific issues. He just talked about things in general, suggested approaches, and let me make my own decisions. It was different this time. He recommended that I read more original English novels in my spare time, use more English dictionaries instead of English-Chinese ones, converse with my close teachers and friends only in English, and recite, recite, recite.

From his own experience, my father told me how important reciting was. He had told me this before, and I was good at memorizing. Now with his renewed emphasis, I started reciting regularly—Shakespeare, Dickens, Hardy, Twain, just about anything I could get my hands on. When I secretly secured a copy of the Declaration of Independence, I memorized it and silently recited it often. The beauty of silent recitation was that I could do it by myself without anybody else knowing. I found it quite useful at our political and newspaper study meetings.

While the Party Secretary was droning on and reading political documents, I stared at him, apparently with my full concentration, while reciting my favorite English passages. My teachers soon observed my rapid progress in written and spoken English. I had my father to thank for that.

When I got back to the Institute, the areas around the furnaces were full of people busily coming and going, sweating, shouting, and laughing. We got the fires going full blast. I was part of the busiest team that fed coke to the furnaces. In order to keep them running continuously, we had to remove the spent coke from the furnaces and fill them with fresh coke as soon as possible. We had to work in extremely high heat with thick, protective clothing. I was the tallest and strongest one on our team. Even though I was the designated model of the White Expert Road, I was the workhorse of my team, pursuing the Red Expert Road toward a noble goal. I would run through the narrow entry to the furnace and shovel the still burning coke out of the furnace at the fastest possible speed. And I had to do this without my eyeglasses. Instead, I wore a face shield. When I got out of the furnace, my work clothes, shoes, and sometimes my gloves were smoking. Old Shun was often there. As soon as I came out, he'd yell, "Come here!" and pour a full bucket of cold water over me.

None of us knew anything about smelting iron and steel, but we did know what iron and steel looked like. When our furnace turned out its first "steel," we didn't recognize it because it was simply a piece of useless junk left over after the smelting process. Something was clearly wrong, but I dared not say what was on my mind, of course. We were ordered to decorate every piece of the junk we produced with red silk ribbons, put them on decorated carts, and report our achievement to the Institute's

CCP Committee and the local government. This was our great contribution to reaching the goal of "1070" and overtaking Britain in steel output. All of us were so excited that we were now on our way to catching up with the US, which Mao had called a "paper tiger."

Other achievements were ballyhooed in the press. In August 1958, the Party decided that people's communes would be the basis of political and economic organization throughout rural China. Private farm plots were forbidden and farmers could not even keep a chicken, let alone a small piece of private land outside their cottages. Communal kitchens were introduced. By year's end, approximately 25,000 communes with an average of 5,000 households each had been established. Wages and money were replaced by work points. Within a year, People's Communes were all over the country. Four hundred million people took their meals in almost four million public canteens. This was when and where the popular term, "Big Pot Meal—eat from the same big pot," originated. The concept that everyone gets the same and equal share of food from the big socialist pot, whether they do a good or a bad job, has become a huge social problem in China that exists even to this day.

The inevitable consequence was that our daily life grew depressing and miserable. As the whole country started feeling the increasing pressure of food shortages, rationing got under way and spread from a few provinces to the whole nation. Starvation affected rural areas more than cities. College students had some of the best quotas, including 14-18 kilograms of corn, flour, and rice and a quarter kilo each of pork and cooking oil per month. Even with 18 kilos of foodstuffs, I soon felt it was far from enough for my survival. Those who have never experienced hunger can never imagine how it felt. I didn't feel deprived at first because I still had my residual body fat to draw on. But as the famine worsened, we began eating tree leaves, weeds, corn and maize cobs, bran, and anything else edible until such items could hardly be found in and around Beijing. With all the reported bumper harvests, why were we eating tree leaves?

Amidst these deplorable conditions, at least one thing was going right. Yuying and I were blissfully in love. One weekend before her graduation from Beijing No. 65 High School, I invited her to go to the Summer Palace. I had been saving my weekly allowance for almost two months in order to afford our excursion. Fees for the public bus and park admission were cheap, but meals were extremely expensive in the restaurants near the palace, and if we wanted to tour the palace by boat, that wasn't cheap either. With my meager savings, Yuying and I could either have a meal and skip the boating on Kunming Lake, or we could go boating and forego having a meal.

We decided to eat and lined up in front of the restaurant next to Long Live Hill. Luckily we got an early number that allowed us to be in the first group to enter the restaurant. After reviewing the menu for a long time, I counted every coin in my pocket to ensure I had enough to pay and finally ordered one meat dish, one vegetable dish, and a bowl of soup for the two of us. I also got a glass of beer. After lunch, we took a walk around Kunming Lake and I deliberately led us to a quiet spot on the southern side of the lake near the Seventeen Arches Bridge. We sat beside the lake under a large weeping willow. It was the perfect place for me to execute the plan I had long prepared.

"Yuying, I have something important to ask you."

"What?"

"Are you planning to register for the China Central Arts & Crafts Institute exam?"

"I don't know."

"What do you mean you don't know? You will miss the opportunity."

"I don't believe I could pass the exam."

"How would you know if you don't try? Your art teachers speak so highly of your drawing and paintings."

Yuying didn't respond.

"May I ask you a direct question?"

"What?" Yuying raised her large, deep eyes and looked right at me.

"Are you worried about your college expenses?"

Yuying lowered her eyes and said nothing.

"If so, my parents want to support you."

"How could I accept that?"

"You could. You know how much my parents like you."

Yuying was silent.

"Would you allow me to ask you one more direct question?"

"What?"

I felt my heart beating loudly and realized that although the day was cool, I was sweating profusely. Suddenly I could not phrase my question.

"What?" Yuying said raising her eyes toward me again.

"Would you . . . ."

"Would I?" Yuying almost whispered.

"W-would you marry me?" I stammered after what seemed like an endless moment.

Now Yuying was also sweating. Her face was suffused with a bashful blush. She lowered her head so deeply that I could not even see her eyes.

"Not immediately, of course," I added. "Not until I graduate from the Institute."

I waited and waited but she uttered not a single word.

After quite a while, I hit on a way out of this impasse. I picked the tip of a small branch from the willow tree.

"If you return this twig to me, it means you agree to marry me. If you throw it into the lake, it means you do not want to. What do you say?"

I didn't get either a yes or no from Yuying, but when I handed the willow twig to her, she took it and promptly threw it back to me. The twig hit my chest and dropped into my hands. I got so excited that I didn't know what to say or do. With one hand holding the twig and the other holding Yuying, I could feel the blood pulsing through my veins. All of a sudden, Yuying started crying and soon went from quiet weeping to uncontrollable sobs. I was scared, confused, and totally at a loss. I pulled out my handkerchief and handed it to her. She buried her face in it and leaned her body into my arms. I clasped her tightly and gently kissed her again and again. It was our first time to kiss after knowing each other for four years.

We sat there in the exquisite sunset, enjoying our embrace. Then Yuying said, "I'll keep this handkerchief forever."

"But don't use it for your tears ever again."

"You don't understand. Those were tears of joy." Yuying's smiling eyes were still wet. "But I'll keep my tears for me and give my smiles to you."

I will never forget Yuying's words. I will never forget that moment.

It was Saturday, May 28, 1960. Yuying was 20 and I was 21.

Chapter 9

BLISS AND FEAR

1961-1965
Beijing, China

AFTER YUYING AND I BECAME engaged, Yuying accepted my parents' offer to pay for all her college expenses and enrolled at the China Central Arts and Crafts Institute. The Institute was small but very well-known. We were so proud that she was admitted. Yuying liked drawing and painting and was good at it. Her teachers had encouraged her to pursue art professionally, but Yuying was modest about her talents. My family wasn't surprised at Yuying's admission, but she was.

My parents helped Yuying in another way that simply delighted me. They were aware of how crowded Yuying's living conditions were. She lived in two tiny rooms with her older sister and brother-in-law, along with their four children. Her sister was expecting their fifth child soon. Five families lived in the small courtyard house they occupied. All tenants had to go outside to use the public toilet because none could afford an inside bathroom. My parents told me to ask Yuying to move into our house. She didn't like being a burden to her sister and brother-in-law but was hesitant to accept my parents' offer. I finally persuaded her that moving in would give us the best of both worlds. She could share a bedroom with my little sister and we would see each other more often. Yuying finally agreed, to the delight of everybody. Even before we were married, Yuying became a much-loved member of the Chen family. Yuying adored my sister and parents and took them as her own.

Yuying and Jiahui were very close to each other and similar in many ways. Both of them wore two long braids that hung almost to their waists, a popular fashion for girls at that time. Whenever they needed to wash their hair, which was quite a job, they would help each other.

My mother treated Yuying and me absolutely equally. We each got two yuan per week as pocket money (Jiahui got only one yuan since she was still in high school). My mother also gave Yuying a wrist watch, her first. It was small and old and ran fast, but Yuying treasured it. She said it was nice that the watch ran fast; she was never late for class. When I got into BFLI, Mother also got me a watch. It was a Russian model, big and ugly, but also very accurate and durable.

During the week, Yuying and I lived in our respective institutes, coming back home on weekends. Those Saturdays and Sundays were a wonderful time for us all. We closed the front door and the family got together in the courtyard, preparing our meager meals, eating together, and catching up on news. Each Saturday, Yuying, Jiahui, and I did the family laundry, pleased that we could do something for the family. The major event for the three of us was going to the movies after we finished the big wash. Movie tickets were very cheap. A fraction of my weekly pocket money was good enough to cover the three of us. At first we saw a lot of Russian movies. "And Quiet Flows the Don" was our favorite. Suddenly, it seemed, China and the Soviets were at loggerheads, and before long there were no more Russian movies on Saturday.

The conflict between the two Communist giants had actually been brewing for years. The time when relations were cordial and Mao had called Stalin his "boss" was long past (and Stalin had died in 1953). China was never happy with the unfavorable terms for assistance that the Soviets had pressed upon the country during the 1950s. The two nations began criticizing each other by proxy. China would direct its charges against Yugoslavia as "Revisionist" and the USSR criticized Albania, which supported China's line. This was an example of "Pointing to the mulberry when reviling the locust tree," a saying in Chinese that described perfectly this war by innuendo.

Khrushchev then openly criticized Mao's outrageous arrogance, ridiculing his claim that the Great Leap Forward would enable China to pass the USSR in their race to lead world Communism. He also denounced Mao with a string of Marxist-Leninist maledictions as a nationalist, a deviationist, and an adventurist. Mao responded in kind, calling Khrushchev a capitalist, a revisionist, and, because he sought "peaceful coexistence" with the West, a coward. The Soviets, for their part, reneged on their promise to help China develop an A-bomb, withdrew all assistance and advisors, and forced onerous terms on the loans it had made to China. In 1964, China ended diplomatic relations with the USSR and all other Warsaw Pact nations, formalizing the Sino-Soviet Split.

One result of the end of Russian movies was that we started seeing movies from other countries—France, Germany, India. Never, of course, would a US film be shown. As a student of the Beijing Foreign Languages Institute, I was privileged to watch American and British films as part of our educational program. I managed to secretly bring Yuying and Jiahui to our Institute to watch "Oliver" and "Great Expectations," based on books by Charles Dickens, and "The One Million Pound Note" from Mark Twain's novel. These were all such great movies. They opened our eyes to the world outside China. Of course, we also enjoyed good Chinese films like "February in Early Spring" and "The Song of Youth." Before long, however, there were no more foreign films of any kind playing in the theaters.

China continued to live under anxious conditions. In 1961, the Great Famine still continued but was beginning to abate. It had begun with the implementation of Mao's flawed vision of a shortcut to industrialization and true Communism. Like most of his visionary plans, they were completely divorced from reality. A series of natural disasters—widespread drought in the north and floods in the south—made things worse, but have no doubt, this was a man-made catastrophe, the greatest single disaster in world history since the Black Plague. The most recent estimates place the death toll at 30-40 million. The birth rate dropped precipitously. Given what we know about the effects of malnutrition on health, especially child development, the number of living victims is virtually impossible to calculate but certainly numbers in the hundreds of millions.

My family managed to buy enough food to get by—often at rather high prices—but we never knew what the next day would bring. We were also lucky to get regular deliveries of wild vegetables and dried turnips from our relatives in

Yanmen. My grandaunt mixed them with a little flour or corn meal and made them into big brown steamed dumplings. They were tasty, and we could fill up on them, which we did once a week. But eventually the packages from Yanmen arrived less frequently and then stopped altogether. We later learned that several of our relatives were victims of the famine, including Shencheng, my cousin and the most faithful of those who had mailed food to us. He was only 45. News we heard from other parts of China also was grim. Anhui was the hardest hit province in North China. A quarter of its population is said to have succumbed to starvation. There were rumors that people were so desperate for food that they ate human flesh. Years later, documented reports showed that this was true in the parts of China most affected by the famine. What irony! China's Great Leap Forward . . . into cannibalism.

These numbers and stories were truly frightening. I just couldn't imagine how terrible the reality must be. But my grandfather knew it firsthand. My father told me that Grandfather had horror stories from when his family escaped the 1876-79 famine in Shanxi and the surrounding four provinces. Over 10 million people starved to death. His family saw dead bodies continually along the road and in the fields as they walked the 600 brutal kilometers from Hongtong to Yanmen.

In those uneasy days, my mother kept telling me that as bad as things were, she felt something worse coming. Although she couldn't say what that might be, she felt it strongly in her heart. And she turned out to be right.

Suddenly one afternoon in May of 1961, we were informed by my father's plant that he had fainted at the boiler shop and been taken to a nearby hospital in Tongzhou, a suburban county under Beijing's jurisdiction. We didn't know what happened beyond that. My mother almost passed out. With shaky hands, she gathered some clothes for my father and told us in a trembling voice to hurry as we quickly made our way to Tongzhou.

My father was old at 64. Already debilitated, he had suffered further from the labor he had been sentenced to do for being a Rightist. His constitution was weakened by the strain of long hours of hard work in the boiler shop of the plant he once owned. My mother had wanted him to see a doctor for some time, but he kept putting her off and refusing to go. He finally collapsed at work. Uncle Lee told us later that, with a barely audible moan, my father had fallen upon the ground senseless with his spade still in his hands and blood on his work clothes. He had coughed up blood.

When we got to the hospital, my father was in the emergency room. A tall, middle-aged physician, Dr. Ren, told us that my father had coughed blood before and during his loss of consciousness. His tuberculosis he first experienced during the 1930s had returned.

"How could you let an old man with tuberculosis work himself almost to death like that?" the doctor asked my mother.

My mother was stricken. Both of us had witnessed my father's decline and should have insisted he go to a doctor. But my father could be a very stubborn man. Of course, he had managed to conceal his condition from all of us. All she could say was, "How is he? How is he?"

Seeing the effect his words had on my mother, Dr. Ren softened his tone. "The situation would have been a lot worse if he had remained untreated much longer, but I believe we will be able to bring him back to health. It will take some time, however. You may see him now. He's resting."

My mother and I stepped into the hospital room and found my father on a small bed with white sheets, a quilt, and a pillow. Lying there perfectly still, he looked peacefully asleep. Without opening his eyes, he knew my mother and I were standing beside the bed and whispered to my mother, "Don't you worry, don't you worry, I'm fine."

"Don't talk. I know you will be fine. Nothing can defeat you. I know that."

"Son, pull a chair over for your mother."

I found a chair and then asked, "Father, how did it happen?"

"Never mind. I am fine in the hospital. You must take good care of your mother. With her long history of high blood pressure, I'm really worried about your mother, not me."

My father was, as usual, being self-effacing. My mother was sobbing quietly. I stood there wondering what we should do, where we could go for help. At that very moment, Uncle Lee came through the doorway and into the room.

"Ah, there you are, Big Sister, I am so sorry. This is all my fault. I didn't take good care of Big Brother."

"How can you say that? Without you, this would have happened a long time ago," my father said.

"I accompanied the clerk of our plant to get all the hospital forms completed. As soon as you are stabilized, you will be transferred to a TB sanatorium for recovery," Uncle Lee said.

"Thank you, thank you so much. I feel so relieved when you are here." My mother was very grateful.

"This is what I should do. You are more than friends; you are family," Uncle Lee said.

I wondered whether the standard of care in the hospital would be any different because my father was a Rightist. These declared enemies of the state were discriminated against in so many ways. I didn't have long to wait for an answer. The second week my father was in the hospital, Dr. Ren invited me to his office. There were only the two of us in the room.

"I just want to tell you that the hospital administrator and I are the only ones here who know your father's status as a Rightist. As long as your father is my patient, I will treat him exactly the same as I treat all my patients. In my book, there are no Rightist patients."

"I am so grateful for your kindness."

"It is not my kindness. It is my duty. Besides," he lowered his voice, "from all I learned about your father, he is a great Rightist. You have a wonderful father."

"I don't know what to say," I said modestly, although of course I agreed with him.

"Don't say anything. Just keep it in your heart," replied Dr. Ren.

My father was soon transferred to the TB sanatorium in Tongzhou. Three times a week, we'd board either a train or a bus to visit him. When we took the bus, we had to get up very early and change buses three times to get there. All my siblings except Wuquan, my sister who worked in Wuhan in distant Hubei Province, saw Father as often as they could. But my mother, Jiahui, and I went there the most. We always brought him food from home. Steamed corn cakes with walnuts and dates were his favorite.

My father shared a small room with another patient, Lao Fang. We often addressed people with either a Lao or a Xiao before their family names. Lao means old, but could refer to anyone who was over 30. I was often called Lao Chen even though I was only 25 simply because I was big. Xiao means little, but not necessarily by size. Your "little" sister could be tall. It was often used to address girls and women. Yuying was called Xiao Meng even after she turned 40.

Lao Fang was a farmer from Tongzhou. Short, thin, and bald, he had suffered a long time from TB but didn't know he had it until he found blood in his sputum. He was admitted to the sanatorium six months before my father. My father and Lao Fang soon became fast friends. They slept in one room, ate at the same table, chatted in the garden, and played chess next to the pond. My father always shared the food my mother brought him with Lao Fang. Ever since he was a child in Yanmen, my father had loved anything made with corn meal. He told us that it was the only food that could make his stomach feel comfortable. Lao Fang liked everything my mother prepared except the corn cakes. I think corn cakes were the only thing they ever disagreed about.

My family was pleased to see the way my father came to life in the sanatorium. He smiled more. Rather than keep silent as he had done for so long, he started talking with Lao Fang and the other patients. I believe the sanatorium provided him with a refuge. Nobody could enter it without permission. Nobody there treated him like a criminal, an enemy. His life started to become normal again. He began getting up at dawn again to do his Tai Chi.

Tai Chi was a popular exercise. My father had learned it from Master Chen years before during his earlier bout with TB. Standing behind Master Chen and my father, I also learned all 108 Tai Chi gestures and positions, although later simplification reduced the number to 36.

Until he fell ill, my father did his exercises every day, in good times and bad, whether it was sunny or rainy, hot or cold. Tai Chi was one way that my father persevered. He often told me that drops of rain could make a hole in a stone by perseverance, not by force. As long as your breathing was correct and you moved naturally from one gesture-position to another until you finished, even 36 gesture-positions were good enough. I didn't have my father's strong will or discipline. Although I could easily do the 36 gesture-positions, I rarely did. I was lazy.

When my father started his Tai Chi exercises in the garden, he was alone. Gradually, more and more people approached him and asked him to teach them the exercises. Soon more than 50 patients, doctors, and nurses were following my father and learning one move after another. Whenever I was there, I hurried to join them. I treasured these moments because I knew they couldn't last. My father was so happy! His Tai Chi group expanded to over 100. And as they got healthier, so did my father. His appetite returned and he started to gain weight. His dreadful pallor was replaced with a healthy glow. My mother was so happy, not only because of my father's quick recovery, but also because she realized how much he was enjoying his time in the sanatorium.

One day, almost a year after he was admitted, the sanatorium director summoned my father and said, "Professor Chen, your most recent exam and X-rays show that you have made great progress. We will be able to send you home soon. But I must say that we cannot let you go until you choose one of your students to lead the Tai Chi exercise group."

"That is not a problem. Lao Fang is fully qualified to be the teacher and leader," my father said.

"Excellent! We could not afford to lose that wonderful program. Those exercises are so therapeutic. They help our patients recover much sooner and more completely. And they are good for our staff as well."

The day my father was discharged from the sanatorium, Mother, Jiahui, and I went there to help him pack. Lao Fang told us that the director was preparing to write a thank-you letter to the Yongtai plant. My father became agitated and blurted out, "No, no, Lao Fang, you must stop the director. Don't do that."

"Why not?" Lao Fang was perplexed.

"If you want me to remember all my time here fondly, please stop the director. The kindness shown to me here is reward enough for whatever contribution I made. Please don't write a letter to my plant."

My mother and I knew exactly what was running through Father's mind; he didn't want to cause any trouble for anyone. Someone might construe allowing a Rightist to teach Tai Chi as a crime.

I still remember clearly that when we prepared to leave, virtually the entire sanatorium—the staff and most of the patients who could walk—gathered in front of the main building. The nurse who took care of my father's ward presented him with a large bouquet of flowers fresh from the garden. The director made a little speech thanking my father, and then everybody applauded him. In his quiet way, my father had made quite an impression.

One month after my father returned home, he was informed by his factory that he had been granted his retirement as a "Cap-removed Rightist." The term "cap-removed" meant he no longer had the legal status of criminal because he had completed five years of "reform through labor," but his history remained in his personal file. My mother didn't understand why Father couldn't retire until his cap was removed. Of course, cap or no cap, none of my father's lost salary or fixed interest payments were ever paid to him.

Encouraged by my father's recovery and retirement, on May 4, 1962, Yuying and I went to the Beijing East District marriage registration office to make our union official. Whether couples had a wedding ceremony or not, this was the only procedure legally joining a husband and wife in China. A pleasant-looking lady in her 40s sat behind a big desk and carefully examined our registration booklets, verified our permanent residence, examined our photos, and read the authorization letters from our institutes.

"How old are you?" she asked me.

"Twenty-three in three months," I replied, although I looked much older.

"How old are you?" she asked Yuying.

"Twenty-two in one month," Yuying answered, although she looked much younger.

At the time, brides had to be at least 18 and grooms 20 (changed to 20 and 22, respectively, in 2005).

"Chen Songsheng, do you want to marry her, Meng Yuying?" she asked me.

"Yes. I do," I answered.

"Meng Yuying, do you want to marry him, Chen Songsheng?" she asked Yuying.

Yuying quickly nodded.

The lady shook her head and chuckled. "Nodding your head doesn't count."

"You must say 'I do,'" I said, trying to help.

"No," the lady interrupted me. "You can't guide her. She must say it herself."

"Let's do it again. Meng Yuying, do you want to marry him, Chen Songsheng?"

"Yes. I do," Yuying replied shyly and blushed.

We didn't have wedding rings, new clothing, or a honeymoon, although I gave Yuying a brooch with two butterflies on a flower as a souvenir of the occasion. That night, Yuying and I had a quiet dinner with my family at home. Later, we had dinner at Yuying's mother's cottage with her family. Although the certificate legally joining us in matrimony was in our hands, we did not consummate our union. That would have to wait until we could have a wedding ceremony that would formalize our relationship in the eyes of our families.

That July, I graduated from Beijing Foreign Languages Institute after five years of study, labor, hunger, discrimination, solitude, and one campaign after another. I was jokingly referred to as the "All-time Champion," but not in an athletic sense. My nickname referred to the fact that I had always been the villain of every political movement that came along. Honestly, I never missed a single one. When I remember my days at the Institute, I cannot help but recall all the big-character posters and movement documents railing against me, the days spent in political or work "classes," and all the worthless writing that was required of us. I was clever with words and could easily finish a 20-page movement summary in 20 minutes proclaiming how much I had learned from the "Great Leap Forward," for instance. It was tough for me to lie, which was an unforgivable sin in our family, but it was easy for me to pretend to toe the party line and imitate what the newspapers reported. Besides, I doubted that anybody ever read those tedious essays.

As her gift for my graduation, Auntie Cheng called me and asked me to perform "Farewell My Concubine" with her. Me? To have the honor of sharing the stage with Auntie Cheng, such a well-known actress? I couldn't believe it. Since 1931, when she was only 14, Auntie Cheng had lived on and for the stage. During our rehearsals, she told me a lot—about her early days of training, about the stage today, about life. She had given much thought to inviting me to perform with her. Other than the fact that she really liked me, she also wanted to express her sincere gratitude to my family for all we had done for her family over the years. To my great surprise, she told me that our presentation would be her farewell performance. Peking Opera had been one of the best-known expressions of Chinese culture for almost two centuries, but Mao would soon draw the curtain on its time of glory and significance in China. Auntie Cheng could see what was coming and, bowing to fate, regretfully decided to retire before the bitter end.

Our performance gave me a much deeper understanding of the nature of beauty because Auntie Cheng exemplified it. Of course, I had seen her perform before, but never from this perspective. Her beauty went so far beyond the physical aspect of what people consider "good looks." On stage, Auntie Cheng transformed herself into the sorrowful concubine through an almost magical combination of elements—her very presence, her exquisite movements and gestures, her powerful singing that evoked such strong emotions, the stylized simplicity of it all. She overwhelmed me with her devotion to her beloved ruler. I could no longer see Auntie Cheng before me, only the distressed concubine. When she committed suicide in my arms, in a flash I understood why Auntie Cheng had selected "Farewell My Concubine" as her last performance. Even to this day, I can still see Auntie Cheng in my mind's eye with all her beauty and hear her singing in my heart. Occasionally she comes to me in my dreams.

Under the national job assignment system then in force in China, all college graduates were assigned jobs by the central and local governments in conjunction with the universities and colleges. Graduates were not allowed to find their own jobs. Most BFLI graduates went into the Ministry of Foreign Affairs or the Ministry of Education. However, those jobs were assigned not on the basis of a good academic record, but rather were based on family origin and class background. As the son of a "Cap-removed Rightist" and the "All-time Champion" of our frequent political campaigns, I didn't have a chance for such a position.

Facing the uncertainty of my employment, I became anxious and found it hard to sleep. Even eating, always a major activity in my life, was less appealing. My mother and Yuying were very concerned about me. Only my father took matters calmly. Of course, he hoped my first job would be in Beijing. After my older brothers and sisters had moved out of our house, I had become a family pillar. But my father's peaceful approach to life enabled him to make the best of things as they were. Early on, he had dealt with tough situations in Yanmen and even more so when he fell victim to China's merciless political storms.

He would often tell me, "There is nothing you can do but let time shape your fate and fly with the wind. If it blows east, go to the east. If it blows west, go to the west."

Fortunately, the winds of fate were gentle with me. I was hired by the Metalworking Technologies Research Institute of the Ministry of Machine Building Industries. I didn't care what kind of job I got just as long as I could be in Beijing, close to those I loved. The Ministry was huge, with oversight of hundreds of state-owned plants. Most of the plants had tens of thousands of workers. They needed English-major graduates to translate advanced metalworking technology research papers and documents from Europe and the United States. I was chosen by that Institute for no other reasons than I was one of only a few English majors left and I happened to have the best exam scores. Of course, the fact that the cap of Rightist had been removed from my father also helped.

Professionally, I was not that happy with the job. I had no interest in metalworking. My father had a totally different view. He explained to me that a foreign language was only a tool, that I must choose my profession by making full use of that tool. I had to answer the important question: "English plus what?" In his opinion, English plus metalworking technologies would be very good for me. He told me, "Just remember, son. The more skills you have, the wider your future choices will be."

When I reported to the Institute, to my surprise I found that it was located exactly on the original site of the Franco-Chinese University where my father had started his teaching career 35 years before. His French textbooks were published by that University's press. It was close to the red buildings of Peking University, from which my father had graduated in 1924. Amazingly, I was following my father's footsteps but on a different track. My father was excited to hear the news. He remembered every corner of the University, especially the library. The library was a two-story building with a basement, which was used to store all kinds of books and magazines. After long years of storage, they were still in good shape.

The Director of the Institute's Personnel Department, a beefy, older woman, welcomed me and told me that she had carefully read my personal files. She knew my family background and urged me to strive extra hard to show my zeal for the country. She explained to me that I must learn metalworking technologies so that I could use my English to translate related documents; the only category left for me was foundry work. The subject was not totally new to me. I had visited the foundry workshop in my father's plant many times. It was the dirtiest and toughest job in the metalworking industry. But I didn't have a choice.

Three senior engineers were assigned to be my tutors. They didn't seem to know very much about my background, and after they learned about me, they didn't seem to care. Senior engineer Feng was especially kind to me. He was a short old man who didn't talk a lot. He was fluent in English and German and had taught in the United States, where he had earned his PhD. He came back to China in 1954, leaving his wife and son behind in Boston.

I was thrilled when I received my first month's salary: 46 yuan! I used it to buy a beautifully carved walking stick for my father. I invited Mother, Jiahui, and Yuying to the department store on Wangfujing, Beijing's major shopping street, to buy gifts for them. My mother tried to choose something cheap, but I wouldn't let her. Finally she picked a very stylish leather handbag. I bought Jiahui and Yuying wool sweaters. And then I invited everyone out to dinner. My father chose the Ji Barbecue Restaurant on Shicha Lake. Twice the restaurant had burned to the ground. Twice it was rebuilt, and each time it became even more prosperous.

Autumn in Beijing was always gorgeous, with comfortable weather. Everyone in our party was happy, but my parents were the happiest. I knew they relished seeing their youngest son becoming a man. While we were enjoying the meal and drinks,

I noticed that my father was absorbed in his thoughts. As we walked out of the restaurant after the meal, he remarked in a low voice, "I assume you know why I chose this restaurant for this memorable moment." Of course I knew: if anything symbolized rebirth, literally rising from the ashes, it was the Ji Restaurant. I cherished this delicious and profound moment with my father.

By the end of 1962, some of the CCP's efforts to correct Mao's mistakes and the worst effects of the Great Leap were gaining traction. Under pressure, Mao had been removed from daily operation of the government. The pragmatists in the Politburo—Deng Xiaoping, Liu Shaoqi, and others—were digging China out of the hole Mao had put it in. Private plots were again allowed. Markets were reopened. More foodstuffs and other goods were available in stores. Through underground exchange dealers, food coupons and daily necessities could be purchased or traded. Commodities in short supply—food, meat, cooking oil, fish, peanuts, sunflower seeds, cloth, cotton, bicycles, furniture, watches—could be bought only with coupons. A bicycle coupon could be exchanged for dozens of kilos of food coupons. Ordinary Chinese citizens were finally awakening from the nightmare of starvation. Mao, meanwhile, was plotting his next mass movement and how it would return him to power.

On October 16, 1964, China exploded its first atomic bomb and became the fifth member of the world's exclusive nuclear club. This was a momentous event for China, and Mao achieved his long-sought goal of beginning to deal with the threat of nuclear blackmail by the US. It also showed that China could make major strides like this despite the withdrawal of Soviet aid. With its 22-megaton explosion at its western desert test site, the PRC made a strong statement. Especially after its breach with the USSR, China had been isolated from the rest of the world, but it had served warning that it could not be ignored.

Domestically, the Four Cleanups Movement was sweeping the nation. Partly in response to the activities of corrupt local officials during the Great Leap and subsequent famine, a reform campaign was begun. It was quickly expanded to cleanse politics, economics, ideology, and organizations. Millions of government officials and employees, workers, and students were formed into work groups and sent to villages in the countryside. In many areas, these efforts became witch hunts with hundreds of thousands of victims killed, tortured, imprisoned, forced into false confessions, fined, or penalized in other ways. Many chose suicide. In this way, the Four Cleanups Movement was no different from other campaigns China waged against its citizens.

Yuying, now a fifth-year college student, was sent to a small village outside Xingtai in Hebei Province as a Four Cleanups work team member. Their mission was to rectify the head and cadre of the poor village. Young, inexperienced students like Yuying and her cohorts at the Art Institute were expected to "clean up" those much older village cadre, who had been born, raised, and worked all their lives in the village. Such was the thinking of China's leaders.

All this was taking place just as China was emerging from the worst famine in a land that was famous for its famines. Extreme poverty and death still stalked the nation. In the village Yuying was "cleansing," peasants used straw to cover themselves at night and substituted the saltpeter that leached from walls for salt in their food. All the students' meals were cooked by the farmers using their meager resources. Bran cakes, which were completely green because wild herbs were the main ingredient, were common fare.

When Yuying took her routine leave home, her face and legs were swollen from edema, a condition caused by malnutrition. My little wife looked like someone had pumped her up like a balloon about to burst. Her clothing was full of lice and fleas. Grandaunt put all her clothing, one batch after another for a whole day, into a large basin of boiling water to get them cleaned. Yuying showed me a picture of a big rally the work team held to criticize the village heads, some of whom were then arrested and imprisoned.

On May 4, 1965, Yuying and I had our simple wedding ceremony. Since Yuying had not yet graduated, and regulations prohibited college students from having wedding ceremonies, we had to keep ours a secret. We might have waited, but my parents were eager to have more grandchildren before they became too old. Although we had legally been husband and wife with our marriage certificate in hand for three years, we lived in different rooms in my parent's house. Yuying still shared a bedroom with Jiahui.

In the Chen family, a certificate may have legalized the marriage, but only the wedding ceremony formalized and completed the vows. Compared with the impressive ceremonies held for my older siblings, ours was small and modest. Only about 20 members of our families gathered for dinner at the Cuihualou Restaurant, where Jiahui and I had taken our lunches during our primary school days 15 years ago. It was the same restaurant, but now the government owned it.

Yuying and I spent our wedding night in our bridal chamber in the west wing of my parents' house. My mother and sisters had furnished and decorated it. The furniture consisted mostly of my old bed, desk, and chairs. There were only two new pieces: a square table in our outside living room and a five-drawer chest (still with us in our current residence in Beijing) in our bedroom. We bought our wedding clothes from a clothing warehouse for national athletes attending international events. Wedding rings or other jewelry, cosmetics, and such items were considered to be sentimental bourgeois artifacts, so there was none of that.

Actually, Yuying didn't need to enhance her beauty in any way. In my eyes and in my heart, her beauty was unmatched. That evening, when I undressed her, it was fully revealed to me for the first time. Her lily-white soft skin and slender body enchanted me with such power that I felt dizzy, like I had just finished two bottles of strong liquor. My heart was pounding. My throat was dry. I couldn't think. Although we were both virgins, we made love as smoothly as if we'd been doing it for years. We were on fire on our own cloud nine.

I was overwhelmed with love for Yuying. I silently vowed that I would devote myself to her, providing for all her material, spiritual, and other needs. In those uncertain times, however, I wondered whether I would be able to keep my vow.

Chapter 10

THE GREAT CULTURAL CATASTROPHE

1965-1966
Beijing, Xi'an, China

FIVE DAYS AFTER OUR LONG overdue wedding ceremony, Yuying went back to Xingtai to continue her assignment with the Four Cleanups Movement. A month later, I was sent almost 1,000 kilometers southwest of Beijing to Xi'an, one of China's oldest cities. My assignment: to inaugurate a Quick Training Class in English.

I was certainly surprised to be entrusted with such a responsible job. When I was called to the Institute Director's office, I thought something terrible was about to happen again. This time, however, the Director told me that I had done an excellent job teaching English after work in the Institute, and my students to a person had praised my approach.

He went on to say that the First Ministry of Machinery Building Industries needed people literate in English in factories all over China. Out of a thousand applicants from 50 factories, the Ministry had chosen 56 engineers and technicians to learn basic English in six months. They would then serve as researchers and translators to introduce advanced metalworking technologies from abroad to improve and modernize production lines at home. I was chosen from among dozens of candidates for this important and challenging job.

The class would start in the summer in a primary school in Xi'an while the students and teachers were on vacation. When I later met with a senior Ministry official, he informed me that I would have no assistants because the Ministry lacked qualified English speakers. We were already paying a price for our years of rejecting everything Western. I would be the only teacher to fulfill this "glorious mission," he intoned, adding that they trusted me and believed that I could do the job well.

I wasn't so sure. I had no textbook, no help, and no experience conducting such a class with so many students. I was expected to compile the textbook as I went along, teach the class, review all the homework, and compose and grade the mid-term and final exams. This was quite a test for me, an untried 25-year-old. I trusted my capabilities, but would I do well enough to satisfy the authorities?

When my father learned about my assignment, he became quite excited.

"Son, that means they really trust you. Training 56 students on your own. That is a huge job."

"I have dozens of thoughts, but no real idea about how to get started."

"Your textbook is the key. Perhaps I can help you by telling you how I wrote my first French texts."

My father told me—as if he were telling the story for the first time—about the summer of 1935. He had spent two months away from home living in a nearby middle school in order to concentrate on producing three bi-lingual textbooks. He showed them to me and explained the principles he had used. He said that once I felt that I had a grip on the concept I was applying and my approach, I needed to plunge into my first few chapters and the rest would follow. He stressed the critical importance of pronunciation and basic grammar. Learning vocabulary must be built into learning English sentence patterns and phrases. Rote memorization was essential. Mnemonics or other memory aids were helpful.

What my father shared with me that night greatly encouraged me and stiffened my resolve. My education at the Institute had also prepared me for my awesome assignment. In three years, I had gained a basic knowledge of metalworking, casting, forging, welding, heat treatment, and mechanics. And during that time, I was also reading and translating English technical papers. When I began, it took me three days to finish a short paper, even with errors. By my last year, however, I had translated and published more technical papers than anyone else in the Institute. I had an excellent foundation for preparing my first English language textbook as well as the many future assignments that would come my way. My career evolved in a way I could never have foreseen, especially in the dark days of the coming Cultural Revolution, from which I often feared there would be no escape.

By mid-June, my English class was in full swing at the primary school in the eastern suburbs of the ancient city of Xi'an. Sometimes called China's "eternal city," Xi'an had served as the capital for 13 dynasties. Today the city is best known as the site of the 8,000 terra cotta warriors of China's first emperor, but their remarkable discovery was still nearly a decade in the future. In 1965, my students and I lived, studied, and played together like one, big, happy family in this beautiful city. For the first time I felt truly respected and useful. The students called me Teacher Chen and treated me with deference, although most of them were much older than I. One of the students with whom I got along especially well was also the CCP Secretary. He was totally in my corner and greatly facilitated the smooth running of the whole training process.

Although I returned to my residence exhausted every day, I was joyful. My only pain was that I missed my family and Yuying dreadfully. When I threw myself onto my bed after a long, hard day, I couldn't stop thinking of them. I wished that they could see how devoted I was to my task and be proud of me and my accomplishments.

To my pleasant surprise, the Party Secretary encouraged me to invite Yuying to spend her last college summer vacation with me. He led the students in turning my residence, which used to be a small reading room, into a humble but decent place for a honeymoon. The female students used their own money to buy new bedding. Yuying and I spent the whole month together.

One real bonus in Xi'an was the discovery there of Zhijie, my second eldest cousin. Zhijie had joined the People's Liberation Army soon after our home town was liberated. After many years of service in the Production and Construction Corps in Xinjiang Province, he was discharged from active military service to become an accountant in Xi'an No. 4 Hospital. Yuying and I were so happy to be able to spend most of our weekends with Zhijie. Yuying learned about our home village and the Chen mansion from my long conversations with Zhijie.

We walked around the Drum Tower and Bell Tower in the downtown area and enjoyed cheap and tasty local foods. Pita bread soaked in lamb soup in Xi'an-style cuisine remains one of my favorite dishes to this very day. Then Zhijie would take us to the Peking Opera show in a big tent theater. Alone, Yuying and I toured other local sights, including the Hua Mountain, some distance from Xi'an. We were fortunate to be able to see the full display in the Forest of Steles before many of them were destroyed as feudalist relics. The high point of our sweet and long overdue honeymoon was conceiving our son Dawei.

When my students graduated, they knew over 2,500 English words, 200 common English phrases, and fundamental English grammar. At their final exam, they translated a 2,500 English-word technical paper into Chinese in four hours with no more than three major mistakes. All 56 students passed. When we had started, only a few of them even knew the English alphabet. We had come together on a common mission and succeeded. While I was eager to get back home, I was sorry to part company with my students.

Upon returning to Beijing, however, I had no time to rest on my laurels. The thank-you letter from my class was still warm in my hand when I first saw the posters around the Institute denouncing me. It was predictable that I would be chosen as a target of the Four Cleanups Campaign. After all, I was "the son of a Landlord, a Capitalist, and a Rightist," who "must be cleaned out of our revolutionary ranks," or so said the big-character posters that were hanging everywhere. As the "All-time Champion" of every past campaign, I was the target of whatever political storm was brewing, the fall guy of every campaign. The labels changed, but nothing else did. I treated this latest crusade as an athlete might deal with participation in yet another sporting event and didn't even bother to tell Yuying and my parents about this version. Why disturb them? Bowing to the inevitable was our only real option.

The political storms again ensnared my father's best friend, Uncle Zhang, who had made such great contributions and sacrifices struggling against the Japanese and Kuomintang and building the new China. We hadn't seen Uncle Zhang since the end of 1959, when he had been labeled as a Mid-Rightist Opportunist because he supported Marshal Peng Dehuai. Peng had been proclaimed an arch-enemy of the state in the summer of 1959. After he became a target, Uncle Zhang didn't want to put us in jeopardy by visiting us, so we hadn't seen him in years.

"Opportunist" was the label used to identify the most dangerous enemies within the Party. It was the equivalent of Counter-revolutionary among the people. Most Opportunists were expelled from the Party and lost their high-ranking positions in the government. Mid-Rightist Opportunists, who went only halfway to the right extreme, could maintain their Party membership after severe criticism, but they were demoted and dispatched to remote areas to atone for their mistakes through meritorious service.

While we had not seen Uncle Zhang for a long time, I did stay in touch with his son, Taiming, and occasionally saw his daughter, Taiqing. Taiming worked in the Scientific Research Academy of the Ministry of Ordnance Industries, not far from my Institute. We often met in the Beijing Library in a quiet corner of its huge reading room. Just before I left for Xi'an, Taiming told me that his father was awaiting transfer to a new job, maybe deep into the mountains of the remote provinces. Although we didn't talk much, I saw the depression and anxiety in Taiming's eyes and on his face. He had lost a lot of weight and looked harried. As we parted, he asked me to tell my father that to learn his second language he was using the French textbooks my father had written almost 30 years ago.

After I returned to Beijing, I met Taiming at our accustomed spot. He told me that his father had finally been assigned a new job after months of rectification. The family was on the verge of leaving the city, but because their destination was a remote area with no inhabitants, he couldn't even give me a name. When I told my father this news, he was most distressed and asked me to visit Uncle Zhang immediately.

I went on a cold and somber day in December 1965. When I got to Uncle Zhang's house in late afternoon, there were no armed guards at the front door as I thought there might be. I knocked at the door several times before Taiming opened it and we exchanged greetings.

Taiming seemed to age every time I saw him. He already looked old although he was only three years my senior. As soon as we reached the courtyard, I saw a high wall partitioning it.

"Is this something new?" I asked.

"It's been this way for two years now. Another family took the bigger part of our house over there." Taiming pointed to the section beyond the wall.

Seeing an old friend's home divided like this made me sad, and I was embarrassed that I had asked. I quickly changed the subject. "Is Uncle Zhang at home?"

"Yes, packing."

"Packing? Did your father's work assignment come through?"

"He'll be working on the third line of defense in Guizhou," Taiming said, referring to one of the interior industrial bases not as exposed to foreign attack as the coast was.

"Who is there? Is that Songsheng?" Uncle Zhang stepped out of his study.

"Uncle Zhang, we all really miss you."

"We also miss all of you. It's been so many years. How are your parents?"

"Fine. They are just fine. Here, my father asked me to bring you some cornbread with dates."

"Splendid! It's so typical of your father to remember such an old favorite of mine."

"Hi, Big Brother." Taiqing practically burst out of her room. With her hair in a bob, she looked gorgeous, but tired.

"Hey, Taiqing. I like your hair. I've brought some of Yuying's and my wedding candies for you all."

Taiqing asked "How could you not tell us about your wedding?" I knew she knew the answer and made no reply.

We all walked into the living room, which was in great disarray.

"Sorry for the mess. We are packing for Guizhou," Taiming explained.

"What will your job be?" I asked Uncle Zhang.

"Relocating military factories from inland to a remote mountainous area in Guizhou Province. Preparing for war."

"For war? Against whom?" I didn't know anything about an impending war.

"US imperialists and Soviet revisionists." Uncle Zhang smiled bitterly.

Clearly in a mood to talk that night, Uncle Zhang told us many secret stories about the internal conflicts between Mao and Peng Dehuai. As Mao's old and close colleague, Peng had served as the Deputy Commander-in-Chief of the Red Army. He led the Chinese People's Volunteers to fight the US troops in Korea. He was Mao's appointed heir in the Central Military Commission. At the 1959 Party Conference at Lushan Mountain, Peng presented an open letter criticizing Mao's Great Leap Forward with its People's Communes and Backyard Steel effort. Mao was already irked by Peng's insubordination and independence. The letter was just like blowing on the embers of Mao's anger until they flared in an explosion of rage. Peng was instantly denounced as the top dog of the Anti-Party Clique and removed as the Defense Minister and Vice Chairman of the Central Military Commission.

Uncle Zhang was soon implicated because he said something similar to Peng's anti-Party criticism during a heart-to-heart meeting with one of his closest colleagues, his chief assistant. It was a breach he would soon regret.

"I kept telling your father to be careful, but I failed to take my own advice. 'Out of a careless mouth comes disaster,' as the saying goes. I told my assistant privately that Peng's letter was fair and square criticism and that he shouldn't be punished like this."

"And my father's assistant reported all this to above." Taiming held his thumb pointing up. Everyone knew what "the above" meant, how many ambitious villains would do anything they could to please their superiors and gain a promotion. "Set a beggar on horseback, and he will ride to the devil."

The chief assistant soon replaced Uncle Zhang and then added insult to injury by dispatching Uncle Zhang to Guizhou.

"Taiqing and I will go with Father," Taiming said.

"We can't let our father go alone and rough it out there in the sticks. I am prepared. I already cut my hair," Taiqing added with a flip of her head and a smile.

Uncle Zhang, Taiming, and Taiqing walked me to the front door. Uncle Zhang saw my concern.

"I'll be fine. Don't you worry. After my experience in the Taihang Mountain guerrillas during the '40s, nothing could conquer me," Uncle said.

"We'll all be fine. Don't worry," Taiming added. I didn't know it at the time, of course, but this would be the last time I saw Taiming.

Uncle Zhang held my hands tightly and said, "Tell your parents, if your father could be a Rightist, then all good-hearted people with a conscience could be Rightists. I am proud to have your father as a friend."

I shook Uncle Zhang's hands. "Uncle, if you could be a Mid-Rightist Opportunist, then all good-hearted people with a conscience could be Mid-Rightist Opportunists. We are proud to have you as a friend and our uncle."

We shared a gleeful chuckle as I felt his big hands—still so strong and so warm—enfold and press mine one last time.

"You must tell your parents, if I told them be careful before, I am telling them to be even more careful now. The rising winds foretell the coming storm."

"Something bad is coming?" I felt the tension in Uncle Zhang's low voice.

"No. Not something bad. Something worse. Something much worse is coming soon."

On that note of foreboding we parted. It didn't take long for Uncle Zhang's prediction to come true.

In March 1966, frustrated by the lack of progress toward his goals for China and seeking to consolidate his power, Mao called for a Cultural Revolution.

In April, Mao urged attacks by the "local" against the "central."

In May, Mao and his followers denounced the Beijing Party and municipal government leaders. The Cultural Revolution was formally launched when Mao's "May 16 Notice" was issued by the CCP Central Committee. Mao created the Leading Group for the Cultural Revolution directly under the standing committee of the CCP Politburo, and Jiang Qing, Mao's wife, was appointed as the Deputy Chief. The "May 16 Notice" called upon the whole country to bring down Representatives of the Bourgeoisie in the Party, government, and army.

The Institute Director and all his deputies were immediately identified as Representatives of the Bourgeoisie. Amidst the big-character posters attacking them that festooned the halls were many posters accusing me of being a Dutiful Son of the Bourgeoisie. While the titles changed, the often deadly process of labeling people went on—Landlord, Counter-revolutionary, Rich Peasant, Bad Element, or Rightist. I was none of those things, but Dutiful Son of the Bourgeoisie was enough to mark me as the enemy. Hadn't Mao proclaimed that China was now in a desperate class struggle in which the proletariat must bring down the bourgeoisie without mercy? As a Dutiful Son of the Bourgeoisie, I was doomed. Despite my outstanding work at the Institute and beyond, I bore this title for years to come. It soon would take me to a cowshed prison cell and eventually to a forlorn labor camp in China's northern desert.

Through the spring, Yuying was getting bigger and bigger with our fast-growing child. She told me with a laugh that because of her protruding belly, she could no longer pull herself close to the table for meals, but it didn't matter because she could just put the dishes on her stomach. My parents were so excited about their coming grandchild but were also very worried about Yuying. She insisted on taking crowded buses to her plant until one day her legs became so swollen that she could hardly walk. I took her to the Peking Union Hospital. Her doctor immediately ordered her to be hospitalized because of her condition and her pregnancy-induced hypertension. Founded by the Rockefeller Foundation in 1921, the hospital was one of the best in China. Coincidently, I was born there in 1939. I had a special feeling of luck and safety there for Yuying and our coming child.

After long, painful attempts to have our child through natural labor, Yuying had to undergo a C-section. Before the operation, I was called into the Office of Obstetrics.

"If you agree with your wife's C-section operation, we need your signature here." A young woman doctor handed me a clutch of papers.

"What are the dangers of the operation?" I was worried.

"It would be far more dangerous not to perform the operation," an older woman doctor kindly explained.

"This is Doctor Lin Qiaozhi," the young doctor said.

"Doctor Lin!" I blurted out her name loudly. "Excuse me, Doctor. Of course you don't recognize me, but you delivered me 27 years ago in this hospital."

All the doctors and nurses were now staring at me.

"Really?" Doctor Lin was pleasantly astonished. "What is your mother's name?"

"Chen. Her maiden name is Fu. Her two sisters, Fu Junrong and Fu Junrui, were also working in this hospital."

"Oh, I remember now. What a remarkable coincidence!" Doctor Lin exclaimed. "You have made my day."

Doctor Lin, now 65 years old, was the well-known former Director of the Department of Gynecology and Obstetrics at the hospital. As soon as the Cultural Revolution started, she was assigned to the lower ranks as a mere resident. Her demotion, however unfair, gave us the unexpected pleasure of having her deliver both father and son. Without any hesitation, we took Doctor Lin's advice and Yuying gave birth to our first child. I had been a large baby at 8.5 pounds, but our big boy weighed in at 11 pounds. Yuying herself stood 5'2" and weighed only 100 pounds.

Without consulting my parents or Yuying, I named our son Wei. It means safeguard, and it was very popular in those days. Millions of Chinese children had Wei as part of their first names: Weidong, safeguard Mao Zedong; Weijun, safeguard the army; Weihong, safeguard "Red." I was definitely not in the flow of this patriotic or Mao-worshipping stream. I simply wished that our son would bring us the good fortune to safeguard my parents and the rest of our family. Since Wei was so big, Dawei, big Wei, became his first name.

The nurses put all the other newborns on a long bed except for Dawei, who was just too big. They found him a small separate bed. Everyone loved him. He was plump with soft, light skin and long, thick, dark hair. He looked more like a two-month-old boy. Dawei never cried unless he was hungry, but he took after his father and had a big appetite, so he occasionally displayed considerable lung power, another trait he may have inherited from his father. With his dark smiling eyes, Dawei became a favorite of the whole hospital. Marvelously, he was born on June 23, sharing that birthday with his mother.

When it came time to leave the hospital, Yuying took Dawei closely in her arms and sat on a flatbed pedicab that I borrowed from my friends. My mother and grandaunt had put a thick quilt on the flatbed. I pedaled slowly and carefully along Dongdan and Dongsi streets. Yuying and I kept silent all the way home as we were buffeted by the big-character posters on virtually every wall and shop window.

"Break Down the Four Olds! Set up the Four News!"
"Destroy Old Customs!
"Destroy Old Culture!"
"Destroy Old Habits!"
"Destroy Old Ideas!"

The destruction inspired by the Cultural Revolution had already begun, and the terrible scenes on the streets gave us chills. We saw many people burning all sorts of things—books, art, scrolls, magazines, photographs, keepsakes, even furniture and screens. People to whom these treasures had belonged were ordered to stand and watch the fire as punishment. Sometimes Yuying had to cover Dawei's mouth with her handkerchief to protect him from the choking smoke. Many shops and buildings had clearly been ransacked. Ripped paintings and shattered porcelain littered the sidewalks. The scene resembled the chaos of a harsh war, which indeed it was. It was much more horrible than 18 years before when Peiping had been surrounded by the Communist Army.

Finally we reached home. "Father and Mother, we are bringing you back a big grandson," I called to my parents while escorting Yuying and Dawei into our house.

"Let us see him, quick." My mother and grandaunt hurried out of the kitchen.

"What a beautiful big boy!" My mother exclaimed, taking Dawei carefully from Yuying. "Are you alright, Yuying?"

"I am fine, Mother. I just don't have enough breast milk for Dawei."

"Don't worry," Grandaunt smiled. "I am cooking you fish soup. It will help you produce more milk for our big boy."

"Let me have a look," my father stepped out of the living room. Mother showed Dawei to him, and he couldn't take his eyes off the newest member of our family.

"High forehead, big eyes, straight nose," my father examined my son attentively. "Broad mouth, round chin, and jaw. Most fortunate good looks!"

Following my father's comments on Dawei's physiognomy, all of us looked at him more closely. Then we retired to our rooms in the west wing, where my mother had prepared a quilt and pillow for the new crib.

"Luckily, we got Dawei a big crib." My mother carefully put him on his comfortable bed. "Songsheng, your father wants to see you in his study."

When I crossed over the threshold into the study, I was shocked to find paintings, pictures, and books all over the floor.

"Father, what are you doing?"

"These items most likely belong to the Four Olds. We have to burn them before it is too late." My father looked around the room anxiously. "There are so many more treasures to discard."

"The scrolls are antiques, aren't they?"

"They are the calligraphy of Zeng Guofan and Zuo Zongtang, now marked as traitors who slaughtered peasants in service to the Qing Dynasty."

"Let me take care of them and the other things."

"Wait until tomorrow. I need you to do another job tonight." My father took out a leather pouch from the inside drawer of his desk.

"Your grandfather gave me this sheepskin pouch and 20 silver coins when I set off to Peking in 1918. I know you have heard the story many times from both me and your grandfather."

"Yes, it was a favorite of his. I wish I had a silver coin for every time I heard it. That story stays with me and inspires me."

"I used the original 20 coins, of course, but now I keep 20 others in the pouch, special ones. Whenever I see this pouch, I see your grandfather."

Father and I grew quiet for several moments, immersed in a reverie of family memories. Then he stirred, untied the dark red cord, took out the coins, and handed them to me.

"These 20 coins were what I managed to save from my first year of teaching in 1925."

I stacked up the silver coins in two piles and gravely pondered them.

"Your mother and I are not planning to leave any money to you or your brothers and sisters. You have all graduated from college except Jiahui, and she will graduate from medical school next year. Your education is the best wealth we could ever give you."

"We all know that."

"But I did want to pass down this pouch and these 20 silver coins to one more generation." He paused for a while. "And now you must throw them away."

"What?" I could not trust my ears.

"Throw them away tonight."

"Why?"

"Saving gold and silver belongs to the Four Olds. And the Party sees this as a threat, the means of restoring reactionary rule by enemies of the country."

"Could we hide them somewhere?"

"Where?"

I did not have an answer.

"Our home is not safe. If we hide them in our close friends' homes, it could possibly get them into big trouble."

Big trouble in the current reign of terror often meant death or suicide. I shivered at the thought.

My father told me that all of the other family gold and silver had been contributed to the China People's Volunteers during the anti-US war in Korea. While these 20 old silver coins had little value, they must be gotten rid of. I told my father I would throw the coins into the moat of the Forbidden City, but that we should keep the pouch.

Although the moat was only three miles from our home, it was a long, lonely walk. The night was thick with darkness. The dim light from the occasional street lamp that penetrated the night made me feel even more miserable. Walking toward the moat, I was suddenly flooded with fond childhood memories and transported to scenes of swimming, skating, and fishing there and sailing toy boats. It was a child's dream to grow up so close to such a wonderful place to play. As the moat came into view, I snapped back to my task at hand. I vigilantly walked along the north bank toward the darkest corner I could spot. Nobody was around. I looked at the water, heaved a sigh, and quickly threw all the coins into the dark waters.

I chose the moat of the Forbidden City as the coins' final destination because it was a part of my family's best times, dear to all of us. But there was more involved. I thought of the word "forbidden," and it seemed appropriate to my mission, throwing away my family's hereditary treasure or at least a symbol of it. A few days later, I accompanied my mother to the local branch of the government-owned China People's Bank to hand in all our bank and deposit books and the deed of our only remaining house. All our bank accounts were frozen, including all the money from the government bonds my mother had purchased. Winds of change swept across the country. Cold winds.

The Anti-Bourgeois Reactionary Line campaign was mounted amidst an unprecedented period of activism. We were urged to speak out freely, air our views fully, write big-character posters, and hold great debates. Combat Teams formed in universities, middle schools, government units, factories, communes, everywhere to promote the revolution. Soon after, the Red Guards sprang up in urban middle schools and colleges and then spread like a wind-whipped wildfire across the land.

Red Guards originally referred to guards with red hearts for Chairman Mao. They wore green army caps and uniforms without military insignia, heavy leather belts with big iron buckles, and red armbands. These young thugs regularly carried Mao's Little Red Book, as did much of the nation, and used it to justify their vicious crimes. They quickly became China's inquisition and scourge, exercising virtually unrestrained power, persecuting and terrorizing an entire country indiscriminately.

Tens of millions of adolescent and older students answered Mao's call to suspend classes and conduct a revolution. Rebelling against authority, humiliating teachers, attacking people on a whim, and stealing their riches were a lot more fun than going to school. On August 18, 1966, Mao received millions of Red

Guards in Tiananmen Square to demonstrate his full support for their revolutionary zeal and activities. At the gate tower, a middle school student from Beijing pinned a red armband on Mao bearing three Chinese characters in Mao's calligraphic style: Red, Guard, Soldier.

"What is your name," Mao asked her.

"Song Binbin," the thin 18 year-old with eyeglasses replied. Binbin means gentle and refined.

"Binbin? That is not good," Mao said. "Don't be gentle. Be fierce and martial."

Mao's words unleashed the Red Guards. They were to be vengeful in following Mao's commands and cleansing the nation. Right away, Song Binbin changed her name to Song Yaowu, meaning martial. Her middle school changed its name to Yaowu School. Under Song Yaowu's leadership, the deputy principal of her school, Bian Zhongyun, had already become the first of many teachers to be beaten to death by their students. "Be fierce and martial" instantly became the principle rule of Red Guards throughout China. An orgy of vandalism and violence followed. Those heavy leather belts with iron buckles beat a nation into submission and terror. In August and September, 1,700 people were murdered in Beijing alone. Shanghai in September recorded 700 suicides and over 500 deaths resulting from the Cultural Revolution.

From August through the end of November, Mao reviewed more than 11 million Red Guards in Tiananmen Square. They had traveled to Beijing from all over the country free of charge. Sometimes the Square was so crowded with Red Guards that the jostling of the throng dislodged some of their ill-gotten gains. Municipal sanitation workers sweeping the street after the crowds had dispersed regularly found silver and gold lost by the Red Guards. The youths enjoyed sight-seeing tours with free room and board and train travel to anywhere they wanted to go in China. What a heady time for a generation growing up without schooling and without restraints!

Of course, the Cultural Revolution needed new slogans, names, and enemies. We went from Sweep Away the Four Olds to Down with the Five Black Breeds, the Black Gang, the Counter-revolutionary Authority, Imperialism, Foreign Religion, and a host of other enemies or evil influences. The Black Gang was made up of virtually all responsible officers and principals of schools, factories, and work units. The Counter-revolutionary Authority consisted of most prominent intellectuals, artists, and other notables. The Five Black Breeds included Former Landlords, Rich Peasants, Counter-revolutionaries, Bad Elements, and Rightists.

All these targets were ordered to wear black armbands proclaiming their crime. Of course, my parents were no exception. Grandaunt made them each their badge of shame. It is hard to describe the anger and resentment that blazed through me when I saw my mother help my father put on his armband. From that day until they were driven from their home, my parents never again stepped foot outside their front door.

Yuying was at home on maternity leave. Jiahui hid in the dorm of her medical college. I was the only one in our family who saw what was happening outside our house. At the Institute, the Red Guards looked at me with hatred and disdain. On the streets, I saw young Red Guards beating men and women of all ages. No one dared to say or do anything. People just looked down at the street and hurried on by.

One night, I suddenly heard someone knocking lightly at our door. I opened it and saw Uncle Yuan with sweat dropping from his face.

"Quiet. I don't want your parents to hear. Something terrible has happened at the Confucius Temple of the Imperial Academy."

"Please come in, Uncle Yuan."

"I can stay only a moment." He stepped in and quickly closed the door behind him. "The Red Guards ordered many members of our community to kneel down around a big fire in front of the temple. They burned Peking Opera costumes and props while beating these poor people with their belts. There was blood all over."

"What?" I said in alarm.

"Yes, I knew quite a few of them. Several were almost beaten to death on the spot." Uncle Yuan took out a handkerchief and put it to his mouth to stifle a sob.

He added quickly, "Don't tell your parents. Let's not worry them any further, but I thought you should know. I didn't think things could get much worse. Little did I know. I must go now."

Before I opened the door, he said in a low, sad voice, "Lao She was also there. They paraded him through the streets and then beat him severely. He drowned himself in Taiping Lake yesterday."

Lao She? Such a kind man and eminent writer? A giant of our literature? Proclaimed as the "People's Artist" by the Beijing Government? Driven to take his own life? For what?

It was August 24, and the bloody month that became known as Red August still had another week to go.

August 27, 1966, Monday

In the hope of avoiding any unforeseen trouble, I rode my bicycle to the Institute very early in the morning. As soon as I entered, I was told by a Red Guard to wait in the meeting room. Someone wanted to see me. I immediately felt the butterflies take flight in my stomach. As I sat and waited for almost two hours, I had plenty of time to conjure up possible scenarios. None of them was good. Finally I was told by tall Yan and short Li, hatchet men of the Red Guards at the Institute, to report to the Director's office. The Director had already been imprisoned on campus as the top dog of the Institute's Capitalist Roaders. His office now served as headquarters for the Wei Dong (Safeguarding Mao Zedong) Red Guard Organization. I entered the office to find an ugly, scowling man I had never seen before. He was in his thirties, short—no more than 5'6"— and slender, wiry and with wire-rimmed glasses. I heard Li call him Captain.

"Chen Songsheng, our Wei Dong Red Guard Organization will now go to your parents' house to sweep away the Four Olds. You must go with us," he announced.

Without waiting for any response I might make, Yan and Li took me to a mid-sized truck, which was already full of Red Guards. I didn't dare say a word for the entire 40-minute trip, which seemed to take hours. When we arrived, several Red Guards were already waiting in front of our house. I knew most of them. They were my colleagues at the Institute.

The still scowling Captain gruffly ordered me, "Go in first and tell your parents to follow our orders strictly. They must obey our every command or they will pay a heavy penalty. Make sure that they understand the consequences of their actions."

I walked into our house to find that my parents were already confined in our north wing. Yuying and Dawei had been ordered into our west wing rooms, and my grandaunt was placed in the east wing kitchen. After I spoke with my parents and passed on the Captain's warnings, I went to our west wing rooms, where I was ordered to stay in the outside room, apart from my wife and child. Some women Red Guards were with Yuying and Dawei in the inner bedroom.

Interrogations started simultaneously in all the rooms. Different groups of Red Guards peppered us with a series of queries.

"Where are you hiding guns and weapons?"

"Where are you hiding gold?"

"Where are you hiding silver coins?"

"Where are you hiding antiques?"

"Where are you hiding US dollars?"

I told them honestly that we weren't hiding anything. What antiques we still had were in the two high cabinets in the end room of our north wing. We had nothing else on their forbidden list. I couldn't hear anything from the other rooms. I could not even hear anything from Yuying's room. I strained to hear any sounds from Dawei, but unbelievably, he didn't cry or even make a peep.

We had nothing for dinner, but then neither did we have any appetite. Two women Red Guards helped Yuying get some hot water to prepare Dawei's powdered milk. From the window, I saw many Red Guards taking antiques and furniture to the center of the courtyard. Two of them checked and registered every item in a small notebook. It soon became dark. Most of the Red Guards left but a few remained on the night watch.

Not all Red Guards were extreme or evil. I asked an older Red Guard to please take some of our hard biscuits to my parents and grandaunt, and I learned later that he had given them the biscuits and also some water. And the women Red

Guards kept sending hot water to Yuying to prepare powdered milk for Dawei.

Yuying, Dawei, and I were restricted to our east wing rooms and not allowed out into the rest of the house. When we needed to use the restroom, we couldn't use our own. Instead, some Red Guards escorted us to the public toilet on the street. I could not see my parents and my grandaunt. Yuying moved Dawei from his crib to our bed, then held and slept with him all night as if in a trance. I couldn't sleep a wink and rose at dawn.

August 28, 1966, Tuesday

Around 3 o'clock in the afternoon, a big group of Red Guards came in. From the window, I saw them lining up in the courtyard. Then the Captain showed up. He walked to the front of the group and began reciting Mao's quotations.

"Chairman Mao taught us, 'Revolution is not a dinner party,'" he shouted.

"Revolution is not a dinner party," the Red Guards replied in unison.

"Or writing an essay,"

"Or painting a picture,"

"Or doing embroidery;"

"It cannot be so refined,"

"Cannot be so leisurely and gentle,"

"Cannot be so temperate, kind, courteous,"

"Cannot be restrained and magnanimous;"

"Revolution is insurrection."

"Revolution is an act of violence with one class overthrowing another."

The chorus grew louder and louder, thundering from the courtyard into all our rooms, piercing not just our ears but our hearts.

Following the Captain, Yan and Li walked toward my parents' room brandishing their wide leather belts with the heavy buckles. I held my breath, hoping against hope that maybe they were only bluffing, just trying to frighten my parents.

Other Red Guards were climbing on the roof of the house and digging deep into the courtyard, searching for hidden weapons. In the center of the courtyard, some Red Guards were setting fire to a huge pile of pictures, paintings, photograph albums, and books that we had not yet destroyed or thought would be "safe." The fire they made filled the house with choking smoke. Suddenly I heard terrible screams coming from my parents' wing. They continued far into the dusk, each one stabbing me to the bone. I couldn't shut my eyes or stop my ears. I felt dazed, as if I had been thrown into a deep hole full of sharp knives. I was too numb to feel pain, but my blood was everywhere in this waking nightmare, red all over. Outside, the flames and swirling smoke lit up the courtyard with a lurid red.

Yuying used all her strength to hold me tight, leaving deep fingerprints impressed upon my arm. She knew I could have done something that might get our whole family slaughtered. I was big and strong, and I practiced Shao Lin boxing all the time. I could easily handle Yan, Li, and the Captain. They were such heroes, beating up my defenseless old parents. I wanted an eye for an eye and a tooth for a tooth. But I had to grit my teeth and control my impulses. I knew what could happen.

In the Chongwen District of Beijing just a few weeks before, a young man had tried to resist the Red Guards who were beating his parents and wounded one of them. He and his father were promptly whipped to death. His wife was forced to prepare many kettles of boiling water that were used to burn his mother to death. His wife then used a cleaver to kill herself. The wounded Red Guard who had led the torture and killing was lauded as a hero. These tragedies were the direct result of Mao's exhortation to his hordes of youngsters to "Be fierce and martial."

The severe beatings and harsh interrogations my family suffered arose partly from the false assumptions and convictions of these Red Guards and their scowling leader. My older brother had been a general in the Nationalist Army; therefore, we must be hiding weapons. And, of course, a rich family such as ours must be hoarding gold and silver! None of our honest denials shook their belief that we were lying and had to be punished.

Before most of the Red Guards left, I caught a glimpse of my parents being moved under guard from their rooms to the kitchen. There was no time for me to alert Yuying. I saw that my mother's long hair had been sheared almost to her scalp. My father supported her. The back of my father's white coarse cloth shirt had been soaked with his blood, now dried. The shirt stuck to his body. Step by slow step, they moved in pain toward the kitchen.

It was another hellish night. I didn't eat. I drank only a few swallows of water. I devoted my full attention to Dawei and Yuying, but my heart and soul were with my parents. My father was 69 years old. My mother had been troubled by high blood pressure for years. Could they survive their brutal torture?

August 29, 1966. Wednesday

No moon or stars. No sound except intermittent moaning from the kitchen, deep and low. It hung in the air, making this wretched night—this terrible, unthinkable night—even more miserable. At dawn, I lay numb, trying to grasp it all. Our house lay smashed and burned. My parents were brutally beaten and locked in the kitchen across the courtyard. Were they even still alive?

Most of the Red Guards had left, although some on night duty were fast asleep and snoring in the living room, unmoved by their evil. A few played chess under a dim light, which attracted moths and mosquitoes. Scattered fires in the courtyard gave a pale reddish glow to the kitchen windows. Tired as I was, as swollen as my eyes were from lack of sleep and all the smoke, I tried to focus. I had watched the kitchen intently all night.

The fires were almost out now. For hours, the Red Guards, led by their Captain, had fed the blaze with what remained of my family's paintings, books, and mementos—criminal possessions of the Four Olds.

Yuying, semi-conscious in the bedroom, groaned in a way that pained me as she stirred from sleep. She was still holding Dawei tightly, as she had ever since the terror began. Her body was in shock. The horrifying sounds of torture, the beating that my parents had suffered at the hands of the Red Guards, and the agony of not knowing what the Red Guards would do to us next had traumatized Yuying. I knew that her groan was not only from the pain of her inflamed incision, but also from her guilt at not being able to produce milk for Dawei and her worry about where his next meals were coming from. I gently pulled Yuying's hands from Dawei's chest and slowly massaged her forehead.

As I gazed across the courtyard, by the dawn's early light, I suddenly saw the silhouette of a slowly moving figure stretching behind the window of the kitchen.

Father! It was my father! My father was alive!

I watched as the form behind the window began to exercise, slowly practicing his Tai Chi, his white shirt, thick with dried blood, stuck to his back. Could he really be strong enough to do his exercises after being tortured so? My heart quickened. I watched, amazed, as my father moved his arms and hands slowly yet firmly toward our room.

I immediately understood the message. The exercises were signals from my father and mother. They were still alive! They had been beaten, but they were not defeated. As his gestures continued, I trembled with joy. Tears ran down my face and onto my chest. Emotion welled up so forcefully in me that I thought my heart would burst.

"Yuying, get up!" I whispered excitedly. "It is Father! Look!" Staring at the slowly exercising figure, Yuying and I held each other closely and sobbed together. Father's silhouette gave us hope and strength in the midst of brutality and loss. He had survived, endured, prevailed. We could also!

As I watched my father, I swore that I would stay alive for my mother, for Yuying and Dawei, but most of all for my father. I would live to tell our tale, the story of the Chen family. I would bear witness against those who had brought such misery to our lives.

I heard a conversation in the courtyard and was shocked to see my sister Jiahui talking with the Red Guard on duty. I so wished she could have kept herself out of this horror, but she had walked right into the trap. The guard brought her to our room. Her face was as pale as could be imagined. Her eyes, big with fright, implored me and Yuying.

"Where are Father and Mother?"

"There, with Grandaunt." I pointed to the kitchen.

"Why didn't you stay in your college?" Yuying asked.

"I couldn't stop thinking of all of you, especially Father and Mother. Besides, all the schools and colleges have shut down. There are no students left at the medical college."

"Maybe it is best that you are with us." I tried to calm Jiahui down.

"And sooner better than later," Yuying agreed.

"How is Dawei?" Jiahui stooped down to pat Dawei, who was still in deep sleep.

"He is fine, though I don't have any breast milk for him." Yuying blamed herself again.

"It is not your fault. Powdered milk is just fine." Jiahui's manner of speaking was just like a doctor.

"Salute Captain Wang," came the call from the courtyard. This was the first time I had actually heard the name of the man who was to exert such a strange influence over my life. I looked out to see a well-dressed, middle-aged man accompanying Wang.

"Did they send all the antiques to the Confucius Temple?" the Captain asked.

"Yes, all except the inkstone. You told us to keep that here."

"Bring it to me. I'll take possession of it now for the Director of the Cultural Relics Bureau," Wang said, indicating the man at his side.

The Red Guard brought a rosewood box from the north wing and handed it to the Captain.

"This is the inkstone of Chu Suiliang from the Tang Dynasty that I told you about. It is an incomparable treasure. Let us go now."

About noon, a small group of Red Guards returned and ordered Jiahui, Yuying, and me to leave our "bourgeois" house immediately. In revolutionary parlance, it was called "Sweep the floor and leave the house." It meant get out and leave everything behind. We were expelled from our home and couldn't take any of our belongings with us.

Jiahui, Yuying holding Dawei, and I walked out of our house without seeing my parents or grandaunt. Other than the clothes we were wearing with literally empty pockets, all we had was Dawei's bamboo baby buggy and his blanket. We didn't know where to go or what to do. We were homeless, penniless, and on the mean streets of a desperate city under siege from within. And Red August wasn't quite over.

Chapter 11

DESPAIR, HOPE, AND SURVIVAL

1966-1969
Beijing, China

UNDER THE BLAZING AUGUST SUN, with Dawei sleeping in his bamboo baby carriage, Yuying, Jiahui, and I anxiously pondered where to go. It was dangerous to linger on the street. Red Guards often stopped passersby and questioned them about their class background and parentage. Offspring of the "Black Five"— Former Landlords, Rich Peasants, Counter-revolutionaries, Bad Elements, and Rightists—weren't even allowed to take the public bus or be served in restaurants. As the son of a Rightist criminal and the brother of a Kuomintang general, I was a marked man, automatically a suspect, whatever the charges.

The only place we could think of to seek shelter was my mother-in-law's ancient, tiny, and already crowded cottage. Two small rooms housed her, her elder son, daughter-in-law, and two grandchildren. But where else could we go? It took us more than an hour to get there, pushing Dawei and trying to avoid any encounters with the Red Guards.

"Mother," Yuying cried as she pushed open the door. "We are all here. You are our only refuge. We have no other place to go." Yuying broke down in tears and Jiahui started to cry, finally able to release her emotions. Their sobs struck deep in my heart.

"Don't cry. Don't frighten my grandson," my mother-in-law quickly urged as she picked up Dawei and put him on her bed. "This is your home. Here is your home."

Before Yuying could even say anything about the Red Guards expelling us, this kind, old lady had guessed what had happened. She was illiterate but smart and tough. As we all stood together in such close quarters, even without the four other residents present, Jiahui, Yuying, and I thought of the inconvenience and discomfort we were bringing to this already overcrowded family. Jiahui said she intended to return to her college dorm the next day.

"No. Everybody must stay," my mother-in-law said. "We'll be one happy family. Where there is a will there is a way."

In the evening, Yuying's brother, sister-in-law, six-year-old niece, and three-year-old nephew all returned. The children immediately threw themselves on the bed to play with Dawei, and laughter, so seldom heard in those days, filled the cottage. The rest of us sat around the table, having our first meal in two days. Yuying and I didn't tell them the whole horrible story, and everyone was sensitive enough not to ask any questions. When we bedded down, we shared the bigger room with Yuying's mother and nephew, who slept in one small bed. Jiahui and Yuying shared the other small bed, while I slept on the floor. Dawei had to sleep in his baby buggy. Yuying pulled down the bamboo-braided panel at the end of the stroller so that Dawei could stretch his long legs, although he didn't have any room to turn over.

The night was a long and restless one for all of us. Yuying got up many times to watch over Dawei. Jiahui couldn't stop crying in her sleep. I was exhausted but worried, half-awake and half-asleep. How were my parents and grandaunt? Did they have anything to drink and eat? My mother didn't have her blood pressure pills with her. How was she coping? A thousand questions played out in my head. If I dozed off, I'd awake with a start and get right back to worrying or, more often, keep on worrying as I even worried in my dreams.

The next day, Jiahui went back to her college dorm. Yuying was still on her extended maternity leave due to her C-section. I had to go to the Research Institute daily. The Red Guards and most of my colleagues kept their distance from me. Through their whispering, I learned that Senior Engineer Feng, my tutor, and his wife had together hanged themselves in their bathroom after a whole day of beating and torture.

Almost overnight it seemed we went from the purgatory of not knowing our fate to the hell of having to face it. The dark shelter on Qianliang Lane that the Institute assigned to me to live in was totally uninhabitable. It used to be a storage room for old and discarded furniture. To welcome us, local Red Guards poured so much sewage into the room that we could smell the offensive odor from a great distance. We had no choice but to return to my mother-in-law's small cottage as our only refuge.

Untold millions of innocent Chinese suffered from the unleashed terror of the Cultural Revolution. Many were beaten to death; others chose suicide. The first person in our extended circle of family and close friends to suffer such a fate was Uncle

Yuan, whom I had talked with less than a week before I learned of his death. In the hope of escaping persecution, Uncle Yuan, Auntie Cheng, and Lifen's two-year-old daughter had moved from their house to a small dwelling on nearby Shisha Lake. But they failed to avoid disaster.

Knowing that Uncle Yuan had owned and managed a private troupe and Auntie Cheng was the leading actress, a group of Red Guards from the Peking Opera circle searched for and finally found them. They were accused of absconding to avoid their deserved punishment. Those adolescent gangsters sheared Auntie Cheng's long hair, cut her colorful dresses and opera costumes into pieces, and ordered her to kneel in front of the gate holding a pair of embroidered shoes in her mouth. The scoundrels used opera props to beat Uncle Yuan. One Red Guard, who had been disciplined by Uncle Yuan because of his adulterous ways within the troupe, used a broadsword to break one of Uncle Yuan's legs. After the Red Guards confiscated everything they wanted, they smashed and burned everything else and then left, shouting revolutionary slogans as if they had just won a glorious battle and done a great deed for the country.

Auntie Cheng said she didn't even have the strength to stand up. She crawled into the small courtyard to find her husband lying flat on the ground and her granddaughter in the inner room, out of breath from crying for so long. At dawn the next day, Uncle Yuan, afraid of encumbering his family with more troubles, put on his gray tunic and trousers, an official Mao suit that he seldom wore. Despite his broken leg, he made his way west to Seeper Lake and drowned himself.

When the Red Guards returned and could not find Uncle Yuan, they accused Auntie Cheng of "covering up the escape of a class enemy." They ordered her to find Uncle Yuan immediately. Otherwise, the Red Guards threatened, she would be punished severely. Carrying her little granddaughter in her arms, Auntie Cheng went in search of her husband. She found him floating face down in the lake. She shuddered at the sight and collapsed. When Auntie Cheng came to, all she could hear was Lifen's daughter crying at the top of her voice. Auntie Cheng stared in horror at Uncle Yuan's body but didn't shed a tear. She told me later that she dared not cry. Her crying at that moment would indicate her sympathy for the enemy and her disloyalty to the Dictatorship of the Proletariat. When Uncle Yuan's body was pulled from the water onto the bank, Auntie Cheng said she felt just as dead as he was.

Another insufferable event to me was the death of Mr. Lao She. I had heard about it from Uncle Yuan in our very last meeting. Without telling Yuying or anyone, I went to the Taiping (Peaceful) Lake quite a few times in the summer and fall of 1966. I wanted to pay my last respects to our greatest writer, the "People's Artist." There was only a sprinkling of visitors around the lake every time I went there. Based on what I learned from some of them, earlier in the summer many red and black goldfish suddenly appeared in the lake and then scrolls, paintings, stoneware, porcelain, and antiques that people were getting rid of as part of the campaign against the Four Olds. And then floating corpses began to appear.

There was no way for me to locate the place where Mr. Lao She had drowned himself, but I did eventually gain some insight into why he chose this form of death when I read what Mr. Lao She wrote in his novel, *Four Generations Living Under One Roof*. "The torrent of the river flew fast, as if it had been impatient. Water sent out a little noise, calling him in a whisper.

Soon, he recalled the things in his lifetime; soon, he forgot everything. Drifting, drifting, drifting, he would drift into the sea, free, cool, clean, happy, and washing off the scarlet letter on his chest."

These grievous events made me even more desperate to devise a safe way to learn how my parents and grandaunt were doing. I was forbidden from returning to my home and didn't want to jeopardize my family by doing so. But sneaking a look at them from a distance would help relieve my worry and anxiety, so I decided to detour in their direction as I biked my way to and from the Institute. I didn't see them the first few days; then just before dawn one morning, as I rode toward their lane, I saw three figures sweeping the street. Nobody else was around. I slowed down to confirm their identity. Indeed, even at a distance, I could tell it was my grandaunt and parents.

My mother and grandaunt wore black scarves to hide their sheared heads. The three of them used long brooms made of twigs tied to a long handle to sweep the lane. My father wielded his broom vigorously and proficiently. I knew he was trying to do more sweeping so my mother and grandaunt would not have to do as much. Suddenly I saw two bicycles riding towards me. I stopped my bike, turned around, and pedaled hard in the opposite direction. As I looked backward, my vision blurred by tears, my loved ones gradually faded from view.

I was sad that I could not sweep the lane for them, yet I was much relieved that they were not only alive but also strong enough for manual labor. For the next several days, I regularly glimpsed them from a distance. Sometimes it was only my father sweeping by the day's first light. He moved the long broom back and forth with a firm rhythm and great energy, making the lane spotless. That was my father, always doing his best regardless of the circumstances. It was painful for me to be close enough to my family to see them but forbidden from returning to my home, separated from them by an invisible man-made barrier. In another sense, no barrier, no government however powerful and capricious, could ever keep our hearts from beating as one. Just as the silhouette of my father practicing his Tai Chi at dawn after being beaten almost senseless is seared on my memory, I will always remember my father's back as he vigorously swept our lane. His silhouette and back are vivid symbols that always enhance my courage and determination in my darkest hours and toughest times.

On September 15, the Neighborhood Committee informed me that we must move all our furniture from our old house because it was going to be converted into a Red Guard Reception Station. It was the first time in more than two weeks that we were allowed to go back to our home and possibly see our family. Yuying and I hurried to our house and saw many Neighborhood Committee activists busy decorating the front gate and each room to welcome the Red Guards from outside Beijing. Transportation, room, and board all over China were provided without charge to these henchmen of Mao, the vanguard of the Cultural Revolution.

To our surprise and shock, our family was nowhere to be found. An old lady told us that they had been moved to another house toward the end of our lane and gave me directions. Yuying said that she would clean out our belongings and urged me to try to find our family. "Be careful. Try to buy them some food," she told me.

Just around the corner, I bought some roasted chicken and other food and then headed back to our lane. My family's new residence was bigger than our old place, but housed seven tenant families. I knew some of them, especially the Dong family. Mr. Dong was a senior researcher on the history of Peking Opera. As soon as I walked into the courtyard, Mrs. Dong, an amiable lady in her fifties, came up to me and pointed to the end of her south wing. I nodded and bowed to thank her and hurried to the designated room.

At the door, I paused and asked softly, "Is anyone there?"

Surprised, my grandaunt slowly opened the door, looking at me as if she was seeing a ghost.

"It is Songsheng," I said quickly. "Don't worry. It's okay for me to be here."

It was only three o'clock in the afternoon. But it was so dark in the room that I could barely discern the old couple sitting on the bed.

"Is that Songsheng?" my mother asked. "Is it you?"

"Yes, it is me, Mother. Could we turn on the light?"

"No." My father pulled himself up. "Are you allowed to come here?"

"Yes. Our house will be used as a reception station. We are moving some furniture out of our rooms to a room next door."

"How is Dawei?" my mother couldn't wait to ask.

"He is fine in Yuying's mother's home. Rest easy. Jiahui and all of us are fine."

I opened my shoulder bag and took out the food. Sesame cakes, biscuits, fried bread sticks, and the roast chicken.

"What is that?" my father asked, looking suspiciously at the bird.

"Roast chicken," I said.

"You take it back. We will keep the rest," my father said almost inaudibly.

"Listen to what your father says," Mother chimed in. "We don't have the appetite anyway."

Father said, "We all must be extremely watchful, always on the alert. A roast chicken could very well indicate to the Red Guards that we have some money hidden somewhere. That could bring us another disaster."

Grandaunt put the roast chicken back into my bag. "As long as Dawei and you all are safe and sound, our minds are at rest."

"Grandaunt, you are a poor peasant by class origin. How could they treat you like this?" I looked at her sheared head resentfully.

"Because I am your mother's aunt," she replied. "There is no escaping fate."

"Sit down," my father told me. "I have something important to tell you."

My father said that during his interrogation and beating he had told the Red Guards about the inkstone.

"Father, why did you mention it?"

My mother answered quickly, "They smashed many pieces of fine Ming and Qing porcelain antiques. When your father saw them taking out the inkstone, he stopped them regardless of the consequences."

"I just told them the truth. The Red Guards kept tormenting your mother and me about where we had hidden all our gold and silver. I told them all those items had been donated to the government long ago. But we had something a thousand times more precious than the gold. The inkstone."

"To whom did you say that? Do you remember?"

"A man of average height with eyeglasses who seemed to be their leader."

"A thin, ugly fellow?"

"Yes, that's him."

"I saw him and an older man in a suit take the inkstone away."
I didn't want to tell my father anything more about the man I
knew to be Captain Wang.

"I told him and the other Red Guards that the inkstone
should be turned over to higher authorities," my father added.

My father had told us many times that he and Mother
intended to donate the inkstone to the Imperial Palace Museum
in the Forbidden City. He said that it belonged to the country
and should be returned to its original home. It had only been
entrusted to the care of the Chen family for a while. All my
siblings fully supported my parents' decision.

I urged them to eat the cakes and fried sticks before they got
cold while I went to find Yuying. With the help of some kind
neighbors, a few pieces of furniture had already been moved
into a room next door. We were told by the Neighborhood
Committee that we could use the room as our temporary
residence. When Yuying told my parents and grandaunt about
the unexpected news, they were just thrilled because soon
they could see Dawei again. We spoke of many other things. It
was so good to be able to converse again. My mother said, "As
long as the green hills are there, there's no need to worry about
firewood." My father repeated this in equivalent literary terms,
saying, "Where there is life, there is hope."

When the time came to say good-bye, I realized what a
turnaround had occurred. Yuying and I came here, trying to
console these three dear souls living in such reduced conditions.
Instead, they were the ones who cheered us up with their
magnanimity and unyielding faith in the future. After that first
reunion, my brothers and sisters and I took practically every
opportunity to visit our parents and grandaunt. Each of us

contributed part of our monthly pay to ensure their comfort and to keep them from worrying about maintaining basic living standards. We also supported Jiahui while she finished her education. The hard times made us stick together all the more.

During the Cultural Revolution, Special Case Teams investigated suspected people. These teams were composed of trusted Party members who interviewed people connected to the persons being investigated. One day, a thin man in his mid-40s from Jiyuan came to the little room where my parents lived. He showed my father a letter of introduction from the local government and ordered my father to write a confession exposing crimes committed by Uncle Zhang. My father couldn't refuse; he had to write something. So he finished several pages of his confession. The man came back, quickly read what my father had written, and yelled at my father because all he read were good things about Uncle Zhang. My father confessed that these were all he truly knew about Uncle Zhang. (We later learned that Uncle Zhang had done the same thing when he was ordered to write his confession about my father.)

The man, Mr. Song Chengjiang, eventually became a good friend of my father and the Chen family. Whenever he came to Beijing, he would visit my father, bringing some local specialties from Jiyuan. He told my father that he could have been promoted if my father had written something bad about Uncle Zhang, the highest-ranking government official in his hometown. Although he didn't get promoted, he was happy to get to know my father.

During those crazed days, the whole country became a sea of red. Complete walls facing the street and slogan-emblazoned signs on all public buildings and other surfaces were painted red to show Mao his nation's "red hearts." No other world leader developed such a passionate personality cult. A collection of his quotations, known in the West as *The Little Red Book*, became the most printed book in history with around six billion copies distributed (the number of bibles printed is estimated at five billion or less). Millions of statues, busts, pins, and other images of Mao were made and sold in China. There were loyalty songs and dances to Mao. His quotations and slogans were a part of virtually every conversation, every commercial exchange. Typical was one occasion when I went to a barber's shop for a haircut.

"Loyal to Chairman Mao, what can I do for you?" the young female shop clerk asked.

"Beating down Capitalist Roaders, I need a haircut."

"Serving the people, please take a number."

"Destroying the Four Olds, how long is the wait?"

"Never forgetting class struggle, about 20 minutes."

"Defeating Counter-revolutionaries, I'll take a number." Afraid that she might ask me my class origin I put an end to the conversation.

"Destroying the Five Black Castes, comrades, it is time for us to practice our loyalty song and loyalty dance to Chairman Mao," said one of the barbers suddenly.

All work stopped and everyone started singing "Forever Loyal to Chairman Mao" with their hands raised up and their heads bowed down toward a plaster bust of Mao. One man, half his head closely shaved and the other half full of hair, sang, danced, and bowed with evident affection. I couldn't believe that I was the only one who felt this exercise was ridiculous. Nevertheless, these displays were taken most seriously. A very old customer who couldn't do the song and dance was actually driven out of the barbershop. Such was the fervor of the times.

Change swept the nation. Relations between the central, provincial, and municipal governments deteriorated as the many factions and splinter groups contended for power. All over China, revolutionary tribunals replaced the governing bodies they had toppled. Those now in power exercised vigilance and zeal in persecuting anyone suspected of counter-revolutionary or reactionary sympathies. The national mandate was to Cleanse Class Ranks. Even minor offenders were often removed from their jobs and their homes and jailed. Many close friends of my parents were ordered to leave Beijing and return to their native towns and villages to be remolded through hard labor under surveillance.

Economic and financial change was also the order of the day. Many factories or other workplaces suspended operations or switched to part-time production. In September 1966, all state and private joint companies and plants were turned into completely state-owned enterprises. All fixed-interest payments to previous private owners were discontinued. My father had lost his fixed-interest payment as early as 1957, when he was labeled a Rightist. His nine years of interest-due payments were totally gone. My mother now officially lost her payments, although she had already stopped claiming them. My parents had long since given up all but the faintest hope that they would ever get their money back from the government. Money meant next to nothing to them. They just needed to keep their heads above water.

We learned about sweeping changes at my father's factory when Uncle Lee and his sons, Zhigong and Zhitong, unexpectedly showed up at my parents' home. I was busy putting in a stove and cooking bench for my mother and grandaunt when they arrived. We were all overjoyed to see these dear old friends.

It was the first time the small room had seen so many people. Uncle Lee held my father's hands. "Elder brother and sister, we have been so worried about all of you."

"We are but a few amongst millions of innocent, suffering people," my mother said. "How about your family?"

"We are fine, but these are risky times. I wish to report what a narrow escape your family had this summer." Uncle Lee told us how in June, Secretary Diao had been marked as a Capitalist Roader and removed from office at my father's old factory. Chairman Wu of the Labor Union became the interim manager of the plant. The Red Guards there wanted to raid my parents' house. Wu stopped them and even allowed Uncle Lee and a few old workers to patrol around our house during the worst of the terror. Then the Red Guards of the plant clamored to send my parents to their home village in Henan province for re-education. Wu again brought their plans to a halt. Uncle Lee said that after he hushed them, Wu asked a simple question. "Do you know who built the dormitory where you sleep at night? It was Professor Chen. People with a conscience wouldn't even think of bringing hardship to this good man." While I appreciated Uncle Lee and Wu intervening on behalf of my parents, in retrospect, I wish they hadn't. I can't imagine my parents faring worse had they been sent back to Yanmen for re-education than they suffered at the hands of the Institute's Red Guards.

Uncle Lee invited my parents to come to his house and stay there for a few days. My father declined, saying that he must sweep the lane everyday. Zhigong, Zhitong, and I all jumped in to say that we'd be happy to do it for him. But my father declined again and said that he really enjoyed sweeping the lane in the early morning fresh air, that it was just as good as doing his Tai Chi.

Uncle Lee and his two sons took over my work, completing the cooking bench and sheltering it somewhat from the weather with a light canopy. Later, with the permission of the Neighborhood Committee, they converted an empty storage closet, formerly a latrine, into a small study for my father. They even put in a small bed and desk in those 120 square feet. There Father could enjoy some sunshine and his reading and writing.

While many of the changes taking place were the direct result of Chairman Mao's orders, others spun out of his control. The ideological conflict fanned by Mao flared up dramatically when armed conflict broke out in the ranks of the Red Guards. Factionalism was rampant in China, making labeling problematic, but some historians call one major side the radicals and the other the conservatives. Perhaps a better way of looking at the fundamental difference was to see one sector fervidly supporting Mao's most revolutionary changes and another sector opposing them, but even that is an oversimplification. All sides claimed to be following the true path and accused their opponents of simply waving the red flag for show.

The rival Red Guards were supported, sometimes behind the scenes and sometimes openly, by contending factions within the Party and the military. Unbelievably, the fighting became fierce and involved full-scale military operations. Hundreds of thousands of Red Guards and innocent civilians in the line of fire were killed in less than two years.

Although the fighting was deadliest in Sichuan Province, perhaps the most dramatic conflict occurred in July of 1967 at Wuhan in the heart of China. There the Red Guards and sympathetic workers, known as the Wuhan Workers' General Headquarters, had attacked the municipal authorities with the goal of replacing them with a Revolutionary Committee, as was happening throughout China. Such tribunals, they believed, could better cleanse the nation of its internal enemies. The Wuhan government was supported by skilled workers and state and local party employees, called the Million Heroes. They were backed by the local Peoples' Liberation Army troops and their intransigent commander, General Chen Zaidao. Each faction numbered about 500,000. What developed in Wuhan and the rest of the nation during the spring and summer of 1967 was a burgeoning rebellion, a civil war really, with widespread bloodshed. In Wuhan about a thousand lives were lost.

Following the failure of the Workers' Headquarters faction to seize power, General Chen gave the Million Heroes arms and besieged the Workers' Headquarters faction. Zhou Enlai ordered General Chen to lift the siege, but Chen ignored him. China's two top troubleshooters for these matters were Xie Fuzhi, Minister of Public Security, and Wang Li, a key member of the Cultural Revolution Group. They ordered General Chen to abandon the Million Heroes and support the Workers' Headquarters. Again Chen refused. Indeed his forces detained and beat Xie Fuzhi and allowed the Million Heroes to kidnap Wang Li.

The government's response was predictable and immediate. Beijing sent three infantry divisions plus naval and air units to end the crisis. Facing these odds, Chen surrendered unconditionally, Wang Li and Xie Fuzhi were released, and the municipal authorities were arrested. General Chen was called back to Beijing for interrogation, criticism, and rehabilitation. Wang and Xie returned to the capital as heroes.

While the Wuhan Incident (called the July 20 Incident in China) was resolved in favor of the radicals, the writing was on the wall. Unless the power of the radicals was curbed, China's leaders faced the prospect of continuous social disorder, economic instability, and mounting casualties. Finally the level of domestic strife, disorganization, and factionalism threatened the Army itself. Only then did the Maoist leadership moderate the revolutionary agenda they had called for and begin to curtail the worst excesses of the Cultural Revolution. The Army took control of government offices, schools, and factories. More than 20 million Red Guards and other young people were sent to the countryside, supposedly to "learn from the peasants." The Cultural Revolution continued, but the zealotry, violence, and chaos that marked its beginnings began to abate.

I did not escape the political upheaval that shook my homeland. On July 14, 1967, a rally was held to criticize the Institute Director, one of the Ministry's top researchers. He was now labeled one of its biggest Capitalist Roaders. A Red Guard leader named Zheng, who everybody called "Big Gun," rebuked me as the Director's loyal follower and supporter. I was again named a Bourgeois Dutiful Son as well as a Reactionary Academic Authority. I had been carrying the Bourgeois Dutiful Son title for quite awhile by then, but since I was only 27 years old, how could I be an Academic Authority? No one ever explained that to me.

Despite my "distinguished" pedigree and several titles, I was considered a low-level offender. The heavyweight Capitalist Roaders, the most dangerous traitors and criminals, were sent to Qincheng Prison north of Beijing. At the time, very few people even knew where it was. Ordinary citizens were not allowed to approach its periphery. Mid-level enemies of the nation were sent to state, provincial, municipal, and prefectural jails, all of which were already full. New jails sprouted everywhere but still could not meet the demand that increased daily. Therefore, makeshift prisons called "cowsheds" were established in countless venues across the country. Instead of cattle, they housed so-called Monsters or Demons. Strictly speaking, we were not criminals under law, but we were treated as such. We lightweight offenders were called many names, including members of the Black Gangs or Five Black Castes, Traitors, Spies, or by no particular name at all. To qualify for the cowshed, you just had to be someone the radicals didn't like, and they certainly didn't like me.

I was not only the son of a Capitalist Rightist, I also did outstanding work. Most of the Red Guards, capable in politics but incompetent in work, were extremely jealous of my performance. They couldn't deal with the fact that my name often showed up on Institute and other publications while none of theirs did. Now they had their chance for revenge and gave vent to their long-simmering resentment. They also needed to imprison as many miscreants as possible so that they would not lose face by lagging behind other institutions. "Big Gun" Zheng was always the first to fire shots on the Demons, and he used the rally to execute his power of "proletarian dictatorship," the popular term at that time for throwing someone in prison. On the spot, I was detained and put into the cowshed.

The cowshed in our Institute was like the prison cells I had seen in movies. It was in the basement of our office building, dark, dank, and stuffy. There were already six prisoners in the cramped room. It took my breath away when I walked into that cell. It was clear that washing and laundry were not a regular part of the cowshed experience. Nobody talked to me and I was in no mood to talk to them. As in a stable, the floor was littered with straw to serve as our beds. I was not given anything to eat and drink. I lay down on the straw with a heavy heart, worrying about Yuying and Dawei, who must be wondering about me and fearful of my fate. Being separated from them was by far the worst effect of my jailing, but none of them was good.

We Demons were regularly tortured and humiliated. The Red Guards and their supporters organized Criticism and Struggle Meetings at which we were denounced. Either in a group or individually, we were ordered to stand on the stage where the Red Guards forced us into what was called the Jet Plane Position. They pushed our heads down as far as they could and then jerked our arms up at a 90-degree angle to our backs, like the two wings of a jet plane. We also had a wooden or metal sign hanging around our necks stating our titles. These signs could weigh 20 pounds or more and the twine that bound them to us would cut into our necks. After a three-hour rally in this position, it was impossible to stand upright. Some of us were practically paralyzed. It was from these rallies that I incurred lumbago, which has stayed with me to this day, a painful reminder of those mad days when justice was absent in China. I have forgotten the torture and hard labor I endured, but I can't wipe from my memory the deliberate humiliation I suffered. Death before dishonor has always been the spirit of intellectuals in China's 5,000-year history. I am a lucky survivor. But I admire Mr. Lao She, Senior Engineer Feng, Uncle Yuan, and countless others who chose death over further disgrace.

Demons also suffered financially. We worked harder than before but our salaries were immediately cut. Instead of my regular monthly pay of 55 yuan, I would now get 12 yuan. I normally spent that amount just for my lunches every month. With only 12 yuan for all my monthly meals and necessities, such as toothpaste and soap, I had to plan my expenditures very carefully. Every day, each of us, no matter how old or young, well or sick, had to put in eight hours of heavy and dirty work. And our guards always made us do it under the harshest conditions possible. We weren't allowed to use wheelbarrows, for instance, to carry heavy or bulky items; we had to move them using brute force or make many trips. In the evening, we had to confess our crimes in writing and then study Mao's works and the *People's Daily* until we were allowed to go to bed.

We were not permitted to communicate with our families. We were dehumanized and demonized. Little Red Guards in primary schools threw stones and trash on us to express their hatred of Demons. In the dining hall, we bought our meals from a separate window beneath a sign saying Monsters and Demons. We were not allowed to eat in the dining hall.

The only easy time for me in the cowshed was working in the Institute's vegetable garden. That was supposed to be part of remolding the bourgeois intellectuals into proletarian intellectuals. Since the Institute's proletarian intellectuals were so busy in their endless campaigns to promote the Cultural Revolution, we Demons were ordered to take their places in the kale yard. Laboring there, I felt like a fish in water. From the time I was four years old, my father had inspired in me a love of working the earth and producing food.

The regular workers in the Institute were amazed by my proficient agricultural skills. We soon became good friends.

They kept me abreast of news from inside and outside the Institute. They told me that Captain Wang, who had led the Red Guards in thrashing Senior Engineer Feng and his wife and had beaten my parents and raided our home, had been promoted. He had divorced his previous wife and married the daughter of a high party official. Now he was the Vice Chairman of the Revolutionary Committee of the Research Academy, the Ministry of Machinery Building Industries' highest authority, with oversight of all the country's research institutes.

After six months of cruelty, deprivation, and hard labor in the cowshed, the lunar New Year was approaching and the rules were relaxed a bit. All prisoners were permitted to write letters to their families, although they were censored. We were also relocated to new quarters, given three days' rest, and allowed to see our family members. No words could possibly describe my excitement at the prospect of seeing my wife and son. I got up early that morning, had my cellmate give me a haircut, took a thorough bath in the Institute's public bathroom, dressed in my cleanest cotton-padded jacket and trousers, and waited expectantly in my new cell. Our new quarters were in the deserted printing building's large workshop, which was temporarily divided by partitions. We used discarded type cases and shelves to construct our beds. In my comparatively spacious living space, I built a huge bed, half of which was for sleeping and the other half for my clothing, books, and sundries.

It was getting to be lunchtime. Quite a few of my cellmates had already welcomed their family visitors. I became anxious and restless. Suddenly, I heard the cell guard calling, "Chen Songsheng, you have visitors."

I dashed out of my cell and saw a little boy with a long cotton jacket running toward me, shouting, "Candies for you. Candies for you."

I took off my eyeglasses that were all covered with tears and found out how big my little boy had grown in my absence. He wasn't just walking, he was running and talking! And he was only 19 months old. I was so proud. Behind him, Yuying shouted, "Dawei, call him Daddy. He is your Daddy."

I ran forward to pick Dawei up and hold him tightly in my arms. He showed me a packet of sweets and murmured in my ear, "Daddy, candy."

With one arm holding Dawei and the other clutching Yuying, whose tears flowed freely, I could not find the words to express my joy. I just kept consoling Yuying, "Don't cry. Don't cry. Look how much stronger I am than before." We went into my cell and sat on my bed. Yuying cleaned my eyeglasses with her handkerchief. I couldn't take my eyes off my wife and son.

"Daddy, candy." Dawei took out many colorful candies from the packet.

"No, these candies are for Dawei," I said.

"No, you," Dawei insisted, peeled the wrapper off a candy, and put it in my mouth.

"Okay. Daddy takes one. Dawei takes one. Mommy takes one." Dawei laughed.

"You have been treated so poorly." Yuying began to cry again.

"Don't cry." I handed her back her handkerchief.

"I can cry in your presence. I don't allow myself to do it in front of others."

"How are Mother, Father, and Grandaunt?"

"They are fine. With the permission of the Neighborhood Committee, Grandaunt moved to our home so that she could give me a hand taking care of Dawei."

"Oh, wonderful. Does Mother now do the cooking for Father?"

"Yes, sometimes," Yuying said. "We all see them often and cook them more food and dumplings than they could use in a week. But..."

"But what?" I asked.

"They are so worried about you."

I didn't know how to reply, and the lull in our conversation was interrupted by one of my cellmates handing me my mess tin.

"Lao Chen, here is your holiday lunch. Hey, who is this fine-looking young man?"

I introduced him to Yuying and then said, "This is my son."

He looked at us admiringly, then a pained look shot across his face. He sighed and went away quietly.

"He is a senior engineer who once worked in the Kuomintang's military plants," I whispered. "His wife divorced him. She and his son and daughter are all in the US."

Yuying opened the aluminium lunch box. "Braised pork!"

"See, you must tell our parents I am doing fine here."

"That's hard for me to believe. If so, why did you ask me to bring you this?" Yuying took out a large can of fried hot peppers.

I didn't answer her. I could afford braised pork once a month. I needed the salty hot peppers to make the corn meal that was our staple diet more palatable. I needed to eat as much as I could to survive the hard labor. Beside the peppers, I had asked Yuying to bring me my thick underpants, which had 17 patches on them.

When the Red Guards had seen them, during the raid on our home, they had sneered at me for pretending to be poor. I had wanted to show them those patches with pride in the thrift that was such a tradition in my family.

The two hours of allotted visiting time elapsed quickly, though Yuying and I still had a lot to talk about. Yuying hadn't said a word about her own tough lot. I knew that to support Dawei and Grandaunt, her 56 yuan monthly pay was quite a stretch.

"Here is some petty cash for you," Yuying said handing me 20 yuan.

This simple gesture made my heart ache. "How can you do that? I already feel conscience-stricken by not being able to send money home."

"Your 12 yuan can't possibly be enough for you. Take it," Yuying persisted.

"If you want me to be happy," I insisted, "use the 20 yuan to buy Dawei and yourself some new winter clothing."

"We are wearing new clothing, can't you see?" Yuying showed off her coat and Dawei's long, cotton jacket. "I altered your old overcoat to make new clothes for us."

"So stylish and well-tailored," I said.

"Trust me; I have not been so pampered in the past that I can't cope with hardship now, as long as you are okay." Yuying looked at me with deep love.

"You should also trust me. I'll be fine. I'll be fine."

I saw Yuying and Dawei to the front gate of the cowshed.

"Mommy, don't go." Dawei cried. "I want Daddy."

Those words and the look in my son's eyes stay with me to this moment. I resolved to stifle the indignation that coursed through me and to endure my daily humiliations—not for me, but for Dawei and Yuying, and the rest of my family. I had no idea when I would see them next. As it turned out, it was a full year.

The leadership's attempts to moderate the worst effects of the class struggle and the endless political campaigns and the dispersal of the Red Guards to the countryside reduced the widespread disorder, but China continued to suffer, especially economically. Industrial output fell 12% between 1966 and 1968. Mao didn't like unreformed intellectuals, but he needed them. Without them, many things simply could not be done. By mid-February 1969, Mao issued instructions about his new Re-education and Offering a Way Out policies for China's intellectuals.

Offering a way out? None of us in the cowshed believed it to be possible and couldn't understand it. What did it mean? Our doubts and suspicions were cleared up when seven cellmates and I were called to the cowshed office. The revolutionary officer first read the document issued by the Central Committee of the Chinese Communist Party and the Central Cultural Revolution Group. Then, he solemnly announced that in order to carry out the new policies, we were free to go back home. It was February 14, 1969, three days before the lunar New Year. Since I was imprisoned on July 14, 1967, I had been in jail for 19 months. The term "liberation" was officially used to refer to releasing the Demons from the cowsheds. When Peiping was liberated in 1948, I had no clue what liberation meant. Now, I understood it. I felt it. Liberation meant I could go back home to my family. That was all I wanted. Nothing more.

Using my bed sheet, I packed up all my things and departed within 10 minutes. I didn't know Yuying's work unit phone number or the public phone station number in our neighborhood. I jumped on the public bus heading toward our home. When I arrived breathless at the fifth floor, I knocked on the door, calling softly, "Grandaunt, I am back home. I am back home."

Grandaunt opened the door. She gulped a mouthful of air and I thought her eyes would pop out. She couldn't even utter a word.

"Don't be afraid. Don't panic. I am alone and everything is fine." I helped her into the bedroom, surprised to find my father and mother there. Father stood up from the bed, asking, "What has happened?"

"Nothing. I am back home. I am liberated."

"Liberated?" my mother, holding Dawei in her arms on the bed, asked.

"Yes. I am allowed to come back home as a free man."

My father and grandaunt fell back in their chairs and were numb with shock, so astonished they were speechless.

My mother quickly came to her senses, "Dawei," she called. "Look at your Daddy. This is your father."

After a year's separation, Dawei didn't recognize me right away. However, he let me take him in my arms and kiss his cheek.

Grandaunt added two more dishes to the dinner she was preparing. Father opened a bottle of red wine. All of us sat around the table, waiting for Yuying. Finally, I heard a sound at our front door. I opened the door and saw Yuying carrying her bicycle upstairs. I didn't dare call her. I went downstairs and quietly took her bicycle from her. She raised her head and opened wide her big eyes. "You?"

"Me! I'm home. Let me carry your bicycle."

All at once, she fell, rather than sat down, on the stairs, sobbing. I put the bicycle down, sat beside her, and cuddled her in my arms.

She took out her handkerchief, wiping her tears. I saw that it was the same white handkerchief I had seen in the cowshed, only she had embroidered two red roses on it.

"It is too good to be true," she said. I stood up and helped her to rise.

She pointed at our front door. "Let's wait a moment. I don't want them to see me crying."

What a wonderful dinner we had that night. We had lots of catching up to do. Our dinner went on until very late. Grandaunt put Dawei to bed in another room. Yuying warmed up the dishes over and over until Father and I had finished the whole bottle of red wine.

During our long conversation, I learned that the previous year Jiahui had become engaged to Gao, her classmate in medical school. They were assigned to a people's commune clinic in Heshui County, Gansu Province. They delayed their wedding until they came back to Beijing from Gansu for no other reason than to enjoy the paid home leave as singles. Married couples weren't entitled to this treatment. They took tractors to get to the county town of Heshui and then took a bus to get to the capital city of Lanzhou. After 36 hours on the train, they got to Beijing. Hardly had Jiahui entered my parent's small room when she burst into tears. My parents scarcely recognized her; she was skinny and pale, and her big eyes looked even bigger.

Sitting close to my mother, tears welled up in their eyes. Jiahui was the youngest child of my family. My parents and siblings loved her so much that they finally convinced her to enroll in the Beijing Second Medical Institute simply because its graduates were normally assigned jobs in Beijing. With similar Five Lowest Castes family backgrounds, Jiahui and Gao were sent to a remote barren village 1,600 kilometers from Beijing. They lived in an adobe shelter and ate a steady diet of salted vegetables, leaves and ground-up vegetable matter—corn cobs, chaff, and other plant waste—that in normal times might be fed to farm animals. Local peasants developed goiters and other ailments because of malnutrition and the lack of iodine. Jiahui didn't dare speak of her bitter hardships with my parents, but she did share them with Yuying.

The two of them were just like sisters. Even now, Jiahui still calls Yuying "Sister Ying" rather than sister-in-law. Yuying helped my sister get married by arranging a simple family dinner in my parents' small room. Jiahui's wedding was the simplest and poorest in our family. No feast. No guests. A few days later, the newlyweds tore themselves away from home and returned to Gansu. My mother didn't feel like eating or sleeping. It was eight years before Jiahui, Gao, and their two daughters were transferred to the city of Baoding, my mother's hometown. Three years later, they came back to Beijing.

Nineteen sixty-nine was the year of the rooster. My Father was 72 years old. I would turn 30 in August. Mao declared the Cultural Revolution officially over in 1969, although historians generally don't consider it ended until the Gang of Four was arrested in 1976.

The Cultural Revolution that spawned the Red Guards was many things. It was the reflection of a power struggle for control of the nation, pitting an increasingly doctrinaire Mao and his cohorts against more pragmatic Party and government officials, such as Liu Shaoqi, Zhou Enlai, and Deng Xiaoping.

It was certainly the most perverse and concerted campaign that a nation has ever waged upon itself. While bloodbaths in Rwanda, Bosnia, and Cambodia may turn the stomach, they were miniscule in scale and duration compared with what happened in China. Conservative estimates place the death toll from the Cultural Revolution at 30 million. Nothing will ever wash the blood, the horror, the waste, the damage, the lying, the demise of morality, the national stain from that decade.

While millions of my countrymen did not survive the beginning of the Cultural Revolution, all the Chens did. After the Red Guards invaded our home on August 27, 1966, we survived 902 atrocious days. We were relieved to still be alive and together. We just didn't know what might come next.

Chapter 12

FIGHT TO LIVE

1969-1971
Beijing, Helan Mountains, Ningxia Province, China

ONLY AFTER I WAS RELEASED from the cowshed did I learn that Yuying had been transferred from the furniture design department to an outdoor manual labor job at the Beijing Lumber Plant where she worked. Her original job was appropriate for Yuying, a graduate of China Central Arts and Crafts Institute. Her new task, however, was to select usable wood from the scraps, an assignment she was given solely because she was the wife of a Monster in the cowshed. Yuying had to work in all kinds of weather, from scorching summers to withering winters. The Red Guards in her plant ordered her to expose "crimes" committed by me and my family in exchange for better treatment. She categorically refused, saying she would rather continue her outdoor job for the rest of her life than tell a lie.

In order to save money to support the family, Yuying rode her old bicycle on the hour-long trip to the lumber plant every day, even in the harshest of weather, hard rain and heavy snow. Often it was dark when she left in the morning and dark when she returned at night. And I was sad to learn that on many evenings, it also stayed dark inside our apartment. In those days, formerly friendly neighbors would gang up on families of the Five Black Breeds to show their scorn for China's enemies and their offspring. Encouraged by tall Yan, who had been my student and the dunce in the English training class at my Institute, teenagers in our building, wearing Red Guard armbands, frequently broke the electrical switch box outside our door. When lights were on in every window in our neighborhood, our apartment was dark. I was overcome with grief and remorse when I learned of the many ordeals Yuying suffered because she was my wife.

"Often when I came home at night, sometimes pedaling hard against a cold wind, the young Red Guards would throw dirt and stones on me and even douse me with buckets of sewage." Yuying took out the handkerchief with two roses. I took it from her, gently wiping away her tears.

"I'd be soaked to the skin with sweat from my ride and completely sopping on the outside from the sewage. All five flights of the stairway up to our apartment were pitch-black," she continued.

"When I put down the bike, I'd have to find the keyhole in the dark. After I opened the door and entered our room ...." Yuying sighed deeply, then suddenly reached for the handkerchief and put it to her mouth, bursting into tears in my arms.

I held her tightly as sobs shook her body.

After a time, she said, "I'd see . . . ," and then she couldn't continue. She lowered her head to hide her tears.

"I, I'd see," she choked back a sob and tried again. "I'd see Grandaunt holding Dawei, sitting still by the window in the dark. Then I'd hear Dawei's fearful little voice calling, 'Mommy, Mommy.'"

Tears spilled down my face. Yuying took off my eyeglasses, and now *she* used the handkerchief to wipe away *my* tears. Together, our tears made the two roses look even redder.

"When I struck a match to light the candle, I could see in the dim light the trail of tears on Dawei's little face as he stretched his arms toward me." When Yuying told me this, I was flooded with a feeling of helplessness. I couldn't even protect my own son.

In silence, Yuying and I held each other on our bed for a long time, anguish wracking our hearts. We cried a lot in those days. We were denied so many rights and forms of release and ways of expressing ourselves as human beings. Crying was one of the few we had left.

The Red Guards at my Institute often raided our apartment at night while I was in the cowshed, supposedly to check on whether we were hiding any strangers. They took away our "bourgeois" belongings, and what they couldn't carry off, they locked in one of our bedrooms. Yuying, Grandaunt, and Dawei had to sleep on the floor because their confiscated beds had spring pads, which made them "bourgeois." Of course, we continued to be charged rent for that locked room.

After paying for rent, electricity, water, coal, and food, Yuying used the little remaining from her 55 yuan monthly pay on Dawei and me. She was so thrifty that when she bought oranges for Dawei and Grandaunt, she saved all the peels. A big basket of dried orange peels was worth one yuan at Chinese medicinal herb shops. Since I was paid only 12 yuan a month, barely enough to pay for my corn cake meals, Yuying tried to supplement my diet. Once she sent me some sausages, which I never received. She learned later that they were confiscated by the Red Guards. Fried and salty hot peppers were the only thing she was allowed to send me through the cowshed gatekeeper. While I loved corn cakes, a steady diet of them was pretty bland and the peppers made them much better. Whenever I received a big jar of peppers, even the jar was dear to me. I touched it as if I were touching Yuying's hands and warming her heart.

As the common people suffered, the political power struggles at the top remained brutal and consumed our leaders. The death of millions of innocent people was trivial as long as the proletarian dictatorship prevailed. At the Ninth Party Congress, the first in a dozen years, the great achievements of the Cultural Revolution were affirmed and acclaimed. Mao proclaimed that such revolutions should be repeated every seven or eight years. The Congress denounced Mao's previous top deputy and heir apparent, Liu Shaoqi, as a traitor yet again, and Lin Biao was formally written into the Constitution as Mao's designated successor and close comrade-in-arms. Lin, a superior military leader and later Defense Minister, was Mao's most important ally in the Cultural Revolution. But Lin helped Mao in other ways beyond his control of the military. Lin had earlier compiled Mao's *Little Red Book* of quotations to re-educate the People's Liberation Army and contributed significantly to building Mao's personality cult.

As Lin reached these lofty heights, Liu Shaoqi fell from power and became the highest-ranking victim of Mao, who was jealous and vengeful and never liked seeing Liu's photo as China's President side by side with his photo as the CCP's Chairman in the *People's Daily*. Liu's pragmatic approach to economic matters conflicted with Mao's radicalism, and Mao came to regard Liu as his chief rival. For a brief period after the disaster of the Great Leap Forward, the pragmatists, led by Liu and Deng Xaoping, had operated the levers of government. But Mao used the Cultural Revolution to destroy or banish his enemies, not only Liu and Deng, but also their supporters. He was an absolute master at political infighting and setting factions against each other.

Liu was assailed as China's biggest Capitalist Roader, followed by Deng Xiaoping. Lin Biao replaced Liu as First Deputy Chairman. Liu was soon placed under house arrest and purged from the party. Then he disappeared. He had actually been removed to a tiny cell in Kaifeng, Henan Province. Tortured, sick with long-term diabetes and then pneumonia, and denied all treatment and medication, Liu died sometime in October 1969, covered in his excrement and vomit. The former president of China was promptly cremated under the name of Liu Weihuang. Cause of death was recorded as "illness" and his occupation listed as "unemployed." It was years before his family learned of his death and a decade before the Chinese people were told. Of course, no details were provided.

As 1970 unfolded, Mao's whims and paranoia and the tyrannical acts of the Gang of Four continued to wreak havoc upon China. The Chairman's latest loony idea was to mobilize the whole nation to "dig deep holes" in preparation for war against the revisionist socialist countries headed by the Soviet Union. The holes, he "reasoned," would also prove useful in times of natural disasters and for storing grain.

All members and friends of the Chen family, even my old father, did our duty and began digging holes at random locations. These large pits started to show up everywhere—on the small lane by our parents' old house, in front of the office building at our Institute, on hospital grounds, in shopping areas, and even under Tiananmen Square. Cement and bricks were in short supply. Without any research, planning, or technical support, countless holes and tunnels all over China simply collapsed or otherwise became hazards.

The hole on the grounds of our Institute was soon full of stagnant water. The "shore" around it was constantly giving way, expanding the pond. Instead of a shelter to shield people against enemy bombs, it became a refuge for wild birds. The soon-polluted waters stank up the whole area around the Institute and became a breeding ground for swarms of mosquitoes and other insects. We later had to transport many truckloads of dirt to fill in that pond, which became a huge patch of sunflowers. Our Institute spent eight months and tens of thousands of man-hours, and all we got out of it was a bumper crop of sunflower seeds. Nobody seemed to care. Everybody got paid by the government anyway regardless of whether anything was actually accomplished.

China also had real achievements that year. On April 24, it launched its first space satellite, "The East Is Red," making China the fifth member of the world's select Space Club. The satellite name refers to the first line of a popular song in China in praise of Mao.

For me, however, the most significant event of 1970 was the birth, two days after the launch, of Yuying's and my second son, Lei, at the Beijing Friendship Hospital. Yuying had to endure another C-section to give birth to another big boy, almost nine pounds. While we were trying to locate the satellite in the sky and hear it broadcast "The East Is Red" in Yuying's ward, I decided the first name of our second son would be Lei.

Lei means thunder in Chinese. I saw the satellite as a thunderous statement. But more importantly, I wanted Lei to be a harbinger of the tremendous thunder we needed to shake the chains and shackles off our bodies and our souls, the thunder that brings the dawn. Lei was such a sweet boy. Very rarely did he cry, but when he did, it was truly like thunder. I took that as a good sign.

By that time, the Uselessness of Academic Study theory permeated the whole country. Curiously, however, after 581 days of imprisonment in the cowshed—essentially for being educated—I was allowed to pursue my advanced studies on foundry technologies and development.

I studied as if I were on a mission. The Institute neither encouraged me, an unreformed intellectual, in my efforts nor did it try to stop me. It had to fulfill its quota of translating and publishing research papers to introduce foreign advanced metalworking technologies to China. That was the Ministry's mandate and mission, and I was helping to do it. As a result, I was one of the leaders in publishing research reports, technical books, and translations. Many of them are still popular and can be Googled on the Internet under my Chinese name.

It took me 17 years of hard work to go from being an English major college student to a foundry researcher and a board director of the Beijing Foundry Society. During my first months at the Institute, I forced myself to study basic metalworking technologies and foundry practices, subjects in which I originally had no interest at all. I needed this basic knowledge, however, to do my job effectively. By that time, I had come to believe that I was born to be a literary scholar. I loved language and literature and considered myself a good teacher. I liked to picture myself at a university. I yearned to read great books and maybe someday to write one. I had no intention of becoming a foundry engineer. However, the more I learned and the deeper I got into the subject, the more I became attracted to the field.

I studied the bronze castings from the Warring States and the Spring and Autumn periods in the Palace Museum of the Forbidden City. I remembered going with my father to Liulihe Township outside of Beijing, where many bronzes of the Yan State during the Western Zhou Dynasty had been cast. I was a fast learner, especially once I got interested in a subject, and found it exciting to discover how metalworking had developed. Very quickly I learned about casting processes, molds, and dies. What I knew about foreign foundry technologies put to shame the primitive casting production lines in the factories under the Ministry. Indeed, even our ancestors had achieved better results than we were now. We basically still used the outdated sand-casting process to deal with more and more complicated jobs. When I finished my dissertation, "On the Orientation and Emphases of China's Foundry Industry," I mailed it to the China Foundry Association.

To my surprise and delight the Association responded with letters to my Institute and me, inviting me to address its annual conference in Jiaxing, Zhejiang Province. It was a difficult decision for the officers of the Institute's Revolutionary Committee. On the one hand, they were reluctant to let an "unrehabilitated intellectual" like me go to the conference. On the other hand, this opportunity was an honor to them as leaders of my work unit and to the Institute. After weighing the pros and cons, they allowed me to go and informed me that my normal monthly salary of 55 yuan was resumed. I was thrilled! The idea of my luck turning, even a bit, gave me hope for my future. If I continued to do good work and bring credit to the Institute, perhaps I could make a name for myself in this field and help my nation grow stronger.

On August 25, 1970, right after I read my paper at the China Foundry Society conference, I was approached by my colleague who had accompanied me to Jiaxing. I thought he was going to congratulate me, but, instead, he told me that I must leave the conference ahead of schedule, go back to Beijing, and prepare to go to the May Seventh Labor School near the Helan Mountains in Ningxia Province bordering Mongolia. As if awakening from a dream, I was brought back to cruel reality. I had been so naïve daydreaming about my future. I had no future. I was just a tool, put to use when needed and thrown away when it was not. I didn't know much about Ningxia, but what I did know wasn't good. The land was dry, rocky, barren, and uninhabited for good reason. How would I tell my parents and Yuying about being banished to the desolate deserts of the wild northwest?

May Seventh Cadre Schools were a perfect example of the Chinese saying "Advertise wine; sell vinegar." Despite their high-sounding names, they were nothing more than labor camps for millions of educated Chinese whom the leaders sought to "re-educate" through hard labor. They replaced the cowsheds, which were too hard to manage and were not a legal part of the justice system. Now everything was legal and controlled. All the "students" in these "schools" took only one "class." It was called hard labor. While most of these camps were called Cadre Schools, a few were designated Labor Schools, and their inmates were treated more harshly. That was the case with my new "school."

This turn of events was no surprise to Yuying, since she always anticipated bad things happening to me and my family. It was easy for her to pack my big wooden crate. I didn't have much to pack, and my stuff from the cowshed was all ready to use the second time. Yuying and I went to see my parents with Dawei and Lei, whom my parents would care for while Yuying saw me off.

My mother was quite worried but not Father. To set my mother's mind at rest, my father pointed to a map of China as he was speaking.

"Look, here is Ningxia. Here are the Helan Mountains. The Yellow River irrigates vast farmlands and benefits millions of people there. As the saying goes, 'The Yellow River spawns a hundred disasters, but always smiles on Ningxia.'" My father inevitably found something hopeful, even in the most desperate situations.

"Don't worry about Dawei and Lei," my mother said as she cuddled the boys on her bed. "We'll look after them. You must take good care of yourself." I smiled half-heartedly at my mother and wondered when I would see my parents again.

Because I had been chosen to address the annual conference of the China Foundry Association, I wasn't part of a large contingent of camp laborers that had left Beijing earlier. I was given a one-way train ticket to Yinchaun, Ningxia Province, leaving September 7, 1970. Yuying and I got up early that day. Grandaunt had already cooked our breakfast. I tied my big wooden crate to the backseat of my bicycle. Yuying and I walked all the way to the Beijing railway station, arriving there early. Yuying bought me some Beijing specialties, candied fruits. We still had a lot to say but didn't know where to start.

"As Mother said, don't worry about us. Take good care of yourself." Yuying repeated variations of this several times.

"As I said, don't worry about me. Take good care of yourself, our parents, Grandaunt, and especially Dawei and Lei." I also repeated myself.

"Take this with you." Yuying took out the handkerchief with two red roses.

"The same handkerchief." I took hold of it tenderly.

"Yes, the same handkerchief," Yuying said, "and the same two red roses."

I softly caressed the roses.

"When you see the two red roses, imagine us. We will always be together regardless of the distance between us," Yuying added, her eyes filled with tenderness and love.

I put the handkerchief in my inside pocket and after a long embrace and one last look, I boarded the train. It pulled away slowly, and I watched Yuying wave at me until I could no longer see her.

The train was so crowded that there was hardly room to breathe. As soon as the train passed over Badaling Mountain, where the Great Wall was situated, all I could see was continuous prairie and then continuous desert. The Mongolian grasslands were endless, but surprisingly I saw no flocks or herds and not a single human being. The farther west the train went, the colder it became. After 26 hours, the train finally reached Yinchuan.

Dilapidated and rustic, the tiny station didn't look like the only train station of a provincial capital. But this was far out in the sticks, as they say in America, almost literally a one-horse town. I walked out of the station, carrying my wooden crate. Xiao Ding, whom I knew from my Institute, stood by a tractor and greeted me from afar. He was an employee of the labor camp, not a prisoner. A young man of medium height and quiet demeanor, Xiao Ding was very bright. In the after-work English class I taught at the Institute, he was one of my best students. After he helped me get my wooden crate onto the trailer for me to sit on, he turned the ignition and with a frightful racket and belching smoke, we were off to the camp.

The tractor was a riding-type, walking tractor, a popular means of transportation in the countryside. Its trailer could carry coal, cement, stone, bricks, and a dozen people. Within 10 minutes, we had left the city limits and made our way on a narrow dirt road that ended all too soon. We continued over rough terrain littered with rocks and boulders toward the distant mountains.

"Those are the Helan Mountains," Xiao Ding said, pointing ahead. "Helan means steed in Mongol."

"So high," I exclaimed.

"The peak is more than 3,500 meters high."

"Wow!"

"Even a brilliant military leader like General Yue Fei couldn't penetrate these mountains in his battles against the Jurchen army." Xiao Ding prided himself upon his historical knowledge.

It was hard to talk over the din of the tractor, so we fell into silence for the rest of the trip. I was awed by the beauty of the layered landscape, the lovely desolation, the mountains that really did resemble a herd of wild horses.

Just before dark, we finally reached camp. If I hadn't seen dozens of large tents on the field, I wouldn't have believed that this was our "school." Xiao Ding told me he'd be one of my tent mates, led me into a large khaki-colored tent, found me an empty "bed" in the corner, and prepared a bunch of straw to serve as my mattress. The beds were simply wooden boards supported by four adobe blocks. The tents had a rigid metal framework and metal bars to support the canvas roof. There was no electricity. Each tent had two kerosene lamps, one hanging from the ceiling and one at the entrance.

When my six other tent mates came back from the field, they greeted me warmly. They were all my mates from the Institute cowshed. A resonant, loud and clear trumpet call interrupted our greetings. Xiao Ding told me that meant it was dinner time. All the camp laborers, with our identical aluminum meal boxes and spoons, went to a big dining tent to get our food, then returned to our own tents to eat. All the cooking was done in the open outside the dining tent. My first meal in camp was hoecakes with soy sauce soup. Corn meal was our main staple—steamed or baked in different shapes and called, among many other names, hoecakes and corn pone. Maybe I inherited my taste for corn meal from my father; I just loved it. To my pleasant surprise, the 12 yuan we paid for food each month allowed us to take as many hoecakes as we liked. My tent mates were amazed that I could eat as many as 16 hoecakes at a sitting. To tell the truth, it was corn meal that saved me and supported me through the long and harsh days in the camp. After dinner, each of us was given a wash basin of cold water from the water wagon that we had to ration carefully to be able to brush our teeth and wash both in the evening and the next morning.

Back in the tent on a full stomach, my tent mates told me of their experiences in camp so far. To a person, they felt they were better off than when we were in the cowshed except for the long distance from loved ones and the indeterminate sentence. Every one of us wondered how long we would have to be students at this "school." Were the rumors true that we had been sent to the desert to work until we died? We didn't talk long that night. My mates were tired from their long day's work, and one by one they dropped off to sleep. While all of them were dead to the world on their beds, I hardly slept a wink. The wind drumming on the canvas blew me back to Dawei, Lei, Yuying, Grandaunt, and my parents. I wondered when I would see them next. And then I thought, "What if I never see them again?" My first night in camp was not restful.

My first full day in camp, however, was strangely peaceful. Autumn was gorgeous in the foothills of the Helan Mountains. The sky was so high, the land so wide. The sun was bright and the breeze gentle. Our job was to dig up the salt marsh alkali flats that stretched for miles. They had never before been cultivated, and we were to prepare them for planting. The soil was so hard that one strike of my heavy pick barely made an impression. After four hours of hard digging, my hands were bloody from broken blisters, and I had succeeded in turning over only a few square feet of earth.

Once the tough crust was broken, the loam beneath was swarthy and rich. A local farmer, who served as a camp instructor, told us that the toughest part of the job was breaking that hard surface. With the Yellow River nearby, irrigation was not a problem, so all we had to do next spring for a good harvest would be to plough and sow. I felt a much greater sense of purpose after hearing this from the old farmer. Field labor on those salt flats under a hot sun was rough, no doubt about it. We worked up to 16 hours a day, but it was not the end of the world, and I always liked working the earth when I could envision the food it would produce.

A bugle call roused us laborers punctually at 6:30 each morning. We'd get ready for breakfast and fall into formation for denunciation by the camp director. When the bugle calls were repeatedly sounded day or night, it meant that one of Chairman Mao's "Supreme Instructions" had been delivered by a cavalryman, who had come from a radio station some distance away, and we should assemble immediately. The camp director would read aloud Mao's instructions, which were often just one or two sentences.

By the end of autumn, it was definitely getting colder, especially after the sun went down. Our tents wouldn't shield us against winter's frigid temperatures, icy blasts, and drifting snow. We were ordered to build our own cabins. In contrast with our previous cramped prison cells, our cabin was huge because we had all the land we wanted, lots of loess for making bricks, and unlimited labor. Using rigid metal frames and cross bars, we built the cabin structure and added a thatched roof, which we covered with a thick layer of clay. We mixed mud and water, shoveled it into wooden forms to make bricks, and let them dry in the sun for several days. The adobe bricks were simple, cheap, and durable. To help shield us against the cold, wind, and snow, we laid down a double course of bricks for all walls. Also using the mud bricks, each of us built a large bed, and we had a big camp stove in the center of our cabin to keep us warm. We had a good supply of coal since the labor camp also owned a small coal mine nearby. By recalling some of Yuying's furniture designs, I built myself a mud brick desk and cabinet. Each one of us enjoyed our own private space with a window close by.

As the 1971 Spring Festival approached, I missed my dear ones more than ever. How much fun I would have with my boys during the holidays if only I could be at home. Images of Dawei and Lei flashed before me continually. I couldn't put them out of my mind. But, of course, we weren't allowed to go back home or receive family visitors. Thankfully, we were allowed to send and receive letters and parcels. I read Yuying's letters over and over again. They gave me so much to think about and cry about. One thing in abundance in a labor camp is time to think about things. I confess that sometimes I plunged deep into the black hole of loneliness and hopelessness. Being so far from loved ones and feeling incapable of hope was the worst part of camp. I didn't mind the hard labor or the rough life. But not knowing whether I would ever be released or see my family again was agony. Being utterly helpless to affect my future was torture.

Without any sense of when I would "graduate" from the labor school, the days seemed like months, the months like years. Only hard work made the time seem to go a little faster. I was assigned lots of jobs besides farm work, but most involved digging. We dug coal from a primitive pit without any safety measures. We dug irrigation channels between the Yellow River and our fields. My most interesting job was when I was ordered to learn how to drive an old truck to transport coal from the pit to other labor camps in the region. The regular driver had taken seriously sick. Why they chose me as his replacement defied reason. I had never even driven a car before. I had a full day of instruction and practice. Then the very next day, I was on my way, driving a big truck with a long trailer, fully loaded with coal. My instructor sat beside me only to my first stop and then I was "driving solo." He told me as long as I didn't get lost before the next stop, I would be fine because there was nothing to hit in the desert.

Well, there wasn't anything big to hit in the desert, but there were plenty of boulders and gullies from the spring rains to avoid. Lots of small rocks and cobbles got kicked up, and I had the noisiest, bumpiest ride of my life. I gripped the wheel tightly and constantly scanned the terrain ahead, vigilant for obstacles and hazards. Finally I reached the next camp. When I stopped in front of the camp gate, a fellow came out and asked me what I wanted. I told him I was there to deliver some coal. He looked at me and then the truck as if I were daft and asked me if I was sure of that. I wondered what sort of idiot I was dealing with. Then he asked me where all the coal was. Wondering whether I was in a labor camp or an insane asylum, I pointed over my shoulder and said, "What do you mean by all? It's right there." Because of the look on his face, I took a look myself and was astounded. The trailer wasn't there! Somehow during that bumpy ride across the desert, I had managed to lose it. I had been concentrating so hard on driving and what was in front of me that I never realized what had happened behind me. We found the trailer about two hours back. People had a good laugh over this, and the worst consequence I faced was the teasing I had to put up with when the story got around.

My favorite job, however, was herding a big flock of sheep far from camp. It seemed like an easy job, but actually it was very demanding and arduous. I ate in the wind, slept in the dew, and endured the hardships of long treks in search of green pastures. But I liked it because I could relish the complete solitude. And watching sheep graze and then rest amidst the lush grass was restful in itself. I took a compass, an umbrella, a blanket, a full canteen of water, a bag of salty hoecakes, and a few bottles of strong white liquor. From the first step on my long journeys with the flock, I felt like a free man.

The dense virgin forests that blanketed the Helan Mountains stretched for hundreds of miles. While they were fearsomely dark at night, I didn't worry about wild animals. Other than the usual small mammals that live in the woods, I never saw anything other than deer, horses, cattle, and goats. I didn't worry about water because cascading streams and ample springs were everywhere. I had no worries about food. If I had finished my own provisions, I could always find friendly herdsmen and mountain folk who shared what they had with me. In return, I invited them to share some white liquor. They loved it. After a few drinks and our meal, they'd start singing Mongolian folk songs and I'd sing my Peking Opera. Before they departed, they always gave me dried venison and other food.

Strangely enough, it was in this idyllic, wooded setting—the best grasslands were on the edge of or just within the forests—that I first began to fantasize about suicide, although I didn't call it that in my mind. I would daydream about how I could shape my future after all, right here in the forest. I could just lie down and refuse to get up. I would neither eat nor drink but gradually slip away from life and become at one with the beautiful nature that surrounded me. I spent several guilty hours thinking of taking control of my destiny in this fashion.

After that experience and my return to camp, I had some serious bouts of depression and, all too often, the thought of suicide would flash before me. It made me—a father, a husband, a son—shiver to even think about it, but I couldn't put it out of my head. My darkest thoughts and greatest resolve to end my life came one night when I was on flood patrol along the river.

Flood control on the Yellow River was always a critical job. It was even more demanding in the summer of 1971 because of unusually heavy rains for that time of year. Our adobe cabins were severely damaged by the endless torrents that fell from the skies. In our soaked clothing, we patrolled the river banks around the clock. Women worked days while men were on night duty. The water had already risen to the top of the banks. We built levees to prevent the river from overflowing. If they failed, the whole valley and all of our crops would be under water. Different camps were responsible for designated areas, coordinated by a central command. Our camp was assigned the most dangerous spot, near a big bend in the river.

One night I was patrolling that stretch alone, one hand holding a flashlight, the other a gong. If I found any weaknesses in the embankment or noticed the water rising quickly, I was to strike the gong loudly and repeatedly until the emergency team arrived. Blinded by the hard rain pelting my eyeglasses, I gingerly picked my way along the narrow, rugged, slippery path. The strong wind blew the rain onto my face. I raised my hand as a shield against the tempest and managed to lose my grip on the flashlight, which knocked my glasses off as it fell. With my bad eyesight I don't see well even in the daylight without my glasses. I was absolutely blind in the pitch black night and pouring rain.

I tried to use my feet to feel for the flashlight and lost my balance and fell into a deep ditch. I heard a sickening sound as my left ankle snapped, and then the pain came. My ankle throbbed and, with every beat of my pulse, sent shivers of pain up my leg. I lay in the ditch like a water-soaked log. I had the gong with me, but I dared not hit it. The gong was only for warning about the threat of flooding, not for signaling that a laborer was hurt. I thought about what life might be like without my glasses. Anyone without bad eyesight probably cannot imagine the panic I felt. If I lost those glasses, who knows when or if I could get another pair?

My helpless misery may have touched the heavenly powers. The rain stopped. In the dark, flat on my back in the ditch water, I wished I were dead. My tortured life seemed hopeless and meaningless. Eternal death promised me lasting peace. I was barely conscious, half-awake and half-asleep. I was thinking about how I might actually die before I finally dozed off.

When I next opened my eyes, the sky was suffused with the soft glow of sunrise. As the sun climbed, never had its morning rays over the river seemed so bright and warm. A sharp glint hit my face and, as I turned to find its source, I saw it was my eyeglasses. Along with the flashlight, they were sitting on the other side of the ditch in plain view. I breathed a sigh of relief. At least I wouldn't have to go through the rest of my life half-blind. As small as it might seem, this moment was a turning point in my life.

As I lay in the ditch, considering this turn of events, I thought of a line from Sunzi's *The Art of War*: "Confront a person with the danger of death and he will fight to live." That was what I had to do. I needed to use all my remaining strength and all the tools I had. Necessity was the mother of invention. I would find the way to survive, and in the end, prevail. With my broken ankle dragging, I hobbled and crawled resolutely bit by bit back to camp, one hand holding the flashlight, the other the gong.

At first, the camp director was furious about my missing the whole night of duty and ordered me back to the riverbank immediately. Then he saw my ankle had swollen to twice its normal size. I was allowed to rest and given some painkillers. Xiao Ding helped me with my meals. One old mate massaged my ankle with some sorghum liquor that he lit. He said this helped it penetrate to the pain. I had taught myself acupuncture in the camp and bought a set of acupuncture needles out of my monthly pay. I applied many needles all over my body, but none helped. The pain was non-stop.

The toughest task for me was going to the toilet. Using my crutch, I could manage to get there, but squatting was tough. I had to crouch down and rise up several times. Even in the cold air, sweat poured from me because of the intolerable pain. After Xiao Ding talked to the camp director a few times, he finally got permission to use the tractor to take me to the central labor camp, which had a clinic.

Although small, the clinic was staffed with top-ranked doctors and nurses, most of whom were camp laborers from well-known hospitals in Beijing and other cities. An X-ray confirmed that my ankle was indeed broken—in two places. With the long delay before treatment, my foot was seriously infected and inflamed. Doctor Liu, an old surgeon, took me immediately into the operating room, not to set the bone, but to drain the pus and blood from the swollen area. He told me that he took three cups of foul liquid from me and that if I had waited a few more days to see him, I might not have survived the blood poisoning.

With my ankle treated and after a few days' rest, I was soon eager to return to camp. My ankle was in a plaster cast, but with a crutch I could walk without too much pain. The clinic beds were in short supply. I asked Doctor Liu to discharge me. He replied that he would be able to do that soon.

The next Sunday morning, a bright, breezy day in early September; I was told that I was being transferred to my camp. A nurse directed me to a truck outside the clinic entrance. Doctor Liu was already in the cab.

"Climb in. You need to see someone before you go."

"Who?" I asked.

"An old friend of yours," Doctor Liu replied with a mischievous grin and said no more.

After about 30 minutes, we stopped in front of a hospital, entered through its broad doors, and took the stairs to the third floor, where two soldiers stood guard in front of the entrance.

"I am Doctor Liu. We have an appointment with the Commander."

"Yes. He is expecting you," one guard said and opened the door.

We followed a long corridor to the room at its end. The door was open.

"Look, Commander, at who I am bringing to see you." Doctor Liu nudged me into the room ahead of him.

It was a big room. On the bed lay an old man with a scraggly beard and deep eyes, pale but brimming with vigor.

"Are you the son of Professor Chen?" the old man on the bed asked.

"Professor Chen?" I was not used to this form of address.

"Yes. Professor Pinzhi Chen," he confirmed.

"Yes, I am his son," I confirmed.

"Do you know Mr. Zhang Hanchen?" he asked.

"Yes, I know him very well," I replied.

"In that case, you should know me." He seemed to be enjoying his game.

I drew a blank. Who was this wizened old man who knew my father and Uncle Zhang? "Could you give me a hint please?" I asked.

"Your garden, 1949." He smiled broadly.

"Oh my God! Commander Liu!" I ditched my crutch and staggered toward my old friend.

"Hold it, young man. The Commander can't afford any excitement in his condition," Doctor Liu said quickly.

"Never mind. Never mind. Come here, 'Overlord'," the old man said as he shook my hand.

"Overlord?" Doctor Liu asked with a quizzical look.

"Yes, Songsheng performed 'Farewell My Concubine' for my troops before we decamped from the garden of his parents' mansion," the old man explained. "Come here, sit by me," he said and motioned to me.

"I never expected to see you here, Commander." I was thrilled.

"I am no longer a commander. Call me Uncle Liu." The old man turned to Doctor Liu. "Doctor, with your permission, could Songsheng and I have lunch together in my room?"

"Let me see what I can do." Doctor Liu walked out of the room.

Commander Liu and I had a long conversation. So many strange and bad things had happened to both of us in the past 20 years. Commander Liu had waged a victorious campaign against Kuomintang troops in south China and fought bravely against the US Army in Korea. He had been wounded in combat eight times. As brilliant as he was in battle, he was naïve when it came to politics and got pulled into an Army power struggle. Framed as a key opponent of Qiu Huizuo, one of Lin Biao's Four

Favorites, he was relieved of his duties, terribly persecuted, and sent to a labor camp next to ours.

"Good news. Lunch will be served in your room right away," Doctor Liu said as he walked into the room. "Bad news. No white liquor as usual. You must be well prepared for your big operation tomorrow."

"What operation?" I asked.

"A subtotal gastrectomy," Doctor Liu said.

"No big deal. Just cutting out part of my stomach. I'm more worried about having to toast you with tea at lunch instead of some good strong liquor."

It was a wonderful lunch all the way around, the food, the companionship, the good spirits (even without the liquor), and the fond memories of that remarkable time in our garden.

Afterward, the Commander said, "Tell me some more news now. Where is your concubine these days?"

"She was a famous Peking Opera actress until the troupes were banned. She got married and had a daughter." I told him just about all I knew of Lifen.

"In Beijing?"

"No. I don't even know where she is now." I had lost contact with Lifen years before.

"You must tell your parents that I still owe them rent for all the time my troops spent in your garden." The old man grew serious.

"What are you talking about?"

"I am talking about the rent for the garden. Your parents refused to discuss it with me, so I asked Hanchen to take care of it. Years later, when I met him, he told me that your parents wouldn't talk to him about it either."

The subject seemed to upset him. I said, "Oh, Commander Liu, I mean Uncle Liu, let it go. That's 25 years ago. It's done and gone. What remains are the good times, the good memories, and the good friends."

"You are right," he sighed. "Even if I do want to pay your parents, what would I use for money?"

Doctor Liu suggested it was time to leave.

"Uncle Liu, you are always my hero." I reluctantly bade him good-bye. "You always triumphed on the battlefield. May your next victory be in the operating room tomorrow."

"Don't worry," the old man said, fully at ease. "Like we said on the battlefield, every bullet has its billet. I'll be fine. I still owe you some rounds of sorghum liquor, your father's favorite."

"I'll anticipate that day with great pleasure," I said.

As we made our way back to the truck, Doctor Liu told me that he was a member of the surgery team for Commander Liu. The word from Beijing's upper levels had come down to the Central Camp to give the commander the highest level of care possible. His life must be saved.

I was warmly welcomed back by my camp mates, managers, and even the director. Word had obviously circulated about my visit with Commander Liu. I felt flattered but a little uneasy. The director called me to his office and handed me a stack of my mail.

"Why didn't you tell me you knew Commander Liu?" he asked.

"I had no idea such a small matter was of any importance."

"Small?" He apparently disagreed. "It's a big matter. From now on, just let me know if you need any help."

Back in my cabin, I couldn't wait to open Yuying's letters. To my pleasant surprise, she had mailed me a photo of her, Dawei, and Lei. My heart melted when I saw how fast my two sons were growing up. Their big eyes were looking at me as if to say, "Come back home, Daddy." Yuying's letter was as warm as her smile in the photo. Holding the photo and her letter, I was so ashamed of my selfishness in contemplating the foolish idea of suicide.

In September, everyone turned to harvesting. The workday started early and ended late every day. We worked before breakfast and after dinner, but no one complained. We were so excited to see and enjoy the fruits of our long, hard labor— fresh corn and all kinds of other vegetables, melons, and rice. We harvested bumper crops, which richly improved the meals that we now ate at long tables in the newly built dining hall. The usual two dishes for lunch and dinner became four dishes and included stewed lamb, other meats, and fish. My Peking Opera singing was an indispensable part of the celebration. In my whole life, I have never devoured so much lamb, drunk so much liquor, and sung so much Peking Opera.

Soon we had even more to be happy about: white liquor and red wines were served at every dinner. We were no longer assigned new jobs. The senior laborers, former high-ranking government officials and army officers, gathered in the camp dining hall for closed meetings several days in a row. By the end of September, the camp was rife with rumors, some simply beyond belief. The wildest was that Lin Biao, Mao's second in command and constitutional successor, Mao's "best student" and most prominent cheerleader, had tried to assassinate Mao and was killed! Before long, everyone was assembled in the dining hall. The camp director read us the latest CCP Red Letter Documents about Lin Biao's Anti-Party Criminal Gang. The Party Central Committee printed these important decrees and edicts in red, hence the name. This time, the documents were so long that it took a whole week for all of us to study them.

The official story was that Lin Biao had tried and failed to assassinate Mao. On September 13, 1971, Lin, his family, and some top aides tried to escape to Russia, but their airplane ran out of gas and crashed in Mongolia with no survivors. Of course, that was only one version of the event, and over the years I have heard many others. But who could have predicted that such a hero of China would come to such an end?

The whole camp turned into one big happy place. We had our own harvest festival with plenty to celebrate beyond the bountiful results of our labor. Most of the camp administrators were army veterans who resented being assigned to a labor camp in the Western desert. With Lin Biao and his cronies dead or purged, their futures were suddenly brighter. At least the faction that sent them into virtual exile was no longer in power.

One day in early November, the camp director summoned me, saying he had something urgent to tell me. I was frightened half to death as I entered his office.

"Sit down, please," he greeted me from behind his desk.

"Is there something wrong?" I asked, uneasy with his politeness.

"No. No. I am now officially informing you that you must go back to Beijing immediately."

"Has something happened to my family?" I was petrified.

"No. No." He held up his hands. "The order comes from high above, and it is top secret," he whispered.

"How soon must I leave?"

"Tomorrow," he said. "My chauffeur will drive you to the train station. Here are your train ticket and an evaluation letter from the school. And this is a note that Commander Liu wanted you to deliver to your parents. You will be met at the Beijing train station."

The next day, November 5, 1971, I left camp on my way to Beijing without a clue as to why I was being called back. What new names or campaigns would I face now? What came after the cowshed and the labor camp? I thought back to the last day I was in Beijing: September 7, 1970. I was scared of being sent to Ningxia, not knowing what to expect. Here I was 424 days later, on my way back to Beijing, fearful of what awaited me. At least I'd be 1,500 kilometers closer to my loved ones.

Chapter 13

LIFE AFTER DEATH

1972-1976
Beijing, China

THE 20-HOUR TRAIN TRIP BACK to Beijing was nerve-wracking. Instead of a hard seat in the coach, I had a sleeper accommodation, but there was no way I could fall asleep. I was so anxious, "fearing the wolf in front and the tiger behind," as the Chinese saying goes. What on earth awaited me in Beijing?

As soon as I got off the train with my big crate, a tall, thin man in his fifties walked up to me and asked, "Are you Chen Songsheng?"

"Yes." I didn't know whether to shake hands with him or not.

"Please come with me." He turned and threaded his way through the crowd, making it easier for me to follow with my burden.

Outside the station, a Jeep was waiting for us. Soon we were making our way past Tiananmen Square, heading toward Beijing's western suburbs. We remained silent all the way until the Jeep stopped in front of a building close to the Beijing Friendship Hotel. The man led me to a big room on the third floor. It seemed like a meeting room but had been rearranged into several workspaces. So many desks, shelves, world maps, foreign magazines, newspapers, and books filled the room that it was hard to move around. I was brought to an old man sitting behind a small desk in a corner of the room that had been screened off as a separate office.

"Sit down, please," he said politely with a simple grace that reminded me of my father's scholar friends. He moved his eyeglasses down his nose and looked at me over their frames. "What I am going to tell you must stay in this room. You must keep everything here confidential—your work, your activities, anything related to this important mission."

He then told me briefly that my assignment was to translate or proofread confidential materials in English. I would work a six-day week and should report for duty in two days. All the work must be done in this building at the highest speed and with the greatest accuracy. Nothing, not even a scrap of paper, was to be taken outside of the office. Any violations would be severely punished.

"Did you bring your evaluation letter from the labor school?"

"Yes." I took it from my bag and handed it to him.

"Any questions?" he asked.

"What about my Research Institute?"

"They have already been informed. Don't worry."

"May I know how long this assignment will last?"

"Until you have no more English materials left to translate." The old man nodded, bid me good-bye without standing up, and went back to his work.

The Jeep then took me to my apartment building. On the way there, I mused on the irony of it all. For years, I had been reviled and scorned, in part because of my pursuit of language and literature, English in particular. Now here I was, plucked from my heavenly hell in the desert because I knew English and, for some strange reason, the government needed my skills. The driver let me off in front of the apartment building. Carrying the crate on my shoulder, I started upstairs. By the time I reached the third floor—we lived on the fifth floor—I heard running steps and a joyful shriek from the stairs below.

"Songsheng, is that you?" It was Yuying's voice.

She must have entered the building just after I did. I put the crate down and turned to see her and Dawei on the landing just below. Stunned with surprise, she halted, staring at me with her mouth open and breathing heavily. Dawei looked at me with wide eyes and total astonishment.

"Dawei, Yuying. I am home. Daddy is fine." I held out my arms and said, "Dawei, come let me see how much you have grown since I last saw you."

"Dawei, run to your father," Yuying urged.

Dawei hesitated only a moment before running up the steps shouting, "Daddy! Daddy!"

Dawei had grown up to be such a big boy. I felt his weight when he jumped into my arms. We left the crate behind, and I carried my big boy up the remaining flights. Yuying ran ahead of me, opened the door, and shouted, "Look, who's here!"

Without even pausing to catch my breath, I rushed into the bedroom to find Grandaunt holding my little boy on the bed.

Dawei, five and a half years old, yelled to Lei, one and a half years old, "Lei, this is Daddy. Call him Daddy."

Lei looked more like a two-year-old. He smiled but wouldn't call me Daddy. But he did put his arms around me and held me tight for the rest of the evening. No one could take him away from me.

"You scared me to death." Grandaunt still could not believe her eyes. "I thought I would never see you again in this life."

"Grandaunt, if we have learned anything through all our years together, isn't it that life is full of surprises?"

Grandaunt looked much older than I remembered. I was so grateful to her. Without her help, Yuying would have had no way to work at the lumber plant and care for our two boys.

It was too late to see my parents that night. I played with Lei and Dawei the whole evening. I had brought them a lot of dried sweet wolfberries, which some call goji berries or medlar. They are one of Ningxia's most famous local products, delicious and good for your health. The jewel-like berries are meaty and sweet and the boys loved them.

For my Mother, Grandaunt, Jiahui, and Yuying, I brought two large young Tanyang lamb skins to be tailored into four fur vests. Called the White Treasure of Ningxia, the fur of these lambs is unparalleled for luster, softness, curl, and warmth. I had bought the skins and Father's gift from the herdsmen and the Helan Mountain folk I encountered while roaming with my sheep.

For my father, I brought the rarest of the gifts, a piece of velvety soft antler from a young spotted deer stag. Such antlers had been used in Chinese medicine for 2,000 years to reinforce kidney yang (the active, masculine, bright qualities to balance the passive, dark, feminine qualities of yin) and replenish blood and vital essence. Not to be confused with hard, ossified antlers, these soft antlers are the living buds that grow from the young stag's head and are usually sold for a king's ransom. My father liked to steep Chinese herbal medicines in his favorite sorghum liquor. He told me that soaking allowed the alcohol to extract more essential elements from the medicines. He had never before used antler, however, let alone the downy antler of a young stag, even when he had the money to purchase those ingredients.

While displaying these gifts to Yuying, I told her of my lonely but lovely experiences as a shepherd in the green pastures and virgin forests of the Helan Mountains. I told her about meeting people strictly by chance who became good friends. I never had more than a couple of bottles of white liquor and a few yuan to offer them. Yet, in return, I got the luxurious lamb skins and the antler. Of course, I didn't tell Yuying about my suicidal thoughts, and I couldn't tell her the real reason for my returning to Beijing. But I did tell her how very much I had missed her every day. Yuying was genuinely moved. She told me that the gifts were really appreciated but that my sweet thoughts were even nicer.

Our reunion that night after such a long separation was even better than our magical wedding night. This time, Yuying's tanned face and hands from her outdoor work contrasted with the lily-white skin on the rest of her body, soft and smooth as before. She couldn't take her hands off my rough face and muscular body, bronzed by the sun and buff from hard work. She sighed deeply as she fondled my broad chest, gazing at me as if I were all she had ever wanted. After discussing it briefly, we decided to take precautions against having a third child, even though both of us yearned for a daughter.

When I awoke in the middle of the night, Yuying was still awake. Touching the soft lamb skin, she whispered, "How wonderful it would be if all people could be like your herdsmen and mountain folk friends."

The next day, Yuying called in to work and Dawei's kindergarten at her plant to ask to take the day off, and we went to see my parents. A strange scene similar to my family's reception of me the previous day played itself out once more when my parents saw me at their door.

"What has happened?" my father asked, looking scared.

I answered immediately, "Everything is fine. Don't worry, Father and Mother. Everything is fine."

We didn't stay long; we took a bus and brought my parents back to our apartment. I could see how happy they and my sons were for all of us to be together again. My mother took many chocolate-covered fruit candies from her handbag for the boys. Dawei took the wrapper off one candy, put it into Lei's mouth, rapidly got one for himself, and said with his mouth full, "We love these candies, Grandma," as he unwrapped a third one.

"Whoa! What's your hurry?" My father tried to slow down his grandsons. "We have plenty here."

Nothing could be better than sitting together with my family at the dinner table again. Grandaunt and Yuying cooked us a full table of delicious dishes. My mother, who rarely drank alcohol, made an exception and joined us with a half cup of red wine. I light-heartedly regaled them with many of my memorable experiences in the labor camp. Without mentioning my broken ankle, I told them of my unexpected meeting with Commander Liu and presented my father with the note, which he then read aloud for all of us to hear.

Dear Chen Family,

How wonderful for me, an old man, not knowing how much longer I may walk this earth, to see my dear Songsheng again and to stir up so many warm memories. What a wonderful son you have. What wonderful parents he has.

Pinzhi, you refused to talk with me about paying rent for your garden, but ever since Hanchen told me you had never been paid, I have felt remiss in not taking care of this myself. I should have been firmer. Please forgive me. Mere words offer scant gratitude for your generosity, but you must know that I am most appreciative of what you did and the friendship we developed.

Songsheng and others have told me of the bad things you went through after the sacrifices you made for China. I too have suffered at the hands of the nation I served faithfully for 40 years and more. But here we stand today, having survived the bite of the tiger. May we all continue to do so.

With fond thoughts of the past and best wishes for the future,

Liu Mingfu

"Survived the bite of the tiger." That is exactly what my family and Commander Liu had done. These were encouraging words to me. I didn't believe my bitterness would end any time soon, but I couldn't let it destroy me. All my hopes for the future had so far ended in ruins. All my dreams had been crushed. I was tired and terribly disillusioned. But I had survived. I had to recover my hope. I had to have a dream for me and my family.

My new job offered me the faint glimmer of a new day, a new dream. Lao Dong, the old gentleman who had received me and who was the manager of the translation team, assigned me my first job. He handed me *Six Crises* by President Richard M. Nixon and several bound pages.

"Read this book carefully but quickly. As soon as you finish it, please start proofreading this translation of Chapter 5, 'Khrushchev,' comparing it with the original English."

Then Xiao Hong, a small young woman with smiling eyes, introduced herself saying, "I am Lao Dong's secretary. Let me give you a tour of our facilities." On the ground floor, there were several offices and a reading room with all sorts of dictionaries and other books. The dining room was just across the hall, and Xiao Hong explained, "Free lunch is served from noon until two o'clock. Free dinner is available for all who need to work late." I got the impression from the way she spoke that working late was a common practice.

She then led me to a desk in an office on the second floor. On it were a typewriter, paper, pencils, several dictionaries, and a tall stack of other reference books in English. Three men and two women occupied the other desks in the room. They raised their heads, nodded perfunctorily, and resumed their work.

"This is your desk. Everyone here is called by his or her family name with the prefix Lao, Xiao, or Da."

Lao means old. Xiao means young or small. Da means big or tall. From that day on, I was called Da Chen. My fellow translators didn't care to know my first name nor did I have any particular desire to learn theirs.

It was, of course, my first time to read *Six Crises*. The book had been published a decade earlier and detailed the key events that shaped Nixon's political career. It was a fascinating book with solid background and insights into Nixon's character. All the English reference materials on my desk were about President Nixon, covering his time as a congressman, senator, vice president, and unsuccessful presidential candidate in his first run for that office. That first day, I stayed reading and waited until 1:30 PM for lunch, hoping to avoid meeting too many people. Noodles, dumplings, boiled eggs, pickles, and other dishes lined a long table. I had a delicious and filling lunch that stuck to my ribs for the rest of the day, but I kept asking myself, what am I doing here?

My uncertainty didn't affect my working hard. Twelve-hour days, seven days a week, were usual during my start-up phase. My capabilities were soon demonstrated and recognized. Instead of carefully comparing the poorly rendered Chinese translation with the English original and making many corrections, I was told to re-translate all of Chapter 5. My handwritten translations were neat and easy to read. I also took the initiative to translate related materials, which analyzed the complicated situation between the US, the Soviet Union, and China. My comprehensive report focused on the changing dynamics of China's superpower relations after it broke with the Soviet Union in 1960. Tension along the border between the two Communist nations reached its peak in 1969 and 1970, presenting the US with an excellent opportunity to play the "China Card" against the Soviet Union. China was playing its cards also.

In April 1971, China signaled a thaw in its relations with the US by inviting an American table tennis team to visit, initiating what came to be known as "Ping Pong Diplomacy." The team was the first group of Americans allowed to enter China since the founding of the PRC. All the translators and staff in our building were given tickets to watch the matches in the Beijing Indoor Stadium. Lao Dong gave me an extra ticket, and I took Yuying. We enjoyed watching how the Chinese team completely dominated but was gracious enough not to let the scores become too lopsided.

Working with these materials, learning so much I didn't know about my country, was an exciting experience—and I was getting noticed.

"Good job on *Six Crises* and the other briefing materials," Lao Dong said after he had called me to his office and gladly shook hands with me. "Again, our conversation mustn't leave the room. I am now allowed to tell you about the important mission we are working on."

Lao Dong shocked me with his information, which was actually old news to the rest of the world and in some quarters of China: President Nixon planned to visit the PRC early in 1972. Nixon's National Security Advisor, Henry Kissinger, helped by Pakistan's President Khan, had made two secret trips to China in July and October of 1971 and talked with Premier Zhou Enlai to set up the visit.

In view of my good work, Lao Dong told me, it was my job now to proofread the whole translation of *Six Crises*.

I also translated background information about Mrs. Patricia Nixon, her miserable childhood, her meeting her husband at a theater group when they were cast in the same play (which reminded me of how I met Yuying), their two daughters, and especially her "spirit of people helping people" and her work with volunteer service programs. The most difficult job for me was proofreading a one-page summary of the alcoholic drinks that the Nixons liked best. It turned out to be a long list, and many terms couldn't be found in the English-Chinese dictionaries I had access to. It took me several days to finish this difficult job (with many mis-translations that I learned about only after I came to the US). I was told later by my colleagues that during their visit, instead of their favorite drinks, the Nixons favored Maotai, the national drink of China. After their visit, Maotai achieved global notice. Subsequent foreign guests often demanded Maotai, President Nixon's drink, at their banquets in China.

From February 21 to 28, 1972, President and Mrs. Nixon and Henry Kissinger visited China, and the President had direct talks with Mao, starting a new era of Chinese-American relations. During his visit, Nixon stated, "There is one China, and Taiwan is a part of China," which satisfied China's prerequisite for signing the Sino-US Joint Communiqué in Shanghai on February 28, 1972. Facing the tough question of how to address the People's Republic of China and Taiwan, which called itself the Republic of China, Zhou Enlai cleverly proposed "the two sides of the Taiwan Straits." Both parties agreed, and this was the terminology used in the communiqué.

The groundbreaking summit between Mao and Nixon began the process of opening up China. Small steps, such as 36 Chinese students being sent to French and British colleges, followed and signified a new direction for my country. By May of 1973, the US and China had established liaison offices in each other's capitals.

Shortly before Nixon's visit, I was released back to my Institute on condition that I stay on call. Although I was never called back, Lao Dong did phone me later to tell me that when Mao met Nixon, he had praised *Six Crises*. I was beside myself with joy when I heard that. Basically it was my translation with Lao Dong's revisions that Mao had read.

On March 8, 1972, one week after I returned to the Institute, I was called to the Director's Office and given a rehabilitation letter with two red seals, one from the Chinese Communist Party Committee of the Institute and the other the seal of the Institute itself. The two seals gave complete authority to the admission of error in labeling me a "Monster and Demon" and mistreating me by raiding my home and imprisoning me in the cowshed. The letter officially rehabilitated my reputation and confirmed that I would be remunerated for lost wages. From July 14, 1967, when I was imprisoned in the cowshed, my ordeal had lasted 1,699 days, and now I was to receive 1,650 yuan retroactive pay. I was genuinely thankful for it. Many other cases in which the charges had been false had not yet been re-examined and the verdicts not yet reversed. Even more sadly, in many cases where the verdicts were reversed, the accused had already died or been killed.

This was the first time that Yuying and I had ever seen that much money. We made a detailed plan of how to use it. Before the lunar New Year, we bought new clothing for Dawei and Lei. They were growing up fast. I bought a case of vermouth for my father. Yuying bought woolen underwear for my mother and grandaunt. We also gave my mother 200 yuan so she would feel more secure and have some cash on hand, and we arranged a big family dinner. Everyone attended except Jiahui, Gao, and their daughter, who were a thousand miles away from us in Gansu. I bought myself the latest editions of the English-Chinese and Chinese-English Dictionaries. I wanted to buy Yuying something special but was stumped on what to get. At the time, jewelry was considered bourgeois and all women wore similar clothing in drab shades of gray, green, or black. I asked her what she might want.

"I don't want anything. As long as you are with me, I don't need anything more."

"No. No way. I have to buy you something. Otherwise, I will feel remorseful."

"How could you say that?" Yuying raised her big eyes. "Don't make me feel remorseful. They gave you 1,650 Yuan for your 1,699 days of tribulation, not even one yuan per day. Every yuan bears your sweat, pain, and misery."

I felt such sweet sorrow as Yuying noted the days of our separation and my long torment.

"I have to buy you something just to keep that memory in our hearts. We will remember it forever." I believe that thought was what convinced her.

For almost five years, I had not been inside a department store. Yuying and I went to the biggest department store on Wangfujing Street, but she didn't find anything she liked. We then walked to the Front Gate Street to the north of Tiananmen Square. Finally, Yuying selected a synthetic wool overcoat. The inner lining looked like sheepskin. She said that with the overcoat she would feel much warmer riding her bicycle against the piercing wind to and from her factory, not only because of the thick lining, but also because I bought it for her with my hard-earned money. It was the biggest gift I had ever given Yuying. I had not yet brought her the good days and good fortune I envisioned when I married her. I renewed my vow that one day I would make Yuying the happiest and most carefree woman in the world.

Despite my rehabilitation and the unexpected remuneration, despite the thaw in China's diplomatic relations and gradually increasing exchange with other countries, these were not easy times for me or China. After the death of Lin Biao and the subsequent purge of his followers, Jiang Qing, Mao's wife since 1938, and the rest of the Gang of Four she headed, wielded their greatest power. It is a mistake to think that these four ran the entire operation. But Jiang—so close to Mao—her protégés, and their supporters did wield a great deal of power and had virtual control over propaganda and the media (an apt role for Jiang, a former star of stage and B-grade movies). The Gang represented the ruling power elite. In private gatherings among close friends, when the Gang of Four (although the term didn't come into common usage until later) was mentioned, five fingers were held up, which meant there was a big potato— Mao—behind the four.

The Gang did not have an exclusive hold on power. During the spring of 1973, backed by Zhou Enlai, Deng Xiaoping was re-instated as a Vice Premier to help restore some order to the economy and the nation. Deng had suffered three years of persecution as the second biggest Capitalist Roader after Liu Shaoqi, plus four years of exile and re-education, laboring in a remote tractor repair plant in Jiangxi Province. But now he was back. It held promise of better things to come.

Anti-intellectualism, always a cardinal principle under Mao, unfortunately reached new extremes at this time. Chinese intellectuals were categorized as the "Stinking Number Nine," indicating that intellectuals were in the same league with all eight previously declared official enemies of China: Landlords, Rich Peasants, Counter-revolutionaries, Bad Elements, Rightists, Traitors, Spies, and Capitalist Roaders.

A case in 1973 dramatized the radical approach to intellectuals and to education. Zhang Tiesheng, a former high school student who had been working in the Liaoning countryside for the previous five years, took a regional college entrance exam and did very poorly. On the blank side of the exam paper, Zhang wrote an open letter to the examiners saying that he had been too busy in the fields to prepare for the exam and shouldn't be penalized. He criticized the students who scored well as "bookworms" who "have done nothing." His story was picked up by the local press and then the national media, including the *People's Daily*. Overnight Zhang became a "model hero," commended for his "blank exam" and "going against the tide" of the elitist and bourgeois model for education.

The most absurd movement of this period was the Criticize Lin, Criticize Confucius Campaign orchestrated by the Gang of Four. What started as a movement to condemn Lin Biao was extended to include Confucius and then the sage from whom Confucius had derived some of his thoughts on governance, the Duke of Zhou or Zhou Gong. His name can also mean "The Honorable Zhou," a phrase sometimes applied to Zhou Enlai.

Confucius, China's most famous philosopher, had long been roundly criticized by reformists of all stripes. Intellectuals and others in the early Republic, for instance, had disdained Confucian ethics and traditional morals as impediments to the un-Confucian ideals of science, technology, and democracy. In the current campaign, however, Confucius was used as a stand-in to attack Premier Zhou Enlai and others who stood in the way of the Gang.

Mao had never liked Confucius and wholly supported the movement, which was composed entirely of innuendo, implication, and indirection. Absurd connections and claims abounded. Lin was tied to Confucius through some epigraphs of Confucius written by Lin and his wife and found in their residence. Confucius was tied to Zhou Gong, a poet and regent of the 12th century BC Zhou Dynasty. And, Zhou Enlai was tied to Zhou Gong through their shared surname. Such was the total power of the totalitarian state that no one dared say that the campaign was ridiculous.

How could I, yearning to be a writer and a scholar, in love with literature and history, hope to advance in a society where the things I most valued were treated as rubbish or worse? These leaders believed that the more books you read, the more dangerous you became. As a confirmed "Stinking Number Nine," the son of a distinguished "Stinking Number Nine," it was hard to ignore the dead-end signs in front of me. But I didn't have a choice. My only possible way out was to work even harder.

I kept plugging away day and night on my research on advanced foundry technologies—ferrous metal die casting, investment casting, ceramic mold casting, uni-directional solidification theory. I moved up from being a mere member of the foundry research team to managing it. I published many volumes of translations and research articles. I was invited to serve as the Chief Advisor for a factory in Hunan Province seeking to modernize its investment casting production line. I helped them move from fairly primitive and labor-intensive methods to more sophisticated and semi-automated lines that increased output, improved quality, and significantly reduced the hard labor previously required. At the feast held to celebrate our achievement, several workers proposed toasts to me. They joked and called me "Aromatic Number Nine." An old worker said that the more Stinking Number Nines like me there were, the better. Maybe my dim appraisal of my prospects was wrong. I certainly was a hit with the workers.

After Premier Zhou Enlai was hospitalized with cancer in May 1974, Deng increasingly assumed the reins of leadership.

By 1975 he was serving as the Party Vice Chairman, First Vice Premier, and Army Chief of Staff. Mao was degenerating further with ALS, Lou Gehrig's disease. He presided over his last Politburo meeting in May. The political reforms Deng pursued and the decisions he made without consulting Mao angered Mao and the other radicals. Despite his titles, Deng's hold on the levers of power suffered when Zhou Enlai, Deng's most important supporter, died on January 8, 1976 at the age of 78 after his long fight with cancer.

For many of us, Zhou's death sounded a death knell for many hopes of the Chinese people. We had hoped that Zhou, five years younger than Mao, would outlive the Chairman, become China's new leader, and save the nation. He was the only top leader whom Mao dared not touch. Mao could get rid of Liu Shaoqi, Deng Xiao-ping (three times!), and Lin Biao, but not Zhou. He realized (quite rightly) that he needed Zhou to clean up the messes he made and deal with the ruined economy. And Zhou knew how to take care of himself. Talk about survivors! Ordinary Chinese people rarely knew about and few understood all the dirty power struggles within the Party that dictated their fate. And none of us knew all the roles that Zhou played, but he was our man and our great leader.

The day after Zhou died, Yuying and I came home from work early on the pretext of a headache. We took Dawei and Lei to Tiananmen Square, close to the Beijing Hospital where Zhou had passed away quietly, hoping to pay our last respects to his hearse. To our surprise, we found huge crowds had already filled on both sides of Chang An (Forever Peace) Boulevard. There must have been a lot of "headaches" in Beijing that afternoon. I held Lei in my arms. Yuying held Dawei's hand.

We stood in the chilly wind for hours without seeing the hearse and returned home disappointed.

The next day was Saturday. Yuying and I left home early in the morning while Dawei and Lei were still asleep. It was too early and too cold to take them with us. Chang An Boulevard was dark and quiet, even solemn. We walked along the street all the way from Fuxing Gate to the Beijing Hotel, trying to find a good spot to wait for the hearse. Hundreds of thousands of people were gathered on either side of the five-kilometer-long street. Sharing their grief and disillusionment silently, throngs of strangers communicated with each other with somber looks and sad nods. We looked expectantly to the east from where the hearse would come. Old people sat on the curb after their long wait. By mid-afternoon, we gave up and went back home.

On January 11, Sunday, Yuying, Dawei, Lei, and I, wearing mourning clothes and white paper flowers, went to Chang An Boulevard again. We could manage only to squeeze in close to Tiananmen Square, which was again packed with tens of thousands of people, all wearing mourning clothes and white flowers. The huge crowd swelled as a spontaneous flood of mourners came to express their sorrow. This time, we took with us some folding chairs that I had made in the labor camp. Yuying and I sat on them, holding Dawei and Lei on our laps, and waited and waited.

Dusk was coming on. The crowd seemed almost bursting with expectation. Suddenly, there it was: The hearse was coming! It was a modified ordinary van with a wreath and funeral bunting on its hood. Holding Dawei and Lei tightly, Yuying and I broke down, crying along with the crowd. When they saw us crying, Dawei and Lei also began crying. I don't think there was a dry eye there. Sobs, wails, and moans broke the still of the dusk.

The hearse passed by and slowly disappeared from view, taking with it our last, best hope for the future.

Many Chinese believe that any irregularities of nature, any disorders in the cosmos, portend coming difficulty for the nation, especially for those in power. For those believers, the signs witnessed March 8, 1976 carried ominous weight. That day, the most massive fall of stony meteorites on record—four tons worth—came to earth near Jilin in northeastern China. Nothing of this proportion had ever happened before. What could it mean? What lay in store for us?

Later in March, demonstrations broke out in many major cities, with slogans of "Safeguard Premier Zhou" and "Down with the Gang of Four!" Before Tomb-sweeping Day, April 4, two million people came together in Tiananmen Square to mourn Premier Zhou and demonstrate their anger at the Gang. Yuying and I went there every night in those days. It was too crowded to bring Dawei and Lei with us. Countless wreaths and white flowers dotted the square along with thousands of heartfelt poems and laments, mourning Premier Zhou and denouncing the Gang, some subtle and some not so subtle. Yuying and I copied many wonderful poems, some written in chalk, others in blood.

With Mao's consent, the Politburo, controlled by the Gang of Four, quickly condemned the demonstration as the "April Fourth Counter-revolutionary Political Event." Tens of thousands of people were arrested. Millions of people were interrogated. Deng Xiaoping, the Gang's real target, was brought down for the third time, booted from all his posts. It was the last triumph for Jiang Qing and her network.

It was strange that amidst all the turmoil, this time I was safe in my Institute. Nobody even bothered to interrogate me. Indeed, it turned out that many people from the Institute were in Tiananmen Square on April 4. An investigation was definitely not in order. What crazy times. We were on edge, wondering what would happen next, but life went on.

That summer, we decided to paint our apartment. After heaping up our furniture in the center of our rooms to prepare to paint the walls the next day, Yuying, Dawei, and Lei bunched up on our big bed. Grandaunt slept in her small room. I slept on the dining table in our kitchen. Early the next morning I was roused from a deep sleep by the table shaking beneath me. Then I saw the large cabinet was tilting and felt the whole building rocking. I jumped down but couldn't walk because the floor was suddenly moving so violently.

"Earthquake!" I shouted. "Stay where you are, Grandaunt. Don't move." The electricity went off. It was pitch black. All around us dishes, vessels, pots and pans, vases were crashing onto the floor. Glass pieces and ceramic shards were everywhere. Luckily I was able to feel around and find a flashlight in the drawer of the kitchen table. I lurched toward the bedroom where Yuying and our sons were.

Yuying, barefoot and wearing only her underwear, rushed out of the bedroom with Lei in her arms and holding Dawei's hand. I took Lei. Yuying stumbled into the small room.

"Grandaunt, don't move." Yuying put Dawei in Grandaunt's arms. The bed frame actually gave them better protection.

Holding Lei, I tried hard to open our front door and failed. The door frame was completely deformed. We were trapped in our apartment. I managed to get to the small room and put Lei in Grandaunt's arms. Silent with fear, Dawei and Lei followed the beam of my flashlight and surveyed the scene with frightened eyes.

"We have no way to get out," I told Yuying. "The door won't open."

"Even if we got out, how could we manage to escape from the fifth floor?"

"We'll have to just take our lot for better or for worse," I agreed.

"As long as we are together and have a clear conscience, we can bear any trouble," Grandaunt tried to reassure us.

After our little conversation, we calmed down. The shaking had stopped and we could take stock of ourselves and our apartment. We had looked death in the face. Yuying and I had conducted ourselves with grace under pressure in our moment of fear. My only thought had been that I was ready to sacrifice my life to protect Lei, Dawei, Yuying, and Grandaunt. The silence that followed the rumbling and tumbling was eerie. My eyes traveled over our messy room revealed by the flashlight, and the beam fell on the clock on the floor, its glass broken but still running. It was 4:14 AM, July 28, 1976.

The earthquake's epicenter was Tangshan, about 160 kilometers northeast of Beijing. It was the most devastating earthquake since the 1556 quake in Shaanxi Province that claimed 820,000 lives, the deadliest earthquake ever recorded. Initial estimates by Tangshan authorities placed the death toll at 650,000, revised downward to 242,000 when the central government released official figures. The true count probably was close to the initial estimate. Under instructions of the Gang of Four, all information about the earthquake was suppressed. All offers of foreign aid and international relief were rejected. The Gang used the earthquake to try to solidify their power and replace Mao, then on his deathbed. One of them supposedly said, "There were merely several hundred thousand deaths.

So what? Denouncing Deng Xiaoping concerns 800 million people."

Luckily, after the first aftershock, our building seemed to heave a deep sigh and settle a little differently than before but still hold together. Our door frame was straighter and the door now opened. I reconnoitered the route and then led the family downstairs. After the earth cracked, the heavens opened. Pouring rain pelted us as strong and numerous aftershocks rocked us. The rain fell in torrents. Even with umbrellas and raincoats, Yuying and I were drenched when we got to my parents' home. All the residents in the area had been ordered to evacuate their unsafe rooms. With their neighbors, we set up camp using plastic sheets and bamboo poles in a bleak spot close to the public toilets. When it rained hard outside the makeshift tent, it dripped hard inside the tent. Potable water and food of any kind were in short supply. My brothers sent water and biscuits to my parents.

We then returned to our neighborhood to set up our own camp on the playground of a nearby middle school. There was no way for us to care for both our parents and our children. After talking with my brothers, except my eldest brother and his family, we decided to go all together to Yanmen, my father's home village.

We took the train to Baoding, our first stop. My two older sisters lived there. They provided us shelter, food, and a chance for an impromptu family reunion on the fly. How good it was that so much of our family could get together at this moment. We missed Jiahui and tried every possible way to inform her that we were all alive and well. Then we left Grandaunt in Baoding with my sisters, while the rest of us continued on our way to Henan Province.

The train got us as far as Zhicheng. There a big group of relatives awaited us at the station. The last time my father had been back to Yanmen was in 1956. It was the first time for the rest of us to set foot on our ancestral grounds. Of all the relatives we met, my brother and I knew only Zhijie, our old cousin who had lived with us in Peiping and settled back in Yanmen after his retirement. He told us that over 50 relatives had met several times to prepare for our arrival after he received our telegram. It was a distance of about a dozen kilometers from Zhicheng to Yanmen. A two-wheel pushcart was prepared for my parents and our luggage. By the time Mother got on the cart, Father was already far ahead, striding energetically back to his old home.

All my father's brothers had passed away long before. My father was the only survivor in his generation. Zhijie's big caveyard became our main residence. With three half-cave, half-brick rooms, it was crowded with so many people. Yuying and I had to sleep on a small bamboo bed in the doorway. A cooking stove had apparently been newly built. Our eldest sister-in-law used a shovel to stir the noodles in the huge pot she cooked in. Our relatives used salty mashed garlic as the dressing for their noodles. The bowls were so big that Lei could have used his as a wash basin. My father quickly finished his full bowl. All of us enjoyed the wonderful handmade noodles. Indeed, I finished three bowls and could have downed a couple more. The warmth and good spirits drove away the horror of the earthquake. It seemed as if we were in another world.

We stayed in Yanmen for about a month. My mother, Dawei, and Lei slept in Zhijie's new north room. My brother's family stayed in the south room. My father insisted on sleeping in the old cave in our eldest sister-in-law's caveyard. She had lost her husband, our eldest cousin, when she was 19. My parents always sent her money and helped her daughter to graduate from a local middle school.

Almost every night and often during the day as well there would be quite a lively exchange of tales about the Chen clan. Many of them were, in fact, "war stories" about the role our relatives played in the fight against the Japanese.

One of the two Chinese words for Japan is "sun." It was said that when the Japanese invaders approached the city of Luoyang, only 25 kilometers from Jiyuan, they hesitated to march on. Luoyang means sunset. The Japanese believed it would be bad luck to get to that city and beyond because then they would be on the way to seeing their sun go down.

The Red Army then had the opportunity to expand their area of control into Shaanxi Province. Its commander-in-chief, Zhu De, decided to lead a group across the Yellow River to the south. My oldest cousin, Xiushan, was in charge of a special unit for covert assignments. He never told anybody, including his wife, what he did. They learned of his adventures only after the war. One of his tasks was actually to find a safe route for Zhu De to cross the Yellow River. The Commander led a platoon down from the Taihang Mountains. Using information provided by Xiushan, they chose the route through Zhicheng to get to the Yellow River. On their way, Xiushan led Zhu De and his group to a grassy area just outside of our caveyard to take a short rest. It was the last time he saw his wife. Of the Yanmen Chens, Xiushan, my eldest cousin, and Jitong, my fifth uncle, were both killed by the Japanese and proclaimed martyrs by the local government.

My most precious memories of that month in Yanmen were the times that my father and I spent together touring all the sites related to our family. We sat in the old, now-collapsed caves where my grandparents had lived; we visited their tombs in the first wheat and cotton fields they farmed; we went to the ridge where my grandfather had given my father the 20 silver coins; and, of course, we drank refreshing water from our sweet well.

My father took me to the well three times. The first time, he only showed me the site of the well. The second time, he asked me to bring a water bucket with a rope. He adroitly pulled up a full bucket of water and drank it with me. The third time, he sat on the edge of the well and asked me a question.

"Do you know why I brought you here three times?"

"When you drink the water, never forget who dug the well," I replied.

"Yes, and?"

I thought a while and responded, "Grandfather spent extra money to earn a chance to dig this well. Compared with a good opportunity, money means nothing."

"Yes, and?"

My father was obviously not yet satisfied. I knitted my brow and thought hard. "The Chen's well was not only for our family, but also for our neighbors and friends."

"Precisely." My father seemed to sigh with relief, and I did so silently. I never liked to fail my father's "exams." After awhile, he used his walking stick to write eight Chinese characters in the dirt: "The gratitude for a drop of water should be repaid with a gushing spring."

Shortly after we returned to Beijing, Mao died on September 9 at the age of 83. We hadn't even reached the last quarter and this was perhaps the most tumultuous year in China's long history—filled with epic disasters, massive change, and widespread misfortune. But it didn't turn out all bad. On October 6, Jiang Qing, Mao's wife, and the other three members of the Gang of

Four were arrested after a bloodless coup d'état. That brought to an end 10 years of the most perverse, insane, destructive series of campaigns that a nation has ever waged upon itself. Although its effects are still felt all these years later, the Cultural Revolution was finally over. Mao was dead and life went on.

PHOTOGRAPHS AND DRAWINGS

During the Cultural Revolution, photographs were thought to reflect bourgeois tastes and loyalties, a nostalgia for times past rather a dedication to Chairman Mao and to building the Peoples' Republic. The Red Guards destroyed any photographs they found during their periodic searches of homes. Of the thousands of photos the Chen family took during the 10 years they lived in their mansion and gardens, only one has survived.

The Chen family caveyard from which
Stephen's father departed for Peking in 1918
(photo taken 2009)

The well outside the Chen family
caveyard, a reliable source of
sweet water (photo taken 2009)

Busts of Stephen's parents,
Professor Chen and
Madame Fu

China's first textbooks on the French language, written by Stephen's father, Professor Chen Pinzhi, 1935-36

Old Peking Union Medical College Hospital, where Stephen was born in 1939 and Dawei in 1966 and where Stephen's mother died in 1981 and his father in 1984

Stephen's first home on Songzhusi Hutong near Peking University, 1939 (photo taken in 2009)

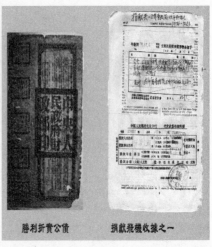

勝利折實公債　　捐獻飛機收據之一

Stephen with Jiahui in the Chen
mansion garden, 1948

Chinese government bond and donation
receipt with Father's note, 1951

Di An Men (Earth Peace Gate), built in 1420, demolished in 1954. Stephen grew
up in this neighborhood.

Stephen with his mother and
sisters (left to right): Siwei,
Wuquan, Jiahui, 1956

"Official" engagement picture, 1960

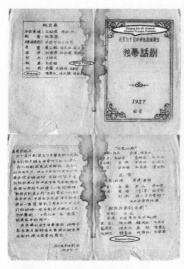

Stephen played the lead and
Yuying was his makeup girl, as
shown on this Beijing Middle
School No. 65 Drama Troupe
program, 1957

Stephen in "Into the Storm," a Russian
drama, during which he got to know Yuying,
1957

Father and three sons (left to right): Yansheng, Songsheng/Stephen, Father, and Jisheng, 1962

Newlyweds Yuying and Stephen at Cuihualou Restaurant, 1965

Siwei, eldest sister; Yao Ying, sister-in-law; Jiahui, youngest sister; Yuying; Wuquan, elder sister (left to right), 1965

The honeymooners in Xi'an at Hua Mountain, 1965

Replicas of shoulder bag, leather pouch, and coins that Father left Yanmen with; homespun cotton shirt much like one Father was wearing the night the Red Guards almost beat him to death.

Illustration of Chu Suiliang's inkstone with Imperial seals, stolen 1966 (from Stephen's memory)

Stephen's parents' house, confiscated and sealed by Red Guards, 1966

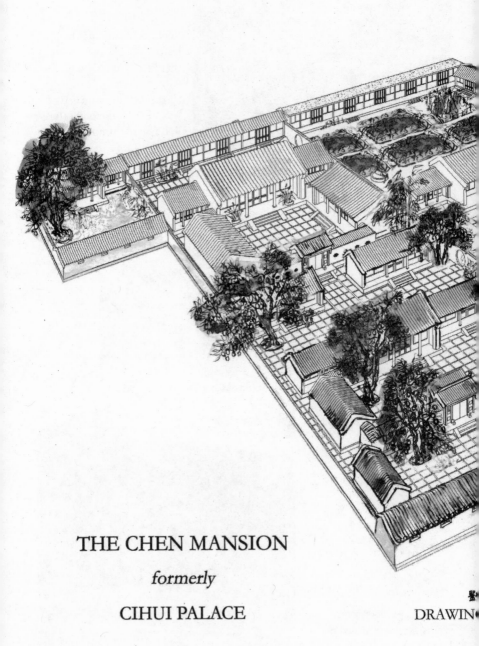

THE CHEN MANSION

formerly

CIHUI PALACE

DRAWIN

陳氏故居
舊稱
慈慧殿

繪
RAINBOW

Photo of Yuying, Dawei, and Lei that Stephen received while in labor camp, 1971

Yuying and Stephen visiting labor camp site near Helan Mountains in Ningxia Province, 1999

Stephen's parents with Dawei and Lei, 1973

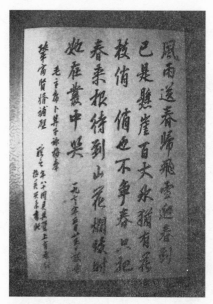

Father's calligraphy of poem by Mao, 1977

Stephen's parents at the Summer Palace, 1979

Stephen with Ambassadors Leonard Woodcock and Zhang Wenjin and their wives, 1984

The family reunited in Detroit, 1985

Stephen (facing camera) at Beijing Jeep reception in Detroit with Vice Premier Chen Muhua (third from right), 1985

Brothers and sisters dedicating their parents' tomb, 1985

GM in China: ancient culture, new promise

CHEN: "China is difficult to ignore."

Stephen with Zhu Rongji, Mayor of Shanghai, 1988

News article about Stephen and GM in China, 1986

Stephen addressing an economic cooperation conference in Nanjing, 1988

Stephen (in costume) with family after performing "Orphan of the Zhao Family" in New York. Dawei (left) and Lei played Stephen's guards, 1989

Amerihua's gift manufacturing base in Xiaoguanzhuang, Baoying County, Jiangsu Province, 1995

Stephen with A.O. Smith friends in Tiananmen Square (son Lei is second from left), 1996

Long overdue wedding photo of Stephen and Yuying at age 60, 1999

Stephen with brother Yansheng and sister Jiahui at the gate of the former Chen mansion, 2000

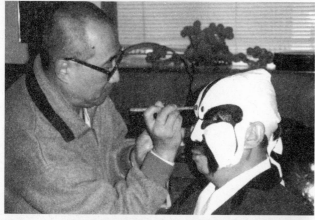

Noted actor Li Changchun painting Stephen's face for a Peking Opera performance, 2001

Stephen with grandsons Michael and Matthew at their great-grandparents' tomb, 2006

Stephen's family (left to right, back row): Ping, Dawei (David), Lei (Leighton), Vivian ; (front row): Yuying, Michael, Stephen, and Matthew, 2007

Memorial ceremony in Yanmen, 2009

Chapter 14

FLYING HIGH AND FAR

1976-1981
Beijing, China

YUYING WAS BOILING DUMPLINGS AT the stove outside my parents' room when I hurried up to her breathlessly.

"The Four are gone," I whispered in her ear and stretched four fingers in front of her.

"What are you talking about?" I knew she understood me but couldn't trust what she had just heard. This was unimaginable news. Just the week before, they had been making speeches glorifying the Cultural Revolution.

I looked around and whispered again, "The Four are gone, finished."

"The Four?" Yuying pointed above.

"The Four. Yes, the Four."

Yuying was thunderstruck and replied, "Nonsense!" I think she actually wanted to say "Fantastic!" but the news was too incredible.

"It's true. Trust me." I dared not, of course, let even my wife know the source of my information. You didn't name names in case an innocent slip could expose a colleague or friend to persecution.

"I can't believe it," she murmured.

"I don't joke about such serious topics. And how could or why would I lie to you?"

We sat down on the steps to the platform that held the stove. For some time, we sat there smiling, alternately shaking our heads in wonderment and nodding at each other with joy, wondering what this great change would mean in our lives. Could we really be emerging from the nightmare that had plagued us for a decade? All of a sudden the pot on the stove began to boil over and Yuying jumped up, saying, "Oh! My dumplings!" Opening the lid, she found a pot full of mush.

I went into my parents' room, and they could not believe their ears when I told them the news. I had to repeat it several times. By the end, we were too excited to speak quietly.

"Be careful; even the walls have ears!" said Yuying as she walked in, carrying the pot of overdone dumplings.

"Truly. Let us not say another word about it. Let's eat," Mother said.

None of us cared a whit about what we ate that night. Mushy dumplings and all, it was a wonderful dinner.

There could have been no greater relief to us—and all of China, except for their supporters—than the arrest of the Gang of Four. When the Party publicly announced their downfall a week later, the country turned to celebrating. Alcohol was sold out in many places. The Gang, with their clawing and grasping ways, their vicious attacks, and their tyrannical tenacity reminded people of crabs, and crabs became their symbol. When the news hit, crabs quickly sold out in Beijing markets. I pedaled my bicycle all over town for hours just to get four crabs and then not in the "ideal" configuration—one female and three males, the female representing Jiang Qing, Mao's wife. (Wang Hongwen, a labor activist; Zhang Chunqiao, a propaganda expert; and Yao Wenyuan, a literary critic were the others.) Some people added a big male crab to stand for Mao.

Steaming and eating the crabs served symbolically to vent the masses' anger. My parents, Yuying, and I finished the four crabs and a whole bottle of red wine, which we drank only to commemorate important and joyful events. During the last part of October, parades and large gatherings of happy people occurred throughout China.

When the facts of the case emerged, it was clear that once Mao was no longer around to protect them, the Gang plotted to consolidate supreme power in their own hands. On October 6, alarmed at their actions, Marshal Ye Jianying, Chair of the Party's Military Commission (and a founder of the Chinese People's Liberation Army) and Party Chairman Hua Guofeng had the Gang of Four and many of their followers arrested. Jiang Qing was detained at her home. The other three were kept in custody in the Hall of Huairentang in the Zhongnanhai, where Party headquarters were located. It was horrible to even contemplate the havoc and destruction that these radical ideologues had caused during the Cultural Revolution. But neither can we focus blame on four people for the decade of atrocities that will forever mar our history. The guilt must be widely shared. It is a national shame.

I never voluntarily read any newspapers during that decade because they just rehashed the same, old stuff in the same, old tone. I never voluntarily went to theaters because there were only eight model operas and movies in the whole country. Starting that fall, however, I began reading newspapers every day hoping I might catch some reference to Deng Xiaoping. Even after the Gang was crushed, though, no immediate changes took place under the policies of Chairman Hua Guofeng's "Two Whatevers": "We will resolutely uphold whatever policy decisions Chairman Mao made, and unswervingly follow whatever instructions Chairman Mao gave."

Making fundamental changes for a better and more open China representing the aspirations of nearly a billion people proved to be a force that no one could stop. In July 1977, Deng Xiaoping was finally reinstated to all his original posts. Under his guidance, the "Two Whatevers" policy was denounced that month at a Party meeting. For the first time in new China's history, a brief period of political liberalization ensued, freed from Mao's autocracy. It became known as the Beijing Spring. The public was allowed unprecedented freedom to express its dissatisfaction and criticize the government. By late summer of 1978, huge wall-posters and hand-written articles condemning Party policies and such actions as the way the government had suppressed the April 1976 Tiananmen Square demonstration appeared on what came to be called the Democracy Wall, a few kilometers west of the Square.

An absolute turning point occurred in December 1978 when the Party's Third Plenary Session of the Eleventh Central Committee established Deng's indisputable supreme leadership. With this meeting, too, the first of a stream of reform measures that would transform China utterly in the following three decades were promulgated. This was the beginning of China's "second revolution." We didn't know, of course, what was going on behind the scenes within the Party. But events beyond our wildest dreams only a few years ago began happening regularly, giving us great expectations for our future.

Deng's pragmatism was neatly captured by some of his oft-repeated statements. He preached that "Practice is the sole standard for testing truth." When Deng said, "It doesn't matter if the cat is black or white so long as it catches mice," we felt great hope that the decisions China would make under his leadership would be based on practical facts rather than rigid ideology.

While the US and China had carried out various cultural exchanges beginning in 1972, it was not until January 1, 1979, that the two countries finally restored diplomatic relations. President Carter was eager to do so during his term in office, and Deng was willing to put aside temporarily the issue of the US selling weapons to Taiwan. The restoration of relations began a new era of economic and cultural exchanges. As soon as it opened in March, I went to look at the new US embassy, where the Stars and Stripes was waving. It was not a sight you could have predicted a few years before. Our former number one enemy was now our most promising partner.

Another surprise that month was my parents receiving a letter from the local branch of the China People's Bank informing them of unclaimed bank deposits in their names. My mother and I went to the branch where a kind lady in her thirties invited us into her small office. She showed us two deposit books. The first recorded the repaid principal with all the interest due from China's first Government Bond, issued in 1950. My mother had set a one-time subscription record for

325

buying bonds in Beijing. At the time, Father was angry with her for taking this step without consulting him. But my mother certainly made a wise decision that resulted in a significant sum of money being restored to the family coffers, allowing the family to improve its quality of life. If my father had prevailed back in 1950, he would have donated the money to China's war to resist US aggression and aid Korea.

The second deposit book showed the dividends from my father's plant from when it became a public-private joint venture in 1956 until October 1957. The dividends were to be issued to all original owners of private businesses for 10 years, but as soon as my father was labeled a Rightist in October 1957, his dividends were terminated. The two deposit books didn't accrue any interest after my mother had handed them over to the bank in August 1966. There was nobody you could reason with about this obvious injustice, nowhere to turn for fair resolution. It was like a robber taking all the money you had and handing you back a tip. Still, we also felt fortunate because no one anticipated this turn. With their windfall income, my parents hosted all our celebrations and meals over the lunar New Year holidays. It was the Year of Sheep in the Chinese zodiac, my mother's birth year. She was 72.

Immediately after the holiday, I got a phone call from my father, who hadn't used a telephone since we had moved from our mansion. (None of our other residences had a phone.) I knew it had to be something urgent. He asked me to visit him and showed me a letter the instant I got there. It was from the Beijing Cultural Relics Bureau telling my father he could go to the Imperial Academy next to the Confucius Temple to claim antiques that had been confiscated.

It was a warm February Saturday in the midst of Beijing's usually cold winter season. I borrowed a flat-bed pedicab for the job. My father and Yuying sat on the flat bed and I pedaled it to Chengxian Street inside of the Anding Gate. The Imperial Academy had been founded in 1306. Its Piyong Palace, the "Emperor's School," was one of Beijing's six grand palaces. The academy was the only extant ancient school in China. Because of Premier Zhou Enlai's unequivocal orders, it had been spared the destruction inflicted by the Red Guards on other such venerable sites. When I pedaled the pedicab through the four memorial archways on the ancient street, all of us admired them silently, in awe. I thought of the countless millions of seekers and believers who had filed past this very spot. How was it possible that such a sacred place could be turned into killing grounds by the Red Guards? How many innocent scholars were tortured, beaten, and killed in this noble school? What a desecration of the place where for almost 700 years, emperors from the Yuan, Ming, and Qing dynasties had offered sacrifices to Confucius!

"Professor Chen, do you still remember me?" An older, slender man with a ready smile opened the door and welcomed us into the Imperial Academy.

"Pardon me. Please refresh my memory as to where we have met before." I could see my father was trying hard to place the man.

"In the Palace Museum of the Forbidden City many years ago when you donated your ancient paintings and antiques to President Ma," the old man said.

"Wait a second. Are you the young secretary of President Ma Heng?" my father exclaimed.

"Yes, but no longer young. I am now 61 years old."

"Perhaps you remember my son Songsheng. He accompanied me that day. And this is his wife, Yuying."

"Well young Songsheng seems to have gained a few inches and added a few pounds since then," Laing observed with a smile as he nodded to Yuying and extended his hand to me.

"I beg your pardon again," my father said. "I cannot recall your name."

"Liang. My name is Liang."

"Mr. Liang, what a pleasant surprise," my father responded.

"I have an even bigger surprise for you. Please follow me."

Mr. Liang led us to the walkway in front of Piyong Hall, the Imperial College's main building. There the emperors had lectured in a square building, which stood for the earth, under a round roof, which represented the heavens, and surrounded by a round lake, which symbolized the oceans. Four stone bridges crossed the waters and wide walks reached to the four gates of the palace, signifying the extension of scholarship to all parts of the world. This glorious site epitomized the high achievements of classic architecture and the richness of Chinese cosmology. The Academy was an inspiring place, offering profound insight into how our ancestors saw their place in the universe.

When we got to the great gallery, our jaws dropped. We could hardly believe our eyes. Along the stone corridor were row after row, batch after batch of antiques and works of art. Attached to every carving, painting, scroll, screen, porcelain, bronze, precious stone, and piece of furniture was a marker with detailed information: the date of receipt and warehousing, brief description of the object, and the original owner's home address. Item after item bore my father's name.

My father seemed by turns stupefied and excited. Tears welled up in his eyes. I know he never thought he would be reunited with some of his lost treasures. In his astonished joy, he could hardly say a word. He took a few steps toward the pieces and then returned and sat down on the stone steps.

"It is a miracle, truly a miracle," he managed to say.

"When I saw your name, Professor, I made the utmost effort to clean up all your valuable pieces. That was the least I could do, and I am afraid it is also the most I can do," Liang said.

"It's awfully kind of you to take such good care of our items during these difficult times. Thank you." My father's voice was quavering.

"You certainly are most welcome. I regret that I also must inform you, Professor Chen, that some confiscated pieces from your collection were designated as Four Olds and can't be returned to you. I have no record of those items." Mr. Liang seemed ashamed to have to give my father this news, and he quickly switched to a different topic. "And, some confiscated pieces from your collection are items that the government wants to buy from you. Here are the details."

"Understood, understood," my father responded instantly.

"Please have a look at the list and the prices offered." Liang handed three pieces of paper to my father.

"There is no need. Everything is fine." My father didn't even bother to read them. I took a quick glance at the first page: four yuan for a mountains-and-waters painting from the Ming Dynasty. Two yuan for an early Qing Dynasty painting. What a joke! With these ridiculous prices, I could use my monthly pay to buy a couple dozen of these pieces and resell them for a fortune. Yuying was also irritated at the prices. I heard her mumble, "Absurd!"

My father quickly signed the paper without saying a word. He gave no indication that he noticed Yuying's and my reaction.

I think he knew the prices offered would be insultingly low and he just wanted to get the transaction over with. He'd been in this position before. And he certainly was overjoyed to get at least some of his beloved pieces back. We were paid 72 Yuan for 41 pieces—paintings, calligraphy, scrolls, and antiques of the Song, Ming, and Qing dynasties—all for less than $50 at the time, about $1.20 per item!

"I can do nothing on those matters." Liang pointed to the pages. "I am bound hand and foot by the policies, rules, and regulations that I must enforce. Please forgive me." Mr. Liang apologized profusely to my father.

"Understood. I am very thankful indeed." My father then added, "Satisfaction is worth more than riches."

"Is there anything else I can do for you, Professor?" Liang asked.

My father hesitated. "I do have a question. It is about the inkstone."

"Inkstone?" Liang asked with a puzzled look.

"Yes, Chu Suiliang's inkstone from the Tang Dynasty."

"What about it?"

"I told the captain of the Red Guards who seized it that the inkstone was a priceless treasure and urged him to turn it over to the government." That event was seared on my father's memory.

"I have never heard of it." Liang was startled.

I quickly added, "The captain came with an official from the Cultural Relics Bureau and took the inkstone away the next day, August 29, 1966." I too recalled the scene as if it had happened yesterday.

"Cultural Relics Bureau?" Liang was agitated. "State or Beijing?"

"We don't know," I said.

"What did they look like?"

"The captain was a short, ugly guy with wire-rimmed glasses named Wang. The official of the Cultural Relics Bureau was a tall, well-dressed, middle-aged man. The captain introduced him to the Red Guards as the Director."

"No way. Impossible. I know all the directors of both the state and Beijing bureaus. All of them were over 60 in 1966 and not one of them was tall. Besides, I'm pretty sure all of them were in prison by that time." Liang smelled a rat right away. And in a flash I realized that Wang had taken the inkstone for himself.

"Father, why don't you tell Mr. Liang the whole story of the inkstone?" I suggested. "Yuying and I need to find a truck to take all these pieces back home."

Our harvest of heirlooms was much more than we expected. There was no way one pedicab could do the job. Yuying and I took it back to our friend and tried to think where we might borrow a truck. Then it dawned on me: why not try my Institute? The Institute's driver was a Peking Opera fan and a good friend of mine. I finally tracked him down. When we got back to the Academy, Mr. Liang had finished his notes about the inkstone, and my father looked like he had been having a most enjoyable conversation with a most compatible colleague. It took us quite a while to carefully pack and load all the items onto the truck. My father bowed his thanks to Mr. Liang. Liang said that he really didn't deserve my father's gratitude and that he would report the inkstone case immediately to his superiors.

It was so ironic. A truck from our Institute had carried the Red Guards who raided our house and confiscated my father's antiques 12 years ago. Now, a truck from the same Institute was carrying us and our long-lost treasures back home. Of course, our home now was not the home we had then. And not all our treasures were returned, including the rarest of all, the inkstone of Chu Suiliang.

On our way back home, my father was quiet and seemed sad. I didn't know why and dared not ask.

Suddenly he spoke, "Son, would you ask your friend to stop at a restaurant soon? He must be hungry."

My father was thoughtful to entertain my driver friend with a dinner. We had instant-boiled mutton at an old restaurant. The truck was safe unattended outside. Pilferage was very rare in those days. After we filled ourselves with good food and drink, my father cocked an eye at me and nodded toward the counter. I followed him to the front desk, where he took out the 72 yuan from his pocket and gave them to me as if he were getting rid of something he couldn't bear to keep.

"Pay the bill."

"I have money." I wanted to take care of it.

"Do as I say."

"Ten yuan should be enough."

"Take all the money and don't tell your mother about it," he cautioned. "Buy something for Dawei and Lei."

He paused for a moment.

"Would you ask your friend to drive us to your apartment?"

"You want to unload these items in our apartment?" I asked.

"Yes, is that alright?"

"That should be no problem for him. Especially at this hour."

"I don't want to disturb my neighbors. Besides, our room is so small," my father said.

And that is how I came to be reunited with many items that I remember from the happy days of my childhood. We were so used to being abused and ill-treated over the past 20 years that when we were treated even a little decently, as we had been lately, we didn't know how to respond or how much to trust our apparently changing fortunes. We were somewhat reassured when over 3,000,000 Rightists were officially relieved of their designated titles. Later, the Party Central Committee removed the titles of all Landlords and Rich Farmers and decreed that they and their offspring should enjoy the same treatment as other Chinese citizens. Although they were still at the foot of the social ladder, more than 20 million people could shed the onerous labels that they had carried, some for more than 30 years.

On January 28, 1979, the first day of the lunar New Year, Deng Xiaoping began his epoch-making visit to the US. During Deng's visit, the two countries signed agreements on science, culture, education, commerce, and space technology. One sign of increased cooperation between the two countries was the rapidly increasing stream of Chinese college students going to study in America.

The year 1979 finished the first 30 years of China's long march to modernity and put an end to the disastrous period of the Cultural Revolution. Deng's reforms began in earnest that year, ostensibly to build "Socialism with Chinese Characteristics." From that time on, we started to hear entirely new terms and policies advocated by Deng: emancipate our minds, use our heads, seek truth from facts, unite as one, and look to the future. As China implemented its reforms and opened up to the outside world, its foremost mission was to correct the most grievous and damaging errors of the past. It had to be done with care because most of them were Mao's errors, and the Party had to maintain Mao's standing as a wise leader. The top leadership feared a domino effect if Mao's standing were to be questioned. It was Deng who navigated these tricky waters, always advocating that practice, not ideology, should be the sole standard determining the truth. After a long and fierce debate that challenged the correctness of the Party's policies and principles, Deng's premise was finally accepted by most of the nation's cadres and the masses. And at least implicitly, Mao was criticized, which paved the way for implementing Deng's openness and reform policies. China entered a period of unprecedented progress.

I still remember the day my father showed me a headline on the front page of the influential *Guangming Daily*: "One person wronged, population increased by 300 million." Mao had severely criticized the famed economist and Peking University President Ma Yinchu because he had proposed that China look to limiting its population growth. Mao went so far as to label Ma's birth control proposition as a "new Malthusian theory of population." (Malthus was, of course, representative of "bourgeois" thought and thus inherently wrong as well as evil.) "Many hands make greater strength" was Mao's policy. The joke at the time was that Mao's idea of birth control was to periodically hold a Cultural Revolution (which claimed so many lives). Ma was marked as a Rightist in 1957 and was terribly persecuted but had never admitted he was wrong. Now he was rehabilitated and named as Honorary President of the Peking University at the age of 96. But it was too late to change the results of this error. China's population swelled from 600 million in 1966 to 900 million by 1976.

To cope with and feed the big population, the newly instituted Household Responsibility System revolutionized the countryside immediately. Freed to work for the benefit of their families, Chinese rural dwellers did what came naturally, and this resulted in truly astounding increases in production, enabling them to have adequate food and clothing. They became "farmers"—small entrepreneurs—again, renting their pieces of land from the government on a long-term basis. They could decide on a rational basis what to plant, and whether to store, process, or sell their produce on the free market (as long as they sold their quotas to the government at fixed prices). The "free" market, although not totally free, played a critical role in the economic development of rural and eventually urban areas. Agricultural output soon rose throughout China, which helped the nation's effort to reform. Reform works best when done on a full stomach.

Under the leadership of Deng, the chief architect of China's "reforms and openness" policies, the cities of Shenzhen, Zhuhai, Shantou, and Xiamen in Guangdong and Fujian provinces became special economic zones, opening to the world. Foreign investment and advanced technologies began to enter China. Deng publically announced that some regions and people would become rich first, and that certainly happened. Private businesses sprang up like bamboo shoots after a spring rain. Privatization supported reform, saved China, and is the backbone of the economy today. More than 70% of the Chinese labor force is now employed by the private sector.

All members of our family benefited from these new policies. My monthly salary, which had been 55 yuan for over 16 years, was raised to 62 yuan. Yuying and my other relatives received similar raises. My siblings and brothers-in-law, who had suffered horrendous discrimination and mistreatment at their universities in Beijing and Baoding, were promoted. Jiahui was transferred to Baoding after eight years working in the poverty-stricken countryside of Gansu Province. She was soon promoted to Chief Physician in the Baoding No. 2 Hospital. I, amazingly, a former dutiful son of a Rightist, was transferred to the China International Trust and Investment Corporation (CITIC), the first and largest foreign trade and investment company in China.

CITIC was founded on October 4, 1979, with the full support of Deng Xiaoping but initially capitalized at only 200 million yuan. The Corporation now has 44 subsidiaries in and outside of China with total assets in 2008 worth 1.6 trillion yuan. In the beginning, with just a few dozen employees, we worked in rooms at the Peace Hotel. We then moved to the 14th and 15th floors of the Chongwenmen Hotel with fewer than 100 employees. As one of the pioneers, I enjoyed, for the first time in my life, a friendly working atmosphere and learned a lot from my elders and colleagues. My English skills and knowledge of metalworking engineering were put to immediate use in negotiating with foreign investors and traders. These experiences laid a solid foundation for my business career in the US.

At the same time, there was a growing demand for my services outside of work because of my English proficiency. While I still felt uneasy interpreting for government officials, I liked doing simultaneous interpretation of English language movies, which were always standing room only for internal audiences at the Institute. It was extremely difficult to get tickets for these shows because most of them were popular new films. I was quite the hero when I distributed the dozens of complimentary tickets I was given. At least once, however, my reputation far exceeded my abilities.

I was invited to interpret "Gone with the Wind." I had read the novel by Margaret Mitchell a few years before and had seen the movie with my elder sisters when I was younger. Its Chinese title was "Beauty in the Time of Misfortune." I thought I could handle the job. Boy, was I wrong. Not a chance! I was supposed to interpret every role in the film over a public address system. With Rhett Butler or Scarlett O'Hara, I might catch every fourth or fifth word, but other than that, I had no idea what they were saying. Mammy, Scarlett's house slave, was on screen a lot and sure spoke up, but I never understood a single word she uttered in her thick accent. Not a single word! And the movie was way too long. Since I didn't understand the dialogue, I tried to tell the story, at least as much as I could remember. I confess, under those conditions, I'm not sure the audience got their money's worth that evening even though their admission was free.

Sitting in the small, overheated, crowded, and closed projection booth with barely time to take a quick sip of water and no time to eat, I fainted toward the end of the show. It was probably a combination of the heat and the pressure. Some people told me later that I was babbling incoherently as they carried me out of the booth, put me on a stretcher, and drove me to a nearby hospital as a precaution. There I was diagnosed with minor heat stroke and told to drink sugar water.

Despite my mishap that night, I made a name for myself and won critical praise as an English language expert. I was invited to host "How to Study English Better and Faster" at China's Central People's Broadcasting Station. When I spoke at a big event in Beijing's Worker's Gymnasium facing 5,000 eager faces, I was momentarily tongue-tied. The last time I had been there, my cowshed cellmates and I were being herded to a rally to denounce Marshal Peng. Now, I was lecturing an even larger audience on how to study English. What a change! Only I knew myself. I was no expert. I was simply a survivor.

Unfortunately, just as my family was beginning to enjoy a more comfortable and worry-free life, my mother passed away. She had a sudden heart attack and died immediately. Although she had long treated it, I think my mother's persistent high blood pressure finally caught up with her. All our other disasters paled in comparison. When we lost Mother, we lost the backbone of our family.

My mother was born into a very poor family. After graduating from primary school in Baoding, she came to Peiping with her family and began working at a boarding house where her father cooked. She could not continue her schooling and soon married my father and became pregnant. Even with no formal education beyond grade two of junior high school, my mother was more involved in our finances and in developing the family fortune than my father. Father cared about his teaching and then the real estate business, but he was an idea man, someone who saw the big picture and thought on a higher plane. He wanted nothing to do with managing money or the details of his businesses'—or the family's—daily workings. How much money did we have in the bank? Only my mother knew. How extensive were our real estate holdings? Only my mother knew. How much money was in my father's pocket? Only my mother knew.

Once my father went out to see his friends, got on the trolley, and found he had no money to pay for a four-cent ticket. He had changed clothes unexpectedly before leaving, and Mother hadn't stuffed any money into the pocket of his new pants. My father finally found a four-cent postage stamp in his eyeglass case and insisted on giving it to the conductor as payment for his fare. My father excelled at some aspects of business, but my mother actually managed everything inside and outside of the family. She stored everything in her nimble mind and thought about matters that others overlooked. Prudent but not over-cautious, diligent and detail-oriented, she and my father formed an excellent team.

I had a hard time dealing with my mother's death. I was absent-minded at home and work. I didn't sleep well and developed dark rings under my eyes. I lost my appetite and lost weight. I shunned company, preferring silence and solitude. I had a lot on my mind. I spent a lot of time in the reading room of the Beijing Library thinking about my mother, her hopes, and my future. Mother's death proved to be a catalyst for me that precipitated quite a turn in the Chen family history. After several long conversations with Yuying and my father, I applied for graduate school in the United States. Three months later, I received a letter of admission as a PhD student from the University of Arizona.

CITIC approved my resignation to pursue my degree. The American Embassy gave me all the help I needed. I soon secured a private passport and an airplane ticket from Beijing to Tucson, Arizona. Everything happened so suddenly, so smoothly. I did have two potential problems, but they were easily resolved. China didn't have a university degree system at the time. I had neither a bachelor's nor a master's degree, only my college graduation diploma. At this critical moment, the Cultural Counselor of the American Embassy and Professor Wang Zuoliang of the Beijing Foreign Languages Institute wrote highly complimentary recommendation letters for me that carried the day. Then to obtain a visa to the US, I had to have an affidavit of support. My sister-in-law's younger brother, Cheng Yao, happily and quickly sent what I needed from Boston. Since my passport was for a private citizen rather than a government official, I had the right to make my own decisions regarding how long I would stay abroad and what I would do afterward. With everything in hand, I was ready to fly high and far.

Not long before I left China, and without letting anyone know, I went to see Uncle Lee, whom I learned was seriously ill. Despite his debilitating respiratory ailments, he still smoked heavily, although he had stopped drinking on his doctor's orders. He'd been depressed for some years now, but he seemed genuinely happy to see me. We reminisced for quite some time, talking about old friends, our mansion, and the tool factory. When he learned I wanted to go to my father's plant to see his workplace in the boiler shop, he insisted on going with me.

"It is too late." I tried to discourage him.

"No matter how late, I must go with you," Uncle Lee said as he grasped my hands. "You might have other chances to go there; I won't."

Uncle Lee knew the gatekeeper of the plant. There was nobody there at this late hour, so he just waved us in. Uncle Lee guided me past the main office and workshops and walked directly to the deserted boiler shop at the east end of the plant. There was a small shelter next to it. Its sole "window" was made with a broken wooden frame holding a stained piece of heavy-duty paper instead of glass.

Uncle Lee opened the crude door of the shelter and let us in. He carefully used his handkerchief to dust off a shabby desk in the corner, took a half bottle from his pocket, and placed it on the desk.

"It's sorghum liquor, your father's favorite."

"That's so thoughtful of you, Uncle."

I looked around. Nothing other than the broken desk was in the room. Despite the emptiness, I felt suffocated by the close walls and low ceiling, but this hovel was precious to me. It was my father's only refuge during his darkest days in the factory.

"I know it's asking for the moon, but I wish I could keep this shelter as a Chen family treasure."

"That's not a real possibility," Uncle Lee said, "but keeping the memory of it alive in your mind honors your father. And every time you tell the story of your father and this factory, this shelter will rise again."

Uncle Lee unscrewed the cap of the bottle, poured half the liquor on the ground, and handed the rest to me.

"I can't drink this stuff anymore. Drink it up to honor your father for both of us."

I raised the bottle above my head, bowed deeply to the desk, and finished off the bottle.

That was the last time I saw Uncle Lee. He died in December 1981.

One week before my departure, my father had all our relatives gather in Beijing. We spent a wonderful day in my apartment. I told them in detail the whole story from when I first thought of going abroad to what I needed to do before my departure. I showed them my passport, ticket, and admission letter from the University of Arizona. The room became silent when my family realized that the ticket was only one-way, Beijing to Tucson. Yuying couldn't quite hold back her tears and went to the kitchen to assist Grandaunt in preparing lunch. Later, we had a reunion dinner in a Henan cuisine restaurant. Except for Dawei and Lei, nobody, even me, ate or drank much. It was a quiet evening.

Three days before my departure, my father arranged a more intimate dinner for the immediate family. Then on the eve of my departure, again through my father's arranging, just the two of us shared dinner in his small room. I bought two of my father's favourite dishes and a bottle of Maotai on my way there.

My father's room, about 120 square feet, was originally a bathroom. The bathtub, basin, and toilet had been removed and it became a storeroom and then a bedroom. Its walls were still covered with white ceramic tiles, giving the room a cold feel. My father and mother had lived there for 15 years. The biggest inconvenience was that they had to use the public toilet outside the house during frigid winters, sweltering and stinky summers, and pelting rain. After my mother passed away, Yuying and I tried to persuade my father to live with us in our apartment, but he refused. Even when he stayed in our apartment for a few days, he always made the same excuse to go back to his small room, saying, "Your mother is waiting for me."

Auntie Sun, my father's nurse, was cooking on the stove outside the room when I arrived.

"Hello, Auntie." I passed the dishes to her. "I didn't buy too much. Otherwise my father would criticize me for my extravagance again. Please warm them up."

"Leave that to me. He's eagerly awaiting you," Auntie Sun said. She was highly regarded in our family. After my mother passed away, my father's health and spirits went downhill fast. He often sat alone weeping. His eyesight was getting worse. But we knew he was in the best possible care with Auntie Sun.

I walked into the room. A double bed was on one side and a single bed on the other. My mother used to sleep on the double bed with Dawei and Lei when they came on weekends. After Mother passed away, Father slept on the double bed. He told us he wanted to be closer to my mother.

I found my father listening to the news, holding a small semiconductor receiver radio close to his ear. I had asked my friends to assemble it as a gift for his 84th birthday that year.

"There you are," Father said as he turned off the radio. "Are you all ready for tomorrow?"

"Yuying is still packing my two suitcases, and I have a few things left to do."

"You will cross the ocean to a place where you will be a stranger. Take an umbrella when the sun shines and food when you are full. Be well prepared."

There were four dishes on the table: boiled peanuts, marinated cucumbers, braised bean curd, and mixed vegetables. During tough times, dishes such as these were all we could afford once a week. And now we served them for my last dinner with my father . . . my last dinner in China until who knew when.

"Father, shall we have Maotai?" I opened the bottle.

"Let's start with the vermouth. Red portends prosperity and good luck." Father pointed at the red wine bottle on the cabinet. Father normally drank only a small cup of medicated liquor every day. Red wine was reserved for special occasions.

The cabinet was the only valuable piece of furniture in the room. One reason for its value to us, however, was never revealed to strangers. Only family members knew it. There was a very secure safe within the cabinet where we kept family treasures. My father took his favorite small antiques that were returned by the government from our apartment and locked them in the safe. From time to time, he would take them out to enjoy.

"Father, first I toast you. I wish you good health and a long life." I looked at my father, lifted my cup, and drained it.

"To your health and a safe journey!" My father drained his cup.

The toasts—full of good wishes—were also sad. My father and I were saying farewell, perhaps forever. Just that moment, I couldn't look directly at my father.

"This is your destiny!" my father said. "I could never imagine that someone in our family would be going to America!" Father drank another cup of wine.

"Take it slowly, Father." I served up some mixed vegetables for him. "We have waited a long time for our luck to change. To be honest, however, I hesitated to take this trip now. This is the year of the rooster, your year. I should be with you."

"Hesitating? What for? This opportunity will come only once in your life. Sixty-three years ago I left Yanmen. I cared nothing about hardships but only for the health of your grandparents. You know what your grandpa said? He told me, 'Your mother and I are both happy from the bottom of our hearts for your great ambition! It is your time.'" My father couldn't continue.

I stood up and handed him a towel. He wiped his eyes and looked up at me. "If your mother were here, she would have said those same words to you. It is your time. It is your time now, Son."

It was my time now! I was so excited by those profound, concise, and powerful words. China held great promise with the new reform and openness policies and the ongoing argument about the roles of capitalism and socialism in our nation. But the Cultural Revolution still cast a long shadow over China. Changes, good or bad, could happen at any time. I knew my ambition could not be realized at home.

"It is my time, now. I'll always remember that, Father. Thank you for those words. I am feeling much better now, although I am still worried about your health."

"I know. But there is no need to worry. Your brothers, sisters, Yuying, and my two grandsons are all with me. Come on! Let's drink some Maotai."

"You've had enough, Father."

"It's a happy day. Let us enjoy it to the fullest."

I filled two small cups with the strong white liquor.

"This toast is the blessing from your mother, wishing that you soar to great heights!"

"Thank you both. I'm hope that Mother's soul may bless me from heaven."

Solemnly, we lifted up our drinks and downed them.

Auntie Sun walked into the room with the last dishes. I invited her to join us, but she said, "I had my meal in the kitchen. You two enjoy your last night together."

"Eat some more," Father said as he finished his bowl of corn meal porridge. "It won't be easy for you to get food like this in America."

I liked everything on the table, but I had no appetite. I was pleased to see, however, that Father enjoyed his food. After he put down his chopsticks he went over to his bed and fished out a small bag from beneath a pillow.

"This is the pouch that your grandfather gave me upon my departure from Yanmen and you saved when you threw the 20 silver coins into the moat. Take it with you now."

I stood up and took the pouch with my two hands. After all these years, the silk cord that fastened the pouch was still a bright red.

STEPHEN SONGSHENG CHEN

"I don't have 20 silver coins for you. The pouch is empty, but it is full of promise and heavy with heritage." It seemed that Father had prepared his words to speak them now. "No money can compare to what you have learned from the Chen family. This tradition, your true inheritance, is more than enough to fill this pouch. Keep it forever."

"Father!" I said quickly and then faltered as my eyes welled up.

"The pouch will remind you of your family, your homeland."

"Pouch or no pouch, family and homeland will never leave my mind. I love our homeland, so rich in natural beauty and human culture. As to my debt to the family, I can never hope to repay it. I must pass it on to my children."

"Son, you make an old man very happy."

"Father, there is one way you could make me and Yuying and the boys very happy. We'd like you to move into our apartment after I leave."

"I'd like that. Yuying is such a good wife to you and so like a daughter to me. And I so enjoy seeing Dawei and Lei grow up. Thank you for asking me."

"Wonderful. That sets my mind at rest. It's getting late. I hate to break up such a wonderful evening, but I should be leaving."

"Yes. It's time."

I stood up slowly, walked to the door, turned back, stared at my father's pale face, and forced back my tears. It was not the custom in our family to embrace and I wouldn't want to embarrass my father by doing so, but I was reluctant to leave my remaining parent.

"Father, I'll write to you as soon as I get there. You must take good care of yourself."

"Don't worry." Father sat there, waving his hand again and again. "Go! Just go!"

After walking out of his room and turning the corner, I stood on tiptoe at the window and peeked in. I saw my father cover his face with a towel, rub his eyes, and whimper softly. I broke down, covered my mouth with my hand, and rushed to the street.

Between thinking of the huge step I was taking and that towel on my father's face, I didn't sleep a wink that night. Early in the morning, I went out and brought home some soybean milk and pancakes. Yuying and I tied the two suitcases with belts and then woke up Dawei and Lei. The car arranged by our friends had already been waiting for us in front of our apartment building for an hour.

There were few cars on the way to the airport. After we pulled up in front of the entrance, Dawei, 15 and already as tall as I, helped with the luggage. Lei, 11, was curious about everything at the airport. We talked for a short while and then heard the announcement that the flight to San Francisco was starting check-in. Yuying, Dawei, Lei, and our friends accompanied me to the security entrance. Yuying, holding Dawei and Lei's hands, didn't know what to say at the last minute. Staring at Yuying, I managed to exclaim, "I'll be fine. Take good care of yourself. Take good care of Grandaunt, Dawei, and Lei. Take good care of Father." I turned to board the plane.

"Wait," Yuying shouted then lifted up a handbag and passed it to me. "I almost forgot. These corn cakes are from Father."

Waving my hand, walking forward while looking back, I soon was no longer able to see my friends and family anymore.

Saturday, September 5th, 1981, I left Beijing on a one-way ticket and started my long, lonely journey.

I had a window seat on the plane. Opening the handbag, I took out a corn cake for breakfast. Corn meal and corn cakes were such a traditional and much-enjoyed food in my family. I'm not sure my father and I could survive without them. They had sustained us in good times and bad. I understood immediately why my father had given me a full bag of corn cakes. They would help me overcome the difficulties and obstacles I faced ahead, taking my first steps toward an unknown world. But there had been countless steps before me. I was both following in my father's footsteps and going beyond them to fulfill his unaccomplished dreams and expectations.

I was surprised at how quickly and easily the huge plane lifted off. We ascended through the morning fog and broke into a brilliant, cloudless sky. The sun, still low and red in the east, suffused the sky with a warm glow. Through patches of ground fog below, I watched as the hills and rivers and cities and villages of my homeland got smaller and smaller. I felt like a kite with a broken string. I had never flown this high and far.

I took out my pen and wrote on my boarding pass: *Like Father, Like Son. The Second Departure.*

Chapter 15

GREAT GAINS, GREAT LOSS

1981-1984
Tucson, Arizona, Detroit, Michigan, US;
Beijing, China

I THOUGHT I WOULD BE totally excited when I left China so full of expectations for what I would find in the new world, the free world. It didn't turn out quite that way. Sure, I was in a high state of energy, but as soon as the plane left the runway in Beijing, my dominant feeling was sorrow at my loss. I looked down at the land where I was born and raised. It wasn't that I was flooded with sweet or bitter memories. All I felt was painful loneliness and self-doubt.

I wondered at what I had just done. I was leaving home on a one-way ticket with $600 in my pocket and didn't know when or even if I would be able to return. I had left my father behind; I had left my wife and two sons behind. I was so alone. Images of a solitary goose honking in the sky or duckweed floating on a pond crossed my mind. I tried to draw some strength from the words I had written on my boarding pass. This second departure was like my father's first one from Yanmen 63 years before. I needed to be brave like my father, resolute in the face of obstacles, but at that moment I didn't feel I could rise to the occasion.

I was wide awake during the flight—wired from all the coffee I had drunk—so I took two treasured books out of my bag, hoping they might distract me. Of all my publications, hundreds of titles and millions of words translated and written over 17 years, I valued these two books the most. One was the first edition of the Modern Foreign Literature Translation Series, published by Canton People's Publishing House. The other was an anthology of H.G. Wells' writings published by Peking University. My translation of the "Loneliness of the Long Distance Runner" by Allan Sillitoe appeared in the first. My translation of *The Island of Dr. Moreau* by H.G. Wells was in the second.

Both books had resulted from the publication of my essay "Rectification and Regret" on the front page of the influential *Guangming Daily* on April 27, 1979. As the title suggests, I used the news that some intellectuals were being posthumously honored as heroes to criticize the Chinese authorities by implication. My point, made indirectly, was that in admitting their error in condemning those intellectuals, the Party should also regret the disaster and damages of the Cultural Revolution. My essay struck a sympathetic chord and resonated with many readers. I received a bushel of letters, forwarded to me by the paper, and responded to several. Soon some correspondents started showing up at my door and before long we began meeting occasionally. Through one of my new friends, I met

Feng Yidai, an editor and well-known translator. We hatched the idea to launch what we called the Modern Foreign Literature Translation Series. I devoted virtually all my spare time to the project.

We applied to China's publishing authorities and proposed several titles, some of which were quickly rejected, including Mario Puzo's *The Godfather*. Many titles were approved, including "The Loneliness of the Long Distance Runner" and *The Island of Dr Moreau*. I picked Sillitoe's little gem because I liked its dark humor and was taken with the word "loneliness." My choice of H.G. Wells' science fiction classic was more complicated. Wells depicted the sinister kingdom of Doctor Moreau on a deceptively beautiful South Sea island. The mad doctor plays a cruel God, turning beasts of the jungle and domesticated animals into half-human hybrids that do beastly things.

I felt that the Cultural Revolution had turned humans into thoughtless creatures who did beastly things and that Mao was a tyrannical dictator who had played the cruel God with his nation. Wells had written a parable that addressed the issues of his day, and by translating his bloody horror story into Chinese, I secretly wished to address what I felt was the burning issue of my day and my country. The project thrilled me and filled me with dread. I completed my translation at night after work during the particularly hot and humid summer of 1979. Using an old trick my father taught me to beat the heat, I put my bare feet into a wash basin full of cold water as I sat and wrote. Nevertheless, perspiration dripped from my head onto the paper and my clothes clung to me. I could almost wring them out when I took them off to go to bed. But my heart was ice-cold as the horrible scenes of the book called up for me the terror my family had experienced. My dread was that someone high up might catch my drift, pick up on the innuendo, and read Wells' novel as I intended. Had the puzzle been solved, I would never have been allowed on this airplane.

Between reading and musing, the flight, even with a stop in Tokyo, went by quickly. Before I had finished Wells' tale, I heard the announcement that we were beginning our descent into San Francisco. What music to my ears! What a beautiful name. It was the home of America's first Chinatown, the largest outside Asia. The promise of the '49er Gold Rush and the ability to make in a day what it took them a year to earn in China caused a mass migration of my countrymen to what they came to call the "Old Golden Mountain." And when the gold fields ran out, the Chinese fanned out, helping to build the railroads, keeping shops, cooking, working in laundries or fields, or becoming servants, anything to earn money and realize their dreams. I was following in countless footsteps.

As the plane landed, I must admit I was overcome with anxiety and began hyperventilating. A stewardess actually asked me if I was okay. The kite with a broken string had crossed the ocean and fallen to earth, and it was a bit of a jar.

The flight to Tucson was a short hop. I arrived to a gorgeous sunset with many rich hues of red, which I took as a good omen. But as soon as I stepped outside the terminal, a wave of heat hit me and almost knocked me to the hot pavement. I knew nothing of Tucson's climate before I got there, and I'm glad I didn't. I don't do well in heat, and this would have given me one more thing to worry about. Even with the sun low in the sky, its rays were so glaring that I couldn't keep my eyes open. When Xianglong Zang, my high school mate, and Danli Lu, an acquaintance from Beijing, picked me up at the airport, they must have thought I had an eye ailment because I was blinking so much. I vowed to get some sunglasses the next day. When I checked the prices for a pair, however, I was shocked at how much I would have to pay. Luckily Xianglong helped me to find a perfectly good, name brand pair at a yard sale for $3. The first photo I sent home to Yuying with the letter telling her of my safe arrival showed me standing at the entrance of the University of Arizona, wearing shorts and the sunglasses. In her reply, Yuying said I looked just like a Western movie star and she couldn't even recognize me.

Xianglong was an engineer at the China Petroleum Research Academy. He had come to the United States one year earlier and was finishing an English Improvement Program at the University before pursuing his master's degree. Danli had come to the United States 10 years before after graduating from the English Department of Taiwan University. A native of Henan Province in her mid-40s, she was involved in developing business ties with China. Danli drove us to our humble studio apartment in an old two-story building where Xianglong had rented a single room for both of us. The price was right, only $60 a month, and it was less than 500 yards to campus. Danli declined with thanks Xianglong's invitation to dinner and left.

Our room was on the second floor. There was a pull-down bed on one wall. The room managed to hold another smaller bed, two small desks, and two folding chairs, which we would have to rearrange when the wall bed was down. Xianglong, much shorter than I, was kind enough to let me use the big bed. Off to one side was a kitchen, an absolute mecca every night for hundreds of cockroaches. Before his infrequent cooking, Xianlong would use several kettles of boiling water to supplement his stomping to kill the damned things. Watching him in the kitchen made me think of the new song I learned my first week in Arizona, "La Cucaracha." We had to use the shared toilet and shower at the end of the hall.

To welcome me, Xianglong invited me to the neighborhood Kentucky Fried Chicken outlet. I just loved their crispy chicken, so tender inside, and found it better than Beijing's savory chicken. I still prefer it and can fully appreciate why KFC is China's most popular global brand. After dinner, we toured the University. Young students were everywhere enjoying the pleasant evening. I had seen photographs of modern dress in the foreign magazines reserved for "select" readers in the "internal reading room" of my Institute, but to actually see tight jeans, short shorts, and micro-minis up close on beautiful coeds was something else again. What a sharp contrast to the Mao suits and coveralls all over China. It was my first meal and my first night in this capitalist country, my former enemy on the other side of the world from home. It was fantastic.

I was late for the semester and needed to take a couple of tough exams before my official admission to the PhD program. I used almost half of my $600 to register for the mandatory courses. After paying my share of the rent, I deposited the remaining $259 in my first checking account at a local bank. I was worried because cash meant everything here. It had been drummed into my head since childhood that the Chens did not borrow money; we never owed anyone a penny. But how long would $259 last? Fortunately my English skills rescued me at that critical moment.

Thanks to a timely introduction from the Oriental Studies Department where I planned to matriculate, I got a job in the library, cataloguing two rooms full of Chinese books and publications. I worked 20 hours per week at $4.35 per hour to start. I needed the money, but I valued even more the opportunity to read so many books that were banned in China. I also found work as a dishwasher in the student union building and took a night shift job at the Tucson Inn Motel. I checked customers in and out and answered and transferred phone calls. The hourly pay was $5.75, and I could use the electric typewriter in the office to type my papers in the wee hours of the morning. That was a definite plus.

The motel job was unbelievably boring, except for one night. It was about 3 AM, and I was in the middle of typing a paper when suddenly I saw a masked man staggering towards me, holding a pistol. Since all the doors and windows were tightly locked, he must have slipped in through the back door of the Inn's dining room next to the office.

"Freeze! Give me all the money," he said, pointing the gun at me, his breath reeking of alcohol.

"Take it slow. Take it easy." I surprised myself with how unruffled I was. I calmly opened the drawer and took all the cash out.

"Here you are. Every penny." I put all the cash and coins, a little more than $100, on the desk.

"That's all ya got?"

"We had a slow night."

"Rubbish! Tell me where you hide the money." He placed his gun directly against my forehead.

"Why should I lie to you? It's not my money. Why should I care?"

"You telling the truth?"

"Trust me. I'm a poor student. Here, take my money." I pulled a $20 bill and a few ones from my pocket and offered them to him.

"I don't want your money. You seem like an honest man. I like you." He sat down in the lobby, pulled a bottle from his back pocket, put it to his lips, and drank deeply.

Then he stood up, took the money, stumbling back in the direction from which he had come.

"Would you like to use the front door?" I asked.

"Yes, it's more convenient." He was drunk but still clear-headed.

I saw nobody around and unlocked the door for him.

"You are a good man. See you around." He staggered out the door.

See me around? I never wanted to see him again. Two days later, I heard that a pizza restaurant two blocks over got robbed. A young clerk was shot dead for less than $100.

After my long hours of work and study, I'm sure I looked haggard in my classes. I think my teachers and classmates were quite surprised when I scored high on almost all my papers. My days were hard, but compared with my time in the cowshed and the labor camp, it was a breeze. With my steady income, I soon sent $200 to Yuying and my father. Early in 1982, I received my certificate of admission to the University. My professors told me I was one of a small handful of students who entered the PhD program without a bachelor's and master's degree.

That fall was an extremely hot one in Tucson, and the central air conditioning in our building was very unreliable. One scorching night, the old system broke down yet again. Our room was as hot as a steam bath. To escape it, Xianglong took me to the Desert Sands Go-Go Club. I had no idea what go-go meant until I saw several strippers dancing on the stage. I had heard about such establishments, but that night was my first experience. To stay in the club, all we had to do was buy two bottles of beer. Xianglong knew the ropes. He chose a table far away from the stage to avoid tipping the dancers. At first, I felt so awkward watching the nude girls dancing that sometimes I looked away from the stage.

One of those times, my attention was drawn to a small, slender, and very pretty young woman preparing to perform. When she went on the stage, the crowd drowned out her accompanying music with cheers. She danced with a presence and grace that differentiated her from the others. She put so much feeling and passion into it, her dance seemed a sort of emotional release. I could feel that she had a story to tell. She was not just another naked body on stage entertaining a roomful of horny men.

The girls worked by turn, one after another. We sat a long time waiting for her turn to come up again and were so enthralled by her performances that we forgot the time. When we finally left, it was already past midnight. Biking our way back to the apartment, we noticed a young woman riding her bicycle past us. Suddenly Xianglong yelled, "Hey, look! It's that girl." I pedaled faster to catch up with her and was thrilled to find that it was indeed our favorite dancer!

"Hello! We very much enjoyed your dancing," I shouted.

"Oh, did you! Thank you," she replied, looking at me with a smile.

Her name was Stephanie. I was surprised to find out that she was a student of the School of Dance at the University. A college student stripper! We arranged to meet again in the library. She asked me to find her some Chinese books about dancing. The only one I could find was about Dunhuang, a cultural crossroads on the Silk Road and one of China's most significant sculptural sites. Some Dunhuang grotto murals date from the Tang Dynasty and feature flying fairies dancing their way to heaven. She loved the book, photocopied many of its pictures, and told me she would include some of those flying movements in her dances.

The more we talked, the more I admired Stephanie. She had lost her parents years before. Without a scholarship, she supported herself by dancing at the club. She had tried working in fast food restaurants, but the pay was too low for her needs. At the strip club, she earned $15 an hour plus tips. She invited me to her school's annual show at the University Theater. Her fabulous solo was the highlight of the evening. She was flying on the stage and also into my heart, not only for her beauty and talent, but also for her great spirit. Although she faced daunting odds in pursuing a career in New York, I believed that she had a bright future. Before she left for the East Coast, I invited Stephanie for a farewell dinner at her favorite Greek restaurant. I asked her where and when I could see her again. She smiled and said that she didn't know when, but she believed it would most probably be in Dunhuang.

Xianglong and I soon bought a used Dodge for $350. I didn't tell him that I selected this make simply because my father had once owned a Dodge. I missed my father even more since the cataracts on both his eyes had worsened. I felt so sorry that now he could barely see. Everything was a blur to him. I was determined to earn enough money to buy him good quality lenses, which weren't available in China. Our Dodge made possible my job of advising Danli Lu on trade with China. She lived 30 miles away from the University. But even with all my jobs, earning enough money to buy my father's lenses wasn't easy until what turned out to be the opportunity of a lifetime presented itself.

On the recommendation of a close friend who worked as a consultant there, American Motors Corporation (AMC) asked me to translate a big contract proposed by the Beijing Auto Works. I had to finish the job within seven days. Using a second-hand electric typewriter I bought at a yard sale for $70, I finished the job in five days, but I didn't know how to write an invoice and had no idea how much to charge. A Chinese colleague in the library helped me. Instead of $800 as he suggested, I wrote $680 on my invoice. Very soon, AMC's International Department sent a thank-you letter and a check for $1,280. The letter praised my fluent translation, which helped them to clarify many confusing issues. The letter also said that my excellent job in a rush deserved much more than I had requested. This was the biggest check I had ever received. The very next day, with the help of Danli Lu, I purchased the artificial lenses my father's doctors had prescribed.

Two weeks after I mailed the lenses to my father, I made my first international call to Yuying. With the permission of the Chinese owner of the Tucson Inn, I used the motel phone. Yuying had to go to the Beijing Long Distance Call Center near Fuxing Gate to take the call. I scheduled the date and time in advance in a letter to Yuying. Yuying registered with the Center and told me the number to call in her return letter. One late night in mid-May 1982, I made the call. An operator answered and then called, "Number 28, booth 6." Suddenly, I heard Yuying's anxious voice, "Songsheng, Songsheng, are you there?"

"Yuying, Yuying, I am here. How are you?" I shouted.

"Let Dawei talk to you."

After a short silence, I heard a low voice say, "Daddy, this is Dawei. We are fine and we all miss you. I'll take good care of

Grandpa. Here is Mother." Every word seemed to have been practiced beforehand.

"Songsheng, we received the lenses. Father will have the surgery soon in Beijing First Hospital. Don't worry. How are you?"

"Everything is fine here. Make sure to have the best doctor perform the operation."

"We will. Grandaunt and Lei are all very well. Lei is now a forward on his soccer team. Don't send us any more money. You need it there." Yuying's voice quivered a little.

We didn't talk long. It was our first conversation in eight months.

My out-of-the-blue translation job provided me with a huge paycheck, but, even more importantly, with a foothold on the corporate mountain I was soon to climb. AMC invited me to Detroit to interview for a summer job. When I showed up on the 19th floor of the AMC Building in Southfield, Michigan, my made-in-China suit and a pair of Arizona leather boots attracted a lot of attention. Folks appeared genuinely impressed by my comprehensive knowledge of China's economic policies and how to do business in China. To their surprise, they found that I was also quite familiar with mechanical engineering. With these qualifications and my spoken and written English skills, they offered me the internship immediately and I accepted it just as quickly.

I worked at AMC the whole summer of 1982. Both AMC and Beijing Auto Works (BAW) were deeply frustrated by the tough, endless, and unproductive negotiations. Both had invested considerable time and money without achieving significant progress. I soon discovered one of the key obstacles: the evaluation of AMC's software and technologies. Out of the $53 million total investment, AMC proposed to invest $16 million split evenly between cash and technologies. The massive collection of related documents—patent specifications, parts and accessory lists, production and assembly procedures, quality and inspection standards—filled half of a large office. The Americans believed the deal to be more than reasonable, but the Chinese thought it was overvalued. We were at a stalemate.

After I had called and spoken to the BAW negotiators dozens of times without any movement on their part, I was totally frustrated by this hopeless situation and ready to give up. Because of the 12-hour time difference, it was already past midnight as I lay on my bed going over my most recent fruitless phone call to China. At that moment, I swear I heard my father's distinctive voice with absolute clarity. "Give it one more try before throwing up your hands," he told me. "Be creative, but be firm." I picked up the phone and called the head of the BAW team.

"Mr. Wu? Sorry to bother you again. I know Beijing Auto Works has been producing and selling Beijing Jeeps. Do you know that Jeep is AMC's trademarked logo?"

"Your colleagues told me about it. Why do you want to tell me again?" Mr. Wu was a little impatient.

"Please understand. The name Jeep can be used *only* by AMC, not by anyone else. *Only* AMC can call its Cherokee a Jeep. Other automakers have to call similar cars four-wheel drive vehicles, or something else, but not Jeeps." I put great emphasis on the word "only."

"What do you mean? We have been producing and selling our BAW Jeeps for many years." He sounded none too happy about my comments.

"But what you are doing is illegal. BAW has been violating international trademark law for many years." I decided to abandon caution and press my case.

After a brief silence, Mr. Wu said, "Nobody cares about that in China."

"But the export market cares. The international market cares. You have emphasized so many times the importance of our joint venture exporting its Jeeps to international markets. Isn't that right?"

After another silence, Wu said, "How much is the name worth, anyway?"

"To be honest, it is priceless. What I am trying to say is that it is hard to put a price on such a valuable asset." I sensed there might be a light at the end of the tunnel and continued. "Perhaps you could tell me how much *you* think it is worth since the first Jeep was built on September 23, 1940, especially since the name is renowned the world over."

Mr. Wu made no response.

"Pardon me for speaking frankly. But AMC could have asked for a lot of money just for the Jeep trademark. Now it's included as part of the $8 million share of our technologies. It's a good deal for BAW and China," I concluded.

"Mr. Chen, would you please mail me a short summary of what you just said as quickly as possible?" Wu's voice was a lot more accommodating.

"No problem. I'll do that immediately."

"Thank you very much for your phone call, Mr. Chen." It was the first time he had ever thanked me.

Before 1977, any attempt at economic relations with capitalist countries was branded as a "national betrayal" by the Gang of Four. Even in the early 1980s, learning advanced science and technology from developed countries was still seen as "blindly worshiping foreign things and toadying up to foreign powers." With rapidly increasing numbers of international contacts, overseas Chinese soon played active roles in helping China and foreign parties to establish their economic ties, but they were often still viewed as being under the malign influence of a decadent ideology. Many BAW executives didn't trust me at the beginning. Some even suspected me of being a spy. When they visited AMC in Detroit, they would dodge and avoid me sometimes and speak among themselves. After my long phone call with Mr. Wu, their attitude toward me changed. Although there were still many differences and disagreements to be ironed out between us, they started talking, calling, and consulting me more and more often. I also learned a critical lesson. Trustworthy friendship must come before or hand-in-hand with successful business ventures. Friendship first, business second.

I enjoyed my summer job. I learned new things every day from my colleagues, and I liked Detroit and the surrounding area. It was the sixth largest city in America, had hosted the 1980 Republican National Convention, and its landmark Renaissance Center was brand new. AMC provided me with a test vehicle, a soft-top Jeep. I rented a room in Dearborn. The landlady, Mrs. Poindexter, was the widow of a retired engineer who had worked his whole life for Ford. Sleeping on the couch in the living room, she rented her only two bedrooms for extra income. One room was rented to a Chinese engineer, a visiting scholar at Ford. I got the other one.

My small room contained a large bed, so large that there was virtually no place to stand and absolutely no place to sit except on the bed. I had to watch my newly bought 13-inch color TV while lying on my side, changing positions frequently to avoid neck pain from watching TV for so long. I stayed there the whole summer and will always remember Mrs. Poindexter, the kindly, old woman who helped to shatter whatever stereotypes of Americans I still carried. We had been taught in China that American citizens were all rich capitalists. Now I realized that ordinary Americans were just like ordinary people at home, good folk who did what they had to do to get by.

When I was ready to return to Arizona after the summer job, I was invited to a farewell dinner. Quite a few AMC senior managers showed up. To my surprise, I was offered a permanent job at AMC right there at the dinner table. Unprepared for this offer, I didn't know how to respond. My AMC friends told me they didn't expect an immediate answer, but they wished I would consider the offer seriously. The easy, warm atmosphere of the dinner, especially after several rounds of scotch and soda, made for candid and convivial conversation. The managers were forceful in presenting this as my golden opportunity. The proposed Beijing Jeep Corporation (BJC) would be the first *manufacturing* joint venture between the US and China. Only the Great Wall Hotel would precede it. How often might such an opportunity come my way?

I couldn't dispute that. America was quickly proving to be the land of opportunity for me, offering me possibilities beyond my greatest ambitions in China. The new Jeep, Cherokee, would be produced and sold in my homeland. The prospect excited me.

Another point they pressed was that all of us overseas Chinese had friends, relatives, or schoolmates with doctorates and no real jobs and no prospects. Some were actually on the dole since jobs were becoming harder to find, especially in the liberal arts. Taking another approach, they said that with my wide-ranging capabilities—English language skills, mechanical engineering, foreign trade experience—my destiny should be in the business world or I would be wasting my talents.

AMC had me pretty convinced, but shifting from literature to business was not an easy decision for me or Yuying. My dream was to get my PhD and become a scholar in comparative literature, specializing in the complementarity of Chinese and foreign literature. But my ambitions extended beyond literature to developing US-China economic ties and sharing mutual experiences, understanding, and wealth. Yuying thought I should first finish my doctorate and make my career decision later. She didn't know there would be no "later." I came to believe it was now or never. My AMC friends didn't want me to rush to an immediate decision. And I did need time to think everything over more thoroughly and to win over Yuying if I decided to accept the AMC offer. Interestingly, neither of us talked about money. I forgot to tell her how much my compensation would be and she didn't ask. I cannot recall today how much it was exactly. I just remember it was over $30,000 to start, which seemed like a lot of money to me.

Instead of flying back to Arizona, I decided to take a Greyhound bus for $99, a special ticket that allowed me to get on and off as often as I liked. I enjoyed my first long bus tour across the beautiful countryside and the opportunity to get a good look at America, its towns, and her citizens. The trip also allowed me time to mull over what was probably the most important decision I would ever face. An event along the way helped me make up my mind.

The bus stopped periodically at stations where the passengers could eat, stretch their legs, buy a magazine. The bus driver's accent made it hard for me to understand his directions. At one stop in one lonesome spot in Missouri, I got off the bus, went to the restroom, bought a Coke from the machine, and couldn't get my change. While I was talking to the manager, I saw the bus pulling away. I ran after it, shouting for the driver to stop but could only watch the bus with my bags on it fade away into the distance. I was so stunned I didn't know what to do. The Greyhound station manager calmed me down and told me that everything would be fine. I could take a later bus to the next station, where my bags would be waiting for me. I wasn't convinced that it would work out that way, but I had no choice. To kill some time, I wandered through the little town. Unbelievably, I found a Chinese restaurant in the middle of nowhere. Out of curiosity, I went in.

It was a family-owned and run restaurant. The husband was the chef, his wife the cashier and waitress. Coming from Taiwan as poor students, they studied hard and earned their master's degrees in mechanical engineering. Both of them worked for companies at various locations in Missouri. After they had their son and daughter, the wife became a full-time housewife and the husband's income fell short of their needs. So they bought the restaurant. Years later, they sent their son to Yale and their daughter to the University of Missouri and still had a small surplus after paying all their bills. They told me that by selling the restaurant when the time came, they would generate sufficient income for their retirement. They said college degrees didn't mean a lot in the US. Scholars with PhDs might have an even harder time finding a job because of their minimum pay standards. The couple refused to give me the bill no matter how much I insisted. They treated me to a free meal and some timely advice.

366

So I ended up accepting AMC's offer. I had so many unfulfilled dreams to accomplish. Compared with the uncertainties—even risks as I had experienced that fateful night at the Tucson Inn—of pursuing a literary career, the exciting Beijing Jeep project was safe and real and had great potential. I would never give up on my dream of writing, of contributing to the world of literature, but I would defer it. My business career would pave the way for accomplishing my larger dreams and achieving my destiny.

I returned to the University with such mixed feelings. I knew it would be many years before I could return to literature. I threw myself into my academic work and finished a major paper on "Weishen," a short story by Mr. Lao She. The story—its title means "a vision"—is a tale of love, recounting Lao She's own first love. I analyzed the piece from a new angle. Mr. Lao She had spent six years teaching and writing in England. Either consciously or subconsciously, he had absorbed and employed many of the techniques then coming into use in English literature, such as stream of consciousness. At the same time, his writing captured the flavor and diction of old Beijing, full of rich details and poignant insights into the human condition. I focused on how Mr. Lao She brilliantly merged Chinese and Western traditions and techniques. Before leaving Tucson, I delivered this, my first and also my last paper, to Professor William Schultz of the Department of Oriental Studies. My paper was more than an academic exercise. It was my lament for Mr. Lao She, the writer I most admired in the world.

Saying good-bye to Xianglong was not easy. We had lived in close friendship under the same roof for 11 months. I left my share of the Dodge to him and invited him and other friends for a dinner at the Chinese restaurant where Xianglong worked to earn money for his studies. All my friends envied me because they didn't know what they would do after they obtained their degrees and I already had a career. Xianglong drove me to the airport and told me that he had made up his mind to go back home to Beijing after he had saved $58,000. (The number 58 is considered lucky in China.) Years later we got together in his nice Beijing apartment. He told me how he drove the Dodge all the way to Las Vegas and then Reno, working 16 hours a day in casinos and restaurants. He never withdrew a penny from his savings account and ended up taking over $80,000 back home. He was driving a Cherokee, working for a foreign trading company, and had a lovely wife and two daughters.

My first full-time job at AMC was as a Senior Analyst for the China Program. I coordinated the negotiating, drafting, finalizing, and translation of all the legal documents, contracts, and appendices of the proposed joint venture. After settling down in my newly rented one-bedroom apartment opposite the AMC building in Southfield, Michigan, I came up against one of the toughest missions in my life.

I didn't know much about international or US business law and regulations, but I got up to speed quickly. When I used my new terminology in conversation with my Chinese counterparts, they were always confused and sometimes indignant. A typical example was the section in the contract on arbitration. There was no such word as arbitration in China. They were furious that the Chinese party had to agree to go to Stockholm for arbitration with the foreign party when the joint venture company was registered in China. In spite of the fact that I, in my heart, felt the same way, I had to persuade them to accept this provision. This single issue took us 17 days to resolve. For the Chinese, it was a major sticking point, a sovereignty issue, a matter of losing face. Only after I showed them contract after contract containing such stipulations did they acknowledge this to be a near-universal standard and accept it.

Even with this progress, the Chinese remained inflexible on BJC's export commitment and salary parity between the American and Chinese executives. Sitting across the negotiation table from each other, our faces were often suffused with a white anger. But at the dinner table, our faces took on the rosy blush of geniality, especially after a few drinks. Our positions didn't change, but our attitudes did. Out of fierce arguments, an easy friendship developed. We could talk straight and even joke with each other. One Chinese negotiator said with a warm smile that his supreme desire was to throw me out the window of our meeting room (on the 19th floor!). I teased him back by saying that I wished his wife would order him to come back home so that we could make progress without him. (He was the most henpecked man I knew.) Then came the day that accelerated our negotiations and brought them to a satisfactory conclusion.

AMC planned meticulously for a visit by top Chinese government officials and executives to its Jeep plant in Toledo, Ohio. The Toledo Parkway Plant, which opened in 1910, was the oldest operating automotive factory in North America. It consisted of two connected units, the Stickney Plant and the Parkway Annex. The operations spread through a labyrinth of buildings and vehicles and components moved by conveyer lines from building to building and through various levels. Showing our guests the entire production line was no small feat! The building was much older than BAW's factories. Parkway began producing military Jeeps at the beginning of

World War II. Its two, tall brick smokestacks bearing the name "Overland" had served as a Jeep brand landmark since 1942. I could see great reverence on the faces of our visitors as they studied the old plant with its long tradition and old-fashioned ethics. Long before the tour was over, all of us were huffing and puffing from our exertions, but I felt our hearts were beating hard together.

Immediately after leaving the plant, we retired to a Chinese restaurant for the concluding presentation. I used a slide projector to tell the Jeep story, starting with its indispensable role during World War II. Jeeps were the first mass-produced off-road vehicles. Their ability to travel through mud, sand, and snow and operate well under the worst conditions soon became legendary. Every Allied country used Jeeps for basic transportation, ambulances, mobile weapons platforms, and supply vehicles with trailers. By war's end, the Jeep had become a veritable "goodwill ambassador" around the world carrying everyone from privates to generals and high-ranking officials. Our Chinese friends knew well that Mao Zedong, Zhu De, and other Red Army leaders all had used Jeeps during and after the war. The vehicles were greatly admired by both military and civilian populations. Chinese people my age, as many of our visitors were, still remembered fondly those Jeep vehicles with their folding tops. For them, the presentation brought back sweet memories, while teaching them something new.

When I reached the last slide, I said, "I am going to tell you a sad story with a happy ending." The slide was a cartoon, showing an American Army general with a pistol in his right hand, covering his eyes with his left hand, about to shoot a badly battered Jeep.

"Like old times in China, when a commander had to put his badly wounded horse out of its misery, the general here has to put down his Jeep and keep the enemy from capturing it alive. But it is clear that old Jeeps never die and they do not even fade away. They are alive in the thoughts and memories of many people today. Our joint venture can capitalize on the glorious fame of the Jeep, the world's most widely imitated vehicle. When we begin to manufacture and assemble Jeeps in Beijing, people in China and around the globe will be able to drive the Cherokee, the descendant of that original Jeep that refuses to die."

My presentation drew hearty applause. Mr. Wu, the owner of the restaurant (with a master's degree in mechanical engineering) presented us with two bottles of Chinese white liquor. He proposed that one bottle stand for China and the other for America and said that when we finished them, the liquor from the two bottles would be blended as one as we should be. Sharing the common feeling of fusion and oneness, we began to discuss how the joint venture could learn from the work ethic and thrift seen in the Toledo Jeep plant. The export issue could be resolved only after BJC had demonstrated that it could produce good quality Jeeps at competitive prices. Everyone was inspired by this sharp turn toward a common goal.

After that, things moved pretty smoothly. To return the concessions on arbitration and export terms that BAW finally agreed to, AMC agreed to pay Chinese executives the same as their American counterparts, even though we knew they were required to give 80-90% of their salaries to BAW's labor union. On May 5, 1983, the Beijing Jeep Corporation became the first US-China industrial joint venture and the 189th Chinese-foreign company to be established. By January 15, 1984, BJC, the first Sino-foreign whole car assembly company, started operations in Beijing after almost four years of negotiations.

I drafted BJC's first press release in Chinese, writing out every word neatly on a piece of typing paper in my apartment, and posted it promptly to the *People's Daily*, China's most authoritative Party organ. In my dark days, it was the *People's Daily* that signaled the political campaigns that persecuted so many millions of Chinese and led me to the cowshed and labor camp. I remembered how the very thought of the paper would make my flesh crawl and how my scalp would prickle as I read its vituperative words: "Knock the enemies down to the ground, and set one foot upon them so that they can never again stand up." That was my father and me, among millions of other innocents that they were talking about! I was dying to call my father and let him know that my announcement would soon be appearing in the *People's Daily*. But Yuying told me that my father's condition had deteriorated rapidly. His cataract surgery had not succeeded, and eventually he could discern only light and dark; otherwise he could no longer see. He missed my mother and cried constantly. And he wasn't eating much.

I saw my father for the last time in June 1984 when I visited Beijing with a delegation from Michigan as Governor James J. Blanchard's advisor. Leonard Woodcock headed up the trade part of the group. The Governor's office had helped me obtain a temporary permit to go back to China while I was seeking my green card. After 32 months of separation, I was thrilled to see Yuying, my two fast-growing sons, and other relatives. But as heart-warming as it was to reunite with my father, it was also a sad sight. Even Yuying's warning had not prepared me for what I found. Father had wasted away to almost nothing. His drawn face made his sunken eye sockets look cavernous and emphasized his clouded blindness. Grim perseverance seemed to be the only thing keeping him alive.

We had our family reunion party at Houdefu, a favorite restaurant of my father's because it served Henan cuisine. I had to lift him into and out of the van that took us there. Sitting next to me in the restaurant, he ate little and talked less. Although he was no longer able to see, he couldn't take his white eyes off me. He put his hand in my lap as if he were trying to feel and follow me while I was talking. This touched me deeply, because touching was not something we did in my family. My father never embraced us, didn't even shake hands with us upon parting. We expressed our feelings for each other through our eyes, and now my father could no longer do that.

When I took my father back to his small room, we sat and talked, although I did all the talking, telling him of my experiences in America. Of course, I didn't tell my father everything. I left out any reference to the Desert Sands Go-Go Club and the night I got robbed.

After about an hour, my father suddenly said, "You should leave now." His feeble voice was almost inaudible.

"It's still early," I replied. I wondered if this might be the last time I would ever see my father. I was loath to bid him farewell.

"You have your duties with the delegation. Just go." He was breathing hard. Simply speaking seemed to tire him.

"Father, please take care of yourself. I'll come back to see you again as soon as I can." I knew lingering would make him uncomfortable. I so wanted to hug him and tell him how much I loved him, but that would have displeased him immensely.

"Fine. I'll wait for that day. Take good care of yourself." Those were the last words I heard from my father.

Again, after walking out of his room and turning the corner, I stood on tiptoes at the window and saw the same heart-breaking scene as 32 months before. My father covered his face with a towel, rubbed his eyes, and appeared to whimper softly.

On September 25, 1984, my father passed away at the age of 87 in the same hospital in which my mother had died, Peking Union Medical College Hospital. As he lay dying, my elder brother leaned over and whispered in his ear, "Do you want me to call Songsheng back?" My father, too weak to speak, nodded his head three times in consent. That I was not able to be with my father at this moment has been a source of deep pain and regret for me ever since.

When my mother died, I was galvanized into action. With my mother's encouragement from heaven, I made my plans to come to America. After my father's death, I felt suddenly older, more mature, and more deeply committed to honoring my father and mother by continuing their unfinished journey and realizing their dreams.

Peking Union Medical College Hospital: Dawei and I were born there; my parents died there. Life is death. Death is life. Death is inevitable. Life is inexhaustible. I am not a religious person, but I do have a god in my heart—my father. With his honest, simple, diligent, frugal, and patriotic ways, he is a model, an inspiration for me and all his descendants. It is so easy to call my father to mind. I see him the morning after the Red Guards beat him almost to death, silhouetted in a window as he rose to begin his Tai Chi. I see his back as he dutifully swept the street as punishment for his "crimes." And I see him in his tiny room, whimpering, a towel covering his face. These images will remain vivid for me until my very last breath and be engraved forever in the pages of Red Circle.

Chapter 16

Losing Touch

1984-1989
Beijing, Tianjin, Datong, China;
Detroit, Michigan; Avon, Connecticut, US

WITH MY INVOLVEMENT IN ESTABLISHING the first US-China joint venture, I seemed to achieve overnight stardom. The *Detroit Free Press* wrote a long front-page article about me, and I was interviewed by other media. I received many phone calls and letters from companies in America and even Europe, offering me first-class tickets for job interviews or for speeches on investment in China's new environment. I was dazzled by all these offers but most attracted to the one from my friend who had led the AMC China team and now worked for General Motors.

There was no reason for me to leave AMC. I had done good work for them, and they had done well by me. AMC had hired an excellent attorney to handle my immigration case. I met the Third Preference requirements, which were used to identify qualified professionals for permanent residency in this country. But after months of waiting, there was no news from the Citizenship and Immigration Services. Then one day, I got a phone call from the local office of the FBI asking for an interview. I had no idea why the FBI would want to see me. I arrived early at its office in downtown Detroit.

"Good afternoon, Mr. Chen." Two gentlemen in their thirties met me. "My name is Wayne. This is Dennis."

"Good afternoon, gentlemen." We all shook hands.

"Mr. Chen, would you please write your Chinese name in both traditional and simplified Chinese?" Wayne, the tall and stout one, asked.

"Certainly." I did it neatly on the piece of paper offered. Dennis took it and left.

"We know you are applying for green cards for you, your wife, and your sons. It's routine procedure for us to ask you some questions." Wayne was very polite.

"No problem. Please."

"Are you a member of the Chinese Communist Party?"

"No."

"If you were not a Party member, how could you serve as a senior level interpreter for Chinese state leaders?" He watched me closely.

"I don't know, but it happened only after I came back from the labor camp."

"Labor camp?"

"Yes, in Ningxia Province. I was there from September 1970 to November 1971."

"Did you join any organizations under the CCP?"

"I was a member of the Chinese Communist Youth League. All good students in my middle school were members," I added.

"I was also a member of the China Young Pioneers in primary school, if you consider that to be an organization under the CCP."

Dennis walked in, holding several pages of paper. "Mr. Chen, these are only part of your record. Look at how many top-level state receptions you attended."

"I was there only as an interpreter," I said.

"Yes, quite a high-level interpreter," Dennis replied.

"Mr. Chen, we must know the truth about why you left China and why you want to become a permanent resident of the United States. After we review further documents, we'll call you to arrange another meeting."

The FBI agents apparently didn't get what they needed from me at our next meeting or the three meetings I was summoned to after that. It took me a while to realize, because it was so far from the truth, that they suspected me of being a Party member and a spy. Finally, during our fifth meeting, Wayne said, "Mr. Chen, you have made many statements about why you could not be a CCP member. Are you willing to take a lie-detector test?"

"A polygraph test?" I knew the technology was flawed. Clever liars could pass with flying colors while honest but nervous test-takers failed.

"Yes, a polygraph."

"May I show you something first?" I asked.

"Go ahead."

I opened my briefcase and took out the rehabilitation letter with its two red seals that my Institute had issued to me after my return from the labor camp.

"For your convenience, I translated them into English. You are welcome to double-check it, of course." I handed the two sheets of paper to Wayne.

The agents read them quickly.

Pointing at the seals, I added, "This is the seal of the Chinese Communist Party Committee of the Institute; the other is the seal of the Institute itself. The letter admits their mistake in labeling me a Monster and Demon and imprisoning me in the labor camp."

"But after that you served as an interpreter for government leaders who were involved with top secrets. Wouldn't such a role have to be filled by a trusted Party member?" Dennis challenged me.

"Those receptions were no more than courtesy calls. Government leaders would never discuss real issues on such occasions."

"If you are telling the truth, you shouldn't mind taking a lie-detector test. Would you mind?" Wayne asked again.

"No. If you actually trust a machine more than an honest man, I'll take your test." My tone was brusque.

After a short pause, Wayne said, "Mr. Chen, we'll call you if we decide to administer the test."

Before I walked out of the office, I turned back and added, "As the son of an enemy of the CCP, how could I become a member? After all the discrimination and suffering my family and I endured in China, I came to America not for the money but for the justice and freedom that are the heart of a democracy. Please don't jeopardize my confidence in your country."

I never heard from them again about the polygraph. On July 16, 1984, I received my green card. Yuying, Dawei, and Lei were approved for permanent residency in the United States at the same time. Wayne and I soon became friends. He told me that he respected my integrity because I had never lied to them, even on trivial issues. Otherwise, he said, I could have been deported immediately.

I liked AMC but was worried about its future after Renault became a major shareholder. The AMC President, assigned by Renault, had voted no on the China project at the company's most recent board meeting. I felt I could never repay the kindness of AMC, but I was deeply concerned because AMC had to agree to dismiss the first and second BJC presidents, both Americans, under pressure from the Chinese side. I didn't want to get involved in this complicated situation. And I didn't want to go back to China for the joint venture company now that my family could finally join me in Detroit. If my father were still alive, returning to Beijing would make sense, but with him gone, it no longer did.

I faced a hard choice. The AMC President and Vice President in charge of the International Department tried hard to persuade me to stay. They matched GM's salary offer and promised to promote me to a directorship. With deep regret, in October 1984, I left AMC and joined GM. My new job was Director of the China Program Planning Office. I had a huge office on the third floor of GM's world headquarters. I started at the bonus level, and my annual salary plus bonus reached six figures for the first time in my life. I soon learned from my colleagues that bonus-level directors almost never got fired. After serving the company for years, many senior managers hadn't achieved this status. For me, it was just the beginning.

Despite the exciting challenges and obvious rewards of my new job, I was not a happy man. The death of my father and the fact that I couldn't be with him in his last days had cast me into a pit. I hadn't felt this low since my time in the cowshed and labor camp. I still had misgivings about leaving AMC, the company that had given me so many opportunities. And I was as vulnerable and lonely as I had been in a long while. I had business associates but no close friends I could talk with—until a chance meeting late one night in the laundry room of my apartment building.

Carrying a laundry basket, she came through the door in a white bathrobe with a blue towel wrapped around her head and immediately filled the room with her delightful after-bath fragrance.

Standing there awkwardly in my pajamas, I said, "Sorry, I wasn't expecting any company at this hour."

"That's all right," she replied with a heavy Russian accent. "Neither was I."

As she bent to begin putting her clothes into the washer, her loose-fitting robe puckered open to reveal much of her beautiful breasts. I felt I dare not gaze. Between the rapid intake of my breath and my heart beating so fast, it was hard for me to breathe. I could feel my face flush. Before anything else could happen, I quickly removed the remaining clothes from the dryer and took my leave with a mumbled, "Dasvidania."

"You speak Russian?" she replied excitedly.

I didn't even realize that I had said "Good-bye" to her in Russian. "Sorry. Good night." Without answering her question, I bolted for my apartment.

A few days later, she knocked at my door to borrow some sugar. I didn't have any, but it gave us the occasion to get to know each other. Her name was Natasha. She was from Moscow and "in between" jobs just then. Before the Soviet Union boycotted the 1984 Summer Olympics in Los Angeles, in retaliation for the US boycott of the 1980 Summer Olympics in Moscow, she had come to America as the interpreter for a business delegation. She subsequently defected. She spoke of her family ties to China. Her ancestors—called White Russians because they opposed the Bolsheviks or Red Russians—had fled to China after the October Revolution in 1917.

I knew a bit about the White Russians. My father's Russian teacher in the early 50s was one, and I told Natasha about him. He was tall and slim with a neatly trimmed brush moustache and a pair of gold-wire-rimmed glasses. I never knew his name. We called him simply "Professor." His scholarly air appealed to my father, who often invited me to be present whenever the Professor showed up. I think my father felt I might be able to learn something from his tutor, and I did. He always smiled bashfully and asked for a cup of red tea and some sweets. Despite his broken Chinese, I grasped the essence of his sad tale. His parents and sisters were all killed by the Red Army. Together with 200,000 other White Russian refugees, he had fled to Hunchun, a small town in China's far Northeast. All he could take with him were the clothes he was wearing and his glasses.

Natasha's company was enticing. We decided to meet later in the week at a Russian restaurant in West Bloomfield Hills. She wore a very sexy see-through blouse to dinner and obviously felt no hesitation about striking provocative poses. Everybody in the place, openly or furtively, looked at her. Waiters, even from other parts of the room, found a reason to walk by our table. I was uncomfortable sitting next to such a center of attention. But as the evening wore on and we shared our life stories, I relaxed and began to enjoy my new friend. She was warm and compassionate and an excellent conversationalist.

She also was a good listener. And that was something I needed. There was a lot on my mind that I needed to get out.

One night not long after our dinner, she invited me to her apartment. Even though I was prepared, both her dress and her demeanor were even more provocative. I had never before seen anything like the garment she was wearing. It was open on both sides and left very little of her voluptuous figure to the imagination. In her high heels, she was almost my height. She led me around her place showing me the artwork on her walls, some of which was frankly erotic. Her graceful and sensual movements reminded me of the dancers I had seen in the Arizona strip club. I wondered if this beautiful woman who lived well despite not working could be a high-priced call girl or have a sugar daddy or both.

"Would you like to taste a White Russian?" she asked suddenly with a seductive smile and inviting look.

"What?" I said, taken aback at her forwardness.

"Taste a White Russian," she repeated, without any trace of embarrassment.

"What do you mean?" I asked, flustered and red-eared.

She raised her cocktail glass, laughing. "A White Russian. It's a drink made from vodka, coffee liqueur, and cream."

The way she flaunted her charms and so easily engaged in sexual banter had a strange effect; it both excited and repulsed me. Natasha was certainly a complex temptress. But my heart and my head told me that I had to leave, and soon. And I did. A mistake then could have caused everlasting regrets and deep wounds that would never heal, all for a few moments of pleasure.

Once it was clear that sex was not going to be part of our relationship, Natasha and I became good friends for each other.

In her own way, she was just as lonely as I was. When she moved to Orlando that December, I was sorry to see her leave, but by that time, the end of my loneliness was in sight. I would soon be with my family.

I used my two years of savings to put a down payment on a house in West Bloomfield Hills and moved out of my apartment. It was my first house in this country and also a gift for Yuying. With her major in interior decorating, Yuying loved pictures and paintings of Western houses and had assembled quite a collection. Now she would have a real Western house of her own.

I flew back to China to collect my family, and on January 15, 1985, Yuying and I, along with Dawei and Lei, boarded a Pan Am 747 in Beijing and took a first class flight to America, thanks to GM's executive relocation program. It was the first time Dawei and Lei had ever flown. They were thrilled by the view, the reclining chairs, and all the drinks and food. Only after I told them that the caviar, chocolate bars, and snacks were all free did they start tasting them. Holding their "Welcome to the United States" documents, the three of them had their pictures taken for their green cards at the New York City airport. We often made fun of Yuying's picture on her green card. As gorgeous as she was, the photo taken at the airport made her look like an old lady in a fur coat, with puffy eyes and her hair flattened against her head.

When we got to the Detroit airport, it turned out to be a dark night following a major snowstorm. We found my Chevrolet Caprice, my newest company car, where I had parked it, half-buried in snow. We drove to our new home, and when my family saw our gorgeous house, their eyes almost popped out of their heads. As I turned into our driveway, they were amazed when I used the remote control to open the garage door. But the snow was too high for us to drive into the garage. After struggling to open the car doors, we all sank in the snow up to our knees. Lei, not quite 15 years old but much stronger than Dawei, carried his mother on his back into our house. After 41 months of living apart, the four of us celebrated our reunion and soon would enjoy the Chinese New Year together.

Meanwhile, General Motors was proving to be an exciting place to work. With more than 600,000 employees, it was the largest private employer in the country, a great and profitable company, even if a somewhat arrogant and extravagant one. GM had reason for its swagger. It dominated the US market and had led the world in global auto sales since 1931. As a then-popular saying put it, misquoting former GM President and Secretary of Defense Charles Wilson, "What's good for General Motors is good for the country." Many of my fellow employees fully believed that assessment. I was overwhelmed by the luxurious, wasteful, over-the-top treatment of executives: first-class international flights, free new test cars every 3,000 miles, free gas, and free lunches. I quickly gained 10 pounds with all the fine food, especially the desserts, in the private dining room.

My mission was to lead 100 executives and senior engineers from GM and five major Chinese corporations to complete an overall feasibility study and issue a report on potential GM-China joint ventures. The total investment was one billion dollars, back at a time when that was still considered a huge investment.

The project's first phase, to identify the right vehicles for China from current and future GM products, took us four months. As the chief coordinator and negotiator, I got total support from GM divisions, the China Automotive Industry Corporation, and the Chinese governmental officials involved. The unique feature of our proposed program was our plan to use the same one-ton chassis to build a Buick passenger car, a light duty truck, and a seven-seat van. Our objective was to establish a low-cost manufacturing base in China to tap not only the great potential of the Chinese market but of the rest of the Far East as well. In addition to my 12 trips to Beijing in 1985, I also traveled to GM subsidiaries in Europe and Brazil.

One benefit of spending so much time in Beijing was that I accomplished one of my long cherished wishes. After the death of my parents, their caskets of ashes were placed temporarily in the Babaoshan Columbarium. With the help of the Beijing authorities, I purchased a lot in Beijing's most hallowed burial ground, Wan An Cemetery in the west suburbs, an area my parents really liked. We erected a tombstone and made the tomb bed in the shape of a book to commemorate my father's publications and academic career.

Every member of the Chen family and our closest friends, except Auntie Cheng, Uncle Lee, and Uncle Zhang, came to the ceremony. In front of a photograph of my parents that was surrounded by wreaths and elegiac couplets, I delivered a short lament on behalf of the Chen family. Then my brother Jisheng, holding my parents' photo, and Jiahui and I, carrying the caskets of ashes, led the gathering to the grave. There we laid the remains of my parents together to eternal rest.

In a corner of the lot, there was a Chinese scholar tree, which the Wan An cemetery allowed us to keep. How apt that a tree with that name would shade my father's grave. It flourishes there still, shielding the grave from dust storms, rain, and snow, symbolically protecting us from grief and calamities. That tree made me think of the persimmon tree in Goose Gate, where my grandfather had buried the silver coins. Without letting anyone know, weeks later I bought 20 silver coins, just as my father had some 40 years before. I had thrown those coins into the Forbidden City moat in 1966, and now I replaced them. I felt a sense of relief when I put the 20 coins into the black leather pouch where they belonged.

Acknowledging the initial success of AMC's Beijing Jeep and GM's initiatives in China, the organizers of the 1985 Automotive World Congress in Detroit invited me to deliver an address. The 35 speakers included the presidents of Chrysler, Hyundai, and Volvo; the vice presidents of Ford and Toyota; and the Chairman of VW. I was the lowest-ranking speaker among them, but my talk got the greatest response. The grand conference hall of the Renaissance Center in downtown Detroit was packed. After the host announced me, I walked toward the podium with some trepidation. Projected on the large curtain at the back of the stage were my name and the GM logo. When I stepped up to the stage, I saw that the first big letter C of Chen was even taller than I was. In the glare of the bright lights and facing a sea of suits, I felt myself turn a little queasy. I credit my Peking Opera performing experience with allowing me to overcome my butterflies.

I started by quoting a quaint Chinese expression that Deng Xiao-ping had made to express his feelings about mixing ideology and economics: "The cat's color doesn't matter, so long as it catches the mouse."

I said that China was committed to doing whatever was needed to join the world's industrial powers and improve Chinese living standards. My message was a simple one: American companies risked missing many opportunities if they didn't have a China policy. China was the last great frontier for marketing motor vehicles and related products. This giant of Asia, with its ancient culture and one billion inhabitants, had been asleep for many years, but its slumber was over. The giant was awakening.

I explained that China's new leaders were just now learning how far their industries had lagged behind other countries, such as Korea, Brazil, and Venezuela, that they had been even with 30 years ago. The Chinese wanted to catch up, and they were ready to accept help to do that. I emphasized the newness of China's open door policy, noting that while China was an ancient civilization, its current economic system was only five years old. China had a long way to go.

I concluded my speech by saying, "Today's Chinese leaders want to create a kind of Chinese socialism, a market-driven economic system that adapts socialism to China's unique social and cultural characteristics. There's a role for GM in this process, as there is for others. It won't be easy. But at the same time, it can't be ignored. It is not a question of whether GM should be in China, it's a question of when and how."

My message and the enthusiastic response to it that night apparently failed to convince GM's board and its Chairman, Roger Smith. As we were completing our feasibility study report, I was asked to make a presentation to the GM Board of Directors. Our 300-page study had to be condensed into a 30-minute report, including the follow-up Q&A. My colleagues and I worked day and night to get the final version done. When we got to the 14th floor of the GM Building, I was both exhausted and exhilarated. There were eight other executives and staff members with me, waiting in a room next to the boardroom. An older man entered the room and told us we were next. I checked my projector sheets for the last time. Then he returned and told me that we must cut the presentation to 20 minutes. My colleagues and I hurriedly began to pull out parts of the report and reorganize it. Then we waited and waited. Finally the older man appeared once more, this time to announce, "Mr. Chen, I'm sorry, your China presentation is canceled. The board has other, more important issues it must address."

My colleagues and I were deeply disappointed—then damn mad. GM was not just canceling my China presentation, they were saying no to their immediate golden opportunity in China. Not until 10 years later did GM finally establish a joint venture in Shanghai. To this day, even after GM's bankruptcy and reorganization, its China operations continue to be among the company's most profitable.

At this time, Karl Krapek, President of the Otis Elevator Company, paid me a visit. A former Manager of Car Assembly Operations for the Pontiac Division of GM, he just walked directly into my office and told me something that carried a lot of weight with me. He didn't want me to make a rash decision, but he suggested it would be a good time for me to visit Otis in Connecticut. Otis was the world's largest elevator company. My tour of its headquarters and my meeting with George David, the Chairman, made quite an impression on me. My one shaky moment came when George kept me in his office until just 30 minutes before my flight back to Detroit. I still don't quite know how the driver made it to the airport in time, but I was the last person to board my flight. I flew home totally committed to the Otis China strategy and their plans to expand operations in Tianjin. I felt this was an opportunity to spread my wings and give full play to my capabilities, not with projects on paper, but in reality.

In October 1987, I left GM and joined the United Technologies Corporation, becoming Vice President for Pacific-China Operations, Otis Elevator Company. Yuying and I sold our house in West Bloomfield, getting $30,000 more for it than we had paid originally. We bought a bigger and much more expensive house on a hill in Avon, Connecticut. From the summit of our hill, I felt that the broad and sweeping vista before me was emblematic of the wonderful opportunities that lay at my feet.

It was an excellent opening for me and a great time for Otis to develop its joint venture company, the China Tianjin Otis Elevator Company. We were in the right place at the right time. Along with Beijing and Shanghai, Tianjin was one of only three Chinese municipalities directly under the Chinese Central Government. The Schindler Elevator Corporation of Switzerland had already established its own joint venture company with the central Ministry of Construction in Beijing. To protect its interest, the Ministry of Construction was unwilling to see another elevator joint venture competing with its own. The Tianjin-Otis application was, therefore, turned down. But Tianjin was determined to make it happen. The only option was to reduce the total investment in the company within the limit of the $5 million US that Tianjin could approve by itself. While this wasn't Otis' original intention, it turned out to be an absolute steal. That tiny initial investment got us through a narrow doorway into China. Starting in 1987, high-rise buildings and shopping malls were mushrooming all along China's coastal areas. Through joint efforts, Tianjin-Otis set up

15 new service centers all over China. Our revenue quadrupled in three years.

While we were developing a major center in Shanghai, I was honored to work with Mayor Zhu Rongji, who later became China's Vice Premier and then Premier. I first came to know Mr. Zhu when I worked for China International Trust & Investment Corporation in 1980. He was only a division chief in the China State Economic Commission then, but I was deeply impressed by his professional knowledge, fluent English, and ideas about how to develop Chinese-foreign projects in the coal power industry. The more I learned about him, the more I respected him. Six years after he graduated from Tsinghua University, he was labeled as a Rightist, which started an ordeal that lasted 20 years and included five years of hard labor in a May Seventh Cadre School.

Since his experience had been so similar to my own and my father's, I felt a strong and warm connection with him when he received me in Shanghai. Many years later, I heard him sing Peking Opera at a gathering sponsored by the State Council. His highly professional singing and playing of the Jinghu, a two-stringed fiddle, surprised the audience. His great accomplishments, varied experience, and range of talents gave me a whole new image of a Communist leader.

As the company Vice Chairman (only the Chinese party could fill the chairman's position at that time), I spent more time in Tianjin than in Avon. But my family flourished in Connecticut. With the support of Karl Krapek, Otis sponsored Dawei to the General Motors Institute in Flint, Michigan, from which Karl had graduated. Majoring in manufacturing engineering, Dawei spent half his time in school and the other half in Bloomington, Indiana, training at an Otis plant. Lei, still in high school, was a good student and one of the best forwards in his soccer league. Yuying, as always, took good care of our family and was in her element, making our big house into a beautiful and comfortable home. Despite often being separated and busy with our own schedules, we still managed to do things as a family. One delightful occasion was in response to the invitation of the Amateur Peking Opera Association to perform the "Orphan of the Zhao Family." I played General Wei while Dawei and Lei played my soldiers. Although we had only one rehearsal, the boys were excellent. As my third elder brother and sister-in-law, my two elder sisters, and Jiahui were visiting us at the time, a lot of our family got to enjoy this singular event.

One day when I returned to the Tianjin Crystal Palace Hotel after work, there was a hand-delivered letter waiting for me at the front desk. It was from my childhood sweetheart, Lifen! My heart jumped. She was visiting a friend in Tianjin and included the address in the letter. I quickly grabbed a taxi to her friend's apartment building and ran up the steps. Lifen herself greeted me at the door. She was still beautiful but looked weak and tired. I invited her for dinner at the Qishilin Restaurant.

When we were seated, I exclaimed to Lifen yet again, "What a pleasant surprise!"

"I thought you might have forgotten me."

"How could you say that?" I felt she must be joking.

"You are such a celebrity now. I can follow you just by the newspaper reports."

From the way she gazed at me with her beautiful eyes and warm smile, I knew she felt proud of me.

"You have never been out of my thoughts. You are vivid in my memory. I can even tell you that our last meeting was

10 years ago when we bumped into each other at the Xidan Democracy Wall."

"Yes, March 17, 1979, a Saturday." She even remembered the exact day of the week.

"I went to see the posters on the wall almost every day."

"So did I. The wall was soon gone and then you vanished." Lifen's sweet smile turned sad.

"I tried to find you before I left. But your home was always locked."

"I sent my mother to Qingdao after my divorce. And then I went to Hong Kong."

"You got divorced?"

"Yes, 10 years ago."

I knew nothing about Lifen's marriage except that it had happened, and I didn't want to inquire further about her divorce for fear of opening up old wounds.

"You settled down in Hong Kong?"

"Yes. I've been teaching and directing Peking Opera there and in Taiwan."

We talked about our careers and old times over the rest of dinner. Lifen used to enjoy the Western food at the Qishilin, but that night she barely touched it. Before we parted, she asked me if we could go together to visit the grave of my parents and then to a place that we had enjoyed so many times as children, the Yungang Grottoes. I gladly agreed.

I visited my parents' grave many times a year. An early April visit was a must whenever I was in China because April 4 is Tomb-sweeping Day in China. But this visit was special. Lifen took a bunch of white chrysanthemums and wept hard as she spread their petals on the grave and the tombstone. Then I took her arm in support, and we walked out of the cemetery.

It was almost dark by the time we caught the train to Datong. The Datong Hotel, built in 1972, was the only one that allowed foreign and overseas Chinese guests. A man and a woman had to show their marriage certificate to share one room. I had already reserved two rooms and a car for us.

At Lifen's request, we got up early, took our breakfast at a small restaurant on the street nearby, and walked to the Yungang Grottoes as soon as it opened. There, in 250 above-ground caves, more than 50,000 statues of Buddha can be found. The grottoes date from the 5th and 6th centuries and are the greatest artistic achievement of Chinese Buddhism. They are so great a treasure that in 2001 they were declared a UNESCO World Heritage Site. Uncle and Auntie Yuan took Lifen and me there many times, long before it had been restored. They had Lifen study and then imitate the various gestures of Buddha to help her study of Peking Opera. Other than sentimental reasons, I didn't know why Lifen wanted to revisit the grottoes with me.

Short of breath and looking drawn, Lifen suggested that we sit down on a bench in front of the biggest Buddha, which reached almost 60 feet high.

"You know I have a daughter," she said suddenly.

"Yes. Your mother told me."

"She is with me in Hong Kong."

"How old is she?"

"Twenty-five. She has graduated from Hong Kong University."

"With a major in the performing arts?"

"No. Journalism."

"What's her name?"

"Ledi. My mother named her. It means happily playing flute."

"Why didn't she follow you and your mother into Peking Opera?"

"Neither of us wanted her to follow our heartbreaking footsteps."

She raised her head, looking up to the face of the tall Buddha.

"May I put Ledi in your care if anything happens to me?" She kept her eyes on the statue as if she were talking to the Buddha.

"Of course. But why are you talking about this now?"

"You are the only one I can trust. Who knows when we will meet again."

The bright morning turned somber. I was troubled by her request, and we lapsed into silence.

"Don't worry. My mother is healthy. I am enjoying my work and earning good money. Ledi always got top grades and is now working for a big newspaper group in Hong Kong."

"I feel there are some words upon your lips that you do not speak. You must tell me the truth."

"I am, but let us go now. We have a train to catch."

April 1, 1989 turned out to be my last meeting with Lifen. I asked for her home address and phone number, but she seemed reluctant to tell me so I didn't press her. She told me she would find me if she needed me.

Later in April, former CCP General Secretary Hu Yaobang suffered a heart attack in the middle of a Party politburo meeting. Before returning to Connecticut, I saw many wreaths on Tiananmen Square, paying respect to Hu, who had been against arresting pro-democracy activists after the

Xidan Democracy Wall was taken down. Several thousand college students sat in front of the Xinhua Gate of the CCP headquarters to protest the unfair treatment Hu had suffered. My close friends at Peking University told me privately that the protest was actually against the sitting "gerontocracy."

That spring proved to be a momentous one. When China had opened its doors a decade earlier, dragons and fishes had jumbled in together. Good and bad things came to pass simultaneously. The most radical economic reform under Deng Xiaoping was first to let a small number of people become rich. This was followed by private ownership in the services, manufacturing and export sectors, and real estate development. In this way, the private sector became part of China's socialist system. Many of these newly legal businesses illegally attempted to bribe government officials, and huge amounts of dirty money changed hands. Corrupt, dishonest, and venal government officials traded their authority for easy money.

Soon, the calls to punish bribery and promote democratization grew louder. The economic transformations had brought into the spotlight the need for corresponding changes in the political system. The result was growing unrest. At the end of May, Yuying, her elder sister in Taiwan, and other relatives of the Meng family gathered in Beijing for a long-planned reunion. I stayed home, but I called Yuying twice a week. She told me she heard that Beijing students had launched more sit-down strikes and that hundreds of thousands of students had swarmed Tiananmen Square, issuing manifestos decrying corruption and discrimination against intellectuals. She heard that 3,000 students went on a hunger strike, requesting direct talks with the central government authorities. One million Beijing residents, workers, and public officials waged demonstrations in support of the students. Yuying told me how much she was touched and inspired by the passion of the students and their compatriots. The whole city maintained extraordinarily good order. Free food and drink poured into the Square for the students. Hundreds of thousands of bicycles were neatly parked in the area without a single recorded theft. The government started talking with representatives of the students.

On May 15, Soviet President Gorbachev visited China. The four-day summit meeting between Deng Xiaoping and Gorbachev ended 30 years of estrangement between the Soviet Union and China. Deng's "Ending the past/Opening the future" set the tone for this event of epochal significance. Yet there was no red carpet out for Gorbachev in Tiananmen Square. He had to use the back door to enter the Great Hall of the People. His schedule was cut and juggled to avoid the legions of protesters occupying the city center.

After May 19, the tide of events unexpectedly turned. The vast hunger strikes by 200,000 students were deemed "reactionary riots" by the central government. At early dawn on May 30, art students, including many from Yuying's alma mater, erected a Statue of Liberty in front of Tiananmen Gate. A curfew was declared and enforced. Armored vehicles showed up on the street close to our apartment building, about five kilometers from the Square. The reunion of the Meng family had turned into a nightmare. All the phone lines to Beijing were cut. We lost touch utterly.

Day and night, I had the TV on, constantly taping the events in Beijing. The intermittent on-the-scene news reports and pictures reminded me of the May 4 Movement that my father had participated in 70 years before. Then it was a protest against traitorous pacts and a call for national unification; now it was a protest against corruption and a call for democracy. On both occasions, heroic students had bravely blazed the trail. My concern escalated steadily. On June 3, my elder brother, sister-in-law, three sisters, and I watched the TV news programs the entire day. That night, I couldn't sleep a wink, watching and recording the events of June 4, which occurred Sunday morning local time in Beijing.

Foreign news agencies and reporters had refused to quit their reporting, arguing with the Chinese authorities that their paid contract for the Deng and Gorbachev summit meeting had not yet expired. In front of the TV, I suddenly heard the CNN reporter shouting far away from the Tiananmen Square, "It sounds like gunfire. I hear gunfire in the distance . . . ." The next moment, the signal went dead. No picture. No sound. In the dark, I left the TV on until receiving official notice from the local channels that they had lost touch with China.

I was entirely at a loss to cope with these developments. I felt helpless, trying to imagine what might happen next. Losing touch with Yuying amidst all the chaos in Beijing drove me mad. When the local NBC affiliate interviewed me at my home, I told them of my deep concern. NBC broadcast the interview nationwide on its evening news, showing Yuying's picture at the end with the short comment, "Chen lost touch with his wife, who is trapped in the violence of Beijing."

Without any hesitation, I accepted an invitation to speak at a public rally in Hartford, protesting the brutal suppression of the unarmed students in Tiananmen Square. Hundreds of Chinese students and foreign friends attended. Despite the risks, I felt I had to do something. At the same time, knowing that Yuying's return ticket had expired and that airline offices were closed, I bought her a new ticket. Through friends at Beijing Jeep, I finally was able to contact a close friend, and I asked him to drive Yuying to the airport. Six days after June 4, Yuying got to the Beijing airport along an almost deserted road and took a practically empty flight to New York's LaGuardia Airport.

I met Yuying at the airport. On our way to Avon, with tears in her eyes, Yuying told me of the many horrible scenes she had witnessed. Her memories are seared into my consciousness. The roaring sounds of gunfire. The panicked retreat of crowds from Chang An Boulevard. Perhaps most touching, the blood around a newspaper kiosk with a pair of small shoes that someone had surrounded with bricks broken by bullets. A hand-written sign next to the shoes read, "A little girl was killed here."

Chapter 17

ONE COUNTRY, TWO SYSTEMS

1989-1995
Avon, Connecticut; Columbus, Ohio, US;
Changzhou, Baoying, Shanghai, China

As I STRUGGLED THROUGH THOSE miserable days after June 4, I reached about the lowest point in my life since arriving in the US. I continued to be absolutely haunted by the image of the blood around the newspaper kiosk with a pair of small shoes and a hand-written sign, "A little girl was killed here." I couldn't get that child's tragic and needless death and what it portended out of my mind. The Chinese people had sacrificed too much to achieve reform and openness to see the door close again and the people's hopes for change crushed. I was sick at heart.

I loved my motherland. I admired Deng Xiaoping's "Practice is the sole standard for testing truth." I was encouraged by China's privatization policies. As the years passed, I thought less about the past and more about the future. The rumble of the tanks on Tiananmen Square was a thunderclap, a wakeup call for me. I was frightened and puzzled. Why had the June 4 Incident happened at all? Why were armed soldiers and tanks used to crack down on the patriotic students who were only demonstrating against corruption and asking for dialogue with the central authorities? Even if there had been provocations during the student demonstrations, these people were our children, our neighbors, our future. They didn't deserve to be treated like this for acting on their ideals. The Chinese people shed tears. The heavens shed tears. In the following months, torrential rains in China led to massive flooding, and landslides caused severe damage. Tens of millions of people lost their homes.

I didn't know whether there would be any political risk for me when I returned to China because of the stance I took, and the speech and interviews I gave regarding the events in Tiananmen Square. Yuying insisted that I at least consult with my schoolmates in the Chinese Embassy in Washington to see what I could learn. They assured me I would be safe, that I would have no trouble continuing to travel to China and conduct business there. At this difficult time, my confidence in China's open policy was unwavering—in public. As long as the door had been opened, I told people, I didn't believe it could be closed again. But in my heart I had my doubts and, even worse, fears for the future of reform in China.

As Co-Chairman of the United Technologies China Committee, I continued my efforts in assisting Carrier, Sikorsky, and Pratt & Whitney to develop their projects in China. As a personal friend of a senior executive of Motorola, I spent several weekends with him and his colleagues, doing my utmost to persuade them to continue Motorola's proposed project in Tianjin. After the June 4 Incident, they were ready to abandon it, to pull out entirely. My persistence and reasoned arguments convinced them otherwise. They did scale back their investment, however. Instead of the original billion dollars they had planned, Motorola invested $100 million. Going into China was a wise decision. I heard later that Motorola Tianjin sold all of its first-year orders in one week.

Another meaningful accomplishment for me in 1989 was helping launch the Committee of 100. Along with I.M. Pei, Shirley Young, Henry S. Tang, Yo-Yo Ma, and Chien-Shiung Wu, I became a founder and Director on the Committee's first board. Our purpose was to increase opportunities in all fields for Chinese Americans and to build mutual understanding between China and America. After the June 4 Incident, I believed this was needed more than ever. Compared with the other, more distinguished founders, I didn't do much for the Committee because of my punishing schedule traveling back and forth to China. I treasure, however, the camaraderie and the memories of our meetings in New York to discuss our goals and how to accomplish them. From those occasions, I gained great insight into the minds of the Overseas Chinese (OC) and the American-born Chinese (ABC). They care for China as deeply as any native of the country and wish the best for China, even as they criticize its flaws.

For stretches of 1990, I neither slept nor ate well. It wasn't just all the travel and demands on my time or thinking about Tiananmen and wondering about the future of reforms in China. I was in conflict with myself, having difficulty making up my mind on an issue with far-reaching implications. I couldn't decide whether to become a US citizen or not. Despite the limitations and inconvenience of being a green card holder,

I couldn't quite make the move. If I did become a US citizen, I would have to renounce my Chinese citizenship, which I was loath to do. I loved my native land, but the two countries did not have an agreement on dual citizenship. Although it was a bitter-sweet choice, I finally became a US citizen on February 8, 1991. The carnage in Tiananmen Square helped me make my decision.

The incident had given me much to think about. I reflected soberly on the past, present, and future. I pondered my father's warning: "The debate between socialism and capitalism is far from reaching its conclusion." How could the debate be brought to an end under the socialist flag carried by the Chinese Communist Party? How far would privatization go and how long would it last? How could the two different systems, publicly owned and privately owned, resolve their apparently irreconcilable differences? I came to no definitive conclusions. All I knew was that China could only be socialistic. In the eyes of China's leadership, democratization and liberalization were the hallmarks of bourgeois capitalism, which aimed to overthrow China's form of socialism and the Chinese Communist Party.

Despite his record of openness and reform, this was Deng's confirmed view as well, and even he could go only so far. The June 4 incident showed Deng's limitations. After General Secretary Zhao Ziyang was removed from his position and placed under house arrest because he advocated a soft line against the protestors, all the top leadership took the view that the demonstrations must be crushed at all costs. But it was Deng who, as chairman of the Central Military Commission, declared martial law and unleashed the events that followed.

In August 1991, my thoughts about Tiananmen Square were stirred when I saw the televised images of tanks rolling into

Moscow's Red Square as part of a coup attempt. Hard-line Soviet Communist Party officials who felt that Gorbachev's reforms had gone too far led the coup. Although their attempt quickly failed, it destabilized the Soviet Union and contributed to both the collapse of the Communist Party and the disintegration of the USSR. I could not help but draw some comparisons. Gorbachev's programs of Perestroika and Glasnost (political and economic restructuring and openness), launched in 1985, were similar to Deng's Reform and Openness programs begun in 1979. But the results could hardly have been more different.

On December 25, 1991, the Soviet flag was lowered for the last time over the Kremlin. Food rationing was in force in Moscow for the first time since World War II. The GDP had been halved since the reforms were begun, and 25% of the population now lived below the poverty line. In contrast, food rationing was about to end in China, where the GDP had almost tripled between 1985 and 1992. Almost 30,000 foreign manufacturing enterprises were registered in China in 1991. Direct foreign investment climbed steadily and was about to explode. By the middle of the decade, businesses from 126 countries would invest $110 billion in China.

In spite of any lingering concerns about the June 4 Incident, the world, especially developing countries, could hardly shut its eyes to these economic realities. China was the last and largest frontier, and the time to make a move was now.

As Otis Elevator Vice President for Pacific-China Operations, I couldn't be based in Connecticut for long. Otis arranged for Yuying and me to tour Singapore and Hong Kong. We were to choose one of those cities for our permanent residence so as to be close to China. We took our tour, which only convinced us that we were not yet ready to head back to Asia. America was where we wanted to live and thrive. Besides, Singapore was too small and Hong Kong was too noisy.

Working for major corporations had given me a steady and substantial income and a wealth of knowledge and experience. But I felt constrained, limited in what I could accomplish as someone else's employee, even as well-compensated as I was. Money was important but mattered little compared with my goal of working for myself. The time had come to act on my dream.

Forty years before, my father had responded to his nation's call to become a Red Capitalist. In return, he was labeled a Rightist and lost all of his investment and dividends. I faced a much different situation now. China had invited overseas Chinese to invest in their homeland and guaranteed that their investment would be legally protected. I saw my opportunity to become an Overseas Red Capitalist and complete my father's unfulfilled dream.

Yuying and I spent many long nights sharing our thoughts in the dim light of our bedroom in our home in Avon. It reminded me of those dark nights in the Chen mansion when my parents would whisper about investing so much of their money in the Yongtai plant and Dasheng Dairy. The big difference was that my parents had such deep fears while Yuying and I had such high hopes. We were confident because of our business plan and all the experience I had gained, contacts made, and reputation I had established over the past decade.

I left Otis at the end of 1991. Yuying fully supported my decision, as usual. That our sons were advancing steadily in their careers made it easier for me to take the leap. Dawei had started working for Otis after graduating from college. Following in the footsteps of his brother, Lei was a freshman manufacturing systems engineering major at the GM Institute, sponsored by GM's Truck and Bus Division. Despite any uncertainties that might arise from my decision, I felt like a freed bird, stretching my wings to their fullest, leaving my gilded cage far behind, and flying into my future.

To gain real experience operating a foreign-Chinese enterprise in China, I accepted the invitation of General Automotive Corporation to negotiate and develop a joint venture there. On September 23, 1992, China Flxible Automotive Corporation (CFAC) was established in Changzhou, Jiangsu Province. Flxible is not a typo. When the parent company was registered in 1919, "Flxible" was purposely used so that this distinctive name could be copyrighted and used as a trademark. CFAC was the first bus manufacturing joint venture in China and the last company whose title could legally start with "China." I became CFAC's President and Chief Executive Officer.

In the two years I lived and worked in Changzhou, I discovered that operating a foreign-Chinese company was far more challenging than simply negotiating its creation, which was invariably difficult in its own right. Many internationally accepted standards and practices were not easily applied in China. Inside the company, the toughest job was to establish and execute a quality assurance (QA) system. Outside the company, the toughest job was to deal with the bureaucracy of the government agencies and the government-owned public transportation enterprises. And then there was the widespread corruption, which seemed to become more rampant with every passing day.

I called these three impediments to doing business "QBC"—Q for quality, B for bureaucracy, and C for corruption.

Quality assurance was actually the easiest one to deal with. Although it took my American colleagues and me more than a year to get our QA system on the right track, at least it was in our hands. The Chinese engineers and workers saw a world of difference between the old buses they had previously produced and the new ones they were turning out. What they didn't grasp, however, was that there was still a huge difference between the new ones they thought were just fine and what was required before we could put the Flxible name on a bus.

The number of rejected busses ran high in the early months and made quite a dent in the workers' collective ego. The American engineers were resolute in maintaining standards. The Chinese workers were frustrated, then angry, and tensions began to run high at the plant. Our patient efforts at training finally paid off, however, and we developed a workforce that understood and cared about quality control, that truly took justified pride in the product. Dozens, hundreds, and then thousands of CFAC's buses were soon running in Beijing, Shanghai, and other cities. Years after I left CFAC, I would delight in jumping on a CFAC bus, paying my two yuan, and enjoying the entire journey. I especially liked watching passengers on a hot day board the bus and realize with relief that it was air-conditioned. I would sometimes tell them that the bus had been made in Changzhou.

Bureaucracy was more difficult to deal with. Just about every government agency seemed so completely composed of red tape that anyone who dealt with it was ensnared. As far as power went, no matter how small the government agency was, it was big. No matter how big the business was, it was small. Small agencies could give a company big headaches, and there were countless numbers of these agencies at every level of government, with countless millions of bureaucrats staffing them. A common belief was that there was one official for every 20 Chinese citizens. If that estimate was even remotely accurate, imagine the ceaseless legions of government officials, quasi-officials, and para-officials. Then add in all the non-government officials, such as executives of state-owned enterprises, banks, and universities. All of these bureaucrats had to do something to justify their positions and win promotions, and many of them had considerable power.

If a township official made an inspection of a company within his jurisdiction, the company would have to tack on the expense of a banquet to any costs of the presentation. Virtually every major business decision had to be approved by the relevant government agencies, or the company could face some real trouble down the line. And then, of course, in every foreign-Chinese company there was a CCP branch and a labor union, which were parties to all decisions. At Beijing Jeep, we streamlined the parties involved by naming the branch Party Secretary as Director of the labor union. I took this approach with all my China projects.

Corruption was the most difficult to deal with. As China's economic growth accelerated, so did the corruption. While no nation is without venality and corruption, the situation in China made corruption inevitable. Every bit of China's 9.6 million square kilometers (3.7 million square miles) is owned by the government. All natural resources above and beneath that land are owned by the government. These are ideal conditions for what economists call "monopoly privilege rent seeking," or deriving profit from an enterprise to which one has added no value.

In China, our term for it is "trading authority for money." From the county level and below on up to the top echelons of government, corrupt officials and their relatives traded their monopolistic authority over land, natural resources, bank loans, major project construction contracts, and access to the national treasury in exchange for a full range of inducements. Cash, of course, always had currency. In one notorious 1991 case, Wang Ju, the Deputy Mayor of Shenzhen, and his clan took 120 million yuan, about $22 million at the time, as part of a sweetheart real estate deal. Other "freebies" commonly offered were credit cards, concubines, international travel, and equity shares in private enterprises. One of the more popular bribes was to sponsor the emigration of the official and his family to another country.

A small fraction of corrupt officials were actually charged with crimes, tried, jailed, and sometimes executed. But it seemed that eliminating one "dirty" bureaucrat just made it possible for two more to take his place. The joke at the time was that if you lined up all the government officials and shot every one of them, a few innocent victims would die. If you shot only every other one, however, many guilty officials would go free.

One result of China's economic restructuring was the depreciation of the RMB, the People's Currency of China. In 1979, the exchange rate was $1 US for 1.47 yuan. The RMB depreciated to 3.76 in 1989, 5.32 in 1991, and 8.61 in 1994. This accelerated China's exports, sourcing, and investments from abroad. Compared with 1979, when China first opened its door, the value of the dollar increased more than five-fold by 1994. Only $1 million was needed to develop the same China project that required $5 million 15 years before. If there ever was a time to do business in China, this was it.

If any doubt existed in anybody's mind, the recently retired Deng Xiaoping dispelled it when he made what came to be called his Southern Tour, visiting Wuchang, Shenzhen, Zhuhai, and Shanghai early in 1992. The catch phrase associated with his Southern Tour was "To Get Rich Is Glorious." While some historians question whether Deng actually said the words during the tour or earlier or at all, the catch phrase caught on. It captured and fanned the spirit of the age. The wave of entrepreneurship that followed in the 1990s contributed greatly to China becoming an economic superpower and continues to fuel the economy today. Deng's tour signaled that despite the critics of reform, including high-ranking Party officials, the reforms would not be reversed. China's merger of socialism and the market economy was permanent.

After my two-year contract was over, I left CFAC in 1993 and devoted myself full time to my own company, Amerihua, in the Columbus, Ohio area, our final destination. After moving from West Bloomfield Hills to Avon, Connecticut, all Yuying and I wanted was to find a place to finally settle down. In order to be sure we were making the right decision, Yuying, Dawei, Lei, and I traveled to Tucson, Houston, and Los Angeles seeking our next home. But all of us chose Columbus in the end. We were most comfortable there, especially with the weather, which is very like Beijing's, although without the sandstorms. We had four seasons. It was neither too hot in summer nor too cold in winter. We often joked that if we dug a deep enough hole through the earth and jumped in, we'd come out in Beijing.

I had registered my trading company in 1981 in Tucson, and I renamed it Amerihua after I moved to Michigan. The name combines America and Hua, meaning China. That's where I wanted to focus my attention, developing commercial opportunities between these two great nations. To take advantage of the economic situation at the time, I changed

Amerihua's emphasis from import to export, expanded our China sourcing, and established more manufacturing bases in China. In addition, I began providing what I called Ad-Manage services to major US companies seeking to do business in China. It wasn't a tough sell. Many firms were eager to enter the market and knew they didn't know how.

Our Ad-Manage consulting and managing program won immediate recognition by Fortune 500 companies and others. The name Ad-Manage was meant to convey our dual roles as advisors and managers. As advisors, we assisted our clients to identify, negotiate, and develop their China projects. As managers, usually serving as the board Director or Secretary, we got our clients off on the right foot as they started up their China operations.

While some opportunities arise from chance, more often than not for me, they come through trusted friends. One of Amerihua's first big projects was suggested by my dear friend Tom Ryan. I got acquainted with Tom when I was with AMC's China Team and he was the Finance Director of AMC's International Department. I couldn't find better words than "true gentleman" to describe him. Tom was tall, white-haired, quiet, and smiled often. He had infectious warmth. It was impossible not to like him. It was from Tom that I gained basic financial knowledge—learning about balance sheets, cash flow, foreign exchange reserves—and which strategies and tactics best supported our auto assembly programs at Beijing Jeep. As a Director on BJC's board, he quickly earned the high regard of Chinese officials and colleagues, as did his beautiful wife Barbara. Indeed, I had to mediate squabbles among the Chinese drivers as to who would serve as Mrs. Ryan's personal chauffeur when she was in Beijing. After I left AMC, Yuying and I stayed in touch with Tom and Barbara, but I was still surprised one day to get a phone call from Tom.

"Hello, my friend. I hope you are still able to recognize my voice," he said.

"Is that you, Tom?" How could I forget his professorial way of talking?

"Yes, indeed. I'm calling from Milwaukee. I'm with A.O. Smith Corporation now. Do you know of them?"

"A little. I know its automotive division supplies chassis to the big auto makers in Detroit."

"That's right. Now, we want to expand our business to China. Are you interested in lending a hand?"

"Of course. I would be only too glad to help."

I flew to Milwaukee the next week. Guided by Tom, our meeting was so productive that we agreed Amerihua would soon arrange an exploratory China tour for a senior executive delegation headed by A.O. Smith Chairman Bob O'Toole. As a result of that successful and productive trip, we worked with A.O. Smith for many years to establish three joint ventures in China—a car chassis plant in Changchun, a fiberglass joint factory in Harbin, and a water heater plant in Nanjing. Our Ad-Manage program enabled me to serve both as a senior advisor as well as the board Secretary of A.O. Smith's major chassis joint venture with China First Auto Works. Lei, using his language skills and what he learned at the GM Institute and the Truck and Bus Division, worked long weeks in Changchun to help both parties prepare the organization chart, salary standards, work and reporting procedures, and corporate policies. It was a wonderful and fruitful experience for all of us.

"Friendship first. Business second." The adage again proved its truth and value. Through Tom and Barbara, we got to know

Sam Safran and his family. Sam recommended that Amerihua enter the Christmas and seasonal gift business, and, in time, this became one of our main operations. Beyond our business connections, the close friendship that joins our three families is remarkable.

My hopes as an Overseas Red Capitalist would not be fulfilled without establishing manufacturing bases in China. They would be needed for Amerihua's seasonal gift business to take off. In August 1995, Yuying and I accepted the invitation of friends to make a site visit to Xiaoguanzhuang village in Baoying County, Jiangsu Province, to see if it might be a good base of operations.

It didn't just rain that day, it poured! All the streams we saw during our drive were running high or had already overflowed their banks. Before we reached the village, we had to abandon the car where a mudflow blocked the road. I took Yuying's arm and we made our way through the muddy fields and along the road as best we could. Our hats and raincoats offered little protection against heaven's torrents, and both of us were soaked to the skin. Finally we reached a small decorative glass plant on the edge of town, only a few minutes after the appointed hour. The workers all stood stoically in the downpour to welcome us. We didn't understand their local dialect very well, but we didn't have to. From their eyes and gestures, Yuying and I felt their warmth and sincerity and pride.

For generations, Xiaoguanzhuang had enjoyed a reputation for producing extraordinarily beautiful glass ornaments. While small, the village was home to numerous families boasting many skilled artisan members. We watched with fascination as some of them demonstrated their talents and produced spun glass birds, dragons, and other figures over a gas torch. Yuying and I didn't take long to decide that here was a good place to establish our manufacturing base.

Before long, I was made an honorary citizen of Baoying County. That modest honor, of course, didn't allow me to be among the 1.2 billion Chinese citizens counted in the 1995 census. But I can't imagine how any of those citizens could have been happier with their investment in China than Yuying and I were with ours. The prospect of creating jobs for my compatriots, perhaps even thousands of them, while fulfilling a Chen family goal, was a dream come true.

Chapter 18

SEEKING SERENITY

1996-1999
Hong Kong, Beijing, Baoying, Ningxia Province,
China; Powell, Ohio, US

IN OCTOBER 1996, YUYING AND I visited Hong Kong at the invitation of local business associates who were also friends. Outside of our usual meetings, the main topic was whether and when they should withdraw capital from Hong Kong to invest in the US and Canada. Without exception, all of them were deeply concerned about the CCP taking over Hong Kong the next year. A significant amount of capital had already fled the crown colony, as had many citizens.

I fully understood that they faced a tough decision. Moving their capital to the US and Canada wasn't a bad strategy to diversify their investments. I had to tell them, however, how my investment in the mainland had benefited from the "one country, two systems" policy. And I told them that after reunification in 1997, stronger economic ties would be developed between Hong Kong and the mainland, generating more business opportunities. Most of my friends opted for soldiering on. The few who went to Canada later came back to Hong Kong.

During the trip, our most pleasant surprise was meeting with Yuying's college classmate, Hu Wenshan, with whom we had lost touch since the late '70s. Wenshan and Yuying had spent five years in the same class at the China Central Arts and Crafts Institute. He soon became my close friend also. After he and his family moved to Hong Kong, he led a major advertising company's efforts to promote trade and investment with China. But then he left the company, and we fell out of contact. Before we left Hong Kong for Beijing, I called the advertising company again; it had previously refused to give me any information about Wenshan. This time, a pleasant older woman gave me his office phone number and told me that he had founded his own company. I called immediately.

Wenshan was delighted to hear our voices. He canceled a planned trip to Shenzhen, and we had a reunion dinner at the Grand Hyatt Hotel. We were overjoyed to see his wife, Chingran, and Weiwei, his very attractive daughter. Weiwei was still in kindergarten in Beijing when we last saw her 18 years earlier. At dinner, she displayed a grace and warmth that charmed Yuying and me. After Weiwei left for her night-shift work, the four of us could hardly wait to ask each other about our children's matrimonial status.

"Are your sons both married?" Wenshan asked.

"No. Lei is still single," Yuying answered.

"How about Weiwei? Does she have a boyfriend?" Yuying asked.

"No. Just friends," Chingran answered.

"How old is Lei?" Wenshan asked.

"Twenty-six," Yuying replied. "How old is Weiwei?"

"Twenty-six," Chingran answered.

"What a perfect match!" I exclaimed, forgetting the power of my Peking Opera singer's voice.

"Songsheng, please don't shout," Yuying said. From her purse, she pulled out a photo of Lei, which Wenshan and Chingran examined carefully.

"What a handsome young man!" Chingran said.

"It's an absolutely perfect match," Wenshan quickly added.

The four of us shared a hearty laugh. Very soon after, Lei traveled to Hong Kong to meet Weiwei, starting a wonderful courtship that culminated in their marriage in 2000. Lei's matrimonial status had been on Yuying's mind for some time. And now fate had intervened and a connection was established across thousands of miles, one end in the US and the other in Hong Kong. Yuying couldn't believe how easily everything seemed to fall into place.

Not long after we returned to the US, I received a phone call one night at home, around midnight. I heard a faint voice speaking with a southern Chinese accent ask, "Are you Mr. Chen?"

"Yes. Who is calling, please?" I asked.

"My name is Wen, the Mayor of Baoying."

"Yes, Mayor Wen. How are you?"

I had met Wen Daocai, a sharp-witted public official in his early 40s, the previous year. He had recently been appointed Chief Operating Officer (called Mayor) for Baoying. In 1995 I had established a base of operations there for making glass ornaments that now employed more than 800 citizens from the region.

"Sorry to bother you. I hope it's not too late," Mayor Wen apologized. While they were more or less aware of the time difference between our two countries, many of my contacts in China were unused to international calling. They called during their business hours, which meant I got calls at all times of night and day. I was a night owl, so taking calls at this hour was all right with me.

"No problem. Anything urgent?"

"No. Everything is fine. We are very glad to hear that you want to expand your production base in Baoying."

"Yes. With strong support in Baoying, our market in America is growing quickly, and we need more capacity."

"We are so excited to hear it, Mr. Chen, and we have a proposal for you."

"Go ahead, please."

"After much thought, we encourage you to buy out your Chinese partner and turn the factory into your wholly owned subsidiary."

The offer was a complete surprise. "Thank you for the proposal. Any particular reasons for your suggestion?"

"Our leadership group has just concluded a meeting and wanted to communicate our proposal to you immediately. Your Chinese partner supports the plan 100%. We believe such an arrangement benefits everyone."

"Please give me some time to think this over."

"Of course. Take your time. We fully support you either way."

"I am very grateful."

"Please let us know if we can be of any help."

"Thank you, Mayor Wen. I'll let you know my decision soon."

Perhaps I shouldn't have been so surprised. The trend of turning foreign-Chinese joint ventures into wholly owned subsidiaries of foreign companies began in the early 90s. For China, these re-arrangements were a welcome source of foreign capital, a good way to transfer American dollars and other currencies to the PRC. Overall, about a third of the joint ventures in China made a profit, a third broke even, and the rest lost money. Often cultural differences between the Chinese and foreign partners, especially involving ways of doing business, led to failure. My American friends regularly complained that they had wasted much of their time in China at meetings and banquets. They now understood the Chinese witticism, "Too many taxes under the KMT; too many meetings under the CCP."

At our new home in Powell, Yuying, Dawei, Lei, and I discussed our options at length. Lei had joined Amerihua in March 1994 after finishing college and his training at GM Truck and Bus. Dawei came on board in May 1995 after completing his assignment with Flxible Bus. My father had never let any of his children work for him in his businesses. But times had changed. Yuying and I felt very differently. We loved having our sons be a part of Amerihua, making it a true family business for the next generation at least. I knew how hard it could be to work for someone else and how tough it was to find a good job. We didn't want to shoulder all the responsibilities of developing a large company, let alone a public company. A family-owned business, with hard-working parents and sons, could and would satisfy our basic needs. We wanted a simple and easy life with enough savings to provide a good education to our grandchildren. We also wanted Amerihua to provide jobs to qualified relatives and friends in China.

Powell is a small, quiet town about 15 miles north of Columbus, Ohio, the state capital. Yuying and I bought a big house from Dennis Hopson, a local hero and former NBA player (and Ohio State University's all-time top scorer). It was about 8,000 square feet with five bedrooms, three entertainment centers, six bathrooms plus a sauna. My Chinese friends teased me that after growing up in a mansion in Peiping, I needed to have one in America. Honestly, I didn't care much about such luxuries. I will say that one feature of the house really appealed to me: its high ceilings. Ever since my time in the basement cowshed and the huts in the labor camp, I couldn't stand being anywhere with low ceilings. What I enjoyed most was that our whole family was now living together under one roof, eating together at one table, driving together in one van on our many sightseeing excursions. What could be better than that? Yuying took great pleasure in cooking our old favorite Beijing specialties. Lei and Dawei quickly gained weight eating their mother's northern Chinese dishes, especially her Beijing noodle soup. You couldn't find better food even in the finest Chinese restaurants or highest state events. No less an authority than the first US ambassador to the PRC, Leonard Woodcock, told Yuying he had never had such tasty Chinese food as he ate in our home. We were flattered by his kind words, given the fact that he had enjoyed so many wonderful feasts in China.

As a family, we carefully considered the benefits and drawbacks of taking over the manufacturing base in Baoying. It didn't take us long to reach the unanimous decision to accept the mayor's proposal, although we all knew greater responsibility would come with this change of ownership. So many employees and their families would depend on us for their futures.

With their training, work experience, natural abilities, and commitment to excellence, Dawei and Lei soon became my right-hand men. Amerihua made great strides in expanding both the consulting and the gifts sides of our business. It was also about this time that Sam Safran, our close friend, helped us raise our gift production to a new and higher level.

I first got to know Sam and his elegant wife, Regina, at a dinner party in Milwaukee hosted by Tom and Barbara Ryan for our family. From the first moment we talked, it was as if we'd known each other all our lives. Sam had been involved in the gift trade for years, developing products, improving production, and importing from China, Europe, and Latin America. I wished we could have met earlier. I immediately invited him to visit Baoying.

When I first set up shop in Baoying, I also bought an abandoned primary school in the village of Zuchuan, 30 minutes walking distance from our plant. I loved the tranquillity and soft sounds of the place, the wind whispering through the silver birches, the murmuring stream, the songbirds. Its huge courtyard was full of Chinese parasol trees with their large leaves and fragrant flowers. The five forlorn rows of classrooms had been vacant for years. I turned the first row into visiting quarters, with two rooms on the right for family, two rooms on the left for guests. To me, it was a veritable paradise, but I hesitated to invite Sam to stay there because it was primitive compared to what he was used to. The shower water, for instance, was often muddy because of sediment in the water tower. We had no TV or telephone. Sam's response was simple: If I could stay there, so could he.

We enjoyed each other's company in this wonderful setting many times over the years. We both felt as if we were in a different world. When I was growing up, my father called the garden parlor of our Peiping mansion Xanadu. He told me that he used the word to call up the thought of an almost unimaginably beautiful place. I named our compound in Zuchuan Xanadu to mean a land of peace away from the turmoil of the world. Sam often told me he was never as relaxed and stimulated as during our time together in Zuchuan. Our very first conversation under the Chinese parasol trees with the setting sun on the horizon was typical of the productive brainstorming and camaraderie that was such a part of the place.

"Sam, I'm thinking about how to speed up production of the Christmas ornaments to meet increasing demand. This means moving from individual to group production. Any suggestions?" I had been pondering this move for some time.

"You mean to develop a sort of production line?" Sam asked.

"Exactly."

"You can't incorporate every step into the line, but the painting of the ornaments is a perfect place to start."

"I'm thinking the same way—painting and packaging." Sam nodded vigorously and a wide smile spread across his face. He and I just clicked.

"When I toured the painting workshop," Sam continued, "some of the women were really master hands. They easily drew beautiful eyes and faces on the figures. Please allow me to say, however, that some were much slower and not as good."

"They need to handle different jobs on the painting line," I interjected.

"You took the words right out of my mouth."

We chuckled over our shared solution and the simultaneity of our thoughts.

I said, "Rookies at the start of the line paint clothing, accessories, base colors. Then come the master hands adding eyes, eyebrows, noses, mouths. Last are the highest-skilled masters, inspecting, correcting, and applying any needed final strokes."

"I guarantee your output will double or even triple." Indeed, Sam's brash prediction proved true, as did his many other assessments.

Sam quickly became a close friend and trusted advisor and later a business partner. We became like brothers. When I look back, I can recall some of the details of launching the painting line, tripling our exports, and building my company into one of the world's major suppliers of glass ornaments. But I remember every one of the wonderful times Sam and I shared at Xanadu. What success I have achieved has usually been accomplished in concert with close friends. Making shared dreams come true makes achievement all the sweeter.

Once our painting line was up and humming and building up inventory, we turned to improving our other lines and revenue streams. We borrowed methods from the foundry to cast low-melting-point metal molds to make glass ornaments with intricate shapes. Skilled workers blew molten glass into molds to produce beautiful Santa Clauses, Snow Whites, Seven Dwarfs, and a raft of licensed items from Disney and other companies. Across the board, we increased production and efficiency while improving product quality.

Xiaoguanzhuang's long tradition of household glasswork served us well. We outsourced glass blanks to hundreds of these family workshops. All we needed to do was provide the molds, inspect their blanks, and pay the workers. The sleepy little village was fast becoming a flourishing township, well-known for its glass exports. Yuying and I enjoyed it especially at night when all the lights inside a growing number of homes with electricity came on, giving a warm glow even to cold evenings.

Heavy traffic of hundreds of container trucks speeded the construction of new paved roads. Eight years earlier, our car got so stuck in the mud that we had to slog our way through the muddy and uneven ground to the plant. Now, it took only 15 minutes to get to our base from downtown Baoying. The most meaningful and rewarding development for Yuying and me was seeing more and more new houses popping up in the small town. Most of the town's residents were farmers. They had more than enough grain from their rented land. They had their own old houses. What they were short of was money. Now they or their children could earn more than 1,000 yuan per month working with us. At peak times, the monthly pay could be over 2,000 yuan. With this extra income came new furniture and new houses everywhere in town. Most of them were two-story buildings with spacious living rooms, multiple bedrooms, and a nice bathroom, something that had never been possible until now. Yuying, Dawei, Lei, and I were often invited by our employees to their homes for dinner. In the past, they were embarrassed to entertain us in their old houses; now they were proud to do so. And what we ate in their new, big dining rooms was much tastier than the food in Baoying's three-star hotel.

On February 19, 1997, Deng Xiaoping passed away at the age of 93. To me, Deng was the greatest leader China had ever had. Without Deng, China wouldn't be the open and progressive nation it is today. Without Deng, I would never have been able to come to America in 1981. Deng, with his three ascents to and three descents from power, never changed his beliefs and never gave up his fight for a better China and better lives for the Chinese people. At the height of his power, he stepped aside for his successors to take the highest positions as the CCP's General Secretary and China's President. Day in and day out, with a few cups of Maotai, the strong Chinese white liquor, and a few packs of Panda brand cigarettes to sustain him, he worked hard and spoke forcefully to speed up China's modernization. When he proclaimed the "One country, two systems" policy for the return of Hong Kong and Macau, his timing was perfect and success was achieved. Over time, the profitable mingling of public and private ownership in China paved the way for accepting and promoting "One country, two systems."

Deng's negotiations with Prime Minister Margaret Thatcher over the return of Hong Kong showed just how tough Deng was, even in dealing with "the Iron Lady." Deng's prerequisite for talking with Thatcher was that China's sovereignty was not negotiable. He resolutely rejected Thatcher's request that British law should govern Hong Kong for 30 years after Hong Kong's return to China. He stood firm that Hong Kong would come directly under China's Central People's Government while enjoying a high degree of autonomy. And China's right to station troops in Hong Kong was not subject to discussion; it was an inalienable right of sovereignty. Unfortunately, Deng didn't live to attend the ceremony on July 1, 1997, when China's flag was hoisted over Hong Kong after more than a century and a half of British rule.

Early July witnessed another significant event in Asia that affected the entire world. An economic crisis started in

Thailand with the collapse of the baht, the floating national currency. Predatory currency speculator George Soros, known as "the man who broke the Bank of England," and several hedge funds gambled that they could drive the baht down and so they did, to their own enrichment and to the ruin of millions, especially the poor. The crisis spread and soon gripped most of Asia, including some of its previous success stories, such as South Korea. The economic bubble—fueled by "hot money," real estate-driven financial over-extension, and huge foreign debt—finally popped. The Asian economic miracle was replaced by an Asian financial crisis that triggered fears of a worldwide economic meltdown.

Once Soros and his fellow speculators had succeeded in Thailand, they set their sights on Hong Kong, mounting their first attack there in October 1997. The next year they began a coordinated and well-planned effort to de-link the Hong Kong dollar from the US dollar and manipulate the stock and futures markets. Affected by the rumor that China would devalue its yuan, great fears swept through the market and sent the Hang Seng Index (Hong Kong's stock exchange index) from 18,000 points to a five-year low of 6,500. The Hong Kong government ended up buying approximately $15 billion worth of securities. More than a hundred thousand families were bankrupted as HK $2.2 trillion evaporated with the collapse of the over-heated real estate market. Many people unable to pay their utility bills unwittingly killed themselves by carbon monoxide poisoning when they burned charcoal in their sealed houses to keep warm. Charcoal was soon in short supply. As a macabre joke, charcoal dealers would ask buyers, "Have you decided to end it all?"

Mainland China was relatively immune to the disaster toppling other nations' economies. With its $140 billion reserves, China firmly maintained its non-convertible currency. Besides, almost all of China's foreign investment took the form of factories on the ground rather than securities, which insulated the country from rapid capital flight. Without internal troubles, China was able to support Hong Kong in fighting back against the speculators. I heard from reliable sources that China's Vice-premier and later Premier Zhu Rongji declared that he would take dozens of billions of dollars to Hong Kong to stack up against George Soros and his gang. Hong Kong survived. China enjoyed a relatively "soft landing" in the widespread turmoil and earned its reputation as a responsible partner and strong regional power in Asia.

Fortunately, following my father's old-fashioned way, the Chen family had developed our businesses in northern China. We never crossed the Yangtze River, let alone strayed as far south as Hong Kong. My father's point was clear and simple: "Stay where you are familiar, close to your home." Amerihua suffered no ill effects from the crisis that destroyed so many other corporations. Indeed, our business was booming.

When 1999 arrived, especially as my August birthday approached, I could hardly believe I was 60 years old. In Chinese terms, I was passing through the Huajia, the 60-year cycle dating back to the very dawn of Chinese history. The birth of time in Chinese civilization is bound up in the sexagenarian cycle, which is the core of the traditional Chinese calendar, cosmology, and astrology. It has been used in China since the second millennium BC and has spread to many other countries in Asia. The 60-year calendar is calculated by combining the Ten Heavenly Stems and the Twelve Earthly Branches (60 is the least common multiple of 10 and 12). These two elements were put to many uses, such as determining the good and bad luck of certain days and years.

My musings on Huajia intensified when I revisited the site of my labor camp at Helan Mountain in Ningxia Province. Yuying and I went to Ningxia in November 1999. After I accepted invitations from Beijing Foreign Studies University, my alma mater, and Hebei University to serve as an adjunct professor, Ningxia University asked me to do the same for them.

I had harsh memories of my time in the camp. According to the secret instructions of CCP Vice-chairman Lin Biao, we laborers were supposed to die in the camps from hard work and old age. Of course, things didn't work out that way. After Lin was killed, his orders were reversed and many of his followers served long prison terms.

Revisiting the Helan Mountains 28 years later, however, also brought back good memories of the Yellow River, the long hours of sunshine, and the vast virgin land that nurtured us. I am forever grateful for those gifts that helped me endure the hard times. When my hosts with the Autonomous Regional People's Government asked what I'd like to do during my stay, without hesitation I replied that I'd like to revisit the site of my labor camp. A Jeep and driver were quickly assigned to the task.

I couldn't tell the driver the address because the camp didn't have one. I couldn't tell the driver the direction because the camp was in the middle of nowhere in a vast mountainous desert. All I could tell the driver was that it was close to a draw between two sharp ridges with steeply sloping sides.

"Well, Mr. Chen, you haven't given me an easy job. That describes a lot of territory out here." The middle-aged driver with closely cropped hair didn't know what to do next.

"You're right. Never mind. Why don't we just take a sightseeing tour?"

"Please, could you give me any other information about the camp?" He refused to give up.

"The site used to be a military horse ranch, not far from rich grasslands used by the local shepherds."

"Ah! I have an idea."

After an hour or so of driving on rugged roads that bounced us all over the Jeep, suddenly I saw some collapsed shelters.

"That's it!" I shouted as soon as I saw a burned-down brick building.

We stopped in front of the destroyed structure, blackened by fire. Amazingly, on its one remaining wall, I found a washed-out slogan of Mao's: "Never forget class struggle." It made my blood run cold. I stood there recalling those unforgettable days.

"This was our meeting and dining room," I said in a low voice.

"This place was abandoned long ago," the driver told me.

"You mean it was completely condemned." I used a different word on purpose.

"Yes. It was too obsolete to be of any use," the driver said.

An obsolete site; an obsolete slogan; an obsolete time. I had survived them all.

I measured my footsteps from the dining room to the south to locate the specific site of my tent. There had been many tents here once, but there was no sign of them now, of course. I left the camp when I was 32. In my mind, I turned over all the twists my life had taken in the last 28 years. But instead of being oppressed or depressed by whatever misery and desolation I suffered, I felt relieved, lighter, almost giddy.

While touring the site, I told Yuying many funny stories. Pointing at a distant spot along the Yellow River, I told her about my horrible night there and how unbelievable it was that I had found my eyeglasses when I crawled out of the ditch with my broken ankle.

"You broke your ankle?" Yuying was shocked.

"Yes, but I soon recovered." I tried to play down the accident.

"Why didn't you tell me?" Yuying was unhappy that I had withheld my injury from her.

"Why should I have bothered you with my troubles when you were also in a devil of a hole?"

I laughed while telling her about my worst experiences. Those crazy times were over, and I really felt they were dead and buried. From my stories, Yuying could imagine more vividly my time here. She didn't laugh and was still and thoughtful most of the time. Before we left, Yuying reached down and put a handful of loess from my tent site into her handkerchief, the one with the two entwined roses she had given to me upon my departure for the camp.

On our way back, I asked our driver to pass through the grasslands where I had contemplated my suicide by walking aimlessly with the sheep flock into the peaceful, deep forest. I kept my silence then and all the way to a restaurant, famous for its local hard bread in mutton broth. It was first rate, but not as tasty as the mutton broth several generals and I had had in camp to celebrate Lin Biao's death. The driver turned out to be a heavy drinker, at least that night. I always prided myself on my capacity, but he could drink me under the table. He was a three-bottle man, and not three bottles of beer, but three bottles of local white liquor, which is stronger than vodka. I normally conk out quickly after a hard drinking bout. Strangely, I was sleepless that night. Deep in thought, I was considering the rest of my life after my Huajia.

In all my life's soul searchings, the *Analects of Confucius* had played a big role. I read it many times without being able to penetrate fully the meaning of its abstruse and abstract words. It was difficult to comprehend in Chinese and almost impossible in English translation. Helped by the explication of Professor Feng Youlan of Peking University, my father's close friend from Henan Province, I grasped the main ideas of Confucius. But many passages still puzzled me, including Confucius' characterization of the stages of his spiritual growth:

At fifteen, I set my heart on study;

At thirty, I understood the rules of appropriate behavior;

At forty, I was no longer perplexed;

At fifty, I knew the biddings of heaven;

At sixty, I heard them with a docile ear;

At seventy, I followed my heart's desires without transgressing any rules.

Revisiting the labor camp site helped open me to new prospects and a new resolve to fulfill my fate. Driving through the sweeping grasslands with the magnificent Helan range on the horizon gave me a broader perspective on life and nature. Lofty views can lead to lofty thoughts. The perception of my own smallness and insignificance was overwhelming. But I wasn't thinking only of myself. So many so-called accomplished, successful men came to pedestrian, even inglorious ends. If they'd known their fate, how would they have conducted their lives? What about me? If I'd known my fate, how would I have conducted my life? I had much to muse on.

At the farewell dinner, our Ningxia hosts toasted the successful launching of China's first spacecraft, Shenzhou, on November 19, 1999. Shenzhou can be translated as "Divine Craft" or "Divine Vessel of the Gods" and is pronounced the same as "Divine Land," one of China's many names. It was a splendid achievement. We toasted more than once.

Perhaps inspired in part by these miracles in outer space, these wonders of the universe and of human endeavor, and certainly warmed by all the toasts, I had some wonderful moments of serenity that night. A sense of peace that had eluded me since my childhood enveloped me. In this blissful state, I wrote a poem for my 60th year.

Not for fame nor fortune did I embark upon my career,
But to achieve balance between mind and body,
And to seek harmony with heaven and earth.
I resolve to return to literature at the height of my worldly success.

Chapter 19

TAKING A NEW TACK

2000-2003
Beijing, Hebei Province, Shanxi Province,
Changchun, China; New York City, Columbus,
Powell, Ohio, US

YUYING AND I HAD LONG planned to celebrate the coming of the 21st century and the new millennium in Beijing, our hometown, where we had shared so many memories—good and bad—and had such high expectations for our future. Foremost in our minds was the May 1, 2000 wedding of our son Lei and Hu Weiwei at Beijing's Shangri-La Hotel. Lei is the youngest of his generation in the whole Chen family, Weiwei the only daughter in her family. A young woman of charm, intelligence, and beauty and a handsome, multi-talented, and mature young man. What a match! What proud parents!

We chose the Shangri-La Hotel because it was next door to our apartment and Amerihua's Beijing Office in the Hua Ao

Center. The Center was the first office and residence building for foreigners to open in Beijing, and we began living there in 1997. We were stunned when we were quoted the price for the two adjoining apartments we wanted to buy—about half a million US dollars for 3,200 square feet, even more expensive than in Columbus, Ohio. But we got a special deal from the builder, who put in a door between the two apartments. With one apartment our office and the other our residence, we no longer had to drive back and forth through heavy traffic everyday. What convenience. We also used these two apartments to receive and entertain friends and relatives from outside Beijing who came for the wedding.

About 100 people attended the ceremony. They lavished compliments upon the newlyweds. It pleased me that I saw them blushing at the praise. Modesty isn't my long suit, but I appreciate it in others. My only regret was that my parents and many old family friends couldn't share this moment. Descendants of Uncle Lee, Mr. Yu, Old Zhu, and Mr. Chang attended. I heard from Mr. Chang's daughter that Taiqing, the last survivor of Uncle Zhang's family, had gone to France and become a teaching nun with the help of Father Clement's family. Taiqing also told her that Uncle Zhang had been buried next to Taiming in a village in Guizhou Province. She could not remember the name of the village.

Looking around at the brightly colored flowers, the beautifully decorated tables, the abundant feast spread before us, and all the dressed-up guests, I couldn't help but recall earlier weddings with bittersweet nostalgia. I remembered my own, 35 years earlier, in a time of such worry and fear. And then there was my younger sister's wedding that I couldn't attend because I was imprisoned in the cowshed. Even with the few immediate family members present, Yuying said my parents' small room was still overcrowded. And now here we were in the expansive, stately ballroom of a world class, five-star hotel. What a change! Indeed, what a miracle!

When Lei returned from his honeymoon, he seemed to plunge into his work with even more zeal than before. He and Dawei were constantly adding to and honing their considerable business skills. As far as Yuying and I were concerned, they were more than ready to assume the reins of Amerihua. Before that could happen, however, I had to clean up a mess that I had made, the biggest business mistake of my career.

I can be arbitrary and headstrong, stubbornly ignoring good advice and shutting out contrary views. Sometimes I simply insist on having my own way. I can be a "Foolish Old Man," but not in the good sense of my grandfather's story. That was the case here. Despite Yuying's and my closest advisors' objections, I made up my mind to invest in a coal trucking business in Baoding. I had a sentimental reason for wanting to accomplish something there; it was my mother's hometown. And I saw this as an inviting opportunity to establish a reliable business.

Transporting coal from China's north to the south had long been profitable. The south is poor in coal and relies on supplies from the north, especially Shanxi Province. We bought over 100 new and used heavy-duty trucks to transport coal from mines in Shanxi to Qinhuangdao, a port in Hebei Province. There it was loaded onto state-owned vessels and shipped south. We didn't have to worry about any of the buying and selling part of the operation. Our Chinese partner handled that. All we had to do was keep our trucks running, deliver the goods, and bank the profits. It all sounded so simple, but it didn't turn out that way at all.

Shanxi and Hebei are neighboring provinces and were hotbeds of provincial protectionism. The highway patrol in Shanxi found every excuse to impose unreasonable fines on our trucks with Hebei plates. They let trucks with Shanxi plates pass by carrying twice as much coal as we did, and fined our trucks for overloading when we knew our carefully weighed loads were below legal limits. Our drivers had to buy the officers off with cash. If our drivers balked at paying the most unreasonable amounts, the authorities simply ordered them to unload "overweight" coal by the roadside. The dumped coal provided regular income to the crooked police. They would rob you one way or the other.

Of course things worked exactly the same way on the other side of the border. The Hebei Highway Patrol used every excuse to impose heavy fines on our trucks bearing Shanxi coal. They'd ask us why we weren't buying our coal in Hebei. They'd confiscate our Hebei license plates. Before long, our business was racking up huge losses. Many of our vehicles were suspended or impounded. Some were stolen and never recovered. The Highway Patrol was too busy enforcing weight restrictions to go after actual criminals. Looking at the rows of heavy-duty trucks—many of them brand new—sitting idle in our parking lot made me sick. There was no way to fix my mistake. I needed to sell our trucks as soon as possible (which meant at bargain prices), absorb heavy losses, and get out of the coal trucking business.

I felt bad that I had lost so much money but even worse that I had lost face. Many people had advised against starting up this business. Most of my anger was directed at myself, but I was outraged at the corruption that forced me to shut down my company. How did we turn into such a nation? Conduct that had been widely condemned before the Cultural Revolution was now standard. The slogan, "We are looking forward to the future," had been revised to "We are looking forward to the money." (In Chinese, "future" and "money" share the same pronunciation.) The Party and the central or local governments occasionally punished officials for taking bribes, but offering bribes was accepted as the way to do business in China. The line between legal commissions and illegal kickbacks was blurred.

I wrote many letters to the central government, suggesting that regulations needed to be strengthened and then enforced. There should be official condemnation of kickbacks, which clearly needed to be treated as crimes. I never got a single response. I was frustrated. Besides writing letters that were never answered, the only thing I could do was promulgate and enforce anti-corruption regulations in our own companies. I fined and demoted a relative from Goose Gate because he had taken kickbacks from a grocery dealer.

One notable business success I did enjoy at this time came about when I helped to negotiate a complex, three-way agreement between China First Auto Works (FAW), Tower Automotive, and A.O. Smith, where I served as a Senior Advisor but would soon be leaving. After 90 years in the automotive industry, A.O. Smith was getting out of the auto business, and I was charged with helping to make that happen with its joint venture company in China. To make the deal work, A.O. Smith had to sell its equity share to Tower Automotive; Tower Automotive had to be willing to become the new shareholder and partner; and FAW had to agree to change partners.

By the time I actually sat down with authorized representatives of all three parties, we had 18 days left to get the job done. I chaired the meetings and discussions. We used

13 days to get the parties to reach a basic agreement on the key issues. After that, we had to turn the agreement into legal documents that would be accepted in both China and the US. I doubted that any of the executives or attorneys party to the negotiations had slept more than 20 hours in the previous five days. The conference room where we met was thick with smoke and hot with arguments that seemed impossible to resolve. As was often the case with such transactions and negotiations, cultural differences complicated the process, but patience and persistence paid off.

On the last day before our deadline, after all the disagreements were ironed out and the language thoroughly vetted by all sides, I presented the bilingual contract in its umpteenth and final revision and the new Tower Golden Ring Automotive Company, Changchun, China, was a reality. My American friends were so exhausted that they declined to celebrate with a last dinner and went back to their hotel instead. My Chinese friends wouldn't let me get away with such a response. They took me to a famous local restaurant that specialized in dog meat, although they didn't tell me that until afterward. As it was, I didn't know what I was eating because I was as drunk as a lord from all the bottles of sorghum liquor we consumed to celebrate our new venture.

I tried to strike a proper balance between hard work and relaxation. In 2001 I booked an end-of-summer cruise from New York to Bermuda for Yuying and me. When our liner left her berth about eight in the morning, you could already tell the day was going to be sunny and warm, a perfect day for cruising the ocean. Shortly after departure, we went up to the afterdeck to take pictures with the receding city as a backdrop. There were too many other passengers there with the same idea, so

Yuying and I retired to our cabin and watched America fading away in the distance.

After the previous day's 10-hour drive from Ohio to New York, I was tired. I lay on the bed, nodding off and waking up, then dozing again. Yuying sat at the foot of the bed watching television. Suddenly, I heard her shout, "Songsheng, look! An airplane is crashing into the World Trade Center."

"It must be a movie," I said groggily.

"No. It doesn't look like any movie to me."

I sat up and watched. The next 15 minutes gave us ample proof that this was no new disaster flick or spy thriller. We stared in horror as smoke billowed from the World Trade Center and people began jumping from the building. At 9:00 AM another airliner slammed into the other tower. What followed was unreal, surreal, like something out of a very scary movie. Unfortunately, it was all too real.

Everyone on the ship was shocked and bewildered. By 11:00 AM both towers had collapsed. The theater onboard was turned into a newsroom. While transmissions occasionally failed, we learned from the big screen that the hijackers had crashed a third airliner into the Pentagon and a fourth plane into a field near Shanksville, Pennsylvania.

The images on the screen were too creepy to believe. People stared at the screen with hopeful disbelief until the awful reality sank in. Many shipmates had relatives or friends who worked in the World Trade Center area or the Pentagon. A few knew people on the flights. They were frantic, trying unsuccessfully to find a way to contact their dear ones. Our whole relaxing trip turned into an anxious ordeal, but we could not turn back. We were watching the world become an utterly changed, terrifying place before our very eyes, all the while smoothly sailing south to our next port-of-call in care-free Bermuda.

Although not vexed by terrorism nor the widespread, long-term damage to America caused by 9/11, China had its own serious problems. They were, to a large extent, overshadowed by the country's fantastic economic growth and its new status as an emerging superpower. China's GNP in 2000 was five times greater than in 1980. The private sector contributed more than a third of China's industrial output and more than two-thirds of consumer goods retail sales. Trade between China and the US in 2001 reached $80.5 billion, 32 times more than in 1979 when the two countries restored diplomatic relations. China was clearly muscling its way onto the world stage as the coming superstar.

At home, though, long-promised political reform was not happening. Human rights were slow to be recognized. Chinese citizens, hoping that democratization would follow their country's economic reforms, were disappointed and grew restive. Unemployment was on the rise, more than doubling between 1996 and 2002. Urban residents were the most affected with rates above 10%. Poverty and lack of opportunity plagued the countryside. Corruption—in and out of government—was a national curse. Bribery, shakedowns, frauds, scams, fake goods, stings, adulterated foods, forged art, wholesale piracy, shoddy public construction at rip-off prices, all sorts of clever schemes and blatant thievery were rampant in China, and nobody seemed to care. What was clear was that China had a "twin-track economy." One track was followed by conscientious civil servants and honest business people while the other attracted the venal bureaucrats and commercial interests who knew how to take care of their friends and get things done.

Despite the acknowledgment of leaders such as former President Jiang Zemin that unchecked corruption could bring down the Party, enforcement was and remains entirely in the hands of the Party. Despite periodic anti-corruption campaigns, the occasional prosecutions and even executions, some tinkering with a corrupt legal system, or trying to raise standards in the civil service, real regulation and reform is nothing more than a vain wish. The Party is not about to shake up the system that serves it so well. Facing so many hard tasks, the current leadership would like to leave the really tough political reform to its successors. But delay has its costs. Economists and others who have studied the problem estimate the loss to China's economy due to the twin-track system exceeds 15% of the GDP. That is a whopping amount to be skimmed off the top for private enrichment in a socialist state.

Notwithstanding these developments and my concerns, our family had much to celebrate in 2002. Michael, our first grandson, was born on April 18 in Riverside Methodist Hospital, Columbus, Ohio. My excitement had grown as the countdown to Weiwei's delivery began, and, after Michael's birth, I was ecstatic when I first saw him through the window in the baby nursery. He was so big and handsome, and yet he had a peaceful air about him, just like his father. I was overwhelmed with the sweet, tender feelings that came with being a grandfather.

Lei and Weiwei asked me to give Michael a Chinese first name. In my study, where I most like to think, I recalled those gloomy days when Dawei and Lei were born, and I ruminated on the bright future of Michael and all his generation. I wrote a long letter in Chinese to Lihong, the Chinese name I gave to Michael. I recorded the details about his birth, his birthday in the Chinese lunar calendar, and his horoscope. I also created three more Chinese names for my grandchildren to come: Liyang, Lizhong, and Lihua. Li means strength. The four characters Hong, Yang, Zhong, and Hua mean "carrying forward China's heritage and culture."

I have long felt remorseful about not being a good father for Dawei and Lei when they were young and we were separated so often. As I sat in my study thinking about the past and the future, I vowed to make up for being so absent in my sons' lives by taking extra good care of my grandchildren. It was while holding Michael in my arms that I first contemplated writing the Chen family history for him and our later descendants. Holding Michael close, feeling him touch me, I felt blessed. This squirming little bundle in my arms was turning my life around.

Late in 2003, two events occurred that also turned my life in a different direction. The first began with a phone call toward the end of Amerihua's year-end review meeting at our Beijing office. Frank, my nephew and Amerihua staff member, came in suddenly.

"Excuse me, Chairman," he whispered. "A Mr. Qi called for you and said it was urgent that he speak with you."

"A Mr. Qi?"

"Yes. He said he is a relative of your father's old friend."

"Qi?" I searched briefly and in vain for the name in my memory, then turned to the meeting participants and said, "Well, this is a good place to stop. Thank you, everyone, for your presentations and the good questions that followed. I think we all know better what we need to do to achieve our goals. Now I have something I must attend to. Excuse me, please." Frank followed me to my office.

"Please call Mr. Qi back," I told Frank. When he had dialed, he handed me the phone.

"This is Stephen Chen. May I have your name, please?"

"I am Qi Jizu, a relative of your father's old friend." The man spoke in old Beijing dialect in a gravelly voice. "I've got something very important to talk to you about."

"And what is that?"

"It's about your missing family heirloom."

"I beg your pardon?"

"I prefer to say no more on the telephone. Let us meet later this evening and continue our conversation."

"Alright. I'll call you shortly to set the time and place." I hung up the phone.

"That's weird, Frank. Would you please arrange a dinner for two at the Fangshan Restaurant this evening at seven? I'm not sure I know who Mr. Qi is or what this concerns, but it sounds as if it might concern the inkstone."

Frank is the younger son of my elder sister, Wuquan. He and his wife, Helen, have worked in the Amerihua Beijing Office since 1995. While I had promised my sister as she lay dying that I would take good care of Frank, and I have, it is Frank who literally takes good care of me. Among his many job titles is chauffeur. On the day we bought the Cherokee, Frank took the keys and the wheel away from me, telling Yuying that it was too dangerous for me to drive in Beijing.

A few hours later, accompanied by Frank, I walked slowly across the stone bridge and along the long approach that led to the Fangshan Restaurant. We were a little early. I looked at the sign by the entrance for a long minute. It was in Mr. Lao She's elegant calligraphy. He liked to dine at Fangshan regularly with my father. Their mutual friends and my father's old schoolmates, Mr. Zhao and Mr. Chang, would often round out the party. I felt so privileged to be present at many of these and other gatherings with Mr. Lao She. He was such a national treasure. That he was branded an enemy and hounded to death will be a stain upon our nation forever.

We entered and shortly after I sat down in the private dining room we reserved, Frank ushered in a middle-aged man of medium build with a narrow, intelligent face.

"Chairman, this is Mr. Qi."

"How do you do, Mr. Chen." The man bowed as he spoke.

"Fine. Thank you. Please don't stand on ceremony." I stood up to return his greeting.

"It is only proper respect for your age and distinction."

Frank said, "Chairman, I will be outside. Just tell me when you want the staff to start serving," and walked out of the room.

"Mr. Chen, did you know a Mr. Qi, the owner of the Select Antiquities Studio once located on Di An Men Street?"

"Mr. Qi?" Suddenly it hit me. "Of course! Mr. Qi was an old friend of my father's. I went to the shop often and he visited us at home."

"He was my uncle."

"Really?"

"Yes. Our family's hometown is Chengde in Hebei Province. After the Communists took over, the antiquities business went from bad to worse. My uncle left Beijing and returned to Chengde."

"That must have been in the early 1950s. I think my father bought many calligraphic scrolls, paintings, and other items from your uncle until about then. I used to accompany him to the shop frequently. Whatever happened to your uncle?"

"He became a Buddhist and led a simple life until he passed away just before the Cultural Revolution."

"Sorry to hear that, but then again, how lucky. He died a peaceful death at least."

"Not exactly. My uncle was troubled by what he saw happening to China. He never succeeded in making his heart immune to the cruelty of the world. I know that he was especially saddened to learn that your father was caught up in the anti-Rightist campaigns and suffered so."

"He knew about that?" I interrupted.

"Yes. My uncle returned to Beijing in the late '50s and tried to look your father up. He found your mansion had already been turned into living quarters for government employees. Mr. Chang told him what had happened to your father."

Neither of us said anything more for some time. It was as if each of us retreated to the depths of our own thoughts and memories of those terrible times.

Finally I asked, "How did you find me?"

"It was easy. I got your contact information from your company website."

"Well, now that we have established our old family ties, let us get down to business. What can I do for you?" I looked directly into his eyes.

"I know the whereabouts of Chu Suiliang's inkstone. My uncle told me how he helped your father buy the treasure from Mr. Jin on the eve of Peiping's liberation." Only the two of us were in the room, but Mr. Qi still lowered his voice.

"My father's inkstone was confiscated by the Red Guards and disappeared after that. No less powerful a person than Vice Premier Gu Mu tried and failed to locate it. Even the Ministry of Public Security has no idea where it is. How did you find it?"

Mr. Qi poured some tea for me and then replied in an even lower voice, "I have special connections. The treasure was purchased by interests in Europe and is now in safekeeping here in Asia."

"What? How did it ever get out of China?" I didn't want to believe Mr. Qi.

"I myself was surprised to learn that it was no longer in China, but then I saw the photos from one of my partners, an antiquities dealer in Singapore."

"How did he get the photos?"

"A rich collector in Singapore spent a decade looking for the inkstone before he found it. Some years after he purchased it, he fell upon hard times and had to sell it. He hired my partner to procure current certificates of authenticity and handle the sale, as it would have to be done most discreetly. My partner sent me several photos and asked if I could identify the piece. I told him it looked exactly like what my uncle had described to me."

"Could it be counterfeit?"

"I believe they have thoroughly documented it as genuine, and the paperwork is impeccable."

"May I see the photos?"

"They are no longer in my hands."

"Does anyone else know about this?"

"Only the people involved in the recent sale. This is not the kind of transaction you want other people to know about. And no one except my Singapore partner and I know that the inkstone belonged to your family."

"I thank you for your kindness in sharing this information." I filled Mr. Qi's cup with tea and quizzed him further.

"Your Singapore partner isn't involved with any illegal trade or looted antiquities, is he?"

"We dare not participate in any illegal business. But I must confess that I do not know how the inkstone appeared after its long absence or how the collector in Singapore acquired it."

"This is a total surprise to me. Let me think about it. It's time for us to eat now." I called to Frank, "Have them serve us please."

Fangshan was among my favorite Beijing restaurants, and I am widely known for my ability to consume large quantities of food, but that night I just didn't have an appetite. My thoughts went back to old times, to our mansion, to that unforgettable night in 1948 when I met Mr. Jin in his fur cap and coat and my father bought his priceless treasure. I remembered those rare times when Father brought the inkstone out to show to special guests. And then I thought back to the last time that I saw the inkstone as Captain Wang removed it from our wrecked home. A chill went down my spine as I remembered my father almost beaten to death, arising the next morning to practice his Tai Chi. And now . . . was it really possible that I might be able to return my family's and my nation's precious treasure to China?

Before we parted that evening, Mr. Qi presented me with his partner's business card. The next day I called him, and he put me in touch with the collector, who gave me the contact information for the Vietnamese businessman in France who had bought the inkstone. That gentleman confirmed that he owned the inkstone and said it might be available for the right price. He said that I'd have to contact his agent in the border city of Dongxing, Guangxi Province, near where the treasure was kept. I asked the agent to meet me in Beijing, but he insisted on meeting in Dongxing. He would then take me to Hạ Long, the capital of Quang Ninh Province, Vietnam, to meet the people who actually possessed the inkstone. He stressed that I must travel by myself because of the need to keep any potential transactions strictly confidential.

It was all too complicated and sounded unreal. And my suspicions were definitely aroused. Things just didn't smell right. My gut instinct was to let it go although I was most curious about what had really happened to the inkstone. My father told us repeatedly that it must be donated to the Palace Museum. I dearly wished to fulfill my father's wishes, but I hesitated and delayed making a decision on traveling to Dongxing.

It was a very busy time in my life. I was just wrapping up post-production of my multi-disc Peking Opera video collection. In my time away from China, Peking Opera continued to be more than simple entertainment. It was a consolation to me, a way to stay in touch with my roots. Singing it anytime, anywhere brought me back immediately to my homeland and close friends. Peking Opera was a powerful medicine to cure my blues and homesickness. I had long planned to produce my own Peking Opera series, and now I was doing it. Over the course of several months, more than 90 producers, directors, actors, accompanists, and professionals in sound and video recording and editing, set design, costuming, and other skills helped me to complete eight discs. During this process, I got acquainted with many new friends in Peking Opera circles.

In late December 2003, I attended a gathering of amateur Peking Opera performers at a private club close to the China World Trade Center. The club was famous for showcasing amateurs from Hong Kong, Taiwan, and other overseas locations along with professional actors and accompanists. Yuying went there with me many times, but not this night. Ever since the birth of our grandson, Michael, she was spending more time at our home in Ohio, where she could be close to Michael, rather than accompanying me to Beijing.

As soon as I got to the club, a tall, beautiful young woman approached me holding a clipboard. Like a soft, warm breeze blowing toward me, her pleasant fragrance greeted me even before she could.

"Good evening. My name is Melody. I'm the mistress of ceremonies for tonight's event. May I know what piece you are going to sing?" She spoke in fluid, almost musical Mandarin.

"Sorry, I am not prepared." I tried to decline her request.

"Please. All of our most accomplished guests here tonight must sing at least one piece, even if it's just an excerpt."

"Is that so?"

"Yes. No exceptions." She replied in a stern voice but with a smile on her lips and a twinkle in her eyes.

"Alright. To respect is to obey. I'll sing a piece from 'The Reconciliation of the General and Premier.'"

"Wonderful. Which role?"

"Should I perform as the General or the Premier?"

Melody cocked her head and examined me from head to toe. "You look more like a general to me," she said in a teasing tone as she marked the program and began to walk away.

"Wait. Without knowing my name, how will you announce me?"

"Oh, I know your name. You are the celebrated Professor Chen."

"Have we met?"

"Well, not formally. I attended your recent lectures at Beijing Foreign Studies University." She turned and walked away from me to solicit another would-be performer. I could dispel neither her image nor her faint but haunting scent—not that I wanted to. While I had just met her, I felt I had known her before. I don't really believe in past lives, but the sense was incredibly strong that we had known each other before. It was uncanny and a little disconcerting but still pleasurable for me to ponder this conundrum.

In the piece I selected, General Lian Po is disappointed that the king has chosen Lian's subordinate as the premier, making him the general's superior. Lian Po, realizing he should not have resented the premier, goes to him, and asks his forgiveness. I often chose this piece when invited to sing Peking Opera for audiences that included visitors from Taiwan. I don't know a better exposition of the theme of reconciliation.

My piece was well-received, and Melody was among the very last of the audience to stop applauding. After she presented the next singer, she passed my seat and handed me a note that read, "Please wait for me."

The evening of wonderful singing lasted almost three hours. I enjoyed the performances—some of these amateurs were as good as many professionals. I was heartened that in the face of declining commercial interest in Peking Opera, amateur clubs were springing up in cities, towns, and colleges all over China. But tonight I couldn't wait for the show to be over.

"I hope I haven't kept you waiting." Melody hurried to the coatroom where I stood. "May I have a few words with you, please?"

"Certainly. And my hope is that you will have more than a few words with me before the evening is over."

"Well, in that case, how would you like to walk me to the China World Hotel where I'm staying? It's only a few blocks away. We can talk as we walk."

A "few" blocks turned out to be seven. There was a distinct chill to the December air. Melody told me she was a journalist from Hong Kong who usually covered business and politics. She had been interested in Peking Opera all her life. She knew me from articles in the *People's Daily* and other Chinese papers, had seen me on television, and then attended my recent public lectures at Beijing Foreign Studies University.

"Despite only meeting you this evening, I feel I know you pretty well," Melody said with a wry smile as we approached the hotel entrance. "I'm almost numb from the cold. How does a cup of hot tea sound?"

"That sounds good to me." How could I turn down such a warm offer when I was cold myself? And it came from such a stunning beauty. When you walked down the street with Melody, you had immediate proof of what a "head-turner" she was. I'd be surprised if some of the men we passed that night didn't get whiplash turning to stare at her.

We sat at the bar until after midnight conversing over two pots of tea on a dozen or more subjects. We talked about global economics, politics, history—ancient and modern—poetry, philosophy, current films, the *Analects of Confucius*, and much more. Melody had real depth and breadth. She spoke well and listened well. Her questions were neatly framed. Those were qualities that I am sure helped her excel at journalism. By the end of the evening I felt I had known Melody a long time. We had spoken so directly, right from the heart, about so much. We communicated on so many levels. She seemed to be as beautiful inside as she was outside. I was already looking forward to our next meeting.

We said goodnight in the lobby of the hotel.

"It was a lovely evening, most entertaining and educational, exhilarating, actually." She smiled and reached her hand out to me.

"L-Likewise," I sort of stammered, lost for words at the moment. She turned, walked a dozen steps, and stepped into an elevator. I stood there for a while, transfixed, lingering where she last was present, smelling her sweet scent. Melody, what an appropriate name. Then I suddenly realized that I didn't even know her last name. I was certain, however, that we would meet again.

I floated back to my apartment on a cloud of pure joy. Although I went to bed, I was too excited to fall asleep that night, absolutely haunted in a lovely way. Melody's eyes looked so familiar. I seemed almost able to recognize her voice. Her fragrance seemed so reminiscent of someone. Trying to puzzle out why I couldn't recognize something so familiar was the last thing I remember before sleep finally overtook me toward dawn. Like a soft, warm breeze, Melody's scent seemed to transport me to a distant past. Was it my past or only a dream?

Chapter 20

RE-EMERGENCE

2004-2007
Beijing, China; Powell, Ohio, US; Singapore

FEBRUARY 4, 2004 WAS THE first day of spring in the Chinese calendar, followed by the Lantern Festival, also known as the Sweet Dumpling Festival. It was the last day of the long Spring Festival vacation. "A year's plan starts with spring," goes the folk saying. I chose this day to publicly announce my "back to literature" plan and hand over the Amerihua business to Dawei and Lei.

As far as the business was concerned, my happiness was complete. And to think that it all started when I flew to America with $600 in my pocket. Although I derived great satisfaction from the fact that Amerihua was a very successful company with over 280 major foreign-Chinese joint ventures to its credit, my greatest pride was that Dawei, 38, and Lei, 34, were more than ready to take over the business. At 65, I had reached the traditional age of retirement and couldn't wait to bid farewell to my business career and get back to my literature. I had been thinking a lot about my book these days.

Before I left our apartment that morning, I told Yuying I would pick up some of our favorite glutinous rice balls for tonight's sweet dumpling dinner. In the Cherokee, I drove down a veritable memory lane of my life—past Wan An Cemetery, the Drum Tower, Cihui Hutong—and then I approached Tiananmen Square. The surrounding streets were festooned with colorful flags, fresh flowers, and all kinds of lanterns for the holidays. They were thronged with people enjoying themselves, despite the chill of Beijing in February. Some of the gorgeously dressed young women wore heavy coats but left them open to show their leather boots and short skirts. Chinese and foreign tourists outnumbered the locals by far. The farm family tourist groups stood out as they took their traditional holiday photos of the entire family. Since farmers were now much better off, coming to the city and "rambling Beijing" had become a favorite annual event.

I stopped at a small shop, picked up the dumplings, then drove north and parked in front of Jingshan Park, just beyond the Forbidden City. The name Jingshan translates as Prospect Hill. As the highest natural point in Beijing, it's aptly named. The park is located on Beijing's central north-south axis and used to be part of the Forbidden City until its walls were demolished in the early 1900s. Before that, it was the royal garden during the Yuan, Ming, and Qing Dynasties. From the base to the top of the hill, there are five pavilions.

Just to the east of the first pavilion stands a replacement for the famed "wryneck" tree (the original was torn out during the Cultural Revolution). To this day it serves as a grim warning to

Chinese leaders. Emperor Chongzhen hanged himself from its branches in 1644, as the corrupt Ming dynasty was toppled by the infamous "100-day emperor," Li Zicheng, and his peasant army. Li had learned horse riding and archery in the Helan Mountains of my labor camp days. He led a revolt that began in Shaanxi, won his most significant battles in Henan, and ended up on the Imperial Throne. Internal conflict and corruption then brought his own reign to an early end. As I gazed at this tree almost four centuries later, I contemplated the potential power of repressed people and the degree of distress they can suffer because of conflict and corruption at the top.

I was out of breath by the time I reached the highest pavilion, which overlooks the city in spectacular fashion. Both the climb and the views from the top are breathtaking. They were even better before the high rises began reaching for the skies, but I so enjoyed the bird's eye view of the Forbidden City and the wonderful vista of my birthplace. I stood there musing on the many memorable events and remarkable people in my life, the stories and characters I would portray in my family history book.

There was my grandfather—thrifty and hardworking all his life. I learned so much from this kind and humble old man. Thank God he died before being marked as a landlord, an enemy of the state. I loved his stories and can repeat many of them word for word, and I do, in part, in this book.

I thought of Grandfather's 20 silver coins in the small leather pouch, his only bequest to my father, and how my father had used them to make himself an influential academic, a successful and wealthy businessman, a philanthropist, a Red Capitalist, and finally a criminal.

I thought about the 20 silver coins I had thrown into the Forbidden City's moat and the empty leather pouch, my sole inheritance, and the $600 I brought to America and what I did with it. I went from a destitute student to high-flying corporate executive; from a daring entrepreneur to overseas Red Capitalist. If I hadn't witnessed some of the amazing events that marked my path through life, I might have a hard time believing them.

I had the feeling—stronger than ever before—that I had traveled a whole circle and was getting back to the starting point. I had followed my father's footsteps, and they had led me to where I stood today.

Now it was time for me to hand down the Chen family business to the fourth generation since my grandfather had built those humble cave dwellings in Yanmen. On paper, the value of this inheritance was incalculably more than 20 silver coins or an empty leather pouch. In fact, nothing could be more valuable than the Chen family tradition that my father and I inherited and which I was now preparing to pass on through my writing.

The prospects for my future from Prospect Hill were magnificent. I made my way down the hill in a state of satisfaction to attend that afternoon's meeting of Amerihua's senior executives in our Beijing office. Generally, I no longer attended executive meetings, but today was an exception. I brought the meeting to order and then said, "Dawei, Lei, please recap the 2004 financial forecast for us."

"On the whole, it doesn't allow for a lot of optimism," Dawei replied quickly. "First, due to tough competition, our export product prices have dropped dramatically, almost 25% last year. Business has slowed. We've had to give up big orders from customers like Wal-Mart because of the extremely low margins. We can't cut ourselves that thin and survive. Prices of raw and other materials are as high as we have ever seen them. Credit is tight. It's tough to secure enough working capital from local banks. The result we see is increased financial pressure on Amerihua in 2004 and a decline in profits that might reach 20%."

Lei continued, "We must either make some fundamental changes in our operation and product line or we face a deteriorating situation."

"Would you be more specific?" I asked.

Lei replied at once, "We need to develop more value-added, high-tech products. We must make better use of our supplier network. We must stop building manufacturing bases and start renting them and make full use of suppliers through sub-contracting."

"I agree," said Mr. Zhou, Amerihua's China finance manager. "Building and operating manufacturing plants is a difficult and risky thing in China today."

"These are times of change," Dawei said. "With an increasingly difficult financial situation and continuously rising labor costs, our export business is facing big trouble, adversely impacting our whole operation. Very soon, both foreign and Chinese enterprises will be paying the same 25% business income tax. Foreign-funded companies will lose their favored status and confront even more tax obligations in the future. This, of course, will put an even greater strain on our dwindling capital. I am sorry to have to present such a grim picture."

"You told the truth and were to the point," said Mr. Gao, Amerihua's senior advisor. "Low labor costs and preferential policies for foreign investment have accomplished their aims and will soon be completely relegated to history in China. It is increasingly hard to run a company or a factory here. As for our future, I am really pessimistic."

"There are plenty of reasons for pessimism, but Mr. Tu and Lei and I have worked up what we think is a good plan," Dawei said. "Our traditional products account for 55% of all current sales. Their revenue is tapering off 15-25% annually, so we need to diversify and invest more in developing high-tech products. While we cannot neglect our foreign market, we need to sell more in China. Let's take advantage of being a sole proprietorship. We can use our ability to make decisions quickly to make the necessary changes now. I think this is the best way out of the current situation."

Mr. Tu, who directed our pump division, adjusted the bifocals perched on his broad nose and cleared his throat. "Let me say something about why there may be reason for optimism. As you know, our young engineering team has developed a line of revolutionary new precision pumps. These peristaltic pumps go beyond state of the art, beyond anything that is in the market. There is an immediate need for these products both in China and abroad, in developing and developed countries. We are now ready to move beyond the prototypes and into production. We will actually be able to produce a demonstrably superior pump at a comparable or lower price than our competitors. And since our production facilities are leased rather than owned, our financial outlay is considerably reduced."

"I've prepared a marketing plan and ads for the new product rollout," Lei said, as he hung a poster from a hook on the wall, handed out a bound document, and shared his findings. As everyone commented on the evident care that had gone into Lei's analysis and presentation, it was clear right away that they liked what they saw. Lei concluded by saying, "I am prepared to assume the leading role in this campaign and for our production base in China."

After a collective intake of breath, the room went silent.

Then Dawei asked, "Do you mean you will move to China with Weiwei and Michael?"

"Yes," Lei replied without hesitation.

I felt everyone in the room had turned to watch my reaction.

"It's a long-term commitment," I said, looking at Lei. "Are you sure?"

"Yes," Lei confirmed once more.

Now was my time to speak. "I'm very pleased with Lei's coming forward to manage this work in China. It's a tough job at a tough time. His decision meshes perfectly with the decision that Yuying and I made recently and which I wish to announce at this meeting. As of today, we are officially stepping down and passing on the oversight and management of all of Amerihua's operations to Dawei and Lei. Dawei will be in charge in the US, and Lei will be responsible for business in China. That will allow me to be responsible for writing my family history. Please wish all of us the best of luck in these new and challenging missions."

At first all the executives, including Lei and Dawei, seemed stunned. When the dropped jaws around the table had mostly closed, everyone applauded. People reached over to congratulate the proud father and mother and their two sons.

Yuying and I invited everyone at the meeting to join us for an early dinner in the suite next door. Family dinners always meant more to us than the banquets at five-star hotels and restaurants. After a half-dozen tasty dishes washed down with inexpensive Beijing beer (far better than the high-priced name brands), we served the sweet dumplings. I don't really have a sweet tooth, but that night I loved the dumplings, enjoying the sweetness in my stomach and in my heart. I never expected my retirement plan to be executed so smoothly. Everything had fallen into place with such good timing and ease. I knew I could begin to devote the time to my writing project that it would require.

I thought my project would be relatively easy—I had so many stories to tell—but I was mistaken and have no one to blame but myself. I started out okay. I bought myself a bound book with blank pages in which to begin writing the actual text. I thought I should first check on some of the things I knew I had to research: dates and names and such. Most of our family photographs and documents had been destroyed by the Red Guards during the Cultural Revolution so there was no trunk full of material to start with. I began by talking with relatives and friends who knew parts of the Chen family story.

"The course of true love never runs smooth," goes the saying. Before I could really begin writing, I got a call from some former partners who were now working out of Las Vegas. They were part of a consortium that was planning a $5.5 billion resort on Sentosa Island in Singapore called Harry's Island. After years of debate, the government there had finally decided to allow casinos, which would be a powerful draw for Singapore's neighbors and for high-rolling Asians, Europeans, and Americans. My once and future partners had a great track record. Several of them had put together the New York, New York casino in Las Vegas. They believed that Harry's Island would become the Eighth Wonder of the World and so named their company. They needed help putting the package together and submitting a bid that would top their competitors. They wanted me, with all my years of experience, to join them.

When they explained that Sentosa meant "serenity" or "tranquility" in Malay, I took it as a good omen. I listened to their pitch with increasing interest. Eighth Wonder had big plans. Creating Harry's Island would be more like building a small city than a large resort. There were many different parts to it: marine research facilities, sports complexes, a 7,500 seat theater in the throat of an ancient volcano, amusement parks, five-star hotels and restaurants, shopping malls and boutiques, a huge conference center, and, of course, world-class gambling. They even had a tree-house hotel with family suites planned for the lush tropical setting of Sentosa Island. I was impressed with how ambitious this project was. It would be the biggest, most expensive project that I had ever been involved with. What a way to cap a career! It also would be lucrative, especially for those of us invited to invest at the start. Then there was the challenge of putting the winning hand together, competing against some of the top players in the world. It was all too irresistible.

Before the end of the year, I was a major investor/partner, board member, and Honorary Chairman of Eighth Wonder USA. I had misgivings from the beginning about being led astray from working on my family book, but I was weak . . . and perhaps greedy. I was greedy not for money but for the plaudits and satisfaction that would come with pulling off this extraordinary project, for having such a monument as an exclamation point at the end of my business career.

The project consumed me but also fed me. It was exciting. As the bid process neared its conclusion, the media virtually declared Eighth Wonder a shoe-in to beat our two competitors, a Malaysian group and an international consortium. Throughout the summer of 2006 and into the fall, headlines in the *Business Times, Asia Times, The Straits Times*, and many other publications around the world proclaimed "Eighth Wonder leads the way for resort casino in Singapore," "Eighth Wonder unveils $5.5 billion proposal for Singapore casino," "Eighth Wonder proposes world's largest living coral reef lagoon." Our executives made innumerable presentations and granted countless interviews. In early October, the Singapore government arranged for us to make our formal presentation. The Vice Prime Minister and three cabinet ministers attended and appeared to be duly impressed by our work and our vision for the future.

Before the press conference that followed, I was surprised to see Melody in the distance. It was not just her striking red and black dress that made her stand out in the conference room. Even from afar, it was her beauty, especially her eyes! She had deep, black, magnetic eyes on her high-cheeked, perfectly oval face. She looked at me as soon as she walked into the room, and it was hard for me to take my eyes off her after that.

As Eighth Wonder's Honorary Chairman, my role was to introduce the project and answer questions—mainly from the Chinese press—or redirect them to one of my colleagues. The media was quite interested in our project, and we had to extend the planned hour-long conference to accommodate all the questions. Melody stayed silent, although she took extensive notes. Afterward, I was surrounded by reporters, asking for my business card and peppering me with more questions. She walked toward me.

"May I have your card, please?" she asked, her eyes locked with mine.

"Certainly." I handed her my card.

"Thanks. Here's mine," she said, then walked away without another word.

I couldn't understand her behavior. How could she not greet me? Then I looked at the card she had given me. It was from the Sentosa Resort & Spa Hotel. On the back she had written: "Room 512. Call me."

I didn't see her at the cocktail reception after the press conference.

"Room 512, please." I called as soon as I got back to my room.

"Hello, Professor Chen?" It was Melody's voice.

"Yes. You didn't even give me a chance to say hello to you."

"Sorry. May I make up for it by inviting you for lunch tomorrow? And I'll be candid. I have a favor to ask."

"That should be fine. I am planning on touring Sentosa Island in the morning but should be free by noon."

"Splendid! My newspaper wanted to cover the Sentosa story for a series we're doing on the business of travel. I volunteered for the job and have been here since Tuesday. The island is quite magical. The right resort project at the right time could profit handsomely because this certainly is the right place. Let's meet in my hotel lobby at noon."

"I look forward to it."

The island tour was well-organized and showed how good a fit Singapore and Eighth Wonder were. Sentosa Island is a paradise for lovers of the sun, the sand, and the sea, and our Harry's Island would add so much more, including 15,000 full-time jobs. Usually I would have paid more attention to the matters at hand, but I couldn't help drifting ahead to lunch. Melody was never far from my thoughts.

We met promptly at noon and went directly to the restaurant. She wasted no time before she asked me to give her some private time for a face-to-face interview after lunch. She had reserved a suite for me at her hotel in advance.

"You seem to have planned this very well from the start." I shot her a glance, smiling.

"I am fascinated by the Stephen Chen I've read about in the media. And the more I know about you, the more I'd like to know about you," she replied.

"More? About what?"

"About your childhood, your life in China, your family. I'd like to do a personal profile on you, if I may. I've cleared it with my editor. My bosses think you are what we call 'good copy.' I agree."

I was flattered but not surprised by her request. I had received similar ones over the years but never from someone as beautiful and intriguing. Again, there was something about her that almost seemed to come into focus and then faded. It wasn't quite a sense of déjà vu, but I had such a strong feeling of familiarity. I wondered why she seemed so interested in my personal history after only one brief meeting at the Peking Opera Club. She seemed to have done a lot of homework on me.

After lunch Melody lost no time in escorting me to my suite, which was perched atop a cliff overlooking the magnificent South China Sea. With a cup of oolong tea imparting a comfortable warmth to my hands, I began telling her the long story of the Chen family, starting with my father leaving Goose Gate with the 20 silver pieces. She sat on a sofa facing me with a reporter's notebook on her knee, but she listened so intently to my stories that it was some time before I saw her take any notes.

She said later, after we had become more than acquaintances, that when I first told her about my father, she sometimes felt I could have been talking about myself. As much as I admired my father, that's how much she admired me. She was deeply touched by several of my stories and said so, although it was also obvious from her reactions. The afternoon passed blissfully and turned all too soon to evening. Melody asked, "Shall we order room service rather than going to a restaurant?"

"That would be fine with me," I said, although I wasn't particularly hungry.

She apparently didn't have much of an appetite either. I finished my soup. She took only a few spoonfuls of hers. We sat there quietly, all the other dishes untouched. It seemed we both had a lot to digest, and it wasn't food.

"Shall we continue the interview?" I asked.

"Unless you are too tired." She looked as if she had something on her mind.

"Well, let me tell you about the night I first fell in love."

Before I could tell her about Lifen, I had to start by recounting how I had befriended Commander Liu and his troops with their shiny German Mauser pistols and all their marching. Then I could tell Melody about the wonderful evening Lifen and I shared before the soldiers moved from our garden.

Melody filled my cup with more tea. I continued, "To express my family's deep appreciation to the Red Army troops, my childhood sweetheart and I were asked to perform 'Farewell My Concubine.'"

"I was 10 and my sweetheart was 12, but I was already big for my age, and she looked like my younger sister, small, exquisite, and charming. She had fetching eyes, just like yours."

Melody leaned forward, taking down every word.

"We had played at performing before, but this was our first time to present the whole scene with musical accompaniment, costumes, and makeup. During our rehearsal, I was embarrassed about our touching and caressing, especially in public. The part where we take leave of each other forever is very intimate. I don't think that either of us realized until that moment that we were no longer innocent playmates."

Melody had stopped taking notes.

"We performed so well that the cheering and applause sometimes drowned out our singing. My sweetheart performed her swordplay dance, her last entertainment for me, and sang her way into my heart. After the swordplay, when the Concubine commits suicide and falls into the arms of the King, she really cried, profusely. I held her tightly and was unwilling to let her go. I knew what love was"

She couldn't wait any longer to ask, "What was her name?"

"Lifen," I said. "Yuan Lifen."

As soon as I uttered Lifen's whole name, Melody sat up straight and let out a gasp. Holding her stomach and her mouth, she bolted for the bathroom.

I was so astonished by her reaction I was speechless. I didn't even call into the bathroom to see if she was okay. I sat there silently awaiting her return and an explanation.

After a while, she came out and said, "Sorry, I have severe abdominal cramps, very painful." Her eyes were swollen with tears.

"Let me take you to the emergency room of Sentosa Main Hospital. It's only a few blocks away. Your pain may be the sign of something serious." I was worried.

"No, that won't be necessary," she replied weakly. "But I would appreciate it if you could take me to my room, please."

"Certainly, but I still think you should see a doctor."

"No, no need. Let's go."

Her suite was only a few dozen steps from mine, but it took us a while to get there. Leaning heavily on me, she seemed almost too weak to walk. She gave me her key to open the door. I helped her to the large bed.

"Are you sure you are alright?" I felt uneasy and continued to hold her arm.

"I'm fine. Don't worry. I just need some rest," she said and sat down on her bed.

By the time I had fetched a glass of water for her and put it on the bed stand, she had slipped out of her shoes and was lying on the bed. She picked up her head as I came back into the room.

"Is there anything else I can do for you?" I asked.

She paused, as though she did not quite know how to say it. "I don't know why, but I feel so lonely tonight. Would you please sit by my side and not leave until after I fall asleep?"

"Of course," I said without hesitation. "That's just what I had in mind."

"How can I ever thank you?" She gave me an affectionate but wan smile.

"Thank me for what? Don't treat me like a stranger. Good night. Sweet dreams."

"I wish for sweet dreams, especially after hearing your sweet stories." She seemed to force a smile, then nodded and put her head on the pillow. "Good night."

I turned off her bedside lamp. Sitting in the dark, I watched Melody fall asleep. Despite the scant light of the waning half moon, I saw tears shining on her eyelids. I don't know how long I sat there before I stopped watching her and left the room.

She had been asleep for some time, but it was a fitful, restless sleep. Once, she called out, but I couldn't understand her words. It left me unsettled, feeling helpless. I wanted to help her but I couldn't.

I didn't sleep well that night. Melody called me early the next morning. As usual, she had everything arranged. She reserved a taxi to pick me up, helped me pack my suitcase, called room service, and managed my departure for the airport. I didn't even remember giving her my flight time, but Melody was resourceful, especially when she was determined to make things happen. She insisted on seeing me off at the airport. We didn't talk much in the car. I thought she was still bothered by her stomach ache. I felt at the same time, however, that something was weighing on her mind. Without the expected heavy traffic, we arrived at the airport early.

"Shall we have some tea?" she asked.

"Perhaps you are run down and should go back home for more rest."

"I'm fine now. Let's go."

We sat in a quiet corner of an airport food court. She ordered for both of us.

"May I ask you a straight question?" Her voice was low and hesitant.

"Certainly."

"And you will give me a straight answer?"

"Of course."

Without looking at me, she asked, "Do you hate those Red Guards who ransacked your house and burned your remaining treasures?"

"I used to but not anymore. Most of them were deceived and misled, caught up in the craziness of the Cultural Revolution."

"How about those who beat your parents?"

"I'll never forgive them—those bullies with belt buckles whipping helpless old people. Shameless sadists without a shred of conscience." I almost spat the words out.

Melody hung her head.

"But I am trying to forget the suffering and injustice and achieve the serenity that will help me as a person and as a writer. It's not easy."

She looked up at me and said, "Nothing really worth doing is ever easy, although part of the challenge of life for me is making it seem easy."

I drank some tea and asked, "Now may I ask you a straight question?"

"Certainly."

"Will you give me a straight answer?"

"Of course."

"How old are you?"

"Forty-two."

"Married?"

"No."

"Any serious boyfriends?"

"I don't date."

"And why is that?"

"I haven't met my prince yet."

"It doesn't seem to me that you are looking for him very hard. What kind of prince are you waiting for?"

Melody lowered her head and her voice, "Someone like you."

"Non-"

She broke in before I could finish, "No, it's not nonsense. It's how I feel about you."

We didn't resume this conversation nor talk much more that day. Melody accompanied me to the check-in counter and wrangled me an upgrade. Before I went to customs, she gave me a long hug, held me close, and whispered in my ear, "I can't wait for you to continue your wonderful story soon." Then she was gone. Her scent lingered on, for which I was thankful. It made the parting less abrupt.

Not long after my return to the States, our family celebrated the birth of Matthew, our second grandson, on October 12, 2006, in the same Riverside Methodist Hospital where Michael had been born. Matthew was very much like his brother, a big, handsome baby, but with a much louder voice. I heard it in the hallway even before I arrived at the nursery window and first saw him. As I had done for Michael, I wrote a letter to Liyang, the Chinese name I had given my second grandson two and a half years earlier. As I composed it, my joy and pride in these two boys, my hope for them filled my heart. But I also had more somber moments and waves of guilt as I considered my future and how differently things were working out from what I had planned. How could I have allowed myself to get so involved with Eighth Wonder that I had virtually abandoned my book? If ours was the winning bid, how long would it be before I could really get back to writing?

On December 8, 2006, the Singapore government announced that the Malaysian Genting International Star Cruises consortium had won the Sentosa Integrated Resort bid. It was no secret that considerable political pressure had been applied. If Genting had lost the bid, it would have seriously strained relations between Singapore and Malaysia. It would probably have made it difficult for Singapore investors and entrepreneurs to participate in the South Johor special economic zone. Before the official announcement was made, I learned the news at home by phone from my own sources. Surprisingly, I wasn't disappointed and sad as my partners were, but I would have had a hard time explaining why. My dominant feeling at this point was tremendous relief at not facing a huge commitment on a tough, multi-year engagement, a responsibility that would stand between me and my destiny, my avowed vocation, my unrealized dream of getting back to literature, of writing my book.

I told friends who commiserated with me that while it was unfortunate that we had lost our bid, it was a wakeup call for me to turn from my vain ambition to my true fate. My time astray had lost money for me, but far more costly were the more than two years I had taken away from my writing. Losing the bid was the best thing that could have happened from my perspective. I was lucky to have dodged a bullet. This cloud was all silver lining as far as I was concerned.

The day after I learned about the bid, I arose from the desk in my study and reached behind me for the bound book of blank pages that I had purchased so many months before. I blew off the dust and sat back down. I looked at the photographs on my desk of my parents and of my grandsons. For my ancestors, for my descendants, I needed finally to make good on my promise to tell the Chen family history. I opened the book before me, crossed out the old title, *Birds in the Cage*, and firmly inscribed two characters on the first page: *Red Circle*.

Chapter 21

ATONEMENT

2007-2008
Beijing, Qingdao, China;
Ho Chi Minh City, Hanoi, Viet Nam

BENEATH LOW CLOUDS AND IN the morning's dim light in early April 2007, Wan An Cemetery looked empty. Frank parked the Cherokee in front of the gate. Carrying a large bunch of white chrysanthemums and a leather bag, I walked through the cemetery entrance. Frank followed me with towels and a half-filled bucket of water that he'd taken from the back of the Jeep.

Frank put the bucket down by the grave. The stone was carved in the form of an open book, a tribute to my father's scholarship and many publications. He began to wipe the gravestone with a dampened towel.

"You clear away the leaves. Let me clean the gravestone and marker," I said and took the other towel, wet it, and began my filial duties. Spending time at my parents' final resting place always filled me with bittersweet memories and a great deal of regret.

I left China for America in September 1981, six months after my mother's death. My father passed away in September 1984, two months after I got my green card. We built my parents' grave in 1985. In January 2007, we added a cast metal marker in memory of my father's 110th and my mother's 100th birthday. Michael and Matthew's names and those of the other great-grandchildren were inscribed on the plaque. Also on it was a poem I wrote, a eulogy extolling my parents' virtues and the ideals they instilled in their descendants.

Father   Sacrifice of 110 Years

Mother   Sacrifice of 100 Years

Honesty and rectitude endured a lifetime of simplicity and hardship.
Neither suffering nor oppression turned their steps from the right path.
We must follow our forebears' footsteps devotedly.
Prosperity over generations is our blissful reward.

I found much to sustain me in this grave marker. It was something small but real, something tangible that I had done for my parents. For years I had been full of self-reproach, believing that I simply hadn't done enough for my mother and father. By the time I earned enough to buy them better food and clothing, they were too old to enjoy such "luxuries." When I finally was able to ask my father to join us in the US, he was too weak to travel. My parents pinned their hopes on me, their youngest son, and I felt I failed them. If I could turn back the calendar and delete the Cultural Revolution, I might have come to the US 10 years earlier and had that extra time to look after my parents. That was my fondest dream, however unattainable.

I stared at the stone in the shape of an open book and suddenly it represented so much more than just a tribute to my father, the scholar and writer. It was a challenge to me to accept and realize my fate—something, according to Confucian teachings, I should have accomplished by the age of 60. Not simply listening to what others told me, but following my heart. I needed to commit—finally—to my writing and practice my aspiration with great devotion. I had to realize my destiny.

Writing *Red Circle* is, in a sense, my way to continue a conversation with my parents. It is the very best way I know to repay and memorialize them. As I stood there I felt remorseful when I considered how far astray I had wandered with the Singapore project and how it had delayed me from my duty. Along with everything else *Red Circle* means to me, it is a healing and rewarding way for me to achieve the atonement I so desperately seek.

"Father and Mother," I silently vowed, "soon I will present you with my *Red Circle*."

In front of the gravestone, in my mind's eye, I imagined a volume of *Red Circle*, my sacrificial offering, consumed entirely by red flames, flying high into the sky and higher still to reach my parents in the kingdom of heaven.

After Frank and I had cleaned the site, the gravestone, and the marker, I plucked the petals from the chrysanthemums and scattered them at the grave's base. An intense, clean, autumnal fragrance suffused the air. After several minutes of reverie, I reached for my leather bag, took out a white cardboard box, and placed it reverently on the grave. I bent my head and prayed. I bowed deeply, bowed again, and once more. I picked up and held the box aloft with both hands, then slowly lowered it and returned it to the bag.

Looking up to Frank, I said quietly, "Let's go."

I asked Frank to take us back to the office by way of my "Number One Road." We passed Tiananmen Square, turned left and entered Nanchizi Street, turned left again onto the street to the East Gate of the Forbidden City, and continued on our way to the moat. We drove through a tower with three gates to reach the Forbidden City's East Meridian Gate. Every time we took this route, I told Frank that it could be our last time to enjoy it. I couldn't believe we were still allowed to pass through the front gate of the world-famous Imperial Palace. In the fast-changing districts of new Beijing, with so many familiar places torn down, we old natives could easily get lost amidst the extensive development. This part of Beijing still had many of its landmarks. Every corner had meaning. Few things in life gave me as much pleasure as driving along my favorite "road" and paging through my book of memories.

As the Cherokee cruised back toward Tiananmen Square, I leaned forward and said, "Drive slowly, would you?"

Above the Square's central gate was a large portrait of Mao. Different versions have been hanging there for the entire 59 years of the People's Republic.

"What's going on over there?" I pointed at the Golden Water Bridges in front of the Tiananmen Tower.

"They're repairing damaged bridge decks and railings. Everything's being spruced up for the big 60th anniversary celebration."

"I wonder if they'll leave Mao's portrait up."

"Who knows?" Frank replied with a shrug. "Who cares?"

I was taken aback. "You would have been thrown into prison if you'd said that 30 years ago," I said sternly.

"Those days are gone. Lao Hu is much better than Lao Mao."

"Who is Lao Hu?" I asked.

"President Hu Jintao."

"How dare you call him that!"

"A lot of people call him Lao Hu. He's a good guy."

"What do you mean, good?"

"He's called for a harmonious society. He said, 'No more toss and turn.'"

"What?"

"No more turmoil," Frank said, paraphrasing.

I fell into thoughtful silence. I had been acutely aware of how different life was now, but hadn't realized how the recent past, still so vivid to me, had become a mere episode in history to younger people who knew little and cared less about China's past. I was shocked by Frank's blasé responses. How times and attitudes had changed in only one generation!

Later in April, as I had carefully planned, I made my very last business tour before leaving Eighth Wonder USA. I flew to Ho Chi Minh City (formerly Saigon) to join my partners in exploring whether Vietnam might provide a venue for our Harry's Island resort project. Whether or not we went in this direction, I was leaving the partnership. I had last been in Vietnam five years earlier. Ho Chi Minh City was now unrecognizable, as were some of my initial contacts in the city. Success had spoiled many of these local acquaintances, turning them from hard-working, small-shop bosses into rich, wasteful, extravagant individuals. One of them even had a zoo in his mansion with hundreds of animals and birds. Most of them loved gambling. There were many casinos in Vietnam, especially along the Chinese border. In theory, the casinos were for foreigners; in fact, many local Vietnamese patronized them.

During the trip, I met with Nguyen Cao Ky, the former Prime Minister and Vice President of South Vietnam. After almost 30 years of exile in the US, he had returned to Vietnam early in 2004 and quickly regained influential status. He was a small, dynamic, yet meticulous man who had a penetrating gaze and made quite an impression on me right from the start. I realized he was a controversial figure in his past, known for his outrageous statements and acts, but all that seemed long ago and far away from the still dashing gentleman I met upon arriving for a dinner meeting.

It was at the Li Bai Chinese Restaurant in the five-star Sheraton Saigon Hotel & Towers. The restaurant was named after Li Bai (701-762), the master poet of the Tang dynasty. The setting was luxurious and the food and drink excellent. Dinner lasted far into the night. Mr. Nguyen was a silver-haired old-timer with a genial smile and a twinkle in his bright eyes. In his tailored gray suit, he looked taller than his actual stature. I respectfully addressed him as General Nguyen. He was nine years older than I. I also wanted to honor his love of his country that had been so torn by civil war, as had mine. In 21 years of brutal fighting, three million divided Vietnamese compatriots lost their lives. This once fanatical, anti-Communist leader of his country, now an old man, and his younger, beautiful partner, his third wife, had in a sense "surrendered" to his former enemies. They returned to their homeland amidst much criticism from the US Vietnamese community and aimed to help revitalize their country. I strongly identified with the General's sentiments and hopes.

At his request, I told him the highlights of my history. While the particulars differed, of course, our stories mirrored each other remarkably, and we took to each other with a mutual admiration that immediately seemed of long standing. General Nguyen told me that he hardly ever cried but had broken down on two occasions: first when he flew his helicopter to flee Vietnam in 1975, and then when he returned to his homeland in 2004. I told him I had experienced the same feelings over a much shorter interval, departing for the US in 1981 and coming back to China in 1984. We talked a lot and drank a lot. We gave many toasts and said ganbei (the Chinese term for bottoms up) often. It was a night to remember—and I have.

With the help of General Nguyen and potential local partners, we toured several possible sites for our resort project. Wherever we went, we were surrounded by a plague of motorcycles. Countless numbers of them swarmed everywhere. Our drivers escaped many accidents that I thought were inevitable. As the guest of honor, I sat in the front seat, constantly afraid that in the next few moments we could kill or seriously maim some poor person on a motor scooter in front of my very eyes. We actually did hit a woman with a baby boy on the back seat of her small motorcycle and a little girl riding behind the handlebars. Our car hit them from behind when the woman tried to speed up and cut in front us. Nobody was hurt. Nobody shouted at anyone. My heart was in my throat for some time after this close call, but for everyone else, it was as if nothing had happened. This incredible, never-ending flow of traffic epitomized Vietnam: fast-moving, fast-changing, flourishing, compelling, but totally disorganized. In a way, Vietnam seemed like China in its early years. I saw banners and slogans everywhere exhorting the Vietnamese and their trading partners to replace China as a place to do business. "Buy in Vietnam, not China." Vietnam's low labor costs averaged $100 per month, less than half of what China's workers were then making. Despite the wage differential and other advantages, such as gorgeous, pristine sites, we decided Vietnam was not a good place for our multi-billion dollar resort project. The overwhelming bureaucracy, insufficient infrastructure, inadequate legal system, and widespread corruption disqualified it.

After a farewell party with our new friends on my last night in town, I returned to my hotel to find a fax delivered to my room and a message marked urgent on my cell phone. The fax was in English and from the Singapore partner of Mr. Qi, whom I had met quite some time ago in the Fangshan Restaurant. He said that he learned of my visit to Vietnam from a report in the local newspapers. Some of his Vietnamese friends had met me when we toured the Da Nang area. With my permission, he would ask his friend to contact me to continue our conversation on that critically important issue.

Surprisingly, the message on my cell phone was from Melody. Addressing me as Professor Chen, she said she had tracked me down through my Beijing office and had a very urgent message for me. Whenever she addressed me as Professor or Mister, I knew she had something important to say. She warned me to be extremely careful with anyone who might contact me about Chinese antiques. She asked me to call her at any time and finished by saying quietly, "Miss you!"

Before I left for Hanoi, my final stop on the trip, I took a phone call from a man who spoke very poor English, a Mr. Giang. He told me he would be honored if I could join him for dinner at the Li Bai Restaurant downstairs. Out of courtesy and considerable curiosity, I accepted his invitation. The two of us were given a private room. He was middle-aged, mid-sized, of seemingly blended gender. Mr. Giang had the most delicate hands, which moved gracefully through the air as he spoke. It was like there was a woman inside the man who was betrayed by her deep voice. Mr. Giang's resonant voice was so powerful that if he whispered, you'd hear him across the room. He drank only tea while constantly urging me to partake of the fine sorghum liquor on our table. He told me excessive drinking had ruined his voice and health. Then suddenly Mr. Giang plunged into the reason for our meeting and told me that on his friend's behalf he was wondering if I would like to buy back a certain art object, the heirloom of my family.

"Exactly what are you talking about?" I asked.

"The precious object your family lost in the Cultural Revolution."

"Are you talking about the inkstone?" I asked him directly.

"Yes. The inkstone from the Tang Dynasty," he replied softly.

"Chu Suiliang's inkstone?"

"Yes. But I don't know the details. I am just passing this message on to you."

"Pardon me?"

"If you are interested, my friends would like to meet you in Mong Cai, a Vietnamese border city. It's just across the border from Dongxing in Guangxi Province."

"Why can't your friends come here to meet me?"

"Mong Cai is a much safer place for you to see the object."

I paused for a while, then raised my cup in a final toast, "Thank you for the dinner. I am not interested." I prepared to leave.

"Understood, understood." He took one sip of his tea. "Let me ask my friends to come here to meet you."

"I'm leaving for Hanoi early tomorrow."

"Then how about meeting you in Hanoi?"

"That might be an option," I hesitated.

"Wonderful! But I am afraid you won't see the real object. You will see only a photo."

"Shouldn't you talk to your friends first?" I wondered how this mere messenger could make such an on-the-spot decision.

"I will, but carrying the priceless object 300 kilometers from Mong Cai to Hanoi is too dangerous." Mr. Giang didn't sound like a messenger to me.

"I will try to arrange for my friends to meet you tomorrow. Where are you staying?"

"The Sheraton Hanoi Hotel. I will need to see the real object or at least a very clear photo of it." What did I have to lose? I was going to Hanoi anyway.

Hanoi is a beautiful, ancient city with 4,000 years of history and, at the time, four million people. I liked its dozens of old districts and narrow streets. I liked its beautiful West Lake. But most of all I liked the Temple of Literature. Built in 1070, the temple was a shrine to Confucius and his disciples. Its royal school admitted sons of mandarins and commoners after they had passed rigorous examinations at the regional level. For 700 years, it was the country's finest university. The names of all its graduates since the late 15th century were inscribed on columns borne by large stone turtles. When I was there, I felt I was in a Chinese temple, very much at home. Despite the many wars and brutal occupations between Vietnam and China, our countries had so much in common.

I loved the name of the place: Temple of Literature. It was inspiring to me. Literature can bring individuals closer, like brothers and sisters. Literature can bring nations of the world closer, like family. The temple was a good place for me to ponder *Red Circle*. If I hadn't been tethered by the planned visit of Mr. Giang's friends, I would have spent more time in the temple.

But I felt I should see if there was a message, and minutes after I got back to my hotel, I got a phone call in Chinese from two gentlemen who were downstairs.

They greeted me in the hotel lobby and invited me to a restaurant on the other side of town. The restaurant wasn't much to look at from the outside but was quite spacious and nicely appointed inside. It was decorated with expensive rosewood furniture, blue porcelain, and Greek figurines. As soon as we entered a private dining room, a tall woman in a very low-cut outfit came forward to greet me.

"Welcome, Professor Chen." She took me firmly by the hand. "I am Mary Giang, Mr. Giang's niece."

"Hello," I said coolly. She spoke fluent Chinese with a trace of Sichuan accent, but her forward manner made me very uncomfortable.

"Professor Chen, what would you like to drink?" the short, fat man asked. I had already forgotten his name.

"A cup of coffee, please." I had decided not to drink any alcohol that night.

"This restaurant has some of the finest French wines in Asia," the thin man remarked. I didn't remember his name either.

"No thanks."

After some preliminary small talk, the short fat man went straight to the point.

"Professor Chen, Mr. Qi, your friend in China, told us your family's treasure was missing, the inkstone."

"Yes." I kept my response brief.

"Is it Chu Suiliang's inkstone from the Tang Dynasty?"

"Yes." I let him carry on.

"It is in our possession," he said in a grave tone.

"How?"

"We are working with interests in Europe," he said.

"Really?"

"Yes."

"How do you know it isn't a fake?"

"It was verified by experts before we bought it."

"We have certificates of authentication by three world-famous appraisers," the thin man added quickly.

"May I see the inkstone?" I challenged them although I already knew what their answer would be.

"As Mr. Giang told you, we can show you only the picture."

The thin man said, "You are welcome to go to Mong Cai to see the real object."

"Let me see the photos first."

"I am terribly sorry," the young woman hurriedly chimed in. "I left them in my hotel room."

I didn't believe her and probably showed it.

"Can you at least tell me how much I will have to pay?"

"We are open to negotiation. Returning the property to its owner is more important to us." She seemed to be the negotiator.

"I need a price," I repeated.

"The food is getting cold. Let us enjoy our meal and discuss business as we eat." Mary Giang raised her glass of liquor and proposed a toast to me.

At first, our table talk concerned their real estate and casino projects along the Vietnamese-Chinese border near Mong Cai, bordering Guangxi and Sichuan Provinces. I wasn't getting the connection to the inkstone, if there was any, when Miss Giang announced that they had paid 12 million euros for the treasure. They would return it to me free of charge if I could raise 12 million euros to invest as a principal shareholder in their enterprises. The thin man quickly added that they would guarantee my investment plus pay high-yield quarterly dividends.

"That sounds too good to be true," I said with a smile.

Mary returned what she probably mistook as an encouraging smile from me and said, "We want you to feel amply rewarded for all the ways you can help us."

"Such as?"

"With your foreign investment, we could all enjoy most-favored terms."

I raised my eyes, looking at her for the first time during our meal.

"We and our influential partners need foreign capital to purchase land use rights in China," she added, avoiding my gaze.

"Influential partners" wasn't a new term to me. These words were common in both China and Vietnam and referred to corrupt government officials and their crooked relatives and associates. Once foreign cash was deposited in their designated bank accounts in foreign countries, they completed the deal by approving the use of prime, government-owned land. The foreign capital invested never made it out of foreign countries.

"Enough talk about casinos and investments," I said. "I need to see the photos." It was time to satisfy my curiosity.

They drove me back to the Sheraton. All of them were staying in the same hotel, but only Miss Giang's room was on my floor. The two men claimed to be tired and went to their rooms, saying their companion could conclude our arrangements.

"Come in, please, and call me Mary." She opened her door, inviting me in.

Quite a selection of spirits and wine, including a venerable bottle of cognac, awaited us on the coffee table in the living room of her suite. She was apparently well-prepared.

"Here are photos of the land sites for our real estate projects. Price per square meter has soared to over $1,000 in this area. We stand to make a lot of money." Without asking my preference, she poured me a full glass of cognac.

"Please show me the photos of the inkstone." I put the site pictures aside.

"Just a moment, please." She walked into her bedroom.

After a few minutes, she came out, wearing a short dressing gown, and said, "I hope you don't mind my slipping into something more comfortable." When she leaned over to show me several photos of the inkstone and its holder, she was obviously hoping I would be more interested in what she revealed under her gown. Her body heat, mixed with the strong perfume she had just put on, almost made me sick. I moved farther away from her and began to study the photos attentively in silence.

After so many years, the inkstone and its holder were only faint recollections. The inkstone was black. The holder cover and bed were deep brown. The ones in the photos looked like them in my misty memory. But how could I tell for sure?

"Is that all?" I asked, looking straight at her.

"Yes." She returned my gaze with uplifted eyes and licked her lower lip.

"Are you sure?"

"Yes. That's all. We think these should be more than enough to convince you." She responded with ease and confidence.

"No other accessories?"

"Well, there is one other accessory—a dowry from me." She moved towards me, opening her gown. "You will have not only the inkstone and your equity share, but me as well."

I stood up quickly and held up my hand to stop her from walking any closer toward me. These swindlers had fabricated and arranged everything almost flawlessly, except they didn't know about the box that contained the inkstone, the one that bore the imperial seal of four emperors. It was even more valuable than the inkstone and would never have been separated from it.

I made my way to the door, opened it, turned back, and said, "I hope you don't find it rude of me that I reject your affections and your inkstone. Both are obviously fake."

I closed the door behind me, my curiosity thoroughly satisfied.

Sitting in my room, overlooking the lush garden, sweeping lawns, and tranquil courtyard, I thought I should return Melody's call. I took my cell phone from my briefcase, turned it on, and found two more messages from Melody. I wasn't accustomed to using my mobile; I hated to be bothered when I wanted to be alone. This time I felt a little rude that I had neglected all her messages of the past few days, especially since they all had been marked "urgent."

When I reached her, she said she wasn't feeling well and asked if I could spare one or two days to meet her in Qingdao. (The local beer, now sold worldwide, goes by the old name for the city, Tsingtao.) She said she would reserve a suite for me at the Shangri-La Hotel, and I re-routed my flight from Hanoi via Guangzhou to Qingdao. Before I left Vietnam, I signed what I hoped would be my last business document. It was a securities redemption agreement withdrawing me as a member of ACV

International, including Eighth Wonder USA. I signed it, sent it to my partners, and felt a great weight taken off my mind. The decks were now officially cleared. There was nothing between me and *Red Circle* except me. At least that's what I thought.

When I arrived in Qingdao and checked into my hotel, a message from Melody already awaited me.

> *Please call a taxi and show him the address on the envelope. I will be waiting for you in my apartment. Miss you.*

That was the way Melody was. She liked to arrange things— everything. I needed only to follow her instructions, relax, and enjoy. She made it easy for me to do just that. She lived in an old five-floor apartment complex within walking distance of the Bay Area. Her apartment was at the top. I was shocked by her appearance when she opened the door. She was thinner and paler than I had ever seen her. She looked weak.

"What's wrong with you?"

"Nothing serious." She cast me a sidelong glance and asked, "Are you trying to avoid me?"

"What a curious thing to say! I just think you look like you belong in the hospital."

"And I just think the only thing I need is for you to take me to the seashore for a breath of fresh air." Before I could even reply, she had turned to change her shoes and put on her jacket.

I always loved walking along the seashore when I visited Qingdao. Starting from Lu Xun Park, named in memory of the founder of modern Chinese literature, the gorgeous beach stretched for miles. Taking me by my arm, Melody leaned heavily into my chest. It wasn't easy walking that way, and we didn't talk much at all. She was so weak that I didn't dare keep her out in the cool breeze for long. On our way back, she bought fresh vegetables and dry noodles and told me she'd like to cook me some soup for dinner. When we got back to her place, she was too feeble to do it. Instead, I made soup for her. She watched me carry a full bowl to her, and it brought tears to her eyes. She told me nobody had cooked such warm and tasty soup for her since she had lived with her mother. We lingered after dinner, but before it got too late she urged me to leave, although her eyes seemed to say just the opposite. I told her to have a good night's sleep and that I would await her call in the morning.

When Melody called around 11, she asked if I could meet her in the lobby in 30 minutes so she could take me to one of her favorite Western restaurants. She showed up acting like a different person from the previous night, lively and with a smile that lit up her entire being and everything around her. She was still pale, but today, in her basic black and white outfit, it seemed to become her. The restaurant was perched high on a hill above the downtown. The food was very good. The scenery was even better. In a quiet corner looking out to the sea, she told me for the first time a little of her family history.

"My apartment here was left to me by my maternal grandmother. I don't have a father."

I didn't know what to say to that.

"He divorced my mother when I was only a year old," she said, sounding bitter.

Now I understood why she never mentioned her parents.

"My grandfather committed suicide in 1966 when I was two years old. My grandmother died here in Qingdao in 2002."

"It saddens me to hear of all your losses." I didn't know what else to say.

"How about your mother?" I asked.

"She's in Hong Kong."

"May I ask you a question?"

"By all means."

"Why did you send me that message in Vietnam?"

"Just to recommend caution."

"That's all?"

"If I tell you why, will you stop asking me more questions?"

"As you wish."

"Someone approached me, asking your whereabouts and mentioning a precious inkstone. It didn't feel right. As an investigative reporter, I have a built-in BS detector, and it was going off big time."

I would have liked to ask her more but kept my promise.

"Let me just say that I am working on an interesting project involving both stolen treasures and forged antiquities. I promise you I will let you know all about it as soon as I learn more."

After lunch, she called a taxi to drive me to the old heart of the city. And then we stopped in front of an old Buddhist temple. Many sites in Qingdao were new to me, but this one, Zhanshan Temple, I knew well. During my many visits there, I got to know a senior engineer who had decided to give away everything he possessed and became a monk. In fluent English, he told me that the once forsaken temple was now frequently visited by old and young alike who came for the inspiration the site offered.

Holding my arm, Melody took me through all the palaces until we entered the Main Shrine.

We stood in awe at the statues and then Melody turned to me and said, "Would you pray with me, please?"

We knelt before the altar and joined hands. She held my hand close to her, closed her eyes tightly, and prayed fervently and long. Then she bowed devoutly three times before the statue of Sakyamuni, and we lit the incense she had purchased earlier.

We finally got to the Pharmacist Buddha Pagoda. People came here to pray for their sick loved ones to be cured. In front of the pagoda, Melody stopped, turned to me, and sought my arms as she began to cry. I didn't know what to do but gently patted her on her back and tried to comfort her.

After a while, she said, "My mother has cancer."

"What?" I was shocked. "Since when?"

"She has been struggling with breast cancer for four years now. She refused to have me at her bedside and told me she wished to leave her healthy image impressed upon my memory. She said she thought her cancer was the punishment she deserved, that she had to pay for the crimes her divorced husband had committed."

"Oh, Lord! How is she now?"

"Not good. I fly to Hong Kong to see her tomorrow."

She nestled up against me on the bench. We sat there quietly, watching the sun go down until the temple was about to close.

In the following months, Melody disappeared from my life. She didn't call or e-mail. I assumed she was with her mother in Hong Kong and didn't want to bother her. And I was preoccupied with *Red Circle*. The more I thought about it, the bigger the project got. If a book, why not a TV series? A movie? So many scenes were so cinematic. There was so much material. I had decided that there was probably more like three books' worth of stories worth retelling. I even had names for the other two—*Red Destiny* and *Red Dust*. But to start, I would focus on just the first one. It was a huge project by itself. I wanted it to cover the 60 years of modern China's history through Chen family stories. No propaganda. No lectures. No prejudice. No attacks. Just telling our stories in honest and plain words.

It wasn't easy. I told my relatives and friends that writing *Red Circle* was much, much tougher than any business transactions I had been involved in, including the four years of negotiations over Beijing Jeep. However, I was far happier. I felt in tune with my inner being and well on my way to realizing my fate.

Chapter 22

DELIVERANCE

2008-2009
Beijing, China

NOT LONG AFTER YUYING AND I returned to our home in Powell in early May, I set right to work. I made a schedule for my writing, began producing regularly, and met my first set of deadlines. Then came an event that literally rocked China and managed to derail me. On May 12, 2008, the Sichuan earthquake struck, peaking at magnitude 8.2. It was the second strongest and second deadliest earthquake in the history of the PRC. Official figures list 88,000 confirmed dead or missing and 375,000 injured. (The 1976 Tangshan quake, after which my family had fled Beijing, was the PRC's deadliest, claiming 240,000 lives, according to the government count, although independent estimates place the toll at two to three times that number.)

Up to 10 million people were left homeless in Sichuan. The devastation and suffering were heart-rending. The dead and injured schoolchildren were the most pitiful and scandalous part of the tragedy. My heart went out to the victims, and I couldn't stop thinking about them. I watched a lot of television, spent time on the phone with friends, and made donations both in the US and China. I didn't return to writing for several weeks.

The tragedy in Sichuan brought back memories of the Tangshan quake, of the terror, the loss, the hardship, the national tragedy that my family and I had witnessed and survived. I thought back to China's attempt to cover up and minimize the 1976 quake, in contrast with the worldwide coverage and global appeal for funds and help for the Sichuan victims. I remembered the Gang of Four's priorities when they announced, "There were merely several hundred thousand deaths. So what? Denouncing Deng Xiaoping concerns 800 million people." Nothing was allowed to get in the way of the Cultural Revolution.

Then came the Olympics, which I watched from beginning to end, filling me with pride for the land of my birth. There was plenty of oohing and aahing in the Chen household, especially during the opening and closing ceremonies. Seeing China and our home town showcased for the world gave Yuying and me much to contemplate and talk about. We discussed national values and priorities. China had spent 520 billion yuan (about $76 billion) building new facilities like the Bird's Nest National Stadium, improving transportation systems, and otherwise preparing for the Games. Of course, China needed to look good on the world stage and for its own citizens, but looking good and being good were two different things.

Yuying and I both felt that there had been a terrible decline in public morals, self-respect, and self-discipline in China since the Cultural Revolution. And, of course, the Party had never thoroughly condemned or renounced the Cultural Revolution, despite the obvious and catastrophic harm it had caused. While it was long over, we were still suffering the effects of that ruinous decade and of Chairman Mao's policies. The popular assessment of Mao, in and out of the Party, was "Feats in founding China; Mistakes in building China; Crimes in the Cultural Revolution." Nevertheless, he remains honored as our greatest hero. How else do you explain his portrait still looming over Tiananmen Square after all these years and into the foreseeable future? Mao's everlasting portrait is a fitting symbol for the Party's everlasting refusal to allow political reform, reform that is the true key to China's future.

Of course, all the problems aren't at the top. The economic reforms and phenomenal growth benefiting China have an underside. We now live in a climate where materialism and the love of money seem to have become the driving force of China. Coupled with corruption, the predictable results are scandals, such as the melamine-adulterated infant formula that sickened 300,000 children and raised the fears of the rest of the world about food safety in China. Money can build the Bird's Nest National Stadium and propel China to economic superpower status, but it can't build a virtuous nation. Not until China raises its ethical standards will it truly be a great power, a world leader.

While I was concentrating on my writing, the unexpected global economic crisis inevitably diverted my attention, especially as it affected the Chen family businesses and our personal investment portfolios. Luckily, I had already divested myself of all my United Technologies and General Motors stock before Wall Street collapsed. I wasn't a genius, able to predict the market. I have *Red Circle* to thank for not getting caught holding my GM stock because I had converted almost all my stock holdings the year before. I didn't want to be worrying about the market when I was trying to concentrate on my book.

The news from friends I knew from my time at GM was bleak. Many of them had already lost or would soon lose their jobs and, most likely, their pensions. GM shares took their final plummet from $60 in 2000 to $1.27 in 2008. In the previous four years, GM had lost $85 billion. Detroit, the world-famous Motor City, was now one of America's most miserable cities, with the country's highest rate of violent crime and second-highest unemployment rate. Around the world, almost the entire automobile industry was in a full-scale slump. American manufacturers were the hardest hit. In contrast, first quarter 2009 figures show that China has moved in front of the US as the world's largest market for cars. Think of that. After leading the world forever, Americans no longer buy more cars than anyone else; the Chinese do. Talk about change!

As far as Amerihua's businesses were affected, steady customers were no longer ordering. We wooed some back with favorable credit terms. We also retrenched and focused on fewer products, stabilizing our high-end gift export business. Meanwhile, our high-tech domestic business is holding steady, and we are considering whether to develop a "green" sheep farm system that my brother, Jisheng, and his student, Li Mingjun, originated. Once again Chen family traditions proved their worth and kept us on solid ground during the financial tsunami. We are faithful to my father's dictum, "Never spend more than you make." Our financial reserves give Amerihua options that many firms lack. And in general, that is true of most Chinese businesses and China as a nation.

High firewalls protected China as most of the world's markets burned. The loss in China's financial sectors was a mere $10 billion, less than 1% of the $1.5 trillion loss worldwide. "Ensuring Eight," the government's guarantee of an 8% GDP growth in 2009, appears to be a reachable goal. Of course, not everything is rosy in my homeland's economy. Export businesses have taken a heavy hit. More than 670,000 privately-owned companies—about 10% of China's total, not including individually owned businesses—have gone bankrupt. Over 23 million rural migrant workers have lost their jobs.

China's $586 billion stimulus package is fueling domestic demand, confidence, and spending. Along with the $124 billion health insurance improvement plan, such unprecedented actions by the Party leadership signal their caution in the face of the unexpected economic downturn, rising unemployment, and, most critically, potential social unrest. Certainly it is far too early to be too optimistic. Compared with most other nations in the world, however, China's version of socialism is showing an unmatched economic vitality.

Despite all these distractions, I made real progress on *Red Circle*, especially after I decided that I wanted to self-publish the book so that I could have it and any related projects under my total control. I didn't want to take time to search for an agent who would search for a publisher, who might or might not see what I saw as the book's tremendous potential. I believed in my book and decided to make it happen on my terms, not according to the timetable and obligations of a publishing contract. And, as excited as I was about the book, I thought the most about the projects that would follow, especially the ones I envisioned for Yanmen. I even saw a role for the local governments in my plans.

Early in 2009, Yuying and I went back to Beijing for our usual Spring Festival family gatherings, but I also had a mission to accomplish during this time in China. I needed to make major headway on *Red Circle* so that it could be published in time to celebrate the PRC's 60th anniversary.

After our exhausting but pleasant holiday activities, I retired to my study to work on *Red Circle*. From where I sat, above the east bank of the Kunyu River, I could see all the way from Kunming Lake in the Summer Palace, where I had proposed to Yuying, to West Hill. Looking farther, I gazed in the direction of Wan An Cemetery, where my parents rest. Beyond that, the far flank of the hills merged with the blue sky and white clouds. Underneath Yuying's and my apartment was the very site of the cowshed where I had been imprisoned for 581 days 40 years ago. A friend of mine who knew many of the coincidences in my life told me, "Stephen, you could hardly make this stuff up." He later e-mailed me a quotation from Mark Twain that he thought was applicable:

Truth is stranger than fiction. Fiction is obliged to stick to possibilities. Truth isn't.

While I was in the middle of researching some historical data related to the book, my cell phone rang. I debated whether to pick it up, but since I hadn't started writing, I thought I would at least see who was calling. It was Melody! She said she was in Beijing and had waited until the holiday season was over to call me. She asked me if I could meet her at her house by Shicha Lake at my earliest convenience.

My earliest convenience was right away. I hailed a cab on Dian An Men Street and was at Melody's place in no time. It was an old house at the north end of Big Flying Phoenix Hutong on the southern bank of Shicha Back Lake. Framed by weeping willows and populated by many teahouses, the area retained the distinctive flavor of old Beijing that I so loved.

When Melody opened the front door, I found her wearing a black armband. Without even greeting me, she threw herself into my arms. She was crying her heart out and unable to speak. I dared not move or ask any questions. After a minute or so in the doorway like that, she said, "My mother passed away."

This took my breath away, even though I knew it was coming. All I could do was mumble, "I'm so sorry." She turned without a word and led me into her living room. To my astonishment, the first things I saw were two gorgeous pictures of Lifen and Auntie Cheng, both in costume for "Farewell My Concubine."

Melody silently turned on the recorder in front of the pictures. It was the well-known aria of the concubine. Pointing at Lifen's picture, she said,

"That is my mother."

"What?" I couldn't believe my ears.

"It is my mother who is singing."

"What?" I repeated, stupefied. I knew perfectly well who was singing. I just couldn't believe Melody was her daughter. But in an instant it all made sense. From the moment I had first met Melody, there was something so familiar about her. Her eyes, her scent, her voice. I never could put my finger on it. How could I? Melody was Lifen's daughter? What were the odds of something like that happening?

"Yuan Lifen is my mother," she repeated.

"Then you are Ledi?" I could barely hear my voice, my heart was pounding so.

"Yes, Ledi is my Chinese name." She paused for a few seconds and continued, "My mother died three weeks ago before the festival of her year of the ox."

I was thunderstruck. I sighed and fell back on the sofa. Lifen's heartbreaking singing filled the room and overwhelmed my heart. The scene almost 60 years ago flashed before me. That late summer night, Lifen and I sang "Farewell My Concubine" for Commander Liu. I fell in love, and now Lifen was dead before turning 72. My first love. Gone. Many memories crowded in on me. Lifen told me often that she would never forget how I protected her by fighting the bigger boys who were teasing her. I could look after her then but not after we grew up. I had not seen or talked with her since our last meeting in 1989 at Yungang Grottoes. Now she was gone forever. I just sat there, my heart heavy with emptiness and loneliness.

Melody turned down the volume of the music. With her mother's sad singing in the background, Melody said, "I'm planning a memorial service for my mother, and you have an important role to play."

"Just tell me what to do and I will do it," I replied quickly.

"I want you to perform 'Farewell My Concubine' with me as a tribute to my mother and grandmother."

My mind raced. I had sung that touching scene with both Lifen and Auntie Cheng. Singing with Melody would complete the circle to comfort the souls of Melody's mother and grandmother resting in heaven. "Of course I will do that," I said, my thoughts poised between the present and the past.

Melody and I sat on the sofa and talked far into the night. She told me about her family. Some of what she told me I knew, but hearing it from her mouth gave me deeper perspective.

She said that the small courtyard dwelling we were in held many sad memories for her. At the start of the Cultural Revolution in 1966, Uncle Yuan, her grandfather, had moved their family from their big house near our mansion to this small dwelling, hoping to avoid the notice of the Red Guards. But they found him and beat him ruthlessly, breaking his leg. Rather than face other cruelties and further jeopardize his family, he drowned himself in a nearby lake the next day.

Melody said that her first memory, one that remained shockingly fresh to her, was when her grandmother told her that they found her grandfather's body floating face down in the lake. When her grandmother turned him over, she saw his pale, puffy face, and this image had haunted Melody ever since.

She told me how, several years later, her grandfather was rehabilitated during an open memorial ceremony. Hundreds of people from the Peking Opera circle came, crowding the hall so much that many people had to stand in the courtyard. From what people said in tribute, Melody came to realize that her grandfather had been a great troupe leader and manager who had helped save many of his colleagues from starvation. When China was liberated, Uncle Yuan handed his troupe over to the government, together with his precious costumes and stage properties, without receiving a cent of compensation. However, all his good deeds were turned into evil crimes during the Cultural Revolution.

His rehabilitation and memorial could recover neither her grandfather's property nor his ashes. His suicide made him a "class enemy who would rather die than surrender." So his body was cremated together with other enemy bodies and their ashes scattered to fertilize a garden close to the crematory.

Twenty years later, Auntie Cheng and Lifen bought a gravesite close to the Ming Tombs Reservoir for Uncle Yuan. As his ashes were not available, her grandfather's glasses and case and his calligraphy brushes were wrapped in his favorite scarf and buried in the grave. No photos. No testament. No last words. The strongest image Melody took from the ceremony was the emptiness of her grandfather's grave.

Melody filled in many details about Lifen's life for me, how she had attracted the attention of a senior government cadre's son, married him, and bore Ledi. Melody said Lifen had married him hoping that his government connections would protect her family. Not long after, Peking Opera was condemned by Mao and his followers and abandoned, along with all the other decadent cultural acts of the academics and the bourgeoisie. No movies, no ballet, no symphony, nor any other cultural or recreational events. The only cultural activity allowed was the Cultural Revolution with its deafening slogans, strident denunciations, and wanton destruction. Of course, we had all sorts of songs and dances glorifying Chairman Mao and the handful of new patriotic operas that replaced Peking Opera's glorious repertoire.

Lifen's meteoric operatic career came to a quick eclipse. So did her marriage. Her husband, active in the Red Guards, divorced her, forcing mother and daughter to move into Grandmother's small cottage. To help erase the memory of the painful marriage and to honor her mother, Lifen changed Melody's family name to Cheng.

In 1979, Lifen took 15-year-old Melody to Hong Kong. Lifen made her living by teaching and directing Peking Opera there and in Taiwan. She saved scrupulously to pay for Melody's education at The University of Hong Kong. After getting her master's degree, Melody was hired by a large newspaper group in Hong Kong as an investigative and beat reporter, specializing in Chinese economic and political matters.

After the Beijing City Government began to return privately owned houses to their original owners, Grandma refitted the little house with much of her savings and then transferred its title to Melody. She had renovated the structure in the traditional style so as to preserve the features of old Beijing. Ancient-looking gate towers, off-white walls, grounds of flashed bricks, red pillars, and green windows were carved and painted as they used to be. All this charm and nostalgia was merged with modern heating, bathrooms, and kitchen. This gem of a house became Melody's home. At first, she felt ill at ease and sad in the place. It certainly held few good memories for her. As time passed, her grief didn't diminish, but she did begin to feel more at home.

"This home is what I have left from my family," she said. "I'm coming to care for it."

Then she returned to Lifen.

"Mother was diagnosed with leukemia in 1979. She thought she might die soon. It was a misdiagnosis, but her health went steadily downhill after that," Melody said quietly.

"She never told me about it. She never let me know her address or phone number in Hong Kong."

"That was Mother. She was so private. She didn't want anybody to know of her condition. By the way, she told me once that you two were potentially a couple." Melody looked at me intently, as if waiting for an answer.

I wondered if I should tell Melody how my parents had discouraged my interest in Lifen and Peking Opera but then answered simply, "Not really, though she was my childhood sweetheart, my first love. We were just kids. And your mother was two years older than I."

"That's not a reason," Melody said. "Otherwise, just think about it, you could have been my father."

Her conclusion left me speechless.

"I just wasn't lucky enough, I guess," Melody said.

I didn't know how to take her comment. Then she said, "One of my mother's last wishes was that I give you something." She stood up, went to her bedroom, and came back with an envelope, which she handed to me.

The envelope was faded and looked decades old. I opened it to find not a letter but two old-fashioned tickets.

Catching my breath, I saw they were two admission tickets to Yungang Grottoes. I recognized Lifen's delicate script on them immediately.

"April 1, 1979" was written on one ticket.

"Ledi in Chinese; Melody in English" was on the other.

"Good heavens!" I cried out.

Memories of my last day with Lifen came rushing back. I thought of Lifen's words as we sat at the foot of the tallest Buddha in the grottoes. She kept her eyes on the statue as if she were talking to it: "May I put Ledi in your care if anything happens to me?"

I said, "Melody, please let us fulfill your mother's wish. From now on, I would love you . . . ," I hesitated, "I would love you to be like Yuying's and my daughter."

"That is not enough for me."

"What else could I do for you, then?"

"You will know when I call you."

I got the call from Melody a few days later. She asked whether I was free the following day. When I said yes, she told me she'd pick me up in front of my apartment building at 10 AM and drive us to a destination about 90 minutes away. She said she would tell me no more until we reached our destination. It was all so mysterious. I tried to figure out what secret Melody might have and why she needed to disclose it to me now and on such short notice. I didn't have a clue. There were always surprises with Melody.

She arrived promptly at 10. We traveled north toward Badaling. Before we came close to the Great Wall, we took an exit and then turned onto some rough side roads clinging to the mountains. After a long drive, we finally stopped at the entrance of an enclosed courtyard surrounded by high walls. Melody showed identification to the guard, and we were admitted to a complex of two- and three-story buildings. We parked and entered the largest and grandest of them. There a male nurse greeted us and took us to the end of the ground floor. He stopped and said to Melody, "Sorry, we've done everything we could. He doesn't have long now."

"Thank you," Melody said and handed him an envelope. "This will take care of your expenses."

The nurse opened the door of the isolation ward and then another door marked Intensive Care and said, "If you want more light, the switch is on your left as you enter. I doubt that he'll recognize you. I'll be in the office in case you need me."

There were two beds in the dark, windowless room. The closest one was empty. In the corner, on the other bed, lay a short, thin old man with his eyes closed. The only light came from a dim lamp above the bed.

Without looking at me, Melody whispered, "That's my father."

I gasped. I understood what she said, but it was such a surprise. The way Melody spoke of her father, I thought he was either dead or at least dead to her, permanently estranged. No contact. What a shock! He was not only alive—if barely—but I was in his presence! And that wasn't all.

Melody continued, "That is Ruzhen Wang, the man who beat your parents and stole the inkstone."

I was thunderstruck and staggered as if I'd taken a heavy blow to my body. I steadied myself at the edge of Wang's bed, bent over, and looked directly into his eyes, which were now open. He seemed to return my gaze, but it didn't look as if he could see me. There weren't any lights on inside. Or without his thick glasses, was everything a blur? It was all too incredible; this pathetic, dying old man was the cursed and vicious Captain Wang? Captain Wang was Melody's father? How could this be?

"That's Wang?" I heard myself asking incredulously.

"That's him," Melody said mournfully. "I am so very sorry for what my family has done to your family."

I probably should have said something to comfort Melody, but I was speechless and couldn't stop staring at Wang. I wouldn't have recognized him if he had passed me on the street in broad daylight. Of course, he had always worn those thick, wire-rim glasses, and I hadn't seen him in 40 years. Only after I peered at him closely did I make out that unforgettable, ugly face, so imprinted on my memory.

Seeing Melody standing there awash with guilt, I felt deeply sad for her. I now understood why she seemed so determined to have a relationship with me, why she waited until Lifen died to tell me Lifen was her mother, why until today she had never told me who her father was. But I couldn't understand why she felt she had to bear the blame and shame of Wang's crimes.

"Let's go," she said, taking my arm and turning us toward the door.

"Wait," I said. "Look."

Despite the dimness of his corner, we saw the dying old man weep. His chest heaved, he let out a quiet whimper, and the tears rolled down his face.

What stirred Wang's tears? Remorse? Frustration? The sight from death's door? A belief in hell? Could he possibly have recognized Melody? I found answers to some long-standing questions seeing Wang on his deathbed. I certainly had greater insight into Melody's motivations, her obsession with me. But seeing Wang also immediately raised questions for me about hatred, punishment, vengeance, and forgiveness. And that was just the start of what Wang eventually inspired me to think about and act on.

Suddenly I felt Melody tugging at me, and we quickly exited the ward. As soon as we reached the hall, Melody broke down in sobs. I put my arms around her and held her somewhat stiffly until she stopped crying. After she calmed down, I said that I would drive us back home. Although Melody always liked to be in the driver's seat, literally and figuratively, this time she acquiesced. On the way back, Melody told me everything about her father.

Wang had chased after and married Lifen because of her beauty. She married him because of his good contacts with high-ranking government officials, hoping to protect her family from the coming storm. Eventually afraid of becoming entangled with her parents' obvious fate as the Cultural Revolution intensified, Wang forced a divorce upon Lifen. Then he married the daughter of a high party official and gained power beyond his Red Guard leadership, eventually becoming involved with the Gang of Four.

In early 2000, Wang, still in government, was arrested for appropriating official funds for his own use and other crimes. In an attempt to escape a long jail term, Wang successfully feigned insanity, but after being committed to Beijing's Fangshan Lunatic Asylum, he actually went mad. As he had ordered his victims to confess their "crimes," a common practice during the Cultural Revolution, he began to write his own confessions and revealed details about his criminal activity. He told how he had stolen my father's inkstone and other valuables and tortured and beaten people to death with his belt, including Senior Engineer Feng and his wife.

Through an old friend of Lifen's still active in Peking Opera circles, Melody had learned that Wang had been committed to an insane asylum. Stirred primarily by a morbid curiosity, she had gone to visit him and settled Wang's bills with the asylum. When she did so, the authorities handed her a thick file of Wang's confessions that they considered to be the scribblings of a lunatic. From them she learned what her father had done to my family and many other helpless victims.

Melody said that however deranged her father actually was, his confessions were lucid and chilling. Then she said that in addition to his writings, her father had drawn several nearly identical maps over the years trying to show where he had hidden the inkstone. He apparently had buried it under a large tree on Ling Mountain about 100 miles west of Beijing. Melody had actually hired people to go out and dig for it but without success. She desperately wanted to return the inkstone to me and had been working on it since she first saw her father's maps two years ago. This explained her curious involvement in my search for the treasure in Vietnam. So many pieces of the puzzle were falling into place.

It was getting dark as I approached the street in front of my apartment. I pulled to the curb, put the Jeep in park without shutting off the ignition, and turned toward Melody. She looked at her watch and said she had an early morning interview lined up and had to get home. After we got out of the car, she came around to the driver's side, paused, and without looking at me said, "I hope that learning who my father is will not keep you from singing at my mother's memorial."

"Of course not, Melody. I don't know how you can even say that."

"Thank you. I'll call you this week about our rehearsal." With a nod and a good night, she slipped behind the wheel and drove away.

Because Melody and I were both familiar with the roles, we felt a single rehearsal would be sufficient. We rehearsed at her house with Sun Xuelin, an accomplished player of the Erhu and Jing-hu and my classmate in primary and junior middle school. Melody seemed to bring a particular intensity to our practice. Her singing filled me with memories of Lifen and Auntie Cheng.

After our session was over and Sun had departed, she said, "This memorial is very important to me. It's not just a tribute to my mother and grandmother. It will be my last performance."

"What?" I said, again amazed at one of Melody's pronouncements. "Why would you stop singing?"

After a pause, Melody replied, "I'd rather not say."

Then she walked me to the door and said, "I'll see you Saturday. Don't be late. We start the program promptly at 7:00." I took a step and turned to say good-bye, but Melody had a strange look on her face and closed the door before I could say anything.

The night of the performance, I entered the private club that Melody had reserved, checked my coat, and found out where the dressing rooms were so I could change into my costume and get made up. Melody had told me that more than 100 guests from Qingdao, Beijing, and Hong Kong would be in attendance. In some ways, it was a strange memorial. Melody had requested no photographs, flowers, or cameras. There were no remembrances or spoken tributes. She said we would be honoring the modesty and wishes of her mother and grandmother by keeping the focus on the performance. The program began with several recordings of Lifen and Auntie Cheng. Their voices were so remarkable and, for such small women, powerful. Even though I was backstage and behind a closed door having my makeup applied, I thrilled to their vibrant singing.

After a short intermission, it was time for our performance. As Melody and I waited in the wings, I was worried. Even through her makeup, she didn't look well. I asked if she felt ill, but she just brushed off my concern. When we went on stage and she began singing, Melody seemed tentative, subdued. And then I realized that was exactly what she was trying to project, the mood and tone of the favorite concubine saying good-bye to her master for the last time. We sang with deep feeling and a dynamic I had never before felt on stage. As the action came to a head and Melody entertained me with her last sword dance, she seemed to be seized by a strange power, as if she were in a zone of her own. Her weakness had such force.

Finally, when she took my sword to cut her throat in front of me, Melody seemed to be on the verge of falling instead of standing still as she should have been. I didn't know where the acting stopped and reality began, but I feared Melody might faint and quickly stepped toward her. Just as I reached her, she collapsed into my arms. I had to sink to one knee to support her weight and hold her. Tears poured from her closed eyes and a shudder went through her body as enthusiastic clapping continued long past the fall of the curtain. Although the audience was small, the response was great. People didn't want to stop applauding.

No one on stage or in the audience had a clue about what had truly happened. After Melody opened her eyes, she wouldn't let go of me even when her makeup girl came over to help her stand up. During our curtain calls, I felt I had to support her to help her keep her balance. With tears blurring her makeup, Melody thanked the audience for coming and bid them all adieu. We stepped behind the curtain, she cast a long, heavy, sad glance at me, then without a word turned and walked to her dressing room.

After I changed out of my costume and washed up, I went to find Melody. The club had pretty much emptied out, and she was not there. When I went to get my coat and asked about her, the coat-check lady told me Melody had left 15 minutes earlier. As I put on my coat, I wondered if this could be the last time I would see Melody. Once outside, I put my hands into my coat pocket and found an envelope. The unsigned note inside read simply:

> *Absence is to love is what wind is to fire.*
> *It puts out the small and inflames the great.*

Epilogue

RETURNING TO GOOSE GATE

2009
Beijing; Yanmen, China

THE CLOSER I CAME TO completing *Red Circle*, the harder it became to write and the more incomplete the circle looked. Trying to decide what to put into the book and what to leave out was not easy. My mind was awash with memories, ideas, bits of dialogue, pieces of stories, and dreams. I couldn't help thinking of all the dreams I had cherished, chased, achieved, and awakened from; all the great expectations, dashed hopes, and fulfillment that had marked my almost 70 years on earth. In the long process of soul searching and seeking the truth by pinning it down on paper, I came to learn and understand many things, especially about liberation. Beijing and China were liberated in 1949; the Chinese people began their liberation in 1979; and now in 2009, I was achieving my own liberation through *Red Circle*. I just needed to honor my vows to my ancestors and descendants and finish the book.

In the months following Melody's and my performance, I completed a draft of the chapters that concerned her and thought it would be appropriate to let her read what I intended to publish if I could get in touch with her. I tried calling her, but her numbers were no longer in service. E-mails to her were returned as undeliverable. I went by her little home on Shicha Lake, but it was shuttered and locked.

Melody had given me some of the most intense and dramatic moments in a life that has been full of them. She was always so full of surprises. That she was Lifen's daughter and Auntie Cheng's granddaughter reinforced the remarkable place of cycles and what others might call coincidences in my life. That I was privileged to sing "Farewell My Concubine" with each of them still gives me shivers when I think about it.

When Melody told me about Wang's many maps and written confessions, it strengthened my sense that Chu Suiliang's inkstone was still in China. I can't quite extinguish the hope that it will surface in my lifetime, but I realize that it might never be seen again. I would love to be able to fulfill my father's wish that the inkstone be donated to the Palace Museum, but that is not within my power.

Seeing Wang on his deathbed was the most cathartic experience of my life. I cannot say exactly how it worked, but it started a healing process. I no longer wanted revenge for the crimes that were committed against my family and hundreds of millions of other Chinese. It began to liberate me from my hatred, a heavy burden to bear all of one's life.

It bothered me that I had no idea what had happened to Melody. I hoped she could finally see things more clearly and stop blaming herself for what Wang had done to my family. I feared that she thought I held his sins against her. I felt strongly that I would never see her again. Given the unsolvable complications of our relationship, that certainly was for the best. Although she might not have realized it, my memories of Melody were mostly sweet ones. I admired her commitment to atoning for Wang's deeds even if I thought it was misguided. I loved her spirit and the beauty of her character.

Facing huge challenges in the unpredictable year of 2009, Yuying and I were fortunate that Dawei and Lei had taken over the reins of the family business and were helping it to weather the global economic crisis. Relieved of those responsibilities, we had more time for each other and our friends and family. Our two grandsons have brought us a joy that we had never before experienced. My work on *Red Circle* was the most satisfying of my life. Yet there were still two more things I needed to do before I could enter wholeheartedly and joyfully into the next cycle of my life.

On the first day of April, Yuying and I got up before dawn to drive the 800 kilometers from Beijing to Goose Gate. We packed lightly. We were only going overnight. I also took along a white leather bag. In it was the most sacred relic of the Chen family. Most of the trip was on expressways, and we made good time, reaching Jiyuan by early afternoon. The roads got poorer as we left the county seat and headed toward Yanmen. Indeed everything in the country seemed poorer. While China's economic advances had raised everybody's standards, rural areas have lagged far behind cities. The number of abandoned homes and deserted caves we saw gave testimony to the many changes that had swept over this land since my father left it more than 90 years earlier.

Instead of embroidering "more flowers on the brocade" back home in Beijing or other cities, I felt that Red Circle projects should provide "fuel in snowy weather" to the countryside. I felt much was needed here. Why not undertake public improvements in the Chen family ancestral home to benefit the poor villagers and their children? A Red Circle library and community center, scholarships, language programs, cultural exchanges, maybe even Red Circle tours. There were so many things that could be done here, so many ways to make these peoples' lives easier and richer. I made up my mind to realize both some of their dreams and my own, right in my father's home village.

Tomb-sweeping Day, April 5, is now one of China's legal holidays, and the whole first half of April is given over to this traditional event. As Yuying and I sped along, we saw many people in the fields visiting their ancestors' graves. The day grew sunnier and warmer the closer we drew to Yanmen. Early spring had followed a green winter in Henan, and everything seemed to be budding, sprouting, or courting, all vibrantly alive. Blossoming wild peach trees colored the hillsides. Yellow mustard plants carpeted the fields. Clumps of violets dotted the roadside. Raucous magpies filled the air. As we approached Yanmen, I was pleased to see one tradition from my father's time still in practice. Farmers had spread wheat on the roadway so that passing vehicles would help thresh the grain from the husks.

We climbed a hill and navigated a switchback, and then the underpass that led to Upper Yanmen came into view. We could see a crowd of our relatives gathered there waiting to greet us. The previous week I had called my cousin Ruiquan and asked him to assemble as many of our family as he could. He obviously had done a good job. More than 50 people, from babes in arms to agile octogenarians, greeted us. We spent some time right there on the road, much of it being introduced to family I had never met or didn't remember. I reunited with my dear cousin Fenglan, 82, whom I think of as my sister, and spent some warm moments with her. Then we made our way down the steep, narrow, and rutted path to my father's caveyard. My cousin and I led the way, followed by Yuying and Ruiquan's wife, arm-in-arm, and the rest of the clan. Ruiquan is 10 years younger than I am but looks 10 years older and seems frail. By the time we reached the bottom of the ravine and turned into the caveyard, however, I was breathing heavily and he wasn't.

One reason we assembled in the caveyard was to honor my grandfather, Chen Fayuan, 1870-1943, and dedicate his tombstone that Ruiquan had recently moved from some nearby farmland originally owned by the Chens but now worked by a different family. Ruiquan had also brought a table down from an adjacent house and set it next to the tombstone in front of the cave entrances. On it were bottles of my grandfather's and father's favorite sorghum liquor, wreaths, incense, joss sticks, joss paper money, some fried dishes and steamed buns, and bronze busts of my father and mother.

Ruiquan looked around and said, "Everyone is here. Shall we start?"

I walked to the table and with others of my generation offered incense to my grandfather and my parents. As I do every time I visit my parents' grave in Wan An cemetery, I used a damp white towel to wipe off my grandfather's tombstone. Then I took from my bag the pouch that was such a relic to my family. I cleared my throat and said, "Ninety-one years ago, my grandfather gave 20 silver coins and this pouch to my father. While those original coins are long gone, years ago I replaced them with 20 vintage coins. I now return this treasure to my grandfather, a small sacrifice to commemorate the great tradition and spirit of the Chen family."

With the help of some of the young people, I dug a hole at the base of the tomb and buried the pouch and coins. After the children finished filling the hole, I tamped the soft earth firm with my shoe and said, "Ruiquan, light the fire."

The youngsters enjoyed burning the wreaths and the paper money. Almost everybody had something to throw on the rising flames. We opened the liquor bottles and filled cups and bowls. Bowing low, we lifted our vessels above our heads, then spilled the spirits upon the ground. Cups and bowls were filled again, and this time we bottomed up with relish. I knelt down and touched my head to the ground three times. Others did the same.

Ruiquan and some of his family had been steadily building the fire. It was blazing when I turned to Yuying and said in a low voice, "It's time."

She handed me my leather bag. I took out a stiff paper box and walked slowly to the fire. I opened the box and with great care took out the bloody, homespun cotton shirt that my father had worn the night Wang and the other Red Guards had beaten him almost to death. My mother had always insisted that we keep it as a reminder of that night and those times. Here I was, 43 years later, ready to consign this gory heirloom to oblivion. It would no longer be a Chen family inheritance. I lifted it with reverence and held it aloft for all to see. Nobody there except Yuying had ever seen the bloody shirt before, but Ruquian told me later that everyone knew the story.

I took one last look at my father's shirt, then resolutely cast it into the flames. My relatives seemed to gasp as one. Firecrackers banged all over the caveyard and whistling bottle rockets shot skyward. The youngsters were having a field day. Amidst this deafening noise, red flames licked at the shirt, which ignited with a fury. The smoke swirled and the fire's updrafts swept glowing particles of the shirt toward the heavens, toward my parents, in a widening gyre. In my imagination, I saw a red phoenix spiraling upward and then spewing forth an enormous red circle. And how much that circle encompassed! All the blood and tears, all the hope and joy, all the inspiration of the past and the promise of the future, a huge red circle, unfinished, beckoning me to my destiny.

At long last, I was reaching toward the end for a new beginning.

AUTHOR'S POEM

红圈　　　　　　七律
不惑無為命自謀，浮萍孤雁闖獨舟。
興衰家世訴真諦，輪回花甲順潮流。
魂系中華千秋業，情歸故里鐘鼓樓。
他鄉莫道宜為客，夢入陽關通燕幽。

RED CIRCLE

Having accomplished nothing by forty,
　　I made unwavering plans for my own life.
Like floating duckweed or a lone goose,
　　I forged ahead in my solitary boat.
As for the vicissitudes of family fortune,
　　I will now reveal the true meaning.
As the sexagenarian cycle completes its revolution,
　　I flow with the tide.
My soul is tied to the millennial destiny
　　of the Middle Kingdom,
As my feelings return to my birthplace,
　　with its Bell and Drum Towers.
Do not suppose that I intend to remain an easy
　　sojourner, far from home,
I have been dreaming of entering the Yangguan pass
　　leading to old Beijing.

Acknowledgments

I WAS INSPIRED TO WRITE a book on the Chen family history when my first grandson, Michael, was born on April 18, 2002. At first I envisioned the book as a novel titled *Birds in the Cage*, but then it evolved into *Red Circle: China and Me, 1949-2009*, a historical novel in the form of a memoir.

From beginning to end, I severely underestimated all that was involved in writing the book. It took me seven years, and yet the book seems to me still unfinished. In the 60-year time span it covers, there are too many stories to tell, too many events to include, and too many scenes to reveal. I set an almost unattainable goal for myself. Therefore, I want first to thank all the readers around the world who have an interest in reading this "incomplete" book.

I don't know how I could possibly have written *Red Circle* without the full and unwavering support of my wife, Yuying; my sons, Dawei (David) and Lei (Leighton); and all the members of the Chen family, including our third and fourth generations. Family and staff members Gong Fan (Frank, my elder sister's son), Xu Hao (Helen, Frank's wife), and Chen Xifan (Ivan, my eldest brother's grandson) also have contributed in countless ways to this project, especially Ivan. The long and tedious process of searching historical materials, collecting Chen family background information, revisiting places of historic events, investigating relevant records, and so forth has provided a rare opportunity for all of us to reacquaint ourselves with Chen family traditions, as well as pass them down to our descendants.

I owe thanks to AuthorHouse—Adalee Cooney, Production Supervisor, and Andrew Mays, Graphic Designer, in particular—for their support, and to Sam Safran, my close friend, who enthusiastically encouraged me to devote my time to writing this book. It was Sam who made a phone call to the University of Chicago and introduced me to Guy Alitto, a professor of Chinese history. I met with Guy in Beijing, and we felt like old friends at first sight. It was Guy who introduced me to Eric Swenson, his high school classmate, a multi-talented writer who edited *Red Circle*. Then Guy introduced me to Susan Alitto and Eric introduced me to Holly Weese, all of us over 60 years old. I thank this old "Dream Team" for their indispensable assistance with the book, and I will treasure our genuine friendship forever.

Yuying and I invited Guy and Susan and Eric and Holly for a *Red Circle* China tour in March 2009. During our 16-day trip, we visited the Forbidden City and many other popular tourist sites that figure in the book. We also traveled to Jiyuan in Henan Province and to the site of my abandoned labor camp near the Helan Mountains in Ningxia. At our farewell party, I asked them what venue they liked the most. Believe it or not, their unanimous answer was Goose Gate, my father's home village. I guess this is the best way to get to know the real China.

STEPHEN SONGSHENG CHEN was born in 1939 in Beijing. He graduated from the Beijing Foreign Languages Institute in 1962 with a major in English. In 1971, after three years in prison and a labor camp in the desert near Mongolia, he was unexpectedly summoned to Beijing to serve as a member of the translation team preparing for the visit of President Nixon and Secretary of State Kissinger. Later he served as an interpreter for top Chinese leaders.

To pursue his PhD studies, Stephen came to the US in 1981, but he was quickly offered and accepted a job with American Motors Corporation. He played a key role in establishing the first US-China joint venture, Beijing Jeep, and later served as director of General Motors' China Program and vice president of Pacific-China Operations for the Otis Elevator Company.

Stephen has helped many major US corporations enter China's and Far East markets. He also founded his own successful manufacturing and trading company, Amerihua International Enterprises Inc. He has been involved in more than 280 joint ventures between the US and China.

An adjunct professor at Beijing Foreign Studies University, Hebei University, and the University of Ningxia, Stephen is well-known for his cultural activities. He has been involved in numerous cultural exchanges, serves as the Chairman of the Overseas Peking Opera Association, and helped to found the Committee of 100, a national non-partisan organization composed of leading American citizens of Chinese descent in a broad range of professions. He has published a dozen volumes of technical papers, literary translations, and essays and been interviewed extensively by the broadcast and print media.

Stephen's wife, Yuying Meng, is the co-founder of Amerihua and an indispensable part of his success. They are blessed with two sons, David and Leighton, and two grandsons, Michael and Matthew.

ERIC SWENSON edited *RED CIRCLE*. An experienced writer, he has published more than 500 articles and six books on a wide variety of subjects. Co-authors of his books include an Olympic athlete and professional sports trainer, a DNA testing pioneer, and Hall of Fame baseball player Dave Winfield. His love and knowledge of history have led Swenson to key roles in television documentaries, oral history programs, and museum exhibits. He currently coordinates the History Project at the University of Washington School of Public Health.

GUY ALITTO provided historical insight and background for the book, as well as all translations in the text. He teaches Chinese history at The University of Chicago and is the author of numerous publications in English and Chinese. Alitto has been a high-level Chinese-English interpreter since 1972, serving with many of the first Chinese delegations to visit the US. His most notable recent service was during the 2001 Hainan Island "spy plane" incident. He is also frequently called upon by the Chinese language media for analysis or commentary on contemporary events.